**W. Michael Reisman
and Chris Antoniou**

THE
LAWS
OF
WAR

W. Michael Reisman is Hohfeld Professor of Jurisprudence at Yale Law School, where he has taught international law for more than twenty years. He is the author of numerous books and articles on international law.

Chris T. Antoniou served for seven years as an officer in the United States Army and graduated from Yale Law School in 1992. He currently practices law in Washington, D.C.

THE
LAWS
OF
WAR

THE LAWS OF WAR

A COMPREHENSIVE COLLECTION OF

PRIMARY DOCUMENTS ON

INTERNATIONAL LAWS GOVERNING

ARMED CONFLICT

EDITED WITH AN INTRODUCTION AND COMMENTARY BY

W. MICHAEL REISMAN AND

CHRIS T. ANTONIOU

VINTAGE BOOKS

A Division of Random House, Inc. • *New York*

A Vintage Original, July 1994
FIRST EDITION

Library of Congress Cataloging-in-Publication Data
Reisman, W. Michael (William Michael), 1939–
    The laws of war : A Comprehensive Collection of Primary Documents on International Laws Governing Armed Conflict / W. Michael Reisman and Chris T. Antoniou.—1st ed.
        p.   cm.
    "A Vintage original."
    ISBN 0-679-73712-X
    1. War (International law)—Sources.   I. Antoniou, Chris T.   II. Title.
JX4505.R465   1991
341.6—dc20   91-50208
                CIP

Book Design by Jennifer Dossin

Manufactured in the United States of America
10 9 8 7 6 5 4 3 2 1

ACKNOWLEDGMENTS

The authors acknowledge, with gratitude, the helpful comments and suggestions of Mahnoush H. Arsanjani, Myres S. McDougal, Andrew R. Willard, and Lydia M. Antoniou. Our editor, Martin Asher, was especially helpful with ideas as to mode of presentation, and showed us great patience and support throughout this project. Captain J. Ashley Roach, United States Navy, was kind enough to review our selection of material and made a number of useful suggestions. Anne Reichel of the United Nations Secretariat kindly provided information about the current status of certain of the multilateral treaties we have reproduced. At Vintage, Edward Kastenmeier edited the manuscript with great skill and courtesy.

The preparation and production of this manuscript was a particularly taxing task. It could not have been done without the skilled and patient administration of Cheryl A. DeFilippo and the assistance of Janet L. DeFilippo.

W. MICHAEL REISMAN
CHRIS T. ANTONIOU
DECEMBER 6, 1993

CONTENTS

Chapter 3: Neutrality   133

Chapter 4: Prisoners of War   149

Chapter 5: Belligerent Occupation   231

A NOTE REGARDING DOCUMENTS

Every effort was made to ensure that the text of each document appearing in this volume was excerpted punctiliously from an authoritative source. Where we have added an explanatory comment within an excerpt, such comment appears within brackets (i.e., [in original]). In addition, where we have corrected spelling errors in the original, such corrections appear within brackets. We add the caveat that while the text of each cited document is the same as that in the authoritative source, certain stylistic features of some documents, such as spacing and highlighting, in particular as to headings, have been altered in the interest of achieving a uniform appearance.

The following abbreviations have been used:

A.J.I.L.: *American Journal of International Law*
Bevans: Treaties and Other International Agreements of the United States of America (1776–1949)
C.M.R.: Court-Martial Reports (United States)
Consol. T.S.: Consolidated Treaty Series
F.2d: Federal Reporter, Second Series (United States)
F. Supp.: Federal Supplement (United States)
I.C.J.: International Court of Justice, *Report of Judgments, Advisory Opinions and Orders*
I.L.M.: *International Legal Materials*
Stat.: United States Statutes at Large
T.S.: Treaty Series (United States, 1778–1945)
U.N. GAOR: United Nations General Assembly Official Records

U.N.T.S.: United Nations Treaty Series
U.S.: Reports of the Supreme Court of the United States
U.S.C.: United States Code
U.S.C.M.A.: Reports of the United States Court of Military
  Appeals
U.S.T.: United States Treaties and Other International
  Agreements (1950 to present).

INTRODUCTION

We often talk of a fight as a "loss of control" or a "breakdown of order." But conflicts between nations are usually highly ordered arrangements in which even antagonists are expected and often do comply with certain commonly shared expectations about the "right way to fight." The adage notwithstanding, all is not fair in love and war. Sometimes views about the right way to fight are remarkably congruent. But because different antagonists may have quite different conceptions of the objectives of war and politics and the relationships between them or they may live by different codes of chivalry or "fair play," and because, since the Industrial Revolution, the technology of weapons has changed rapidly and competitively, key expectations about the "right way to fight" have often been unstable or uncertain for certain weapons or certain types of tactics. The rules about fighting, like all law, are continuously tested under stress. Throughout history, nations who feel that particular legal arrangements favor the enemy and discriminate against them in some current or prospective conflict have struggled to replace them with more advantageous arrangements.

Efforts toward limitations and prohibitions on the use of certain armaments are part and parcel of the history of warfare, and professional soldiers have always had an obvious common interest in arrangements that were mutually beneficial. The laws of war, however, have always been what anthropologists would call an "unorganized" legal system. There have never been courts in continuous session, nor an international legislature, nor an international executive to enforce the laws of war. Like international law of which it is part, the law of armed conflict has been respected and enforced in an ongoing process of reciprocation and retaliation. Arrangements that seemed to be in the common interest of the antagonists would be respected as long as compliance was reciprocal. Violations usually would excite retaliations that, in turn, might reestablish respect for the norms.

Of course, the possibilities of reaching even minimal accommodation depend ultimately on the type of war under way. "Wars of annihilation," in which one group's objective is the obliteration of the other, do not lend themselves to anything approximating what we would call a law of war. "Wars of control," in contrast, have proven to be a more fertile ground for legal development. Modern international law recognizes certain military actions as lawful and prohibits uses of force whose principal goal is annihilation.

Alas, wars of annihilation, under various sobriquets, continue to occur, in part because there is often only a subjective line between these two types of conflict goals.[1] And as conflicts take their toll and begin to escalate, both sides may begin to diabolize the other and to view the stakes—that until then were quite limited—in apocalyptic terms.

By the nineteenth century, a range of popular organizations and movements sought to condemn war, to temper its severity when it occurred and, even more ambitiously, to create international dispute mechanisms that might obviate it entirely. As the "Peace Movement," as it came to be known in the United States and in Western Europe, gained in numbers and political influence, many of these citizen-stimulated organizations began to press their governments to conclude agreements with other governments and even to establish permanent international organizations to accomplish their objectives.

Some governments also saw advantages in negotiating restrictions on the development and deployment of certain weapons. The reasons, however, were not always pacifistic. In the last decade of the nineteenth century, when told that Russia simply did not have the revenue necessary to develop the weapons to counter those that Prussia was producing, the czar called an international conference at The Hague in the hope that it would declare a moratorium on the development of these particular weapons—at least until the exchequer of the Holy Russian Empire could be replenished.

The relentless complexity and expense of ever newer weapons systems and the inability of one or more of the antagonists to bear the costs have been a continuing incentive for securing arms control agreements, which maintain existing power balances but at lower levels of military parity. Meanwhile, line and staff officers in many countries began to see common disadvantages in the widespread use of certain new weapons and began to consider ways of restraining or prohibiting their production or use. With customary practices and various chivalric codes in the background, these new sources of political energy began to fashion the modern law of armed conflict.

The sources of the law of armed conflict, like international law of which it is a part, are more diverse and complex than in domestic legal systems. In the United States, there is the Constitution, the statutes produced by Congress and the various state legislatures, and the decisions of courts. In the international political system, no such organizations exist. While there is an International Court of Justice (ICJ) in The Hague, its competence in each case depends upon the prior agreement of the states concerned. If states have not agreed to submit a particular dispute or type of dispute to the ICJ, it simply cannot act. And there is certainly no international executive comparable to the executive branch of the United States with the ability to enforce the court's decisions.

Historically, much of the law of armed conflict on sea and land developed from practices that gradually were recognized as "customary law." The International Military Tribunal at Nuremberg, which was established to try the major war criminals of World War II in the European theater (and which we will consider in Chapter 7), said:

> The law of war is to be found not only in treaties, but in the customs and practices of states which gradually obtained universal recognition, and from the general principles of justice applied by jurists and practised by military courts. This law is not static, but by continual adaptation follows the needs of a changing world.[2]

Treaties, which are formal written agreements between states, are a relatively late development in the law of war. Since a treaty ordinarily binds only the states that have signed and ratified it, a particular treaty, despite its general language, may actually have a very limited range of application. If one state to a conflict is party to a treaty, but the other state is not, the restrictions in the treaty, insofar as they are based on treaty law, will not apply. Consider, for example, the problem of the use of gas and chemical weapons in the Iran-Iraq War of 1980–89. The 1925 Protocol[3] prohibits, in the most general and absolute terms, the use of gases and bacteriological methods in warfare. Iran never became party to that treaty. Iraq, which became party in 1931, subjected its accession to a reservation to the effect that the Protocol would be binding only as regards states which themselves were party to the Convention. Many states also indicated, when they joined, that the treaty would cease to operate if a belligerent violated any of the prohibitions in it. Thus these weapons may not have been prohibited in the Iran-Iraq War.

Because of these limitations on the applicability of treaty-made law, those states and scholars, who are anxious to extend the application of certain treaties, sometimes contend that rules that commenced in a treaty have subsequently been transformed into custom because of the widespread practice of states. This may be very subjective, for the evidence of transformation into custom is often sparse and ambiguous. When inferences overshoot the actual expectations of combatants, whichever side initially seeks to comply with the law suffers a disadvantage, and the credibility of the law of war as a whole is depreciated.

If custom has the advantage of applying to everyone while treaties, like contracts, apply only to the states that have become parties to them, customary law has the disadvantage of often being hard to identify. The *Annotated Supplement to the Commander's Handbook on the Law of Naval Operations*, a remarkable and, in our view, outstanding document on the law of armed conflict, which was released by the United States Navy in 1989, notes:

> The customary international law of armed conflict derives from the practice of military and naval forces in the field, at sea, and in the air during hostilities. When such a practice attains a degree of regularity and is accompanied by the general conviction among nations that behavior in conformity with that practice is obligatory, it can be said to have become a rule of customary law binding upon all nations. It is frequently difficult to determine the precise point in time at which a usage or practice of warfare evolves into a customary rule of law. In a period marked by rapid developments in technology, coupled with the broadening of the spectrum of warfare to encompass insurgencies and state-sponsored terrorism, it is not surprising that nations often disagree as to the precise content of an accepted practice of warfare and to its status as a rule of law.[4]

The fact that custom is so hard to identify, and that in some conflicts the failure of one of the belligerents to conform to it may indicate its suspension or inapplicability, presents major problems to soldiers in the field, and to students and judges after the fact. Furthermore, it is quite difficult to tell a soldier, whose life may hang in the balance, that it is not clear whether certain actions may be taken—especially if the adversary is taking them.

Because most of the law dealing explicitly with conduct in the course of armed conflict initially was codified at conferences in The Hague, that part of the law of war dealing with armed conflict was often referred to as "Hague Law." The International Committee of the Red Cross (ICRC) was founded in Geneva in 1864 by Henry Dunant, a Geneva banker who had witnessed and been traumatized by the massive horrors of the Battle of Solferino in northern Italy in 1859. The ICRC, which concerns itself with reinforcing and extending humanitarian aspects of the laws of war and, in particular, securing the protection of prisoners of war and other noncombatants, has convened many of its conferences in Geneva where it maintains its headquarters. Therefore the stream of codification of the laws of war that the ICRC initiated has been referred to as "Geneva Law."

Since 1977, the International Committee of the Red Cross has sought to merge the two streams of codification into a single comprehensive body of what it would like to be known as "humanitarian law." Humanitarian law also seeks to incorporate key aspects of that part of contemporary international law that is concerned with the protection of human rights.

There are certain common goals in the modern law of war and the international protection of human rights, for both seek to restrain governments' use of power against people subject to them. But the commonality cannot be pressed too far. Human rights documents generally speak in terms of absolute prohibitions on certain government actions against people, while the law of war is premised on the existence of a belligerent situation in which high levels of violence will be directed by governments and their agents against people. Rather than the absolute prohibitions of human rights law, the question in the law of war, more often than not, is what level of violence is reasonably necessary and proportional in the context.

Because the outcome of the 1977 codification effort is still uncertain and the similarity in names of human rights law and humanitarian law could be confusing, we feel that, despite the indelicacy of the terms, a certain clarity is secured by continuing to use the terms "law of armed conflict" and "law of war."

The identification of what constitutes the law of war at any moment is further complicated by an odd-sounding international legal term called "soft law." For some time, people who study international law have noted that some of the production of the international law-making system lacks certain critical features of law, yet is still viewed, for some purposes, as law. A "law" that has some of the features of law but lacks others has come to be called a "soft law." There are three distinct forms of soft law:

(1) Law can be soft with regard to its content. For example, a prohibition on the use of gases may not indicate whether tear gas is included. Ambiguity with regard to the reach of a particular law is a fairly common legislative technique in domestic law. When parties crafting a legislative instrument are unable to agree about one particular part, they often paper over their difference with some general language, appreciating that the courts can be counted on to clarify the matter in the course of litigation. But because there are no compulsory courts in the international system, the soft quality of the content of the particular norm may not be firmed up for a long time, if ever.

(2) A norm can also be soft with regard to the law-making authority of those purporting to establish it. The General Assembly of the United Nations, for example, may make recommendations, but it does not have the authority to pass resolutions that bind member-states. Yet the Assembly often purports to do this. Some of these resolutions may, indeed, become part of international law. But this occurs because of factors external to the United Nations. When the resolution was passed, their authority was soft. Nongovernmental organizations frequently convene and in solemn fashion and using the appropriate legislative symbols pass resolutions that purport to express international law, but they certainly lack the authority to do this and, like resolutions of the General Assembly, these products will become law only after they have been accepted by the international community.

In other instances, states that have the authority to make law may go through some of the motions and even couch their conclusions in familiar legislative terms, but it is doubtful if they have intended to make law for themselves.

(3) A critical distinguishing feature of law is its "sanction," which essentially means the credible commitment of those making the

law to see to it that there is compliance. Because the international political system lacks a centralized enforcement agency, the commitment to make a law effective depends on the political will of powerful states. Laws will be soft or become soft when the commitment to making them effective is either very low at the moment of enactment or bleeds off, for various reasons, afterward. Parts of the modern law of war that do not or no longer have the commitment of stronger states for their enforcement are soft in this sense.

Soft law frequently is characterized as a pathology of the international legal system. From the standpoint of the soldier in the field or the commander responsible for him, however, the additional uncertainty as to whether or not a particular legal formulation is soft or hard may well be less desirable than having no legal regulation. Yet soft laws may serve important functions. Sometimes, soft laws gradually firm into effective prescription. In other cases, the mere establishment of standards serves larger political purposes. The application of soft law, particularly in war, is more problematic.

It is not uncommon for legal aspiration to outstrip political reach. In the nineteenth century, conferences would characterize statements, which all the participants knew were aspirational but could not be made effective, at least at that time, as *voeux*—i.e., wishes or aspirations. These *voeux* were expressed in an unmistakable fashion that clearly indicated to anyone who had occasion to use them that they were not binding in a legal sense.

Unfortunately, those formal distinctions are no longer maintained. The problems of identifying law in its customary form and determining the "legality" of a particular formulation are made even more complex by an increasingly common international legal practice of expressing in conventional legal form policies that the parties understand are only aspirational and cannot be made effective.

Soft law and aspirational law may seem legally misleading, yet they perform an important function in the emergence and application of the laws of war. In a developmental sense, statements of aspiration often point in the direction toward which key agents of social change are directing themselves and may be an indication of what the law will be in the future. Where this is the general perception, parties who may be unable to accept that particular formula as law at that moment are able to begin to make the necessary internal political changes and to position themselves so that they may accept it at some point in the future.

In an even more general sense, popular perceptions of what the law of armed conflict is, or should be, may become self-fulfilling when the support of the population is a critical factor in the continuing conduct of the war. In modern popular democracies, even a limited armed conflict requires a substantial base of popular support. That support can erode or even reverse itself rapidly, no matter how worthy the political objective, if people believe that the war is being conducted in an unfair, inhumane, or iniquitous way. Precisely because of this, adversaries who are able to take advantage of mass media frequently go out of their way to depict or even invent military actions against them as violations of some general legal or moral standard or to hide or downplay their own actions. Legal purists may insist that the legal standards that are being invoked in these sorts of public and media exchanges are not law. Technically they are correct, but as a practical matter, those expectations may force changes in military conduct by one side and possibly influence the future content of the common standards.

The media play an important role in this process by conveying information about the conduct of war. During World War II, there appeared to be a fundamental agreement between the press and the military command of the great democracies. The national elite press was privy to all plans but practiced a type of self-censorship. Transformations in the nature of warfare and the structure of the mass media in democratic systems have wrought major changes in this relationship. During the Vietnam War, the selection of images to be reported to the public at large as well as the characterization of the moral and legal significance of those images was essentially the province of journalists. In the operations in Grenada, the Falkland Islands, and Panama, access by journalists was restricted carefully, and military spokesmen began to assume a substantial part of the function of transmitting images to the population at large. Observers of the United States–led coalition against the Iraqi aggression in Kuwait noted the extent to which individual members of the press corps were restricted and, in a sense, manipulated by both sides; the care with which military spokesmen explained their objectives and accomplishments; and the skill with which they presented their conception of what the law of war prescribes, focusing attention, as best they could, on certain issues and attempting to deflect it from others. This development in the law of armed conflict is particularly fascinating. The consequences of this process of participation on the application of the law of armed conflict and on the corpus of the law may prove to be substantial.

International law relates to every aspect of armed conflict, though particular sectors are more developed than others. Efforts have been made to prescribe for the preparation of war and to impose limits on types of armaments that may be developed and quantities that may be stockpiled. Major efforts have been mounted to prescribe for the conditions under which force may be resorted to and, of course, the ways that force may be used. Historically, the law also has distinguished between internal and international conflict, a distinction that will be considered in one of the commentaries in the book. There is an elaborate law of neutrality concerning the rights and obligations of states that are not participating in a conflict. A substantial body of law has developed to deal with prisoners of war and other noncombatants. When territory is seized, the law of belligerent occupation is supposed to apply. Violations of all these laws of war are treated under the rubric of war crimes.

In this book, the focus is essentially on the actual law concerning armed conflict and not on the many rules concerned with regulating its longer-term preparation. But it is not always easy to maintain that distinction. In the Gulf War, for example, United States officials spoke about the need to reduce Iraq's war-making capacity for the future and, in particular, to destroy nuclear, biological, and chemical production facilities. After "Desert Storm," the United Nations mounted a major effort to accomplish this.[5] While these particular sites may be lawful targets under the law of war, it is clear that a concurrent objective in their selection was to render Iraq militarily incapable of mounting other adventures like its invasion of Kuwait on August 2, 1990. In this respect, the lawfulness of these actions also has to be appraised in terms of that part of the law regulating preparation.

While the humanitarian element plays a significant role in the law of armed conflict, particularly in Western Europe and the United States, certain ultimate limits on this particular body of law should be appreciated. Armed conflict is one of the strategic modes available to actors in international politics—recall the view of Carl von Clausewitz, the nineteenth-century Prussian military officer and author, that war is a continuation of politics by other means—whether used for defensive and conservatory or offensive and expansive purposes. By war's very nature, the practices that become effective (rather than aspirational) law will be influenced decisively by the concerns of military specialists to protect their own personnel and assets and to use them effectively. When attempts by the various groups that participate in making the law of armed conflict overshoot this core interest, documents expressed in the legal formula may be produced, but they will be rejected by states that contemplate the probability of having to go to war. Even if accepted, they are likely to prove ineffective once the first shot is fired. This particular development is exemplified, to an extent, by certain ambitious sections of the Protocols Additional to the Geneva Conventions, which we will consider in Chapter 2, and which remain among the more controversial recent efforts to develop the law of armed conflict.

Because the international political system lacks the institutions found in national law, the law of armed conflict's application is as complex as is the procedure by which it is made.

Instead of a single system of hierarchical courts capped by a supreme tribunal, as one finds in the United States, the law of armed conflict has, for the most part, been explicitly applied by a range of national courts and military commissions. Therefore a fair amount of the "case law" in this book was produced by national courts and commissions. The few examples of true international war crimes tribunals, for example the Nuremberg Tribunal and the Far Eastern Military Tribunal, have been exceptions, though efforts continue in some quarters to establish a standing international war crimes tribunal. As we go to press, the United Nations has decided to establish a War Crimes Tribunal, but its competence and jurisdiction have yet to be decided.

To an extent, one might expect officers, judging their own men and usually conscious of and sympathetic to the stresses under which they have been, to be biased in the application of the law of war. This may be the case, but what is surprising overall has been the extent to which national agencies in a number of states have reflected a sufficient concern for the continuation of the law of war to secure its application even in the course of conflicts.

Nuremberg and the Far Eastern Military Tribunal involved applications of a different order. Each was obliged, in the context of some of the criminal cases before it, to make the law which was thereupon applied. The decisions of both tribunals are not without controversy, but each was able to enunciate more general principles, many of which appear to have been incorporated into the body of the law of armed conflict.

In much the same way that some lawmaking is soft, there are also softer applications of the law of war. During the Vietnam War, Bertrand Russell initiated a "tribunal" to "judge" the United States' compliance with the laws of war. Other private groups have established "commissions" to examine allegations of violations of the law of war in parts of the

Middle East and in Afghanistan. A privately established "court" in the United States examined Stalin's crimes in Ukraine.

Characterizing these various efforts as "courts" or "commissions" is more than a bit pretentious, for they have no governmental authority, and their findings are in no sense binding. But that does not mean that they have no effect on public opinion. If the individual members are jurists of repute and the procedures followed are satisfactory, they can play a role in the application of the law of war. For it would be a mistake to assume that law is only applied by intergovernmental courts or commissions. In a more general sense, all of the agencies involved in armed conflict that incorporate the law of war, into their own decision procedures and implement it on a regular basis may be considered as part of the application function. Even the training in the law of war given to officers and people in the ranks is an important part of application. It is patent that if those engaged in hostilities have not been exposed to the prescriptions of the law of armed conflict, then they hardly can be expected to comply with them. Military manuals, special training in the law of war, and dissemination of the laws of war by nongovernmental organizations such as the International Committee of the Red Cross are important parts of its application.

Access to and familiarity with the basic instruments of the law of war is indispensable. We believe that discussion within the government, in the media, in places of worship, and in other places in which citizens discuss issues of war and peace must take into account the basic documents of the law of war. But the way these documents are implemented must also be understood. This book rests on the belief that in a democracy all citizens may play a role in the shaping and implementation of law.

Contrary to popular belief, law is not a process in which rules are selected and automatically applied to particular factual situations. In all legal application, critical elements of judgment or what medieval jurists called "prudence" are required. Sometimes, judgment is relatively easy because the facts and the context make it so. But more often, in applications of the law of war, the responsibility of judgment looms large. Consider two recent examples.

On December 23, 1989, during the United States military action in Panama, First Sergeant Roberto Bryan, a nineteen-year veteran of the U.S. infantry, and other members of his unit stopped a carload of five Panamanians at a roadblock. One of the passengers of the car tossed a hand grenade at the American soldiers, injuring ten of them. The American soldiers opened fire, killing four of the Panamanians and wounding the fifth. The wounded man, who had been taken prisoner and was lying on the ground, allegedly moved, and First Sergeant Bryan, who claimed later that he believed the prisoner had concealed a second hand grenade and might have thrown it toward the U.S. soldiers, shot and killed the man. A U.S. officer who was present, First Lieutenant Brandon Thomas, accused Bryan of committing a war crime—shooting the Panamanian to avenge the wounds to his fellow U.S. soldiers—and Bryan was tried by court-martial. Although the law of war prohibits shooting combatants who have been taken prisoner, First Sergeant Bryan would have acted lawfully if it were reasonable, in the circumstances, for him to believe that the Panamanian prisoner posed an immediate threat, even if the belief proved subsequently to have been unfounded. Bryan was acquitted. Apparently, the members of the court-martial thought that there were reasonable doubts about Bryan's act.

Historically, the law of armed conflict has prohibited actions injuring the environment. In the early phases of the war against Iraq, the Iraqi government, consistent with threats made before the outbreak of hostilities, (i) released a large amount of crude oil into the Persian Gulf, apparently with the intention of hindering an amphibious invasion and also of fouling Saudi desalination plants that were providing potable water to the coalition forces, and (ii) set scores of oil wells ablaze, presumably to limit the visibility of coalition pilots attempting to engage targets on the ground. Two international legal instruments prohibit intentional destruction of the environment as a weapon if the results are of long duration. But the hindering of an amphibious invasion and aerial attacks certainly was a lawful objective, and the destruction of desalination plants providing water for the enemy could have been a legitimate target.

A number of political leaders in the international coalition and many commentators in the media promptly characterized the Iraqi action as a violation of the law of war and a war crime. But, wholly apart from the question of whether the instruments invoked are effective law, many judgments and appraisals must be made before the use of the oil weapon in these two fashions can be characterized as a war crime. In the Iraqi case, criteria of the necessity of the action from a military standpoint and the proportionality of the damage wrought vis-à-vis the military objectives sought have to be factored in before a conclusion of unlawfulness can be drawn. While much evidence is not yet available, it is quite possible that these particular Iraqi actions were not a violation of the law of war. The case is somewhat comparable to the United States use of Agent Orange and other defoliants in Vietnam. Its longer-term environmental consequences are still unclear.

We cite these two examples at the outset of this book as a precautionary measure. Legal judgment is a complex deliberative process that requires familiarity with the facts and law and the ability to consider impartially the different points of view. In no legal application should one rush to judgment. In the law of war, this caution is all the more urgent, because characterizations of war crimes serve to generate greater indignation and determination and may make the prosecution of the war easier but nastier.

Hasty conclusions that war crimes have been committed also depreciate the value and respect for this body of law. In addition, because international politics frequently settles for compromise solutions, the emotive rhetoric of war crimes allegations can sometimes hinder political settlements with adversaries who, in the heat of conflict, have been vilified. On the other hand, to subordinate the law of war to political objectives and to fail to draw the appropriate judgments can itself undermine the efficacy of this body of law.

In 1949, in the wake of World War II, most of the nations of the world, under the auspices of the International Committee of the Red Cross, convened in Geneva and produced four conventions dealing with a large number of humanitarian aspects of armed conflict on land and sea. The Geneva Conventions, which came into force in 1954, have been accepted by almost all states of the world and are an important conventional base of the modern law of armed conflict.

By the early 1960s decolonization, including "wars of national liberation," had become a major feature of international politics. But the Geneva Conventions had focused on the type of conflict experienced in World War II. In order to address the challenges of new forms of warfare, the International Committee of the Red Cross convened a new conference in Geneva. It culminated, in 1977, in two additional Protocols to the Geneva Conventions. These Protocols, while largely in consonance with the bulk of the provisions of the four Geneva Conventions of 1949, have been criticized sharply on several grounds by the United States and a number of states in Western Europe. In particular the Protocols have been criticized because they attempt to classify as combatants individuals who operate in the military arena without wearing a military uniform and without carrying arms openly, so long as the arms are carried openly immediately preceding the armed attack. Critics fear that this may result in an unfortunate blurring in the distinction between combatants and noncombatants. The Reagan administration decided not to submit Protocol I to the Senate for advice and consent, though it did agree to submit Protocol II, which addresses so-called noninternational conflict. Some other states that have ratified these additional Protocols insist that they are representative of the contemporary international law of armed conflict and, indeed, the United States supports a number of developments contained in Protocol I. The possibilities for dispute and misunderstanding in this sort of legal uncertainty are rife.

In addition to these developments, the United Nations General Assembly has passed resolutions dealing with a wide range of different aspects of the law of war. Some of the resolutions also have been expressed in the form of international conventions, but relatively few states have subscribed to them. The International Court of Justice, in the *Nicaragua*[6] case, to which the United States was a party but from which it withdrew after the jurisdictional decision, also purported to clarify and expand certain aspects of the modern law of war. A number of national courts have rendered important decisions as well. All of these various exercises may have some relevance for determining what the contemporary law in these matters is and must be considered by anyone trying to understand and follow the contemporary law of war.

In the United States, we tend to think of ourselves as living in a time of "peace." But in the last twenty years, we have engaged in two major wars (Vietnam and the Persian Gulf), three major invasions and occupations of countries, several punitive or reprisory activities, and a large number of threats. War is too much with us. Because it is, war is too important, in modern democracies, to be left only to the generals and, indeed, even to the politicians. Decisions about when to use force and how to use it are increasingly parts of national political debate. In this context, it is vital that citizens who wish to participate intelligently in these decisions understand the international law of war. Obviously, no generalist can be expected to master all of the fine points of this body of law or any other on a single reading. But anyone who believes in democracy also believes that the responsible citizen, given access to basic materials, may use them to facilitate his or her evaluation of options.

Our book is a contribution to that end. The idea for the book emerged from the many telephone calls received from journalists, politicians, and clergy seeking views on some aspect of the law of war. It was apparent that this was a subject of wide public concern. We have tried to address that concern by selecting the basic documents, judgments, and other decisions that comprise, together, the modern law of war. Inevitably, subjective evaluations play some role in the process of selection and exclusion. Some scholars may disagree with our selections; we readily acknowledge that this is a subject on which reasonable people may disagree. We have, however, tried to be thorough and to include those portions of the law that are most useful while pruning the ceremonial or administrative sections of the instruments. In addition to the basic material, we also have added a number of introductory notes and comments about application, currency, degree of controversiality, and "softness" of some of the selections.

As to treaties reproduced in this volume, a chart at the back of the book indicates the states that are parties to some of the more important conventions. Any special conditions they attached to their participation— so-called "reservations" or "objections"—are noted on the chart. We have not, however, followed the practice of a number of other collections and indicated states that have only *signed* particular treaties but have not ratified or otherwise acceded to them. In international law, the signature of a state's representative on a draft treaty means little more than authentication of the text. Compiling long lists of signatures of states that have not gone on to ratify may lead nonspecialists to believe that there is much greater adherence to the instrument in question than there really is. An effective law of war is an urgent necessity for the international community, but we believe no purpose is served by creating illusions that there may be more law than there really is.

We would hope that this material will serve to better inform the citizen, the journalist, the clergyman, and the politician, all of whom play roles in the making and application of the modern law of war.

W. Michael Reisman
Chris T. Antoniou
December 6, 1993
New Haven, Connecticut

ENDNOTES

1. "Wars of expulsion," now referred to euphemistically as "ethnic cleansing," seem to be a variant of "wars of annihilation."
2. *Trial of the Major War Criminals Before the International Military Tribunal*, vol. 1, p. 221 (1947).

3. Reproduced in part at p. 60.
4. The United States Navy, *Annotated Supplement to the Commander's Handbook on the Law of Naval Operations*, pp. 5–10 (Naval Warfare Publication [NWP] 9 [Rev. A] 1989).
5. United Nations Security Council Resolution 687, April 3, 1991.
6. Military and Paramilitary Activities in and Against Nicaragua (*Nicar.* v. *U.S.*), 1984 I.C.J., p. 392; 1986 I.C.J., p. 1.

THE
LAWS
OF
WAR

RESORTING TO MILITARY FORCE

Until this century, the unilateral resort to military force by a state for any reason it deemed appropriate was lawful. Early in the century international tribunals began to try to establish limitations on the right of states to engage in minor coercions or reprisals. Efforts to restrict the right to use force soon accelerated—spurred on by revulsion over the carnage of the Great War. The Covenant of the League of Nations (Part I of the Treaty of Peace With Germany), the first postwar effort, did not outlaw war as such, but did impose several restraints and preconditions on member states of the League before they could resort to war.

THE COVENANT OF THE LEAGUE OF NATIONS

[225 Consol. T.S. 188, 195, signed on June 28, 1919, at Versailles and entered into force among contracting parties on January 10, 1920; the United States did not ratify the Covenant]

. . .

Article 4
[Council]

1. The Council shall consist of Representatives of the Principal Allied and Associated Powers [the United States of America, the British Empire,

France, Italy, and Japan], together with Representatives of four other Members of the League. . . .

Article 11
[Action in Case of War or Threat of War]
1. Any war or threat of war, whether immediately affecting any of the Members of the League or not, is hereby declared a matter of concern to the whole League. . . .

Article 16
[Sanctions of Pacific Settlement]
1. Should any Member of the League resort to war in disregard of its covenants under Articles 12, 13 or 15, it shall *ipso facto* be deemed to have committed an act of war against all other Members of the League, which hereby undertake immediately to subject it to the severance of all trade or financial relations. . . .

2. It shall be the duty of the Council in such case to recommend to the several Governments concerned what effective military, naval or air force the Members of the League shall severally contribute to the armed forces to be used to protect the covenants of the League.

· · ·

NOTE: The Treaty for the Renunciation of War as an Instrument of National Policy of August 27, 1928, more generally known as the Pact of Paris or the Kellogg-Briand Pact, ambitiously sought to prohibit warfare. Most of the major powers of the day—including China, France, Germany, Great Britain, Japan, and the United States— became parties to the treaty.

THE KELLOGG-BRIAND PACT
[T.S. No. 796]

· · ·

Article I
The High Contracting Parties solemnly declare in the names of their respective peoples that they condemn recourse to war for the solution of

international controversies, and renounce it as an instrument of national policy in their relations with one another.

Article II

The High Contracting Parties agree that the settlement or solution of all disputes or conflicts of whatever nature or of whatever origin they may be, which may arise among them, shall never be sought except by pacific means.

.   .   .

NOTE: Because the Kellogg-Briand Pact was embedded in the larger institutional regime of the League of Nations, its effectiveness depended on the League, which proved to be unsuccessful.

The United Nations Charter in 1945 made an explicit effort to terminate the right of a state to engage in war. The spine of the United Nations system was its collective security mechanisms. Article 2(4) of the Charter set out the fundamental principle in this scheme while other provisions elaborated the machinery for its implementation.

CHARTER OF THE UNITED NATIONS

[T.S. No. 993, signed on June 26, 1945, at New York]

.   .   .

Article 2

.   .

4. All Members shall refrain in their international relations from the threat or use of force against the territorial integrity or political independence of any state, or in any other manner inconsistent with the Purposes of the United Nations.
[This scheme was to be effected by special procedures:]

.   .   .

THE SECURITY COUNCIL

Article 27
1. Each member of the Security Council shall have one vote.

.   .   .

3. Decisions of the Security Council on all other matters shall be made by an affirmative vote of seven members including the concurring votes of the permanent members. . . .

PACIFIC SETTLEMENT OF DISPUTES

Article 33
1. The parties to any dispute, the continuance of which is likely to endanger the maintenance of international peace and security, shall, first of all, seek a solution by negotiation, enquiry, mediation, conciliation, arbitration, judicial settlement, resort to regional agencies or arrangements, or other peaceful means of their own choice.
2. The Security Council shall, when it deems necessary, call upon the parties to settle their dispute by such means. . . .

ACTION WITH RESPECT TO THREATS TO THE PEACE, BREACHES OF THE PEACE, AND ACTS OF AGGRESSION

Article 39
The Security Council shall determine the existence of any threat to the peace, breach of the peace, or act of aggression and shall make recommendations, or decide what measures shall be taken in accordance with Articles 41 and 42, to maintain or restore international peace and security.

.   .   .

Article 41
The Security Council may decide what measures not involving the use of armed force are to be employed to give effect to its decisions, and it may call upon the Members of the United Nations to apply such measures. These may include complete or partial interruption of economic relations and of rail, sea, air, postal, telegraphic, radio, and other means of communication, and the severance of diplomatic relations.

Article 42

Should the Security Council consider that measures provided for in Article 41 would be inadequate or have proved to be inadequate, it may take such action by air, sea, or land forces as may be necessary to maintain or restore international peace and security. Such action may include demonstrations, blockade, and other operations by air, sea, or land forces of Members of the United Nations.

. . .

Article 45

In order to enable the United Nations to take urgent military measures, Members shall hold immediately available national air-force contingents for combined international enforcement action. . . .

Article 46

Plans for the application of armed force shall be made by the Security Council with the assistance of the Military Staff Committee.

. . .

Article 47

1. There shall be established a Military Staff Committee to advise and assist the Security Council on all questions relating to the Security Council's military requirements for the maintenance of international peace and security, the employment and command of forces placed at its disposal, the regulation of armaments, and possible disarmament.

. . .

Article 48

1. The action required to carry out the decisions of the Security Council for the maintenance of international peace and security shall be taken by all the Members of the United Nations or by some of them, as the Security Council may determine. . . .

Article 49

The Members of the United Nations shall join in affording mutual assistance in carrying out the measures decided upon by the Security Council.

. . .

Article 51

Nothing in the present Charter shall impair the inherent right of individual or collective self-defense if an armed attack occurs against a Member of the United Nations, until the Security Council has taken the measures necessary to maintain international peace and security. Measures taken by Members in the exercise of this right of self-defense shall be immediately reported to the Security Council and shall not in any way affect the authority and responsibility of the Security Council under the present Charter to take at any time such action as it deems necessary in order to maintain or restore international peace and security.

. . .

REGIONAL ARRANGEMENTS

Article 52

1. Nothing in the present Charter precludes the existence of regional arrangements or agencies for dealing with such matters relating to the maintenance of international peace and security as are appropriate for regional action, provided that such arrangements or agencies and their activities are consistent with the Purposes and Principles of the United Nations.

. . .

NOTE: The scheme in the Charter was a comprehensive collective security system in which the most powerful states, which were assigned permanent seats in the Security Council—the United States, the Soviet Union (now Russia), China, the United Kingdom, and France—were given primary responsibility for the maintenance of peace and security. If an event occurred that was deemed to threaten or breach the peace or constitute an act of aggression, the Security Council could decide on what it deemed to be an appropriate response. All other members of the United Nations were obliged to comply with the decision of the Security Council. The council also could draw upon certain military assets of UN members to effect its decision. But action by the council depended upon the unanimous agreement of the five permanent members. If any one of these states decided to veto the action, the council was paralyzed.

Shortly after the United Nations was established, the consensus between the United States and the Soviet Union, which had been one of the preconditions for its existence, disintegrated. Thereafter, each superpower could be expected to veto any action proposed for the Security Council that it deemed offensive to its interests. As a result, the council was paralyzed. For the next forty years, "the Charter gave you a 911 number to call when you were in trouble," a diplomat put it, "but there was no one at the other end of the line to pick up the phone."

Because Article 51 provided a backup procedure when the Security Council was unable to act, the United States began to develop a broad reading of this provision and to insist upon a right of individual or collective self-defense when the council was not operating. That interpretation, while not accepted by many other members of the United Nations, remained the American modus operandi of the postwar world. The United States still asserts this view.

◆

DEFINITION OF AGGRESSION

While a number of scholars have argued that the terms that are contingencies for the use of force—"aggression" and "self-defense"—should not be defined but in each case should be matters of appreciation, the General Assembly of the United Nations has sought to define the term "aggression" and, as a result, to regulate, to a greater extent, the conditions for lawful unilateral resort to self-defense by states. On December 4, 1974, the General Assembly adopted a "Definition of Aggression."

DEFINITION OF AGGRESSION

[G.A. Res. 3314, U.N. GAOR, 29th Sess., Supp. No. 31, at 142, U.N. Doc. A/9631 (1974)]

. . .

Article 1

Aggression is the use of armed force by a State against the sovereignty, territorial integrity or political independence of another State, or in any other manner inconsistent with the Charter of the United Nations, as set out in this Definition. . . .

Article 2

The first use of armed force by a State in contravention of the Charter shall constitute *prima facie* evidence of an act of aggression although the Security Council may, in conformity with the Charter, conclude that a determination that an act of aggression has been committed would not be justified in the light of other relevant circumstances, including the fact that the acts concerned or their consequences are not of sufficient gravity.

Article 3

Any of the following acts, regardless of a declaration of war, shall, subject to and in accordance with the provision of article 2, qualify as an act of aggression:

(a) The invasion or attack by the armed forces of a State of the territory of another State, or any military occupation, however temporary, resulting from such invasion or attack, or any annexation by the use of force of the territory of another State or part thereof;

(b) Bombardment by the armed forces of a State against the territory of another State or the use of any weapons by a State against the territory of another State;

(c) The blockade of the ports or coasts of a State by the armed forces of another State;

(d) An attack by the armed forces of a State on the land, sea or air forces, or marine and air fleets of another State;

(e) The use of armed forces of one State which are within the territory of another State with the agreement of the receiving State, in contravention of the conditions provided for in the agreement or any extension of their presence in such territory beyond the termination of the agreement;

(*f*) The action of a State in allowing its territory, which it has placed at the disposal of another State, to be used by that other State for perpetrating an act of aggression against a third State;

(*g*) The sending by or on behalf of a State of armed bands, groups, irregulars or mercenaries, which carry out acts of armed force against another State of such gravity as to amount to the acts listed above, or its substantial involvement therein.

Article 4

The acts enumerated above are not exhaustive and the Security Council may determine that other acts constitute aggression under the provisions of the Charter.

Article 5

1. No consideration of whatever nature, whether political, economic, military or otherwise, may serve as a justification for aggression.

2. A war of aggression is a crime against international peace. Aggression gives rise to international responsibility.

3. No territorial acquisition or special advantage resulting from aggression is or shall be recognized as lawful.

Article 6

Nothing in this Definition shall be construed as in any way enlarging or diminishing the scope of the Charter, including its provisions concerning cases in which the use of force is lawful.

Article 7

Nothing in this Definition, and in particular article 3, could in any way prejudice the right to self-determination, freedom and independence, as derived from the Charter, of peoples forcibly deprived of that right and referred to in the Declaration on Principles of International Law concerning Friendly Relations and Co-operation among States in accordance with the Charter of the United Nations, particularly peoples under colonial and racist régimes or other forms of alien domination; nor the right of these peoples to struggle to that end and to seek and receive support, in accordance with the principles of the Charter and in conformity with the above-mentioned Declaration.

. . .

NOTE: A resolution of the General Assembly of the United Nations is not binding under the Charter but is only a recommendation. Hence some scholars consider the General Assembly's definition to be "soft." But others have argued that it shows what a majority of states think international law on this point is and, as such, is customary law. The International Court of Justice relied on the Definition in its controversial decision in the Case Concerning Military and Paramilitary Activities in and Against Nicaragua (*Nicaragua* v. *United States of America*). That case had been brought by Nicaragua against the United States to challenge American support of the contra forces then operating against the Sandinista government in Nicaragua. The United States objected to the court's preliminary decision that it had jurisdiction and withdrew from the case. But the court proceeded to render judgment in the absence of the United States.

NICARAGUA v. UNITED STATES OF AMERICA

[1986 I.C.J. 1 (June 27, 1986) (opinion of the Court)]

.   .   .

18. The dispute before the Court between Nicaragua and the United States concerns events in Nicaragua subsequent to the fall of the Government of President Anastasio Somoza Debayle in Nicaragua in July 1979, and activities of the Government of the United States in relation to Nicaragua since that time. Following the departure of President Somoza, a Junta of National Reconstruction and an 18-member government was installed by the body which had led the armed opposition to President Somoza, the Frente Sandinista de Liberación Nacional (FSLN). That body had initially an extensive share in the new government, described as a "democratic coalition", and as a result of later resignations and reshuffles, became almost its sole component. Certain opponents of the new Government, primarily supporters of the former Somoza Government and in particular ex-members of the National Guard, formed themselves into irregular military forces, and commenced a policy of armed opposition, though initially on a limited scale.

19. The attitude of the United States Government to the "democratic coalition government" was at first favourable; and a programme of economic aid to Nicaragua was adopted. However by 1981 this attitude had changed. United States aid to Nicaragua was suspended in January 1981

and terminated in April 1981. According to the United States, the reason for this change of attitude was reports of involvement of the Government of Nicaragua in logistical support, including provision of arms, for guerrillas in El Salvador. . . .

20. The armed opposition to the new Government in Nicaragua, which originally comprised various movements, subsequently became organized into two main groups: the Fuerza Democrática Nicaragüense (FDN) and the Alianza Revolucionaria Democrática (ARDE). The first of these grew from 1981 onwards into a trained fighting force, operating along the borders with Honduras; the second, formed in 1982, operated along the borders with Costa Rica. . . . [I]t was made clear, not only in the United States press, but also in Congress and in official statements by the President and high United States officials, that the United States Government had been giving support to the *contras*, a term employed to describe those fighting against the present Nicaraguan Government. . . . According to Nicaragua, the *contras* have caused it considerable material damage and widespread loss of life. . . . It is contended by Nicaragua that the United States Government is effectively in control of the *contras*, that it devised their strategy and directed their tactics, and that the purpose of that Government was, from the beginning, to overthrow the Government of Nicaragua.

21. Nicaragua claims furthermore that certain military or paramilitary operations against it were carried out, not by the *contras*, who at the time claimed responsibility, but by persons in the pay of the United States Government, and under the direct command of United States personnel, who also participated to some extent in the operations . . . [that] include[d] the mining of certain Nicaraguan ports in early 1984, and attacks on ports, oil installations, a naval base . . .

24. As already noted, the United States has not filed any pleading on the merits of the case, and was not represented at the hearings devoted thereto. It did however make clear in its Counter-Memorial on the questions of jurisdiction and admissibility that "by providing, upon request, proportionate and appropriate assistance to third States not before the Court" it claims to be acting in reliance on the inherent right of self-defence "guaranteed . . . by Article 51 of the Charter" of the United Nations, that is to say the right of collective self-defence.

. . .

77. . . . According to a press report, the *contras* announced on 8 January 1984, that they were mining all Nicaraguan ports, and warning

all ships to stay away from them; but according to the same report, nobody paid much attention to this announcement. It does not appear that the United States Government itself issued any warning or notification to other States of the existence and location of the mines.

· · ·

80. On this basis, the Court finds it established that, on a date in late 1983 or early 1984, the President of the United States authorized a United States government agency to lay mines in Nicaraguan ports; that in early 1984 mines were laid in or close to the ports of El Bluff, Corinto and Puerto Sandino, either in Nicaraguan internal waters or in its territorial sea or both, by persons in the pay and acting on the instructions of that agency, under the supervision and with the logistic support of United States agents; that neither before the laying of the mines, nor subsequently, did the United States Government issue any public and official warning to international shipping of the existence and location of the mines; and that personal and material injury was caused by the explosion of the mines, which also created risks causing a rise in marine insurance rates.

· · ·

94. . . . [T]he Court is unable to find that the United States created an armed opposition in Nicaragua. However, according to press articles citing official sources close to the United States Congress, the size of the *contra* force increased dramatically once United States financial and other assistance became available.

· · ·

106. . . . [T]he Court is not satisfied that all the operations launched by the *contra* force, at every stage of the conflict, reflected strategy and tactics wholly devised by the United States. However, it is in the Court's view established that the support of the United States authorities for the activities of the *contras* took various forms over the years, such as logistic support, the supply of information on the location and movements of the Sandinista troops, the use of sophisticated methods of communication, the deployment of field broadcasting networks, radar coverage, etc. The Court finds it clear that a number of military and paramilitary operations by this force were decided and planned, if not actually by United States advisers, then at least in close collaboration with them, and on the basis of the intelligence and logistic support which the United

States was able to offer, particularly the supply aircraft provided to the *contras* by the United States.

. . .

126. The Court has before it, in the Counter-Memorial on jurisdiction and admissibility filed by the United States, the assertion that the United States, pursuant to the inherent right of individual and collective self-defence, and in accordance with the Inter-American Treaty of Reciprocal Assistance, has responded to requests from El Salvador, Honduras and Costa Rica, for assistance in their self-defence against aggression by Nicaragua. The Court has therefore to ascertain, so far as possible, the facts on which this claim is or may be based, in order to determine whether collective self-defence constitutes a justification of the activities of the United States here complained of. . . .

127. . . . In the Court's view . . . if Nicaragua has been giving support to the armed opposition in El Salvador, and if this constitutes an armed attack on El Salvador and the other appropriate conditions are met, collective self-defence could be legally invoked by the United States . . .

128. In its Counter-Memorial on jurisdiction and admissibility, the United States claims that Nicaragua has "promoted and supported guerrilla violence in neighboring countries", particularly in El Salvador; and has openly conducted cross-border military attacks on its neighbours, Honduras and Costa Rica.

. . .

195. In the case of individual self-defence, the exercise of this right is subject to the State concerned having been the victim of an armed attack. Reliance on collective self-defence of course does not remove the need for this. There appears now to be general agreement on the nature of the acts which can be treated as constituting armed attacks. In particular, it may be considered to be agreed that an armed attack must be understood as including not merely action by regular armed forces across an international border, but also "the sending by or on behalf of a State of armed bands, groups, irregulars or mercenaries, which carry out acts of armed force against another State of such gravity as to amount to" (*inter alia*) an actual armed attack conducted by regular forces, "or its substantial involvement therein". This description, contained in Article 3, paragraph (*g*), of the Definition of Aggression annexed to General Assembly resolution 3314 (XXIX), may be taken to reflect customary international law. The Court sees no reason to deny that, in customary

law, the prohibition of armed attacks may apply to the sending by a State of armed bands to the territory of another State, if such an operation, because of its scale and effects, would have been classified as an armed attack rather than as a mere frontier incident had it been carried out by regular armed forces. But the Court does not believe that the concept of "armed attack" includes not only acts by armed bands where such acts occur on a significant scale but also assistance to rebels in the form of the provision of weapons or logistical or other support. Such assistance may be regarded as a threat or use of force, or amount to intervention in the internal or external affairs of other States. It is also clear that it is the State which is the victim of an armed attack which must form and declare the view that it has been so attacked. There is no rule in customary international law permitting another State to exercise the right of collective self-defence on the basis of its own assessment of the situation. Where collective self-defence is invoked, it is to be expected that the State for whose benefit this right is used will have declared itself to be the victim of an armed attack.

· · · ·

229. . . . For the Court to conclude that the United States was lawfully exercising its right of collective self-defence, it must first find that Nicaragua engaged in an armed attack against El Salvador, Honduras or Costa Rica.

230. As regards El Salvador, the Court has found . . . that it is satisfied that between July 1979 and the early months of 1981, an intermittent flow of arms was routed via the territory of Nicaragua to the armed opposition in that country. The Court was not however satisfied that assistance had reached the Salvadorian armed opposition, on a scale of any significance, since the early months of 1981, or that the Government of Nicaragua was responsible for any flow of arms at either period. Even assuming that the supply of arms to the opposition in El Salvador could be treated as imputable to the Government of Nicaragua, to justify invocation of the right of collective self-defence in customary international law, it would have to be equated with an armed attack by Nicaragua on El Salvador. . . . [T]he Court is unable to consider that, in customary international law, the provision of arms to the opposition in another State constitutes an armed attack on that State. Even at a time when the arms flow was at its peak, and again assuming the participation of the Nicaraguan Government, that would not constitute such armed attack.

· · · ·

233. . . . So far as El Salvador is concerned, it appears to the Court that while El Salvador did in fact officially declare itself the victim of an armed attack, and did ask for the United States to exercise its right of collective self-defence, this occurred only on a date much later than the commencement of the United States activities which were allegedly justified by this request.

· · ·

238. Accordingly, the Court concludes that the plea of collective self-defence against an alleged armed attack on El Salvador, Honduras or Costa Rica, advanced by the United States to justify its conduct toward Nicaragua, cannot be upheld; and accordingly that the United States has violated the principle prohibiting recourse to the threat or use of force . . . and by its assistance to the *contras* [italics supplied] to the extent that this assistance "involve[s] [in original] a threat or use of force" . . .

· · ·

292. For these reasons,

· · ·

(2) By twelve votes to three,
Rejects the justification of collective self-defence maintained by the United States of America in connection with the military and paramilitary activities in and against Nicaragua the subject of this case;

· · ·

(3) By twelve votes to three,
Decides that the United States of America, by training, arming, equipping, financing and supplying the *contra* forces or otherwise encouraging, supporting and aiding military and paramilitary activities in and against Nicaragua, has acted, against the Republic of Nicaragua, in breach of its obligation under customary international law not to intervene in the affairs of another State;

· · ·

(4) By twelve votes to three,
Decides that the United States of America, by certain attacks on Nicaraguan territory in 1983–1984, namely attacks on Puerto Sandino on 13 September and 14 October 1983 . . . and further by those acts of

intervention referred to in subparagraph (3) hereof which involve the use of force, has acted, against the Republic of Nicaragua, in breach of its obligation under customary international law not to use force against another State;

. . .

(6) By twelve votes to three,

Decides that, by laying mines in the internal or territorial waters of the Republic of Nicaragua during the first months of 1984, the United States of America has acted, against the Republic of Nicaragua, in breach of its obligations under customary international law not to use force against another State. . . .

NOTE: The American judge, Stephen M. Schwebel, the British judge, Sir Robert Jennings, and the Japanese judge, Shigeru Oda, dissented. Portions of the opinions of judges Schwebel and Jennings are set out in the excerpts below.

DISSENTING OPINION OF JUDGE SCHWEBEL

176. In my view, the Court's reasoning, certainly as it applies to the case before the Court, is erroneous for the following reasons:

(a) A State is not necessarily and absolutely confined to responding in self-defence only if it is the object of armed attack.

(b) Armed attack in any event is not only the movement of regular armed forces across international frontiers; it is not only the sending by State A of armed bands across an international frontier to attack State B or overthrow its government; it is, as the Definition of Aggression puts it, "substantial involvement therein"—for example, the very sort of substantial involvement which Nicaragua's multifaceted involvement in promoting and sustaining the Salvadoran insurgency illustrates.

(c) In a case such as the case before the Court, where Nicaragua has carried out and continues to carry out the acts of support of armed insurgency against the Government of El Salvador which El Salvador and the United States have charged and the appendix to this opinion establishes, the Government of El Salvador has had the choice of acting in self-defence or capitulating. Lesser measures of counter-intervention could not suffice. It has chosen to act in self-defence, but it lacks the power to carry the battle to the territory of the aggressor, Nicaragua.

(d) In such a case, El Salvador is entitled to seek assistance in collective self-defence. Such assistance may in any event take place on the territory of El Salvador, as by the financing, provisioning and training of its troops by the United States. But, as shown below, contemporary international law recognizes that a third State is entitled to exert measures of force against the aggressor on its own territory and against its own armed forces and military resources.

177. I find the Court's enunciation of what it finds to be the law of counter-intervention as applied to this case unpersuasive for all these reasons. More generally, I believe that it raises worrisome questions. Let us suppose that State A's support of the subversion of State B, while serious and effective enough to place the political independence of State B in jeopardy, does not amount to an armed attack upon State B. Let us further suppose that State A acts against State B not only on its behalf but together with a Great Power and an organized international movement with a long and successful history of ideology and achievement in the cause of subversion and aggrandizement, and with the power and will to stimulate further the progress of what that movement regards as historically determined. If the Court's *obiter dictum* were to be treated as the law to which States deferred, other Great Powers and other States would be or could be essentially powerless to intervene effectively to preserve the political independence of State B and all other similarly situated States, most of which will be small. According to the Court, State B could take counter-measures against State A, but whether they would include measures of force is not said. What is said is that third States could not use force, whether or not the preservation of the political independence—or territorial integrity—of State B depended on the exertion of such measures. In short, the Court appears to offer—quite gratuitously—a prescription for overthrow of weaker governments by predatory governments while denying potential victims what in some cases may be their only hope of survival.

.   .   .

As the State which First Used Armed Force in Contravention of the Charter, the Aggressor is Nicaragua

262. The Government of the Republic of Nicaragua has come before the Court alleging that it is the victim of unlawful acts of the use of force and of intervention. At the same time, it has been demonstrated that

(a) the Nicaraguan Government came to power on the back of some of the very forms of foreign use of force and intervention of which it now complains;

(b) since coming to power, it has violated the undertakings which it gave to the OAS and its Members, some of whom facilitated its taking power;

(c) the Nicaraguan Government has itself committed acts tantamount to an armed attack upon El Salvador, and engaged in multiple acts of intervention in El Salvador and other neighbouring States; and that

(d) these aggressive acts of the Nicaraguan Government were committed "first", that is, they were committed before the United States undertook the responsive actions of which Nicaragua complains. In the light of these considerations, the boldness of the Nicaraguan case is remarkable.

263. The Definition of Aggression adopted by the General Assembly of the United Nations on 14 December 1974 not only provides that among the acts that qualify as acts of aggression is, "The sending by or on behalf of a State of armed bands, groups, irregulars or mercenaries, which carry out acts of armed force against another State . . . or its substantial involvement therein" but that, "The first use of armed force by a State in contravention of the Charter shall constitute prima facie evidence of an act of aggression . . .". This interpretation of Charter obligations is consistent rather than inconsistent with customary international law.

264. It is plain in this case that the first international use of armed force—consisting of Nicaragua's "substantial involvement" in the "sending" of armed bands to El Salvador which have carried out acts of armed force against El Salvador—was committed by Nicaragua. Sandinista involvement with the arming, training, and command and control of the Salvadoran insurgents, whose leadership has frequently been "sent" from Nicaragua to El Salvador and back, has been shown to go back to 1979, to have reached an early peak in January 1981, and to have fluctuated since. Nicaragua's own evidence establishes no exertions of force, indirect

or direct, by the United States against Nicaragua before December 1981 or early 1982. Thus the prima facie aggressor in this case is Nicaragua.

. . . .

DISSENTING OPINION OF
JUDGE SIR ROBERT JENNINGS

. . . The Court (para. 195) allows that, where a State is involved with the organization of "armed bands" operating in the territory of another State, this, "because of its scale and effects", could amount to "armed attack" under Article 51; but that this does not extend to "assistance to rebels in the form of the provision of weapons or logistical or other support" (*ibid.*). Such conduct, the Court goes on to say, may not amount to an armed attack; but "may be regarded as a threat or use of force, or amount to intervention in the internal or external affairs of other States" (*ibid.*).

It may readily be agreed that the mere provision of arms cannot be said to amount to an armed attack. But the provision of arms may, nevertheless, be a very important element in what might be thought to amount to armed attack, where it is coupled with other kinds of involvement. Accordingly, it seems to me that to say that the provision of arms, coupled with "logistical or other support" is not armed attack is going much too far. Logistical support may itself be crucial. According to the dictionary, logistics covers the "art of moving, lodging, and supplying troops and equipment" (*Concise Oxford English Dictionary*, 7th ed., 1982). If there is added to all this "other support", it becomes difficult to understand what it is, short of direct attack by a State's own forces, that may not be done apparently without a lawful response in the form of collective self-defence; nor indeed may be responded to at all by the use of force or threat of force, for, to cite the Court again, "States do not have a right of 'collective' armed response to acts which do not constitute an 'armed attack' " (see para. 211).

This looks to me neither realistic nor just in the world where power struggles are in every continent carried on by destabilization, interference in civil strife, comfort, aid and encouragement to rebels, and the like. The original scheme of the United Nations Charter, whereby force would be deployed by the United Nations itself, in accordance with the provisions of Chapter VII of the Charter, has never come into effect. Therefore an essential element in the Charter design is totally missing. In this situation it seems dangerous to define unnecessarily strictly the conditions for lawful self-defence, so as to leave a large area where both a forcible response to force is forbidden, and yet the United Nations employment of force, which was intended to fill that gap, is absent.

.   .   .

NOTE: The implications of these developments for the question of the right to resort to force under the law of armed conflict are considerable. The court concluded that the General Assembly's Definition means that a small-scale attack by an armed band from one state into another state does not amount to an "armed attack." In other words, it does not justify a forcible armed response. Quite the contrary. An armed response to those attacks would itself be considered an act of aggression. After the International Court illuminated this innovation in the *Nicaragua* case, this version of law appeared to allow provocative, low-intensity conflict, as it came to be known, and, ironically, encouraged states that felt they were victims of it to respond in kind. The court's holding is consistent with the position enunciated in Article 1 of Protocol I Additional to the Geneva Conventions, of 1977, which is not yet in force for the United States and many other states:

> *Article 1.* General Principles and Scope of Application.
>
> .   .   .
>
> 3. This Protocol, which supplements the Geneva Conventions of 12 August 1949 for the protection of war victims, shall apply in the situations referred to in Article 2 common to those Conventions [Article 2 is set out at page 153 herein].
> 4. The situations referred to in the preceding paragraph include armed conflicts in which peoples are fighting against colonial domination and alien occupation and against racist régimes in the exercise of their right of self-determination, as enshrined in the Charter of the United Nations and the Declaration on Principles of International Law concerning Friendly Relations and Co-operation among States in accordance with the Charter of the United Nations.[1]

AN EXCEPTION TO THE PRESCRIPTION AGAINST USE OF FORCE—REPRISALS

Traditionally, the law of armed conflict permitted states to engage in short-term, roughly proportional, but not necessarily symmetrical, punitive actions for violations of particular rights. These actions are known as "reprisals" and could be taken in peacetime in response to a general violation of international law or in wartime in response to some violation of the law of war. The two arbitral cases extracted below arose out of purported reprisals that took place during World War I. The tribunals set out the requirements for a legal reprisal—requirements that were not met in either case.

PORTUGAL V. GERMANY
(THE NAULILAA CASE)

[*Annual Digest of Public International Law Cases Years*
1927 and 1928 526
(Arnold D. McNair and Sir Hersch Lauterpacht, eds., 1931)]
Special Arbitral Tribunal. 31 July, 1928.
(Meuron, Fazy, Guex.)

THE FACTS.—On 19 October, 1914, [footnote omitted] a German official and two German officers of German South-West Africa were killed by members of a Portuguese frontier post at Naulilaa. Two other Germans were wounded and interned. As a measure of reprisals, and at the order of the Governor of German South-West Africa, German forces attacked and destroyed a number of forts and posts in the frontier region of Portuguese territory. In addition, the German Governor sent a military expedition in the direction of the fort of Naulilaa, whose garrison offered resistance but was finally forced to give up the fort and to retire. The retreat continued well into Portuguese territory, although the German troops withdrew, after the engagement, into the German colony. As the result of the Portuguese retreat the evacuated regions were subjected to looting and pillage on the part of the native population.

. . . Portugal contended that the reprisals were unjustified, and that Germany was responsible for the damage caused by the invasion.

After examining the circumstances accompanying the death of the three Germans on 19 October, 1914, the Commission found that the incident was entirely due to a misunderstanding caused largely by the fact that the Germans did not speak Portuguese and that the Portuguese officer who gave the order to fire believed himself to be in danger.

Held: That Germany was responsible.

(a) *Justification of reprisals.* A necessary condition for the legitimate exercise of the right of reprisals is the violation of a rule of international law by the State against which the reprisals are directed. There was no such violation in the present case, seeing that the death of the German officers was due to an accident caused by a misunderstanding. Neither could the internment of the two surviving Germans be regarded as an act contrary to the law of nations. A neutral State is entitled to disarm and intern members of belligerent forces which come into its territory.

(b) *Necessity of Request to Redress the Injury.*—Reprisals are illegal if they are not preceded by a request to remedy the alleged wrong. There is no justification for using force except in cases of necessity. It was true that this principle was not denied by Germany, who pleaded that the German Governor informed all German posts by wireless of the assassination of German officers, and this notice, which must have reached the Portuguese authorities, should have been sufficient warning. Germany also pleaded that the Governor refrained from sending a party with a flag of truce because he feared that the members of the party might be put to death or imprisoned. However, the Tribunal was not prepared to regard these reasons as sufficient.

(c) *Question of Proportionality.*—Reprisals which are altogether out of proportion with the act which prompted them, are excessive and therefore illegal. This is so even if it is not admitted that international law requires that reprisals should be approximately of the same degree as the injury to which they are meant as an answer. In addition, Germany did not, in the pleadings, deny the requirement of proportionality. There was an obvious lack of proportion between the incident of Naulilaa and the reprisals which followed the incident.

PORTUGAL v. GERMANY
(THE CYSNE)

[*Annual Digest of Public International Law Cases Years 1929 and 1930* 487 (Sir Hersch Lauterpacht, ed., 1935)]
(Meuron, Fazy, Guex.)

30 June, 1930

THE FACTS.—. . . On 28 May, 1915, *The Cysne*, a Portuguese cargo steamer, sailed with a cargo of pit props from Porto (Portugal) to New Port. When in the Channel she was stopped by a German submarine which, after examining the ship's papers, ordered the crew to take to the boats within five minutes and then sank the steamer. . . .

The German Government submitted:

. . .

(*b*) that the placing of pit props on the list of absolute contraband was a measure adopted in pursuance of reprisals against similar measures by Great Britain and her allies. . . .

Held: . . . [R]eprisals are not admissible against neutrals. There is no legal justification for reprisals except when they have been provoked by an act contrary to international law. This means that they are not admissible except against the State held guilty of the original violation of international law. It is conceivable that such legitimate reprisals may indirectly injure the subjects of the innocent neutral (*e.g.*, when the property of neutral subjects suffers in the course of a bombardment). But in the present case the reprisals were aimed directly and deliberately against neutral subjects. As Portugal had not violated, in relation to Germany, any rule of international law, acts of reprisals directed against her were contrary to international law.

. . .

NOTE: Article 50 of the 1907 Hague Convention on Land Warfare, which is considered in more detail in subsequent chapters, provides:

> No general penalty, pecuniary or otherwise, shall be inflicted upon the population on account of the acts of individuals for which they cannot be regarded as jointly and severally responsible.[2]

This provision does not appear to have been interpreted as a prohibition of reprisals. Sir Hersch Lauterpacht, one of the leading international jurists of this century, wrote: "Probably Article 50 of the Hague Regulations, enacting that no general penalty, pecuniary or otherwise, may be inflicted on the population on account of the acts of individuals for which it cannot be regarded as collectively responsible, does not prevent the burning, by way of reprisals, of villages or even towns, for a treacherous attack committed there on enemy soldiers by unknown individuals, and, this being so, a brutal belligerent has his opportunity."[3] But Protocol I Additional to the Geneva Conventions, of 1977,[4] which, as previously noted, is not yet in force for the United States and many other states, provides:

> 1. Civilian objects shall not be the object of attack or of reprisals. Civilian objects are all objects which are not military objectives as defined in paragraph 2.
> 2. Attacks shall be limited strictly to military objectives. In so far as objects are concerned, military objectives are limited to those objects which by their nature, location, purpose or use make an effective contribution to military action and whose total or partial destruction, capture or neutralization, in the circumstances ruling at the time, offers a definite military advantage.
> 3. In case of doubt whether an object which is normally dedicated to civilian purposes, such as a place of worship, a house or other dwelling or a school, is being used to make an effective contribution to military action, it shall be presumed not to be so used.[5]

Protocol I does not preclude resort to reprisals as such; it only addresses their appropriate target and scope. The question of whether states are entitled, under the modern law of war, to undertake forcible reprisals or reactions is uncertain. The International Law Commission, an organ of the General Assembly of the United Nations, in a draft on State Responsibility, has stated in Article 30:

> The wrongfulness of an act of a State not in conformity with an obligation of that State towards another State is precluded if the act constitutes a measure legitimate under international law against that other State, in con-

sequence of an internationally wrongful act of that other State.[6]

This is an inelegant and confusing formulation, not uncommon in legal writing. What it says, in effect, is that a state may be permitted to act illegally against another state in response to a wrong the other state inflicted on it. That, of course, is the core of the doctrine of reprisal.

The American Law Institute's Restatement of Foreign Relations Law provides:

> [A] State victim of a violation of an international obligation by another state may resort to countermeasures that might otherwise be unlawful, if such measures (a) are necessary to terminate the violation or prevent further violation, or to remedy the violation; and (b) are not out of proportion to the violation and the injury suffered.[7]

But the American Law Institute qualifies this right of resort to force by reference to international law:

> The threat or use of force in response to a violation of international law is subject to prohibitions on the threat or use of force in the United Nations Charter . . .[8]

In response to questions about the United States' position concerning the resort to force in the form of reprisals in general and by Israel in particular, the Office of the Legal Adviser at the Department of State released the following statement in 1979:

> Initially, the United States joined in the adoption of Security Council resolutions which isolated and condemned as illegal Israeli armed reprisals regardless of the provocations involved. [1953–1964] [in original] . . . While the United States has modified its initial position of willingness to isolate armed reprisals and condemn them as illegal by insisting on a balanced condemnation of both the provocative acts, especially acts of terrorism, and the armed reprisals, the United States has not changed its position that reprisals involving the use of force are illegal. . . . In addition to

the above possible examples of United States conduct of reprisal actions involving the use of force and threat of such use of force, it is clear that the United States recognizes that patterns of attacks or infiltration can rise to the level of an "armed attack" thus justifying a responding use of force in the exercise of the right of self-defense. . . . In conclusion, it is clear that the United States has taken the categorical position that reprisals involving the use of force are illegal under international law; that it is generally not willing to condemn reprisals without also condemning provocative terrorist acts; and that it recognizes the difficulty of distinguishing between proportionate self-defense and reprisals but maintains the distinction. Where the United States has itself possibly engaged in reprisal action involving the use of force, characterization of the action has been confused by equating it also with self-defense. These so-called reprisal incidents took place in the context of a war justified by the United States Government as collective self-defense, and on this basis, could be distinguished from the reprisal raids conducted by Israel. It is also clear that the United States has determined that patterns of attacks can constitute a level of "armed attack" justifying the use of force in self-defense.[9]

◆

SOME OTHER EXCEPTIONS TO THE PRESCRIPTION AGAINST USE OF FORCE

A. Decolonization

The United Nations General Assembly has tended to condemn uses of force by and against states. But it also has developed a number of exceptions. One is for military force used to secure decolonization and self-determination. The Assembly's Declaration on Principles of International Law concerning Friendly Relations, which was approved in 1970, provides:

By virtue of the principle of equal rights and self-determination of peoples enshrined in the Charter of the United Nations, all peoples have the right freely to determine, without external interference, their political status and to pursue their economic, social and cultural development, and every State has the duty to respect this right in accordance with the provisions of the Charter. [10]

The operational implications of this right are spelled out three paragraphs later.

Every State has the duty to refrain from any forcible action which deprives peoples . . . of their right to self-determination and freedom and independence. *In their actions against, and resistance to, such forcible action in pursuit of the exercise of their right to self-determination, such peoples are entitled to seek and to receive support in accordance with the purposes and principles of the Charter.* [11] [italics supplied]

Note here the beginning of an attempt at inverting customary law. "Peoples" have the right to "self-determination" and "freedom and independence." The state against which these groups are struggling must refrain from any action that impedes the struggle, i.e., it must refrain from actions that could otherwise be characterized as self-defense. Third states are obliged to help the struggling groups but cannot be held legally responsible by the targeted state.

The Convention against the Taking of Hostages of 1979[12] is even more explicit in setting out the implications of the inversion. Article 1(1) defines the offense prohibited by the Convention as follows:

Any person who seizes or detains and threatens to kill, to injure or to continue to detain another person (hereinafter referred to as the "hostage") in order to compel a third party, namely, a State, an international intergovernmental organization, a natural or juridical person, or a group of persons, to do or abstain from doing any act as an explicit or implicit condition for the release of the hostage commits the offence of taking of hostages ("hostage-taking") within the meaning of this Convention. [13]

But Article 12 of the same Convention provides in pertinent part:

> [T]he present Convention shall not apply to an act of
> hostage-taking committed in the course of armed con-
> flicts, as defined in the Geneva Conventions of 1949
> and the Protocols thereto, including armed conflicts,
> mentioned in article 1, paragraph 4, of Additional Pro-
> tocol I of 1977, [footnote omitted] in which peoples
> are fighting against colonial domination and alien oc-
> cupation and against racist régimes in the exercise of
> their right of self-determination, as enshrined in the
> Charter of the United Nations and the Declaration on
> Principles of International Law concerning Friendly
> Relations and Co-operation among States in accordance
> with the Charter of the United Nations.[14]

B. Brezhnev and Reagan Doctrines

Both the United States and the former Soviet Union, at various
times, have asserted the right to: (1) intervene militarily in strategic
areas close to them, and (2) to provide covert support to selected
insurgencies against existing governments. The genesis of these claims
can be traced as far back as the Monroe Doctrine for the United States
and the first Congresses of the Communist International (COMIN-
TERN) for the former Soviet Union. Neither claim has been endorsed
in any formal way by the international community, but particular
actions effected under them sometimes have been tolerated or even
accepted.

C. The United States' Perspective

As the remaining superpower and the critical force in the United
Nations security system, the United States has defined for itself a
special role and special prerogatives with regard to the use of force.
In a speech on January 5, 1993, then President Bush, speaking at
West Point, said,

> . . . Military force is never a tool to be used lightly, or
> universally. In some circumstances it may be essential.
> In others, counterproductive. I know that many people
> would like to find some formula, some easy formula to

apply, to tell us with precision when and where to intervene with force.

. . .

But to warn against a futile quest for a set of hard and fast rules to govern the use of military force is not to say there cannot be some principles to inform our decisions. Such guidelines can prove useful in sizing and indeed shaping our forces, and in helping us to think our way through this key question.

Using military force makes sense as a policy where the stakes warrant, where and when force can be effective, where no other policies are likely to prove effective, where its application can be limited in scope and time, and where the potential benefits justify the potential costs and sacrifice.

Once we are satisfied that force makes sense, we must act with the maximum possible support. The United States can and should lead, but we will want to act in concert, where possible, involving the United Nations or other multinational grouping.

. . .

But in every case involving the use of force, it will be essential to have a clear and achievable mission, a realistic plan for accomplishing the mission, and criteria no less realistic for withdrawing U.S. forces once the mission is complete.[15]

In his inaugural address shortly thereafter, President Clinton said,

. . . When our vital interests are challenged, or the will and conscience of the international community defied, we will act—with peaceful diplomacy when possible, with force when necessary. The brave Americans serving our nation in the Persian Gulf, in Somalia, and wherever else they stand are testament to our resolve.[16]

One month later, in an address to the European Institute in Washington, a member of President Clinton's National Security Council said, "I think you will see us willing to use force again on a case-by-case basis, but in a variety of combinations."[17] Plainly, the United States sees its unilateral use of force in circumstances it deems appropriate as consistent with, and an implementation of, international law. This self-perception continues to be controversial.

◆

CONCLUSION

International legal prohibitions on the use of force are clearer than they were at the beginning of the century but are still fuzzy around the edges. The major texts since the League of Nations have sought to prohibit unilateral uses of force. But the pattern of condemnation of violations of the law regarding the resort to force over the past forty-five years has been irregular. A careful examination of the pattern suggests that not all initiatives using force have been deemed unlawful. It is clear that uses of force *across* international boundaries have been viewed as much more threatening to the international system than have uses of force *within* national boundaries. Hence gross human rights violations in particular countries that were effected by massive uses of military force, for example, Syria's brutal suppression of the uprising of Hama or Iraq's massacre of Kurdish noncombatants with chemical weapons at Halabjah, aroused some popular indignation but excited relatively little formal international condemnation. But actions across state boundaries, for example, the former Soviet Union in Afghanistan, the United States in Grenada and Panama, Iraq in Kuwait and so on, while all treated differently, usually were subjects of immediate and formal international consideration. It appears that international decision makers still feel that cross-boundary violations are the most threatening to the international political system and require a clear and forceful response. Situations that can be defined as internal rather than international, such as Soviet suppression of self-determination in Estonia, Latvia, and Lithuania, appear to have been viewed by many as internal efforts to control domestic violence and have not excited as clear an international condemnation as a cross-border incursion. Reaction to Serb conduct in Bosnia-Hercegovina and Croatia has been more complicated. While the international community has recognized the sovereignty of these two new states and condemned Serb conduct therein, the community has been reticent to use the military instrument to quell the carnage.

One exception to prohibitions on national resort to force seems to have developed for decolonization, the historic process in which the major European empires, created over the past five centuries, were rolled back, with new states, under indigenous governments, created in their place. Thus, there has been remarkably little condemnation of cross-boundary violence in decolonization cases such as India in Goa, and Indonesia in East Timor. When Argentina sought to regain control of the Falkland Islands from the United Kingdom, which it has claimed for more than a century, the Security Council characterized the Argentine action as a "breach of the peace" but refrained from using the term "act of aggression."

There is some evidence of a rather uncertain toleration for cross-boundary uses of force that are directed at removing intolerably vicious governments and replacing them with popularly based governments. Historically, this was called "humanitarian intervention." In 1979, the Tanzanian army expelled the Amin government from Uganda without international condemnation. In the same year, French paratroopers expelled the Bokassa government from the Central African Republic and placed David Dakko in power, again without international condemnation. When Vietnam entered Cambodia in 1979 to expel the Pol Pot regime, there was no initial condemnation, but condemnation swelled when it became apparent that Vietnam intended to install a puppet government in Phnom Penh. In the case of the United States' removal of Manuel Noriega from Panama and the installation of the internationally confirmed government of President Endara, there was formal condemnation, but it subsided quite quickly. The international community approved of the dispatch by the United States of over 25,000 Marines to Somalia to deter factional fighting and to expedite delivery of relief supplies. One may infer from cases such as these that an operational code has developed that tolerates the use of force to quell internal strife, to overthrow colonial or racist regimes, and for certain humanitarian purposes. But the matter continues to be controversial and this uncertainty makes a continuing law of war all the more relevant and urgent.

ENDNOTES

1. Protocol Additional to the Geneva Conventions of 1949, Relating to Protection of Victims of International Armed Conflicts (Protocol I), June 8, 1977, 1125 U.N.T.S. 3.
2. Convention on Laws and Customs of War on Land (Hague, IV), Oct. 18, 1907, 1 Bevans 631, 652.
3. L. Oppenheim, *International Law*, Vol. II, *Disputes, War and Neutrality* 565 (Sir Hersch Lauterpacht, ed., 7th ed., 1952).
4. Protocol Additional to the Geneva Conventions of 1949, Relating to Protection of Victims of International Armed Conflicts (Protocol I), June 8, 1977, 1125 U.N.T.S. 3.
5. *Ibid.* at 27.
6. *Report of the International Law Commission to the General Assembly*, [1980] 2 Y.B. Int'l. L. Comm'n. 33.
7. Restatement (Third) of Foreign Relations Law of the United States, § 905 (1987).
8. *Ibid.*
9. Marian L. Nash, *Digest of United States Practice in International Law 1979* 1749–1752 (1983).
10. G.A. Res. 2625, U.N. GAOR, 25th Sess., Supp. No. 28, at 123, U.N. Doc. A/8028 (1971).
11. *Ibid.* at 124.
12. International Convention Against the Taking of Hostages, Dec. 17, 1979, G.A. Res. 146, U.N. GAOR, 34th Sess., Supp. No. 46, at 245, U.N. Doc. A/34/46 (1980).
13. *Ibid.*
14. *Ibid.* at 246–47.
15. "Bush's Talk to Cadets: When 'Force Makes Sense,' " *The New York Times*, Jan. 6, 1993, p. A6.
16. Advance Text of President Bill Clinton's Inaugural Address, Prepared for Delivery at 12:05 P.M., U.S. Capitol, Washington, D.C., Wednesday, January 20, 1993.
17. Jennone Walker, quoted in Martin, "U.S. Message in Bosnia Air-drop Plan," *Financial Times*, Feb. 26, 1993, p. 3.

USING FORCE

The Declaration of St. Petersburg of 1868, in which the parties renounced the use of projectiles below a certain weight, was one of the earliest international efforts to develop explicit limitations on how war is to be conducted.[1] The object of the Declaration itself is more of historical than practical interest, but its Preamble is still important, for it explains eloquently yet economically the concerns underlying this part of the law of war and in a more general sense the new conceptions and objectives of warfare that made it possible.

THE DECLARATION OF ST. PETERSBURG

[1 A.J.I.L. (Supp.) 95–96 (1907), signed on November 29, 1868, at St. Petersburg]

[T]he progress of civilization should have the effect of alleviating as much as possible the calamities of war . . .

[T]he only legitimate object which states should endeavor to accomplish during war is to weaken the military force of the enemy . . .

[F]or this purpose, it is sufficient to disable the greatest possible number of men . . .

[T]his object would be exceeded by the employment of arms which uselessly aggravate the sufferings of disabled men, or render their death inevitable . . .

[T]he employment of such arms would, therefore, be contrary to the laws of humanity . . .

NOTE: The more general proposition to which this approach leads was expressed in Article 22 of the 1907 Hague Convention (IV) Respecting the Laws and Customs of War on Land: "The right of belligerents to adopt a means of injuring the enemy is not unlimited."[2] The same principles underlie the United States Army's view of the law of war, as expressed in the following extract from a United States Army field manual:

THE LAW OF LAND WARFARE[3]

. . .

CHAPTER 1: BASIC RULES AND PRINCIPLES

. . .

2. *Purposes of the Law of War*
. . . [T]he law of land warfare . . . desire[s] to diminish the evils of war by:

  a. Protecting both combatants and noncombatants from unnecessary suffering;
  b. Safeguarding certain fundamental human rights of persons who fall into the hands of the enemy, particularly prisoners of war, the wounded and sick, and civilians; and
  c. Facilitating the restoration of peace.

3. *Basic Principles*
  a. *Prohibitory Effect.* The law of war places limits on the exercise of a belligerent's power in the interests mentioned in paragraph 2 and requires that belligerents refrain from employing any kind or degree of violence which is not actually necessary for military purposes and that they conduct hostilities with regard for the principles of humanity and chivalry.
  The prohibitory effect of the law of war is not minimized by

"military necessity" which has been defined as that principle which justifies those measures not forbidden by international law which are indispensable for securing the complete submission of the enemy as soon as possible. Military necessity has been generally rejected as a defense for acts forbidden by the customary and conventional laws of war inasmuch as the latter have been developed and framed with consideration for the concept of military necessity.

. . . . .

41. Unnecessary Killing and Devastation
. . . [L]oss of life and damage to property must not be out of proportion to the military advantage to be gained. Once a fort or defended locality has surrendered, only such further damage is permitted as is demanded by the exigencies of war . . .[4]

NOTE: Each successive effort to codify the law of armed conflict has attempted to expand and illuminate these principles and propositions. Customary international law, in a development that has paralleled and sometimes intersected with efforts at formal codification, has emphasized that each lawful use of force must be militarily necessary and proportional to that necessity. Proportionality frequently has focused on the selection of weapons that are effective in the theater in which they are being used but still capable of discriminating between combatants and noncombatants. The late Waldemar Solf, former chief of the International Affairs Division of the U.S. Army's Office of the Judge Advocate General, along with professors Bothe and Partsch, two leading German authorities on the law of war, offered the following discussion of how one determines if a particular use of force provides sufficient military benefits to qualify it as proportional to the collateral damage it also causes:

> The principle of proportionality is a general principle of the law of armed conflict which has found its expression in such provisions as the prohibition of "unnecessary" suffering (Art. 23(c) of the Hague Convention no. IV of 1907). It is not restricted to the question of the protection of the civilian population for which it has now been codified by Part IV of Protocol I. An obvious example that medical units cannot be ex-

empted by law from suffering collateral damage is the existence of sickbays on men of war. If it were inadmissible to subject medical units to collateral damage, no attempt to sink a warship with a sickbay aboard would be permissible. In applying the proportionality test to the protection of medical units against collateral damage, everything depends on the concrete situation. The yardstick of proportionality is the concrete and direct military advantage anticipated. If a medical unit operates near an important firing position (which it often has to do), the neutralization of this position constitutes a great advantage for the enemy and the enemy is consequently entitled to run the risk of causing a high degree of collateral damage within the medical unit as a result of the attack directed against the firing position. On the other hand, small and unimportant military objectives may not be attacked if this may be expected to cause important collateral damage within major medical units such as field hospitals.[5]

◆

THE DUTY TO INSTRUCT SOLDIERS IN THE LAW OF WAR

Hague Convention (IV) Respecting the Laws and Customs of War on Land

[1 Bevans 631, signed on October 18, 1907, at The Hague]

. . .

Article 1
The Contracting Powers shall issue instructions to their armed land forces which shall be in conformity with the Regulations respecting the Laws and Customs of War on Land, annexed to the present Convention.

. . .

GENEVA CONVENTION RELATIVE TO THE TREATMENT OF PRISONERS OF WAR (GENEVA III)

[6 U.S.T. 3317, signed on August 12, 1949, at Geneva; the other three Geneva Conventions of 1949 contain a corresponding article—Geneva I (Article 47), Geneva II (Article 48), and Geneva IV (Article 144)]

. . .

Article 127

The High Contracting Parties undertake, in time of peace as in time of war, to disseminate the text of the present Convention as widely as possible in their respective countries, and, in particular, to include the study thereof in their programmes of military and, if possible, civil instruction, so that the principles thereof may become known to all their armed forces and to the entire population. Any military or other authorities, who in time of war assume responsibilities in respect of prisoners of war, must possess the text of the Convention and be specially instructed as to its provisions.

. . .

NOTE: This is a critical position in the law of armed conflict, in many ways the linchpin of its effectiveness. If the rules set out in treaties are not available to the actual fighters, the rules will have little effect. Unfortunately, relatively few states appear to teach the law of war to their military forces. When the ranks and officer corps are illiterate, the possibilities of fulfilling the duties imposed by the articles noted above are severely restricted.

◆

DUTY OF NOTIFICATION

HAGUE CONVENTION (III) RELATIVE TO THE OPENING OF HOSTILITIES

[1 Bevans 619, signed on October 18, 1907, at The Hague]

. . .

Article 1
The Contracting Powers recognize that hostilities between themselves must not commence without previous and explicit warning, in the form either of a reasoned declaration of war or of an ultimatum with conditional declaration of war.

Article 2
The existence of a state of war must be notified to the neutral Powers without delay, and shall not take effect in regard to them until after the receipt of a notification, which may, however, be given by telegraph. Neutral Powers, nevertheless, cannot rely on the absence of notification if it is clearly established that they were in fact aware of the existence of a state of war.

NOTE: Formal declarations of war have fallen into obsolescence, but the basic principle here continues to be important. A requirement that nations about to engage in war ensure that their adversaries, as well as neutral third parties, know of their intentions limits the possibilities of surprise attacks. If surprise attacks were generally permitted, the level of expectation of violence would always be high, and the incentive to preempt even the possibility of a surprise attack would make the occurrence of wars more frequent. What appears to be demanded is not notification of the precise moment at which conflict will commence, but notice that the nature of the relationship has changed or that certain contingent acts by the other party will lead to forceful reaction.

♦

QUALIFYING BELLIGERENTS

Both customary and conventional law have sought, at least until 1977, to maintain the distinction between combatants and noncombatants with as much clarity as possible. Hence great attention was given to developing distinctive means of identification of belligerents and, as an incentive and, to an extent, a reward, assuring those who were so identified of the special protections available to prisoners of war.[6] Because of the centrality of the distinction between belligerents and civilians, great attention also was given to regulating "ruses" and tricks to avoid "perfidy" (unlawful ruses). Perfidious tricks are intolerable to the contemporary law of war because they break down the distinction between fighters and civilians.

HAGUE CONVENTION (IV) RESPECTING THE LAWS AND CUSTOMS OF WAR ON LAND, ANNEX TO THE CONVENTION

[1 Bevans 631, signed on October 18, 1907, at The Hague]

. . .

THE QUALIFICATIONS OF BELLIGERENTS

Article 1
The laws, rights, and duties of war apply not only to armies, but also to militia and volunteer corps fulfilling the following conditions:
1. To be commanded by a person responsible for his subordinates;
2. To have a fixed distinctive emblem recognizable at a distance;
3. To carry arms openly; and
4. To conduct their operations in accordance with the laws and customs of war.

In countries where militia or volunteer corps constitute the army, or form part of it, they are included under the denomination "army."

Article 2

The inhabitants of a territory which has not been occupied, who, on the approach of the enemy, spontaneously take up arms to resist the invading troops without having had time to organize themselves in accordance with Article 1, shall be regarded as belligerents *if they carry arms openly* and if they respect the laws and customs of war. [italics added]

Article 3

The armed forces of the belligerent parties may consist of combatants and noncombatants. In the case of capture by the enemy, both have a right to be treated as prisoners of war.

. . .

SPIES

Article 29

A person can only be considered a spy when, acting clandestinely or on false pretences, he obtains or endeavours to obtain information in the zone of operations of a belligerent, with the intention of communicating it to the hostile party.

Thus, soldiers not wearing a disguise who have penetrated into the zone of operations of the hostile army, for the purpose of obtaining information, are not considered spies. Similarly, the following are not considered spies: Soldiers and civilians, carrying out their mission openly, intrusted with the delivery of despatches intended either for their own army or for the enemy's army. To this class belong likewise persons sent in balloons for the purpose of carrying despatches and, generally, of maintaining communications between the different parts of an army or a territory.

Article 30

A spy taken in the act shall not be punished without previous trial.

Article 31

A spy who, after rejoining the army to which he belongs, is subsequently captured by the enemy, is treated as a prisoner of war, and incurs no responsibility for his previous acts of espionage.

. . .

PROTOCOL I ADDITIONAL TO THE GENEVA CONVENTIONS OF 1949

[1125 U.N.T.S. 3, adopted on June 8, 1977, at Geneva]

. . .

Article 44
Combatants and Prisoners of War

1. Any combatant, as defined in Article 43, who falls into the power of an adverse Party shall be a prisoner of war.

2. While all combatants are obliged to comply with the rules of international law applicable in armed conflict, violations of these rules shall not deprive a combatant of his right to be a combatant or, if he falls into the power of an adverse Party, of his right to be a prisoner of war, except as provided in paragraphs 3 and 4.

3. In order to promote the protection of the civilian population from the effects of hostilities, combatants are obliged to distinguish themselves from the civilian population while they are engaged in an attack or in a military operation preparatory to an attack. Recognizing, however, that there are situations in armed conflicts where, owing to the nature of the hostilities an armed combatant cannot so distinguish himself, he shall retain his status as a combatant, provided that, in such situations, he carries his arms openly:

  (a) During each military engagement, and
  (b) During such time as he is visible to the adversary while he is engaged in a military deployment preceding the launching of an attack in which he is to participate.

Acts which comply with the requirements of this paragraph shall not be considered as perfidious within the meaning of Article 37, paragraph 1(c).

. . .

NOTE: When combatants are clearly marked as such, noncombatants also are apparent, and the capacity of fighters to distinguish them and to avoid firing on them in error is enhanced. Hence the emphasis in many of the earlier Conventions on uniforms and on carrying arms openly. A majority of the states that participated in the international conferences that adopted the Additional Protocols of 1977 were sympathetic to the insurgent sides in the so-called "wars of national liberation." Such insurgents usually did not wear uniforms or carry their arms openly, but concealed themselves among the population at large.

The concealed combatant certainly has an advantage over the uniformed soldier, but the advantage comes with a price that others must pay. It inevitably leads to increased casualties among the civilian population, as the uniformed adversary can no longer clearly distinguish between combatant and noncombatant. In some wars of national liberation, this side effect may have been intentionally sought by the guerrilla forces as a way of forcing the government to act in ways that would alienate the population and drive it into the guerrilla camp. These provisions have been of particular concern to states that have refused to become party to Additional Protocol I.

Protocol I attempts to expand the category of individuals considered combatants to include concealed guerrilla forces. It also attempts to exclude a class of individuals that always had been considered combatants—mercenaries. The effect of Protocol I's downgrading of the status of mercenaries, however, is unclear. On December 4, 1989, the United Nations General Assembly adopted the International Convention against the Recruitment, Use, Financing and Training of Mercenaries (29 I.L.M. 89 (1990)). The convention will enter into force on the thirtieth day following the deposit of the twenty-second instrument of ratification or accession with the United Nations Secretary-General; but as of November 29, 1993, only five accessions (Barbados, Cyprus, Maldives, Seychelles, and Togo) and two ratifications (Suriname and Ukraine) had been received.[7] This limited international participation in the Convention on Mercenaries is evidence, perhaps, that while the proscription on mercenaries is to be found in Protocol I, there remains at present limited support for such a proposition.

PROTOCOL I ADDITIONAL TO THE GENEVA CONVENTIONS OF 1949

[1125 U.N.T.S. 3, adopted on June 8, 1977, at Geneva]

. . . .

Article 47
Mercenaries

1. A mercenary shall not have the right to be a combatant or a prisoner of war.

2. A mercenary is any person who:
 (a) Is specially recruited locally or abroad in order to fight in an armed conflict;
 (b) Does, in fact, take a direct part in the hostilities;
 (c) Is motivated to take part in the hostilities essentially by the desire for private gain and, in fact, is promised, by or on behalf of a Party to the conflict, material compensation substantially in excess of that promised or paid to combatants of similar ranks and functions in the armed forces of that Party;
 (d) Is neither a national of a Party to the conflict nor a resident of territory controlled by a Party to the conflict;
 (e) Is not a member of the armed forces of a Party to the conflict; and
 (f) Has not been sent by a State which is not a Party to the conflict on official duty as a member of its armed forces.

.   .   .

NOTE: The Hague Rules of Aërial Warfare distinguish between combatant and noncombatant aircraft. The Rules never entered into force and their status as law has been doubtful, even more so in the light of technological changes. Most of the techniques of visual identification are not relevant in an environment of supersonic flight, night operations, long-range communications, and weapon systems that rely on radar.

Given the complex network of civil aviation about the globe and its continued operation during many small wars, rules and procedures for distinguishing civilian from military craft are urgent. As the recent downing of the Iranian Airbus by the U.S.S. *Vincennes* showed, the opportunities for tragic mistakes here are great. The reader may ponder what measures military forces take to not engage noncombatant aircraft. While most aircraft, civilian and military, are equipped with a transponder that may be used to emit an electronic transmission of a four-digit number (provided by civil or military authorities) between 0000 and 9999 (with each number signifying a particular aircraft or type of aircraft), the Identify Friend or Foe (IFF) system, as it is called by the military, is of little importance. Due in part to administrative difficulties in continuously acquiring updated codes from civil authorities and, perhaps more importantly, the fear that enemy military aircraft may use civilian aircraft codes, the U.S. military, and probably the military of other states instead rely upon a combination of things to determine the status of an aircraft. The following criteria are often used to determine if an aircraft is a combatant and, consequently, may be fired upon: (1) whether the aircraft is within a predesignated civilian flight corridor; (2) whether the aircraft is flying through the corridor at a time normally scheduled for civilian flights; (3) whether the aircraft appears to be heading on a vector toward friendly ships or other sites; (4) whether the aircraft has the flight profile of a civilian aircraft, that is whether it is flying at speeds commensurate with civil aircraft capabilities; (5) whether the aircraft is descending in an attack mode; (6) whether the aircraft responds to communication queries to identify itself and its intentions; (7) whether it has been observed by friendly force fliers, and (8) whether it has closed to within engagement range of weapons commonly associated with enemy aircraft. The large number of factors that must be weighed by military decision makers and the dramatically increased lethal character of precision munitions (as demonstrated, for example, by the damage wrought by the attack by an Iraqi fighter aircraft upon the U.S.S. *Stark* in 1987) makes their task an extremely difficult one during what Clausewitz called the "fog of war."

.   .   .

◆

BASIC RULES GOVERNING WARFARE

HAGUE CONVENTION (IV) RESPECTING THE LAWS AND CUSTOMS OF WAR ON LAND, ANNEX TO THE CONVENTION

[1 Bevans 631, signed on October 18, 1907, at The Hague]

. . .

MEANS OF INJURING THE ENEMY, SIEGES, AND BOMBARDMENTS

Article 22

The right of belligerents to adopt means of injuring the enemy is not unlimited.

Article 23

In addition to the prohibitions provided by special Conventions, it is especially forbidden:
- (*a*) To employ poison or poisoned weapons;
- (*b*) To kill or wound treacherously individuals belonging to the hostile nation or army;
- (*c*) To kill or wound an enemy who, having laid down his arms, or having no longer means of defence, has surrendered at discretion;
- (*d*) To declare that no quarter will be given;
- (*e*) To employ arms, projectiles, or material calculated to cause unnecessary suffering;
- (*f*) To make improper use of a flag of truce, of the national flag, or of the military insignia and uniform of the enemy, as well as the distinctive badges of the Geneva Convention;
- (*g*) To destroy or seize the enemy's property, unless such destruction or seizure be imperatively demanded by the necessities of war;
- (*h*) To declare abolished, suspended, or inadmissible in a court of law the rights and actions of the nationals of the hostile party.

A belligerent is likewise forbidden to compel the nationals of the hostile party to take part in the operations of war directed against their own country, even if they were in the belligerent's service before the commencement of the war.

Article 24

Ruses of war and the employment of measures necessary for obtaining information about the enemy and the country are considered permissible.

. . .

NOTE: The Declaration of St. Petersburg, part of which was set out at the beginning of this chapter, is the progenitor of modern international efforts to restrain adopting industrial and scientific innovations to produce more destructive weapons. Like its many successors, it was only partially successful. The International Military Commission was unable to agree on a general principle about scientific applications to weapons development but did, however, establish as "contrary to the laws of humanity," "the employment of arms which uselessly aggravate the sufferings of disabled men, or render their death inevitable." To that end, the states party thereto agreed to refrain from using exploding bullets against each other.

THE DECLARATION OF ST. PETERSBURG

[1 A.J.I.L. (Supp.) 95 (1907), signed on November 29, 1868, and December 11, 1868, at St. Petersburg]

. . .

The contracting parties engage, mutually, to renounce, in case of war among themselves, the employment, by their military or naval forces, of any projectile of less weight than 400 grammes, which is explosive, or is charged with fulminating or inflammable substances.

. . .

Hague Declaration (IV, 3) Concerning Expanding Bullets

[1 A.J.I.L. (Supp.) 155 (1907), signed on July 29, 1899,
at The Hague]

. . .

The Contracting Parties agree to abstain from the use of bullets which expand or flatten easily in the human body, such as bullets with a hard envelope which does not entirely cover the core, or is pierced with incisions.

The present Declaration is only binding for the Contracting Powers in the case of a war between two or more of them.

. . .

Convention on Prohibitions or Restrictions on the Use of Certain Conventional Weapons Which May be Deemed to be Excessively Injurious or to Have Indiscriminate Effects

[U.N. Doc. A/CONF./95/15 (1980), reprinted in 19 I.L.M. 1523
(1980), adopted on October 10, 1980, at Geneva]

. . .

Article 1
Scope of Application

This Convention and its annexed Protocols shall apply in the situations referred to in Article 2 common to the Geneva Conventions of 12 August 1949 for the Protection of War Victims, including any situation described in paragraph 4 of Article 1 of Additional Protocol I to these Conventions.[8]

. . .

Protocol on Non-Detectable Fragments (Protocol I)

It is prohibited to use any weapon the primary effect of which is to injure by fragments which in the human body escape detection by X-rays.

·   ·   ·

Protocol on Prohibitions or Restrictions on the Use of Mines, Booby-Traps and Other Devices (Protocol II)

Article 1
Material scope of application

This Protocol relates to the use on land of the mines, booby-traps and other devices defined herein, including mines laid to interdict beaches, waterway crossings or river crossings, but does not apply to the use of anti-ship mines at sea or in inland waterways.

Article 2
Definitions

For the purpose of this Protocol:

1. "Mine" means any munition placed under, on or near the ground or other surface area and designed to be detonated or exploded by the presence, proximity or contact of a person or vehicle, and "remotely delivered mine" means any mine so defined delivered by artillery, rocket, mortar or similar means or dropped from an aircraft.

2. "Booby-trap" means any device or material which is designed, constructed or adapted to kill or injure and which functions unexpectedly when a person disturbs or approaches an apparently harmless object or performs an apparently safe act.

3. "Other devices" means manually-emplaced munitions and devices designed to kill, injure or damage and which are actuated by remote control or automatically after a lapse of time.

4. "Military objective" means, so far as objects are concerned, any object which by its nature, location, purpose or use makes an effective contribution to military action and whose total or partial destruction,

capture or neutralization, in the circumstances ruling at the time, offers a definite military advantage.

5. "Civilian objects" are all objects which are not military objectives as defined in paragraph 4.

6. "Recording" means a physical, administrative and technical operation designed to obtain, for the purpose of registration in the official records, all available information facilitating the location of minefields, mines and booby-traps.

Article 3
General restrictions on the use of mines, booby-traps and other devices

1. This Article applies to:
(a) mines
(b) booby-traps; and
(c) other devices.

2. It is prohibited in all circumstances to direct weapons to which this Article applies, either in offence, defence or by way of reprisals, against the civilian population as such or against individual civilians.

3. The indiscriminate use of weapons to which this Article applies is prohibited. Indiscriminate use is any placement of such weapons:
(a) Which is not on, or directed against, a military objective; or
(b) Which employs a method or means of delivery which cannot be directed at a specific military objective; or
(c) Which may be expected to cause incidental loss of civilian life, injury to civilians, damage to civilian objects, or a combination thereof, which would be excessive in relation to the concrete and direct military advantage anticipated.

4. All feasible precautions shall be taken to protect civilians from the effects of weapons to which this Article applies. Feasible precautions are those precautions which are practicable or practically possible taking into account all circumstances ruling at the time, including humanitarian and military considerations.

Article 4
Restrictions on the use of mines other than remotely delivered mines, booby-traps and other devices in populated areas

1. This Article applies to:
(a) mines other than remotely delivered mines;

(b) booby-traps; and

(c) other devices.

2. It is prohibited to use weapons to which this Article applies in any city, town, village or other area containing a similar concentration of civilians in which combat between ground forces is not taking place or does not appear to be imminent, unless either:

(a) They are placed on or in the close vicinity of a military objective belonging to or under the control of an adverse party; or

(b) Measures are taken to protect civilians from their effects, for example, the posting of warning signs, the posting of sentries, the issue of warnings or the provision of fences.

Article 5
Restrictions on the use of remotely delivered mines

1. The use of remotely delivered mines is prohibited unless such mines are only used within an area which is itself a military objective or which contains military objectives, and unless:

(a) Their location can be accurately recorded in accordance with Article 7(1)(a); or

(b) An effective neutralizing mechanism is used on each such mine, that is to say, a self-actuating mechanism which is designed to render a mine harmless or cause it to destroy itself when it is anticipated that the mine will no longer serve the military purpose for which it was placed in position, or a remotely-controlled mechanism which is designed to render harmless or destroy a mine when the mine no longer serves the military purpose for which it was placed in position.

2. Effective advance warning shall be given of any delivery or dropping of remotely[-]delivered mines which may affect the civilian population, unless circumstances do not permit.

Article 6
Prohibition on the use of certain booby[-]traps

1. Without prejudice to the rules of international law applicable in armed conflict relating to treachery and perfidy, it is prohibited in all circumstances to use:

(a) Any booby-trap in the form of an apparently harmless portable object which is specifically designed and constructed to contain explosive material and to detonate when it is disturbed or approached, or

(b) Booby-traps which are in any way attached to or associated with:
  (i) Internationally recognized protective emblems, signs or signals;
  (ii) Sick, wounded or dead persons;
  (iii) Burial or cremation sites or graves;
  (iv) Medical facilities, medical equipment, medical supplies or medical transportation;
  (v) Children's toys or other portable objects or products specially designed for the feeding, health, hygiene, clothing or education of children;
  (vi) Food or drink;
  (vii) Kitchen utensils or appliances except in military establishments, military locations or military supply depots;
  (viii) Objects clearly of a religious nature;
  (ix) Historic monuments, works of art or places of worship which constitute the cultural or spiritual heritage of peoples;
  (x) Animals or their carcasses.

2. It is prohibited in all circumstances to use any booby-trap which is designed to cause superfluous injury or unnecessary suffering.

Article 7
Recording and publication of the location of minefields, mines and booby-traps

1. The parties to a conflict shall record the location of:
(a) All pre-planned minefields laid by them; and
(b) All areas in which they have made large-scale and pre-planned use of booby-traps.

2. The parties shall endeavour to ensure the recording of the location of all other minefields, mines and booby-traps which they have laid or placed in position.

3. All such records shall be retained by the parties who shall:
(a) Immediately after the cessation of active hostilities:
  (i) Take all necessary and appropriate measures, including the use of such records, to protect civilians from the effects of minefields, mines and booby-traps; and either
  (ii) In cases where the forces of neither party are in the territory of the adverse party, make available to each other and to the Secretary General of the United Nations all information in their possession concerning the location of minefields, mines and booby-traps in the territory of the adverse party; or

(iii) Once complete withdrawal of the forces of the parties from the territory of the adverse party has taken place, make available to the adverse party and to the Secretary-General of the United Nations all information in their possession concerning the location of minefields, mines and booby[-]traps in the territory of the adverse party;

(b) When a United Nations force or mission performs functions in any area, make available to the authority mentioned in Article 8 such information as is required by that Article;

(c) Whenever possible, by mutual agreement, provide for the release of information concerning the location of minefields, mines and booby[-]traps, particularly in agreements governing the cessation of hostilities.

PROTOCOL ON PROHIBITIONS OR RESTRICTIONS ON THE USE OF INCENDIARY WEAPONS (PROTOCOL III)

Article 1
Definitions

For the purpose of this Protocol:

1. "Incendiary weapon" means any weapon or munition which is primarily designed to set fire to objects or to cause burn injury to persons through the action of flame, heat, or a combination thereof, produced by a chemical reaction of a substance delivered on the target.

(a) Incendiary weapons can take the form of, for example, flame throwers, fougasses, shells, rockets, grenades, mines, bombs and other containers of incendiary substances.

(b) Incendiary weapons do not include:

(i) Munitions which may have incidental incendiary effects, such as illuminants, tracers, smoke or signalling systems;

(ii) Munitions designed to combine penetration, blast or fragmentation effects with an additional incendiary effect, such as armour-piercing projectiles, fragmentation shells, explosive bombs and similar combined-effects munitions in which the incendiary effect is not specifically designed to cause burn injury to persons, but to be used against military objectives, such as armoured vehicles, aircraft and installations or facilities.

2. "Concentration of civilians" means any concentration of civilians, be it permanent or temporary, such as in inhabited parts of cities, or inhabited towns or villages, or as in camps or columns of refugees or evacuees, or groups of nomads.

3. "Military objective" means, so far as objects are concerned, any object which by its nature, location, purpose or use makes an effective contribution to military action and whose total or partial destruction, capture or neutralization, in the circumstances ruling at the time, offers a definite military advantage.

4. "Civilian objects" are all objects which are not military objectives as defined in paragraph 3.

5. "Feasible precautions" are those precautions which are practicable or practically possible taking into account all circumstances ruling at the time, including humanitarian and military considerations.

Article 2
Protection of civilians and civilian objects

1. It is prohibited in all circumstances to make the civilian population as such, individual civilians or civilian objects the object of attack by incendiary weapons.

2. It is prohibited in all circumstances to make any military objective located within a concentration of civilians the object of attack by air-delivered incendiary weapons.

3. It is further prohibited to make any military objective located within a concentration of civilians the object of attack by means of incendiary weapons other than air-delivered incendiary weapons, except when such military objective is clearly separated from the concentration of civilians and all feasible precautions are taken with a view to limiting the incendiary effects to the military objective and to avoiding, and in any event to minimizing, incidental loss of civilian life, injury to civilians and damage to civilian objects.

4. It is prohibited to make forests or other kinds of plant cover the object of attack by incendiary weapons except when such natural elements are used to cover, conceal or camouflage combatants or other military objectives, or are themselves military objectives.

Hague Convention (VIII) Relative to the Laying of Automatic Submarine Contact Mines

[1 Bevans 669, signed on October 18, 1907, at The Hague]

. . .

Article 1. It is forbidden—

1. To lay unanchored automatic contact mines, except when they are so constructed as to become harmless one hour at most after the person who laid them ceases to control them;

2. To lay anchored automatic contact mines which do not become harmless as soon as they have broken loose from their moorings;

3. To use torpedoes which do not become harmless when they have missed their mark.

Article 2. It is forbidden to lay automatic contact mines off the coast and ports of the enemy, with the sole object of intercepting commercial shipping.

Article 3. When anchored automatic contact mines are employed, every possible precaution must be taken for the security of peaceful shipping.

The belligerents undertake to do their utmost to render these mines harmless within a limited time, and, should they cease to be under surveillance, to notify the danger zones as soon as military exigencies permit, by a notice addressed to ship owners, which must also be communicated to the governments through the diplomatic channel.

. . .

Article 5. At the close of the war, the Contracting Powers undertake to do their utmost to remove the mines which they have laid, each Power removing its own mines.

As regards anchored automatic contact mines laid by one of the belligerents off the coast of the other, their position must be notified to the other party by the Power which laid them, and each Power must proceed with the least possible delay to remove the mines in its own waters.

. . .

Hague Rules of Aërial Warfare

[32 A.J.I.L. (Supp.) 12 (1938), signed on February 19, 1923,
at The Hague; not in force]

. . .

Article 18.
The use of tracer, incendiary or explosive projectiles by or against
aircraft is not prohibited.

. . .

◆

PROHIBITIONS ON USE OF CHEMICAL
AND BIOLOGICAL WEAPONS

Hague Declaration (IV, 2) Concerning
Asphyxiating Gases

[1 A.J.I.L. (Supp.) 157 (1907), signed on July 29, 1899,
at The Hague]

. . .

The Contracting Powers agree to abstain from the use of projectiles
the object of which is the diffusion of asphyxiating or deleterious gases.

. . .

Protocol for the Prohibition of the Use
in War of Asphyxiating, Poisonous or
Other Gases, and of Bacteriological
Methods of Warfare

[26 U.S.T. 571, signed on June 17, 1925, at Geneva]

. . .

Whereas the use in war of asphyxiating, poisonous or other gases, and of analogous liquids, materials or devices, has been justly condemned by the general opinion of the civilized world; and

Whereas the prohibition of such use has been declared in Treaties to which the majority of Powers of the world are Parties; and

To the end that this prohibition shall be universally accepted as a part of International Law, binding alike the conscience and the practice of nations;

. . .

[T]he High Contracting Parties, so far as they are not already Parties to Treaties prohibiting such use, accept this prohibition, agree to extend this prohibition to the use of bacteriological methods of warfare and agree to be bound as between themselves according to the terms of this declaration.

. . .

NOTE: The exact meaning of this Protocol is contested, and for some states its prohibition is contingent. The United States has interpreted the Protocol of 1925 as not prohibiting the use of riot control agents such as tear gas. A number of Western European allies have interpreted the Protocol as prohibiting all such gases. Additionally, a significant number of nations, including the United States, issued a reservation stating that first use by a belligerent of chemical and biological weapons authorizes the state subject to the attack to respond in kind, that is, to retaliate with chemical and biological weapons.

CONVENTION ON THE PROHIBITION OF THE DEVELOPMENT, PRODUCTION AND STOCKPILING OF BACTERIOLOGICAL (BIOLOGICAL) AND TOXIN WEAPONS AND ON THEIR DESTRUCTION

[26 U.S.T. 583, opened for signature on April 10, 1972, at London, Moscow, and Washington]

. . .

Article I
Each State Party to this Convention undertakes never in any circumstances to develop, produce, stockpile or otherwise acquire or retain:

1. Microbial or other biological agents, or toxins whatever their origin or method of production, of types and in quantities that have no justification for prophylactic, protective or other peaceful purposes:
2. Weapons, equipment or means of delivery designed to use such agents or toxins for hostile purposes or in armed conflict.

Article II

Each State Party to this Convention undertakes to destroy, or to divert to peaceful purposes, as soon as possible but not later than nine months after the entry into force of the Convention, all agents, toxins, weapons, equipment and means of delivery specified in Article I of the Convention, which are in its possession or under its jurisdiction or control. In implementing the provisions of this article all necessary safety precautions shall be observed to protect populations and the environment.

Article III

Each State Party to this Convention undertakes not to transfer to any recipient whatsoever, directly or indirectly, and not in any way to assist, encourage, or induce any State, group of States or international organizations to manufacture or otherwise acquire any of the agents, toxins, weapons, equipment or means of delivery specified in article 1 of the Convention.

. . .

Article XIII

1. This Convention shall be of unlimited duration.
2. Each State Party to this Convention shall in exercising its national sovereignty have the right to withdraw from the Convention if it decides that extraordinary events, related to the subject matter of the Convention, have jeopardized the supreme interests of its country. It shall give notice of such withdrawal to all other States Parties to the Convention and to the United Nations Security Council three months in advance. Such notice shall include a statement of the extraordinary events it regards as having jeopardized its supreme interests.

NOTE: The most recent and most ambitious effort to prohibit chemical weapons was signed in 1993 by 144 countries; as of May 13, 1993, it had been ratified by only three (Fiji, Mauritius, and Seychelles). In addition to its prohibitions, the Convention also establishes an international organization to oversee the implementation of its terms.

CONVENTION ON THE PROHIBITION OF THE DEVELOPMENT, PRODUCTION, STOCKPILING AND USE OF CHEMICAL WEAPONS AND ON THEIR DESTRUCTION

[31 I.L.M. 800 (1993), signed on January 13, 1993, at Paris; not in force]

. . .

Article I
General Obligations

1. Each State Party to this Convention undertakes never under any circumstances:

(a) To develop, produce, otherwise acquire, stockpile or retain chemical weapons, or transfer, directly or indirectly, chemical weapons to anyone;

(b) To use chemical weapons;

(c) To engage in any military preparations to use chemical weapons;

(d) To assist, encourage or induce, in any way, anyone to engage in any activity prohibited to a State Party under this Convention.

2. Each State Party undertakes to destroy chemical weapons it owns or possesses, or that are located in any place under its jurisdiction or control, in accordance with the provisions of this Convention.

3. Each State Party undertakes to destroy all chemical weapons it abandoned on the territory of another State Party, in accordance with the provisions of this Convention.

4. Each State Party undertakes to destroy any chemical weapons production facilities it owns or possesses, or that are located in any place under its jurisdiction or control, in accordance with the provisions of this Convention.

5. Each State Party undertakes not to use riot control agents as a method of warfare.

. . .

Article III
Declarations

1. Each State Party shall submit to the Organization [Organization for the Prohibition of Chemical Weapons, established pursuant to Article VIII of the Convention], not later than 30 days after this Convention enters into force for it, the following declarations, in which it shall:

(a) With respect to chemical weapons:
  (i) Declare whether it owns or possesses any chemical weapons, or whether there are any chemical weapons located in any place under its jurisdiction or control;
  (ii) Specify the precise location, aggregate quantity and detailed inventory of chemical weapons it owns or possesses, or that are located in any place under its jurisdiction or control, in accordance with Part IV (A), paragraphs 1 to 3, of the Verification Annex, except for those chemical weapons referred to in sub-subparagraph (iii);
  (iii) Report any chemical weapons on its territory that are owned and possessed by another State and located in any place under the jurisdiction or control of another State, in accordance with Part IV (A), paragraph 4, of the Verification Annex;
  (iv) Declare whether it has transferred or received, directly or indirectly, any chemical weapons since 1 January 1946 and specify the transfer or receipt of such weapons, in accordance with Part IV (A), paragraph 5, of the Verification Annex;
  (v) Provide its general plan for destruction of chemical weapons that it owns or possesses, or that are located in any place under its jurisdiction or control, in accordance with Part IV (A), paragraph 6, of the Verification Annex;
(b) With respect to old chemical weapons [chemical weapons produced before 1925 or between 1925 and 1946 that have deteriorated to such an extent that they can no longer be used as chemical weapons] and abandoned chemical weapons [chemical weapons abandoned by a state after January 1, 1925, on the territory of another state without the consent of the latter]:
  (i) Declare whether it has on its territory old chemical weapons and provide all available information in accordance with Part IV (B), paragraph 3, of the Verification Annex;
  (ii) Declare whether there are abandoned chemical weapons on its territory and provide all available information in accordance with Part IV (B), paragraph 8, of the Verification Annex;
  (iii) Declare whether it has abandoned chemical weapons on the territory of other States and provide all available information in accordance with Part IV (B), paragraph 10, of the Verification Annex;
(c) With respect to chemical weapons production facilities:

(i) Declare whether it has or has had any chemical weapons production facility under its ownership or possession, or that is or has been located in any place under its jurisdiction or control at any time since 1 January 1946;

(ii) Specify any chemical weapons production facility it has or has had under its ownership or possession or that is or has been located in any place under its jurisdiction or control at any time since 1 January 1946, in accordance with Part V, paragraph 1, of the Verification Annex, except for those facilities referred to in sub-subparagraph (iii);

(iii) Report any chemical weapons production facility on its territory that another State has or has had under its ownership and possession and that is or has been located in any place under the jurisdiction or control of another State at any time since 1 January 1946, in accordance with Part V, paragraph 2, of the Verification Annex;

(iv) Declare whether it has transferred or received, directly or indirectly, any equipment for the production of chemical weapons since 1 January 1946 and specify the transfer or receipt of such equipment, in accordance with Part V, paragraphs 3 to 5, of the Verification Annex;

(v) Provide its general plan for destruction of any chemical weapons production facility it owns or possesses, or that is located in any place under its jurisdiction or control, in accordance with Part V, paragraph 6, of the Verification Annex;

(vi) Specify actions to be taken for closure of any chemical weapons production facility it owns or possesses, or that is located in any place under its jurisdiction or control, into a chemical weapons destruction facility, in accordance with Part V, paragraph 1(i), of the Verification Annex;

(vii) Provide its general plan for any temporary conversion of any chemical weapons production facility it owns or possesses, or that is located in any place under its jurisdiction or control, into a chemical weapons destruction facility, in accordance with Part V, paragraph 7, of the Verification Annex;

(d) With respect to other facilities: Specify the precise location, nature and general scope of activities of any facility or establishment under its ownership or possession, or located in any place under its jurisdiction or control, and that has been designed, constructed or used since 1 January 1946 primarily for development of chemical weapons. Such declaration shall include, *inter alia*, laboratories and test and evaluation sites;

(e) With respect to riot control agents: Specify the chemical name, structural formula and Chemical Abstracts Service (CAS) registry number, if assigned, of each chemical it holds for riot control purposes. This declaration shall be updated not later than 30 days after any change becomes effective.

2. The provisions of this Article and the relevant provisions of Part IV of the Verification Annex shall not, at the discretion of a State Party, apply to chemical weapons buried on its territory before 1 January 1977 and which remain buried, or which had been dumped at sea before 1 January 1985.

Article IV
Chemical Weapons

1. The provisions of this Article and the detailed procedures for its implementation shall apply to all chemical weapons owned or possessed by a State Party, or that are located in any place under its jurisdiction or control, except old chemical weapons and abandoned chemical weapons to which Part IV (B) of the Verification Annex applies.

2. Detailed procedures for the implementation of this Article are set forth in the Verification Annex.

3. All locations at which chemical weapons specified in paragraph 1 are stored or destroyed shall be subject to systematic verification through on-site inspection and monitoring with on-site instruments, in accordance with Part IV (A) of the Verification Annex.

4. Each State Party shall, immediately after the declaration under Article III, paragraph 1 (a), has been submitted, provide access to chemical weapons specified in paragraph 1 for the purpose of systematic verification of the declaration through on-site inspection. Thereafter, each State Party shall not remove any of these chemical weapons, except to a chemical weapons destruction facility. It shall provide access to such chemical weapons, for the purpose of systematic on-site verification.

5. Each State Party shall provide access to any chemical weapons destruction facilities and their storage areas, that it owns or possesses, or that are located in any place under its jurisdiction or control, for the purpose of systematic verification through on-site inspection and monitoring with on-site instruments.

6. Each State Party shall destroy all chemical weapons specified in paragraph 1 pursuant to the Verification Annex and in accordance with

the agreed rate and sequence of destruction (hereinafter referred to as "order of destruction"). Such destruction shall begin not later than two years after this Convention enters into force for it and shall finish not later than 10 years after entry into force of this Convention. A State Party is not precluded from destroying such chemical weapons at a faster rate.

7. Each State Party shall:

(a) Submit detailed plans for the destruction of chemical weapons specified in paragraph 1 not later than 60 days before each annual destruction period begins, in accordance with Part IV (A), paragraph 29, of the Verification Annex; the detailed plans shall encompass all stocks to be destroyed during the next annual destruction period;

(b) Submit declarations annually regarding the implementation of its plans for destruction of chemical weapons specified in paragraph 1, not later than 60 days after the end of each annual destruction period; and

(c) Certify, not later than 30 days after the destruction process has been completed, that all chemical weapons specified in paragraph 1 have been destroyed.

8. If a State ratifies or accedes to this Convention after the 10-year period for destruction set forth in paragraph 6, it shall destroy chemical weapons specified in paragraph 1 as soon as possible. The order of destruction and procedures for stringent verification for such a State Party shall be determined by the Executive Council.

9. Any chemical weapons discovered by a State Party after the initial declaration of chemical weapons shall be reported, secured and destroyed in accordance with Part IV (A) of the Verification Annex.

10. Each State Party, during transportation, sampling, storage and destruction of chemical weapons, shall assign the highest priority to ensuring the safety of people and to protecting the environment. Each State Party shall transport, sample, store and destroy chemical weapons in accordance with its national standards for safety and emissions.

11. Any State Party which has on its territory chemical weapons that are owned or possessed by another State, or that are located in any place under the jurisdiction or control of another State, shall make the fullest efforts to ensure that these chemical weapons are removed from its territory not later than one year after this Convention enters into force for it. If they are not removed within one year, the State Party may request the Organization and other States Parties to provide assistance in the destruction of these chemical weapons.

12. Each State Party undertakes to cooperate with other States Parties

that request information or assistance on a bilateral basis or through the Technical Secretariat regarding methods and technologies for the safe and efficient destruction of chemical weapons.

13. In carrying out verification activities pursuant to this Article and Part IV (A) of the Verification Annex, the Organization shall consider measures to avoid unnecessary duplication of bilateral or multilateral agreements on verification of chemical weapons storage and their destruction among States Parties.

To this end, the Executive Council shall decide to limit verification to measures complementary to those undertaken pursuant to such a bilateral or multilateral agreement, if it considers that:

(a) Verification provisions of such an agreement are consistent with the verification provisions of this Article and Part IV (A) of the Verification Annex;

(b) Implementation of such an agreement provides for sufficient assurance of compliance with the relevant provisions of this Convention; and

(c) Parties to the bilateral or multilateral agreement keep the Organization fully informed about their verification activities.

14. If the Executive Council takes a decision pursuant to paragraph 13, the Organization shall have the right to monitor the implementation of the bilateral or multilateral agreement.

15. Nothing in paragraphs 13 and 14 shall affect the obligation of a State Party to provide declarations pursuant to Article III, this Article and Part IV (A) of the Verification Annex.

16. Each State Party shall meet the costs of destruction of chemical weapons it is obliged to destroy. It shall also meet the costs of verification of storage and destruction of these chemical weapons unless the Executive Council decides otherwise. If the Executive Council decides to limit verification measures of the Organization pursuant to paragraph 13, the costs of complementary verification and monitoring by the Organization shall be paid in accordance with the United Nations scale of assessment, as specified in Article VIII, paragraph 7.

17. The provisions of this Article and the relevant provisions of Part IV of the Verification Annex shall not, at the discretion of a State Party, apply to chemical weapons buried on its territory before 1 January 1977 and which remain buried, or which had been dumped at sea before 1 January 1985.

.   .   .

◆

PROHIBITION ON USE OF NUCLEAR WEAPONS

DECLARATION ON THE PROHIBITION OF THE USE OF NUCLEAR AND THERMO-NUCLEAR WEAPONS

[Resolution 1653 of the United Nations General Assembly, adopted on November 24, 1961, G.A. Res. 1653, U.N. GAOR, 16th Sess., Supp. No. 17, at 4, U.N. Doc. A/5100 (1962)]

. . .

The General Assembly,

. . .

1. *Declares* that:
   (a) The use of nuclear and thermo-nuclear weapons is contrary to the spirit, letter and aims of the United Nations and, as such, a direct violation of the Charter of the United Nations;
   (b) The use of nuclear and thermo-nuclear weapons would exceed even the scope of war and cause indiscriminate suffering and destruction to mankind and civilization and, as such, is contrary to the rules of international law and to the laws of humanity;
   (c) The use of nuclear and thermo-nuclear weapons is a war directed not against an enemy or enemies alone but also against mankind in general, since the peoples of the world not involved in such a war will be subjected to all the evils generated by the use of such weapons;
   (d) Any State using nuclear and thermo-nuclear weapons is to be considered as violating the Charter of the United Nations, as acting contrary to the laws of humanity and as committing a crime against mankind and civilization;

. . .

Non-Use of Force in International Relations and Permanent Prohibition of the Use of Nuclear Weapons

[Resolution 2936 of the United Nations General
Assembly, adopted on November 29, 1972, G.A. Res. 2936,
U.N. GAOR, 27th Sess., Supp. No. 30, at 5, U.N. Doc.
A/8730 (1973)]

. . .

The General Assembly,

. . .

1. *Solemnly declares,* on behalf of the States Members of the Organization, their renunciation of the use or threat of force in all its forms and manifestations in international relations, in accordance with the Charter of the United Nations, and the permanent prohibition of the use of nuclear weapons;

. . .

NOTE: No general treaty prohibits the use of nuclear weapons. Efforts to prohibit their use have come principally from the General Assembly, whose resolutions are recommendatory. Notwithstanding the superpower rapprochement of the early 1990s, the specter of nuclear war still hangs over humanity. Indeed, with the proliferation of nuclear weapons and ballistic missile delivery systems to many states that lack internal control mechanisms, the likelihood of nuclear war may be increasing. In limited scenarios, perhaps such as one in which Iraq's troops would have provided sustained stiff resistance to coalition forces in 1991, the question of the lawfulness of use of nuclear weapons could become acutely relevant and difficult to resolve.

As we go to press, the World Health Organization has asked the International Court of Justice for an advisory opinion on the lawfulness of the use of nuclear weapons. In the meanwhile, neither the United States nor Russia is now committed to a "no first use" policy.

◆

"ENVIRONMENTAL" WARFARE

CONVENTION ON THE PROHIBITION OF MILITARY OR ANY OTHER HOSTILE USE OF ENVIRONMENTAL MODIFICATION TECHNIQUES

[31 U.S.T. 333, adopted by Resolution 31/72 of the
United Nations General Assembly on December 10, 1976,
and opened for signature on May 18, 1977, at Geneva]

.　　.　　.

Article I

1. Each State Party to this Convention undertak[e]s not to engage in military or any other hostile use of environmental modification techniques having widespread, long-lasting or severe effects as the means of destruction, damage or injury to any other State Party.

2. Each State Party to this Convention undertakes not to assist, encourage or induce any State, group of States or international organization to engage in activities contrary to the provisions of paragraph 1 of this article.

Article II

As used in article I, the term "environmental modification techniques" refers to any technique for changing—through the deliberate manipulation of natural processes—the dynamics, composition or structure of the Earth, including its biota, lithosphere, hydrosphere and atmosphere, or of outer space.

Article III

1. The provisions of this Convention shall not hinder the use of environmental modification techniques for peaceful purposes and shall be without prejudice to the generally recognized principles and applicable rules of international law concerning such use.

.　　.　　.

Article VII

This Convention shall be of unlimited duration.

.　　.　　.

PROTOCOL I ADDITIONAL TO THE GENEVA CONVENTIONS, 1977

[1125 U.N.T.S. 3, adopted on June 8, 1977, at Geneva]

. . .

Article 55
Protection of the natural environment

1. Care shall be taken in warfare to protect the natural environment against widespread, long-term and severe damage. This protection includes a prohibition of the use of methods or means of warfare which are intended or may be expected to cause such damage to the natural environment and thereby to prejudice the health or survival of the population.

2. Attacks against the natural environment by way of reprisals are prohibited.

. . .

NOTE: Concern for the effects of the use of certain types of weapons on the environment has grown rapidly since the Vietnam War. The longer-term consequences of the use of defoliants such as Agent Orange are still uncertain, but they have been the subject of numerous lawsuits and legislative settlements in the United States.

In the Gulf War, the coalition accused Iraq of violation of environmental warfare prohibitions with regard to intentional oil spills in the Persian Gulf and the igniting of Kuwaiti oil wells. Neither of those accusations seems to have been pursued after the war ended. Perhaps one reason they were not pursued is that the two pertinent conventions (Environmental Modification and Protocol I) did not formally bind the parties to the conflict: Iraq is not bound by the Environmental Modification Convention, and Iraq, as well as several members of the coalition, including the United States and France, are not parties to Protocol I.

Even if the two conventions did bind the parties to the conflict, it is not clear, as stated in the introduction to this book, that these actions are violations of the laws of war. By forestalling coalition amphibious landings and limiting coalition supplies of potable water, via the release of oil into the Persian Gulf, and by limiting the capability of coalition fliers to strike their targets, via the haze resulting from the burning of oil, Iraq surely attempted to achieve military objectives. Whether the objectives achieved were proportional to the environmental damage sustained, and whether that damage is "widespread, long-lasting, or severe" within the meaning of the 1976 Convention and 1977 Protocol is difficult to resolve. This uncertainty is echoed by the Department of Defense Report:

> During that treaty's [Protocol I] negotiation, there was general agreement that one of its criteria for determining whether a violation had taken place ("long term") was measured in decades. It is not clear the damage Iraq caused, while severe in a layman's sense of the term, would meet the technical-legal use of that term in Protocol I. The prohibitions on damage to the environment contained in Protocol I were not intended to prohibit battlefield damage caused by conventional operations and, in all likelihood, would not apply to Iraq's actions in the Persian Gulf War.[9]

The military objectives Iraq is thought to have pursued in releasing oil into the Persian Gulf and in igniting oil wells, however, may have been secondary to the primary aim Iraq is believed by many commentators to have had: punitive destruction of Kuwaiti natural resources. Such a view is expressed in the Department of Defense Report:

> [O]il well fires to create obscurants could have been accomplished simply through the opening of valves; instead, Iraqi forces set explosive charges on many wells to ensure the greatest possible destruction and maximum difficulty in stopping each fire. Likewise, the Ar-Rumaylah oil field spreads across the Iraq-Kuwait border. Had the purpose of the fires been to create an obscurant, oil wells in that field on each side of the border undoubtedly would have been set ablaze; Iraqi destruction was limited to oil wells on the Kuwaiti side only.[10]

Assuming that Iraq punitively destroyed the resources of Kuwait, such action probably would be a violation of the laws of war. Article 23(g) of Hague IV (1907) deems it unlawful "To destroy or seize the enemy's property, unless such destruction or seizure be imperatively demanded by the necessities of war." And Article 147 of Geneva IV (1949)[11] states that it is a grave breach of the law of war to conduct "extensive destruction and appropriation of property, not justified by military necessity and carried out unlawfully and wantonly." The Department of Defense Report notes that the government of Canada, in conjunction with the United Nations secretary-general, hosted a conference of international legal scholars to consider Iraq's actions in the Gulf War. These scholars generally agreed that Iraq's actions relating to the release and burning of oil constituted violations of Article 23(g) of Hague IV and Article 147 of Geneva IV.[12]

In September 1992 the United States and the Kingdom of Jordan submitted a joint letter to the United Nations General Assembly specifying which provisions, in their view, provided protection for the environment during armed conflict.

PROTECTION OF THE ENVIRONMENT IN TIMES OF ARMED CONFLICT

[Letter dated 28 September 1992 from the Permanent Missions of the Hashemite Kingdom of Jordan and of the United States of America addressed to the Chairman of the Sixth Committee]

(a) The fundamental rule, set out in article 22 of the Regulations annexed to the Hague Convention [IV] of 1907 respecting the laws and customs of war on land, that the right of belligerents to adopt means of injuring the enemy is not unlimited;

(b) The rules governing the means of injuring the enemy reflected in article 23 of the Hague Regulations that prohibit the employment of poison and the destruction of the enemy's property unless such destruction be imperatively demanded by the necessities of war, and in article 28 of the Hague Regulations that prohibit pillage;

(c) The rule, set out in article 55 of the Hague Regulations, that the occupying State is only an administrator and usufructuary of the real estate of the occupied State and consequently is required to safeguard the capital of these properties and administer them in accordance with the rules of usufruct;

(d) The rule, set out in article 53 of the Geneva Convention of 1949 relative to the Protection of Civilian Persons in Time of War, that any des[t]ruction by the occupying Power of real or personal property belonging individually or collectively to private persons, or to the State, or to other public authorities, is prohibited, except where such destruction is rendered absolutely necessary by military operations;

(e) It is a grave breach of international humanitarian law, and is a war crime, as set out in article 147 of the Fourth Geneva Convention of 1949, to extensively destroy and appropriate property when not justified by military necessity and carried out unlawfully and wantonly;

(f) The rule, reflected in articles 49 and 52 of Additional Protocol I, that military operations may only be directed against military objectives and that acts of violence, whether in offence or defence ("attacks"), shall be strictly directed at military objectives;

(g) It is a war crime to employ acts of violence not directed at specific military objectives, to employ a method or means of combat which cannot be directed at a specific military objective, or to employ a means or method of combat the effects of which cannot be limited as required by the law of armed conflict;

(h) The customary law rule that prohibits attacks which reasonably may be expected at the time to cause incidental loss of civilian life, injury to civilians, damage to civilian objects, or a combination thereof, which would be excessive in relation to the concrete and direct military advantage anticipated, are prohibited; and

(i) The customary law rule that, in so far as objects are concerned, military objectives are limited to those objects which by their nature, location, purpose or use make an effective contribution to military action and whose total or partial destruction, capture or neutralization in the circumstances ruling at the time, offers a definite military advantage.

2. For States parties the following principles of international law, as applicable, provide additional protection for the environment in times of armed conflict:

(a) Article 55 of Additional Protocol I requires States parties to take care in warfare to protect the natural environment against widespread, long-term and severe damage;

(b) Articles 35(3) and 55 of Additional Protocol I also prohibit States parties from using methods or means of warfare which are intended or may be expected to cause such damage to the natural environment and thereby to prejudice the health or survival of the population;

(c) Article 55(2) of Additional Protocol I prohibits States parties from attacking the natural environment by way of reprisals;

(d) Article 2(4) of Protocol III to the 1980 Convention on Prohibitions or Restrictions on the Use of Certain Conventional Weapons Which May Be Deemed to Be Excessively Injurious or to Have Indiscriminate Effects prohibits States parties from making forests or other kinds of plant cover the object of attack by incendiary weapons except when such natural elements are used to cover, conceal or camouflage combatants or other military objectives, or are themselves military objectives; and

(e) The 1977 Convention on the Prohibition of Military or Any Other Hostile Use of Environmental Modification Techniques (ENMOD) prohibits States parties from engaging in military or any other hostile use of environmental modification techniques (i.e., any technique for changing—through the deliberate manipulation of natural processes—the dynamics, composition or structure of the earth, its biota, lithosphere, hydrosphere and atmosphere, or of outer space) having widespread, long-lasting or severe effects as the means of destruction, damage or injury to any other State party.

◆

PRESCRIPTIONS CONCERNING CIVILIAN AND MERCHANT SEA AND AIR VESSELS

HAGUE CONVENTION (VI) RELATIVE TO THE STATUS OF ENEMY MERCHANT SHIPS AT THE OUTBREAK OF HOSTILITIES

[2 A.J.I.L. (Supp.) 127 (1908), signed on October 18, 1907, at The Hague]

.   .   .

Article 1. When a merchant ship belonging to one of the belligerent powers is at the commencement of hostilities in an enemy port, it is desirable that it should be allowed to depart freely, either immediately, or after a reasonable number of days of grace, and to proceed, after being furnished with a pass, direct to its port of destination or any other port indicated.

The same rule should apply in the case of a ship which has left its last port of departure before the commencement of the war and entered a port belonging to the enemy while still ignorant that hostilities had broken out.

Article 2. A merchant ship unable, owing to circumstances of *vis major*, to leave the enemy port within the period contemplated in the above article, or which was not allowed to leave, cannot be confiscated.

The belligerent may detain it, without payment of compensation, subject to the obligation of restoring it after the war, or requisition it on payment of compensation.

Article 3. Enemy merchant ships which left their last port of departure before the commencement of the war, and are encountered on the high seas while still ignorant of the outbreak of hostilities, cannot be confiscated. They are only liable to detention on the understanding that they shall be restored after the war without compensation, or to be requisitioned, or even destroyed, on payment of compensation, but in such case provision must be made for the safety of the persons on board as well as the security of the ship's papers.

After touching at a port in their own country or at a neutral port, these ships are subject to the laws and customs of maritime war.

Article 4. Enemy cargo on board the vessels referred to in articles 1 and 2 is likewise liable to be detained and restored after the termination of the war without payment of compensation, or to be requisitioned on payment of compensation, with or without the ship.

The same rule applies in the case of cargo on board the vessels referred to in article 3.

Article 5. The present convention does not affect merchant ships whose build shows that they are intended for conversion into war ships.

Article 6. The provisions of the present convention do not apply except between contracting powers, and then only if all the belligerents are parties to the convention.

. . .

Hague Convention (VII) Relative to the Conversion of Merchant Ships into War Ships

[2 A.J.I.L. (Supp.) 133 (1908), signed on October 18, 1907, at The Hague]

. . .

Article 1. A merchant ship converted into a war ship cannot have the rights and duties accruing to such vessels unless it is placed under the direct authority, immediate control, and responsibility of the power whose flag it flies.

Article 2. Merchant ships converted into war ships must carry the external signs which are characteristic of the war ships of their state.

Article 3. The commander must be in the service of the state and duly commissioned by the competent authorities. His name must figure on the list of the officers of the navy.

Article 4. The crew must be under military discipline.

Article 5. Every merchant ship converted into a war ship must follow in its operations the laws and customs of war.

Article 6. A belligerent who converts a merchant ship into a war ship must, as soon as possible, announce such conversion in the list of the navy.

Article 7. The provisions of the present convention do not apply except between contracting powers, and then only if all the belligerents are parties to the convention.

. . .

Hague Convention (XI) on Restrictions with Regard to Right of Capture in Naval War

[1 Bevans 711, signed on October 18, 1907, at The Hague]

. . .

Postal Correspondence

Article 1. The postal correspondence of neutrals or belligerents, whatever its official or private character may be, found on the high seas on board a neutral or enemy ship, is inviolable. If the ship is detained, the correspondence is forwarded by the captor with the least possible delay.

The provisions of the preceding paragraph do not apply, in case of violation of blockade, to correspondence destined for or proceeding from a blockaded port.

Article 2. The inviolability of postal correspondence does not exempt a neutral mail ship from the laws and customs of maritime war as to neutral merchant-ships in general. The ship, however, may not be searched except when absolutely necessary, and then only with as much consideration and expedition as possible.

. . .

The Exemption from Capture of Certain Vessels

Article 3. Vessels used exclusively for fishing along the coast or small boats employed in local trade are exempt from capture, as well as their appliances, rigging, tackle, and cargo.

They cease to be exempt as soon as they take any part whatever in hostilities.

The Contracting Powers agree not to take advantage of the harmless character of the said vessels in order to use them for military purposes while preserving their peaceful appearance.

Article 4. Vessels charged with religious, scientific, or philanthropic missions are likewise exempt from capture.

. . .

Regulations Regarding the Crews
of Enemy Merchant-Ships Captured by a Belligerent

Article 5. When an enemy merchant-ship is captured by a belligerent, such of its crew as are nationals of a neutral State are not made prisoners of war.

The same rule applies in the case of the captain and officers likewise nationals of a neutral State, if they promise formally in writing not to serve on an enemy ship while the war lasts.

Article 6. The captain, officers, and members of the crew, when nationals of the enemy State, are not made prisoners of war, on condition that they make a formal promise in writing, not to undertake, while hostilities last, any service connected with the operations of the war.

Article 7. The names of the persons retaining their liberty under the conditions laid down in Article 5, paragraph 2, and in Article 6, are notified by the belligerent captor to the other belligerent. The latter is forbidden knowingly to employ the said persons.

Article 8. The provisions of the three preceding Articles do not apply to ships taking part in the hostilities.

Proces-Verbal Relating to the Rules of Submarine Warfare Set Forth in Part IV of the London Naval Treaty of 1930

[3 Bevans 298, signed on November 6, 1936, at London]

. . .

(1) In their action with regard to merchant ships, submarines must conform to the rules of International Law to which surface vessels are subject.

(2) In particular, except in the case of persistent refusal to stop on being duly summoned, or of active resistance to visit or search, a warship, whether surface vessel or submarine, may not sink or render incapable of navigation a merchant vessel without having first placed passengers, crew and ship's papers in a place of safety. For this purpose the ship's boats are not regarded as a place of safety unless the safety of the passengers and crew is assured, in the existing sea and weather conditions, by the

proximity of land, or the presence of another vessel which is in a position to take them on board.

. . .

NOTE: Like many efforts at codifying the law of war, the London Rules did not receive wide acceptance. Because of developments in communications and aviation, they were obsolete with regard to submarine warfare by the time they were drafted. Since a merchant vessel could radio its plight and likely bring its air force over the scene in a short time, a submarine that tried to comply with Rule 2 would not last long. There is some indication that Germany tried to comply with Rule 2 early in World War II, but Allied reactions deterred it from further compliance. Thereafter, the war was marked by unrestricted submarine warfare by all belligerents. With the introduction of surface-to-surface missiles that may be launched far beyond the range of visibility and which may, with a single strike, destroy a ship, the London Rules have been rendered completely unworkable.

HAGUE RULES OF AËRIAL WARFARE

[32 A.J.I.L. (Supp.) 12 (1938), signed on February 19, 1923, at The Hague; not in force]

. . .

MILITARY AUTHORITY OVER ENEMY AND NEUTRAL AIRCRAFT AND PERSONS ON BOARD

. . .

Article 30. In case a belligerent commanding officer considers that the presence of aircraft is likely to prejudice the success of the operations in which he is engaged at the moment, he may prohibit the passing of neutral aircraft in the immediate vicinity of his forces or may oblige them to follow a particular route. A neutral aircraft which does not conform to such directions, of which he has had notice issued by the belligerent commanding officer, may be fired upon.

. . .

Article 33. Belligerent non-military aircraft, whether public or private, flying within the jurisdiction of their own state, are liable to be fired upon unless they make the nearest available landing on the approach of enemy military aircraft.

. . .

Article 34. Belligerent non-military aircraft, whether public or private, are liable to be fired upon, if they fly (1) within the jurisdiction of the enemy, or (2) in the immediate vicinity thereof and outside the jurisdiction of their own state, or (3) in the immediate vicinity of the military operations of the enemy by land or sea.

. . .

Article 35. Neutral aircraft flying within the jurisdiction of a belligerent, and warned of the approach of military aircraft of the opposing belligerent, must make the nearest available landing. Failure to do so exposes them to the risk of being fired upon.

. . .

VISIT AND SEARCH, CAPTURE AND CONDEMNATION

. . .

Article 49. Private aircraft are liable to visit and search and to capture by belligerent military aircraft.

. . .

Article 50. Belligerent military aircraft have the right to order public non-military and private aircraft to alight in or proceed for visit and search to a suitable locality reasonably accessible.

Refusal, after warning, to obey such orders to alight or to proceed to such a locality for examination exposes an aircraft to the risk of being fired upon.

. . .

Article 51. Neutral public non-military aircraft, other than those which are to be treated as private aircraft, are subject only to visit for the purpose of the verification of their papers.

. . .

Article 53. A neutral private aircraft is liable to capture if it—

(a) Resists the legitimate exercise of belligerent rights.

(b) Violates a prohibition of which it has had notice issued by a belligerent commanding officer under Article 30.

(c) Is engaged in unneutral service.

(d) Is armed in time of war when outside the jurisdiction of its own country.

(e) Has no external marks or uses false marks.

(f) Has no papers or insufficient or irregular papers.

(g) Is manifestly out of the line between the point of departure and the point of destination indicated in its papers and after such enquiries as the belligerent may deem necessary, no good cause is shown for the deviation. The aircraft, together with its crew and passengers, if any, may be detained by the belligerent, pending such enquiries.

(h) Carries, or itself constitutes, contraband of war.

(i) Is engaged in breach of a blockade duly established and effectively maintained.

(k) Has been transferred from belligerent to neutral nationality at a date and in circumstances indicating an intention of evading the consequences to which an enemy aircraft, as such, is exposed.

Provided that in each case (except (k)) the ground for capture shall be an act carried out in the flight in which the neutral aircraft came into belligerent hands, i.e., since it left its point of departure and before it reached its point of destination.

· · ·

◆

PROTECTION OF CIVILIANS; RULES ABOUT BOMBARDMENT

During the Gulf War, the coalition attacked targets within major Iraqi population centers that, in some cases, resulted in the injury and death of noncombatants. Iraq launched Scud missiles into Israel and Saudi Arabia, also inflicting injury and death upon noncombatants. Coalition attacks upon Iraq and Iraqi attacks upon Saudi Arabia clearly envisaged, to varying degrees, the destruction of military targets. Iraqi attacks upon Israel, however, clearly targeted civilians; these attacks certainly represent a grave breach of the laws of war. The lawfulness of certain of the coalition attacks upon Iraq and Iraqi attacks upon Saudi Arabia is more difficult to assess.

HAGUE CONVENTION (IV) RESPECTING THE LAWS AND CUSTOMS OF WAR ON LAND, ANNEX TO THE CONVENTION

[1 Bevans 631, signed on October 18, 1907, at The Hague]

. . . .

Article 25. The attack or bombardment, by whatever means, of towns, villages, dwellings, or buildings which are undefended is prohibited.
Article 26. The officer in command of an attacking force must, before commencing a bombardment, except in cases of assault, do all in his power to warn the authorities.

. . . .

Article 28. The pillage of a town or place, even when taken by assault, is prohibited.

. . . .

HAGUE CONVENTION (IX) CONCERNING BOMBARDMENT BY NAVAL FORCES IN TIME OF WAR

[1 Bevans 681, signed on October 18, 1907, at The Hague]

. . . .

Article 1. The bombardment by naval forces of undefended ports, towns, villages, dwellings, or buildings is forbidden.

A place cannot be bombarded solely because automatic submarine contact mines are anchored off the harbour.

Article 2. Military works, military or naval establishments, depots of arms or war matériel, workshops or plant[s] which could be utilized for the needs of the hostile fleet or army, and the ships of war in the harbour, are not, however, included in this prohibition. The commander of a naval force may destroy them with artillery, after a summons followed by a reasonable time of waiting, if all other means are impossible, and when the local authorities have not themselves destroyed them within the time fixed.

He incurs no responsibility for any unavoidable damage which may be caused by a bombardment under such circumstances.

If for military reasons immediate action is necessary, and no delay can be allowed the enemy, it is understood that the prohibition to bombard the undefended town holds good, as in the case given in paragraph 1, and that the commander shall take all due measures in order that the town may suffer as little harm as possible.

Article 3. After due notice has been given, the bombardment of undefended ports, towns, villages, dwellings, or buildings may be commenced, if the local authorities, after a formal summons has been made to them, decline to comply with requisitions for provisions or supplies necessary for the immediate use of the naval force before the place in question.

These requisitions shall be in proportion to the resources of the place. They shall only be demanded in the name of the commander of the said naval force, and they shall, as far as possible, be paid for in cash; if not, they shall be evidenced by receipts.

Article 4. Undefended ports, towns, villages, dwellings, or buildings may not be bombarded on account of failure to pay money contributions.

.   .   .

Article 6. If the military situation permits, the commander of the attacking naval force, before commencing the bombardment, must do his utmost to warn the authorities.

Article 7. A town or place, even when taken by storm, may not be pillaged.

.   .   .

Hague Rules of Aërial Warfare

[32 A.J.I.L. (Supp.) 12 (1938), signed on February 19, 1923, at
The Hague; not in force]

. . .

Bombardment

Article 22. Aërial bombardment for the purpose of terrorizing the civilian population, of destroying or damaging private property not of military character, or of injuring non-combatants is prohibited.

. . .

Article 23. Aërial bombardment for the purpose of enforcing compliance with requisitions in kind or payment of contributions in money is prohibited.

. . .

Article 24. (1) Aërial bombardment is legitimate only when directed at a military objective, that is to say, an object of which the destruction or injury would constitute a distinct military advantage to the belligerent.

(2) Such bombardment is legitimate only when directed exclusively at the following objectives: military forces; military works; military establishments or depots; factories constituting important and well-known centers engaged in the manufacture of arms, ammunition or distinctively military supplies; lines of communication or transportation used for military purposes.

(3) The bombardment of cities, towns, villages, dwellings or buildings not in the immediate neighborhood of the operations of land forces is prohibited. In cases where the objectives specified in paragraph (2) are so situated that they cannot be bombarded without the indiscriminate bombardment of the civilian population, the aircraft must abstain from bombardment.

(4) In the immediate neighborhood of the operations of land forces, the bombardment of cities, towns, villages, dwellings or buildings is legitimate provided that there exists a reasonable presumption that the military concentration is sufficiently important to justify such bombardment, having regard to the danger thus caused to the civilian population.

(5) A belligerent state is liable to pay compensation for injuries to

person or to property caused by the violation by any of its officers or forces of the provisions of this article.

. . .

♦

GENOCIDE AND PROTECTION OF CIVILIANS

The Convention on the Prevention and Punishment of the Crime of Genocide was in large part a reaction to the Nazis' systematic murder of Jews and members of certain other groups of people.

CONVENTION ON THE PREVENTION AND PUNISHMENT OF THE CRIME OF GENOCIDE

[78 U.N.T.S. 277, adopted by Resolution 260 (III) A of the General Assembly of the United Nations on December 9, 1948]

. . .

Article I. The Contracting Parties confirm that genocide, whether committed in time of peace or in time of war, is a crime under international law which they undertake to prevent and to punish.

Article II. In the present Convention, genocide means any of the following acts committed with intent to destroy, in whole or in part, a national, ethnical, racial or religious group, as such:

  (a) Killing members of the group;

  (b) Causing serious bodily or mental harm to members of the group;

  (c) Deliberately inflicting on the group conditions of life calculated to bring about its physical destruction in whole or in part;

  (d) Imposing measures intended to prevent births within the group;

(e) Forcibly transferring children of the group to another group.

Article III. The following acts shall be punishable:

(a) Genocide;

(b) Conspiracy to commit genocide;

(c) Direct and public incitement to commit genocide;

(d) Attempt to commit genocide;

(e) Complicity in genocide.

Article IV. Persons committing genocide or any of the other acts enumerated in article III shall be punished, whether they are constitutionally responsible rulers, public officials or private individuals.

Article V. The Contracting Parties undertake to enact, in accordance with their respective Constitutions, the necessary legislation to give effect to the provisions of the present Convention and, in particular, to provide effective penalties for persons guilty of genocide or of any of the other acts enumerated in article III.

Article VI. Persons charged with genocide or any of the other acts enumerated in article III shall be tried by a competent tribunal of the State in the territory of which the act was committed, or by such international penal tribunal as may have jurisdiction with respect to those Contracting Parties which shall have accepted its jurisdiction.

Article VII. Genocide and the other acts enumerated in article III shall not be considered as political crimes for the purpose of extradition.

The Contracting Parties pledge themselves in such cases to grant extradition in accordance with their laws and treaties in force.

Article VIII. Any Contracting Party may call upon the competent organs of the United Nations to take such action under the Charter of the United Nations as they consider appropriate for the prevention and suppression of acts of genocide or any of the other acts enumerated in article III.

Article IX. Disputes between the Contracting Parties relating to the interpretation, application or fulfilment of the present Convention, including those relating to the responsibility of a State for genocide or for any of the other acts enumerated in article III, shall be submitted to the International Court of Justice at the request of any of the parties to the dispute.

.　　.　　.

NOTE: The Convention establishes that the international community will not tolerate grave crimes against targeted groups of people as occurred in World War II. Yet such crimes have not ceased. Consider several recent examples. In the civil war in Somalia, competing ethnic groups purposely starved members of rival ethnic groups, bringing about tragedy on a scale unseen since the fighting and famine in Ethiopia in the 1980s and the exterminations perpetrated by the Khmer Rouge in the 1970s. More than 150,000 people perished in civil strife in Burundi in 1993. Consider also the crimes committed in the Balkans, which may seem more shocking because of, among other things, greater media attention. A report by Helsinki Watch, a nongovernmental human rights organization, documents these abuses:

> The findings in this report, and the reports from Bosnia-Hercegovina by independent news media, provide at the very least *prima facie* evidence that genocide is taking place. The "ethnic cleansing" that is being practiced by Serbian forces is directed particularly against Muslims and Croats on the basis of their religion and ethnicity. The victims of such "ethnic cleansing" have been expelled from their homes and villages; rounded up and held in detention camps; deported; killed in indiscriminate attacks; and summarily executed. . . . To varying degrees, all parties to the conflict in Bosnia-Hercegovina have violated humanitarian law, or the laws of war. Croatian and Muslim forces have taken hostages, mistreated persons in their custody and harassed Serbs in areas which they control. Serbian forces have committed the same abuses but on a broader scale. Helsinki Watch has found that Serbian forces are summarily executing, detaining and deporting non-Serbs in areas under their control in an effort to "ethnically cleanse" such areas of Muslims and Croats. Such practices were employed in Serbian-occupied areas of Croatia. Similarly, Serbian paramilitary groups are responsible for the forcible displacement of Hungarians, Croats, Ruthenians and others living in Serbia, particularly in the province of Vojvodina.[13]

Protocol I Additional to the Geneva Conventions of 1949

[1125 U.N.T.S. 3, adopted on June 8, 1977, at Geneva]

. . .

Article 43—Armed Forces

1. The armed forces of a Party to a conflict consist of all organized armed forces, groups and units which are under a command responsible to that Party for the conduct of its subordinates, even if that Party is represented by a government or an authority not recognized by an adverse Party. Such armed forces shall be subject to an internal disciplinary system which, *inter alia*, shall enforce compliance with the rules of international law applicable in armed conflict.

2. Members of the armed forces of a Party to a conflict (other than medical personnel and chaplains covered by Article 33 of the Third Convention) are combatants, that is to say, they have the right to participate in hostilities.

3. Whenever a Party to a conflict incorporates a paramilitary or armed law enforcement agency into its armed forces it shall so notify the other Parties to the conflict.

. . .

CIVILIAN POPULATION
SECTION I. GENERAL PROTECTION AGAINST EFFECTS OF HOSTILITIES

. . .

Article 48—Basic Rule

In order to ensure respect for and protection of the civilian population and civilian objects, the Parties to the conflict shall at all times distinguish between the civilian population and combatants and between civilian objects and military objectives and accordingly shall direct their operations only against military objectives.

Article 49—Definition of Attacks and Scope of Application

1. "Attacks" means acts of violence against the adversary, whether in offence or in defence.

2. The provisions of this Protocol with respect to attacks apply to all attacks in whatever territory conducted, including the national territory

belonging to a Party to the conflict but under the control of an adverse Party.

3. The provisions of this Section apply to any land, air or sea warfare which may affect the civilian population, individual civilians or civilian objects on land. They further apply to all attacks from the sea or from the air against objectives on land but do not otherwise affect the rules of international law applicable in armed conflict at sea or in the air.

4. The provisions of this Section are additional to the rules concerning humanitarian protection contained in the Fourth Convention, particularly in Part II thereof, and in other international agreements binding upon the High Contracting Parties, as well as to other rules of international law relating to the protection of civilians and civilian objects on land, at sea or in the air against the effects of hostilities.

. . .

Article 50—Definition of Civilians and Civilian Population

1. A civilian is any person who does not belong to one of the categories of persons referred to in Article 4 A (1), (2), (3) and (6) of the Third Convention and in Article 43 of this Protocol. In case of doubt whether a person is a civilian, that person shall be considered to be a civilian.

2. The civilian population comprises all persons who are civilians.

3. The presence within the civilian population of individuals who do not come within the definition of civilians does not deprive the population of its civilian character.

Article 51—Protection of the Civilian Population

1. The civilian population and individual civilians shall enjoy general protection against dangers arising from military operations. To give effect to this protection, the following rules, which are additional to other applicable rules of international law, shall be observed in all circumstances.

2. The civilian population as such, as well as individual civilians, shall not be the object of attack. Acts or threats of violence the primary purpose of which is to spread terror among the civilian population are prohibited.

3. Civilians shall enjoy the protection afforded by this Section, unless and for such time as they take a direct part in hostilities.

4. Indiscriminate attacks are prohibited. Indiscriminate attacks are:

(a) those which are not directed at a specific military objective;

(b) those which employ a method or means of combat which cannot be directed at a specific military objective; or

(c) those which employ a method or means of combat the effects of which cannot be limited as required by this Protocol;

and consequently, in each such case, are of a nature to strike military objectives and civilians or civilian objects without distinction.

5. Among others, the following types of attacks are to be considered as indiscriminate:

(a) an attack by bombardment by any methods or means which treats as a single military objective a number of clearly separated and distinct military objectives located in a city, town, village or other area containing a similar concentration of civilians or civil[i]an objects; and

(b) an attack which may be expected to cause incidental loss of civilian life, injury to civilians, damage to civilian objects, or a combination thereof, which would be excessive in relation to the concrete and direct military advantage anticipated.

6. Attacks against the civilian population or civilians by way of reprisals are prohibited.

7. The presence or movements of the civilian population or individual civilians shall not be used to render certain points or areas immune from military operations, in particular in attempts to shield military objectives from attacks or to shield, favour or impede military operations. The Parties to the conflict shall not direct the movement of the civilian population or individual civilians in order to attempt to shield military objectives from attacks or to shield military operations.

8. Any violation of these prohibitions shall not release the Parties to the conflict from their legal obligations with respect to the civilian population and civilians, including the obligation to take the precautionary measures provided for in Article 57.

. . .

Civilian Objects

Article 52—General Protection of Civilian Objects

1. Civilian objects shall not be the object of attack or of reprisals. Civilian objects are all objects which are not military objectives as defined in paragraph 2.

2. Attacks shall be limited strictly to military objectives. In so far as

objects are concerned, military objectives are limited to those objects which by their nature, location, purpose or use make an effective contribution to military action and whose total or partial destruction, capture or neutralization, in the circumstances ruling at the time, offers a definite military advantage.

3. In case of doubt whether an object which is normally dedicated to civilian purposes, such as a place of worship, a house or other dwelling or a school, is being used to make an effective contribution to military action, it shall be presumed not to be so used.

. . .

Article 54—Protection of Objects Indispensable to the Survival of the Civilian Population

1. Starvation of civilians as a method of warfare is prohibited.

2. It is prohibited to attack, destroy, remove or render useless objects indispensable to the survival of the civilian population, such as foodstuffs, agricultural areas for the production of foodstuffs, crops, livestock, drinking water installations and supplies and irrigation works, for the specific purpose of denying them for their sustenance value to the civilian population or to the adverse Party, whatever the motive, whether in order to starve out civilians, to cause them to move away, or for any other motive.

3. The prohibitions in paragraph 2 shall not apply to such of the objects covered by it as are used by an adverse Party:

(a) as sustenance solely for the members of its armed forces; or

(b) if not as sustenance, then in direct support of military action, provided, however, that in no event shall actions against these objects be taken which may be expected to leave the civilian population with such inadequate food or water as to cause its starvation or force its movement.

4. These objects shall not be made the object of reprisals.

5. In recognition of the vital requirements of any Party to the conflict in the defence of its national territory against invasion, derogation from the prohibitions contained in paragraph 2 may be made by a Party to the conflict within such territory under its own control where required by imperative military necessity.

. . .

Article 56—Protection of Works and Installations Containing Dangerous Forces

1. Works or installations containing dangerous forces, namely dams, dykes and nuclear electrical generating stations, shall not be made the object of attack, even where these objects are military objectives, if such attack may cause the release of dangerous forces and consequent severe losses among the civilian population. Other military objectives located at or in the vicinity of these works or installations shall not be made the object of attack if such attack may cause the release of dangerous forces from the works or installations and consequent severe losses among the civilian population.

2. The special protection against attack provided by paragraph 1 shall cease:

 (a) for a dam or a dyke only if it is used for other than its normal function and in regular, significant and direct support of military operations and if such attack is the only feasible way to terminate such support;

 (b) for a nuclear electrical generating station only if it provides electric power in regular, significant and direct support of military operations and if such attack is the only feasible way to terminate such support;

 (c) for other military objectives located at or in the vicinity of these works or installations only if they are used in regular, significant and direct support of military operations and if such attack is the only feasible way to terminate such support.

3. In all cases, the civilian population and individual civilians shall remain entitled to all the protection accorded them by international law, including the protection of the precautionary measures provided for in Article 57. If the protection ceases and any of the works, installations or military objectives mentioned in paragraph 1 is attacked, all practical precautions shall be taken to avoid the release of the dangerous forces.

4. It is prohibited to make any of the works, installations or military objectives mentioned in paragraph 1 the object of reprisals.

5. The Parties to the conflict shall endeavour to avoid locating any military objectives in the vicinity of the works or installations mentioned in paragraph 1. Nevertheless, installations erected for the sole purpose of defending the protected works or installations from attack are permissible and shall not themselves be made the object of attack, provided that they are not used in hostilities except for defensive actions necessary to respond to attacks against the protected works or installations and that

their armament is limited to weapons capable only of repelling hostile action against the protected works or installations.

. . .

7. In order to facilitate the identification of the objects protected by this Article, the Parties to the conflict may mark them with a special sign consisting of a group of three bright orange circles placed on the same axis, as specified in Article 16 of Annex I to this Protocol. The absence of such marking in no way relieves any Party to the conflict of its obligations under this Article.

. . .

PRECAUTIONARY MEASURES

Article 57—Precautions in Attack

1. In the conduct of military operations, constant care shall be taken to spare the civilian population, civilians and civilian objects.

2. With respect to attacks, the following precautions shall be taken:

(a) Those who plan or decide upon an attack shall:

(i) Do everything feasible to verify that the objectives to be attacked are neither civilians nor civilian objects and are not subject to special protection but are military objectives within the meaning of paragraph 2 of Article 52 and that it is not prohibited by the provisions of this Protocol to attack them;

(ii) Take all feasible precautions in the choice of means and methods of attack with a view to avoiding, and in any event to minimizing, incidental loss of civilian life, injury to civilians and damage to civilian objects;

(iii) Refrain from deciding to launch any attack which may be expected to cause incidental loss of civilian life, injury to civilians, damage to civilian objects, or a combination thereof, which would be excessive in relation to the concrete and direct military advantage anticipated;

(b) An attack shall be cancelled or suspended if it becomes apparent that the objective is not a military one or is subject to special protection or that the attack may be expected to cause incidental loss of civilian life, injury to civilians, damage to civilian objects, or a combination thereof, which would be excessive in relation to the concrete and direct military advantage anticipated;

(c) Effective advance warning shall be given of attacks which may affect the civilian population, unless circumstances do not permit.

3. When a choice is possible between several military objectives for obtaining a similar military advantage, the objective to be selected shall be that the attack on which may be expected to cause the least danger to civilian lives and to civilian objects.

4. In the conduct of military operations at sea or in the air, each Party to the conflict shall, in conformity with its rights and duties under the rules of international law applicable in armed conflict, take all reasonable precautions to avoid losses of civilian lives and damage to civilian objects.

5. No provision of this Article may be construed as authorizing any attacks against the civilian population, civilians or civilian objects.

Article 58   Precautions Against the Effects of Attacks

The Parties to the conflict shall, to the maximum extent feasible:

(a) without prejudice to Article 49 of the Fourth Convention, endeavour to remove the civilian population, individual civilians and civilian objects under their control from the vicinity of military objectives;

(b) avoid locating military objectives within or near densely populated areas;

(c) take the other necessary precautions to protect the civilian population, individual civilians and civilian objects under their control against the dangers resulting from military operations.

NOTE: Because a significant part of the Geneva Convention Relative to the Protection of Civilian Persons in Time of War of August 12, 1949, prescribes rules of belligerent occupation, it has been included in Chapter 5. This chapter includes portions of Protocol I to the Convention that generally refer to rules governing which civilian objects may be targeted by military forces.

The primary innovations of Protocol I concern the prohibition of targeting objects indispensable to the survival of the civilian population such as foodstuffs and water (Article 54) and objects that contain dangerous forces, such as dams, dikes, and nuclear power stations (Article 56).

◆

PROHIBITIONS ON USE OF FORCE AGAINST CULTURAL AND OTHER PROTECTED PROPERTY

HAGUE CONVENTION (IV) RESPECTING THE LAWS AND CUSTOMS OF WAR ON LAND, ANNEX TO THE CONVENTION

[1 Bevans 631, signed on October 18, 1907, at The Hague]

. . .

Article 27. In sieges and bombardments all necessary steps must be taken to spare, as far as possible, buildings dedicated to religion, art, science, or charitable purposes, historic monuments, hospitals, and places where the sick and wounded are collected, provided they are not being used at the time for military purposes.

It is the duty of the besieged to indicate the presence of such buildings or places by distinctive and visible signs, which shall be notified to the enemy beforehand.

HAGUE CONVENTION (IX) CONCERNING BOMBARDMENT BY NAVAL FORCES IN TIME OF WAR

[1 Bevans 681, signed on October 18, 1907, at The Hague]

. . .

Article 5. In bombardments by naval forces all the necessary measures must be taken by the commander to spare as far as possible sacred edifices, buildings used for artistic, scientific, or charitable purposes, historic monuments, hospitals, and places where the sick or wounded are collected, on the understanding that they are not used at the same time for military purposes.

It is the duty of the inhabitants to indicate such monuments, edifices, or places by visible signs, which shall consist of large stiff rectangular panels divided diagonally into two coloured triangular portions, the upper portion black, the lower portion white.

HAGUE RULES OF AËRIAL WARFARE 1922/23

[32 A.J.I.L. (Supp.) 12 (1938), signed on February 19, 1923, at The Hague; not in force]

. . .

Article 25. In bombardment by aircraft, all necessary steps must be taken by the commander to spare as far as possible buildings dedicated to public worship, art, science, or charitable purposes, historic monuments, hospital ships, hospitals and other places where the sick and wounded are collected, provided such buildings, objects or places are not at the time used for military purposes. Such buildings, objects and places must by day be indicated by marks visible to aircraft. The use of marks to indicate other buildings, objects or places than those specified above is to be deemed an act of perfidy. The marks used as aforesaid shall be in the case of buildings protected under the Geneva Convention the red cross on a white ground, and in the case of other protected buildings a large rectangular panel divided diagonally into two pointed triangular portions, one black and the other white.

A belligerent who desires to secure by night the protection for the hospitals and other privileged buildings above mentioned must take the necessary measures to render the special signs referred to sufficiently visible.

. . .

Article 26. The following special rules are adopted for the purpose of enabling states to obtain more efficient protection for important historic monuments situated within their territory, provided that they are willing to refrain from the use of such monuments and a surrounding zone for military purposes, and to accept a special régime for their inspection:

(1) A state shall be entitled, if it sees fit, to establish a zone of protection round such monuments situated in its territory. Such zones shall in time of war enjoy immunity from bombardment.

(2) The monuments round which a zone is to be established shall be notified to other Powers in peacetime through the diplomatic channel; the notification shall also indicate the limits of the zones. The notification may not be withdrawn in time of war.

(3) The zone of protection may include, in addition to the area actually occupied by the monument or group of monuments, an outer zone, not exceeding 500 metres in width, measured from the circumference of the said area.

(4) Marks clearly visible from aircraft either by day or by night will be employed for the purpose of ensuring the identification by belligerent airmen of the limits of the zones.

(5) The marks on the monuments themselves will be those defined in Article 25. The marks employed for indicating the surrounding zones will be fixed by each state adopting the provisions of this article, and will be notified to other Powers at the same time as the monuments and zones are notified.

(6) Any abusive use of the marks indicating the zones referred to in paragraph 5 will be regarded as an act of perfidy.

(7) A state adopting the provisions of this article must abstain from using the monument and the surrounding zone for military purposes, or for the benefit in any way whatever of its military organization, or from committing within such monument or zone any act with a military purpose in view.

. . .

EISENHOWER MEMORANDUM [TO SUBORDINATE COMMANDERS], MAY 26, 1944

Secret
Subject: Preservation of Historical Monuments

1. Shortly we will be fighting our way across the Continent of Europe in battles designed to preserve our civilization. Inevitably, in the path of our advance will be found historical monuments and cultural centers which symbolize to the world all that we are fighting to preserve.

2. It is the responsibility of every commander to protect and respect these symbols whenever possible.

3. In some circumstances the success of the military operation may be prejudiced in our reluctance to destroy these revered objects. Then, as at Cassino, where the enemy relied on our emotional attachments to shield his defense, the lives of our men are paramount. So, where military necessity dictates, commanders may order the required action even though it involves destruction of some honored site.

4. But there are many circumstances in which damage and destruction are not necessary and cannot be justified. In such cases, through the exercise of restraint and discipline, commanders will preserve centers and objects of historical and cultural significance. Civil Affairs Staffs at higher echelons will advise commanders of the locations of historical

monuments of this type, both in advance of the front lines and in occupied areas. This information, together with the necessary instructions, will be passed down through command channels to all echelons.[14]

CONVENTION FOR THE PROTECTION OF CULTURAL PROPERTY IN THE EVENT OF ARMED CONFLICT

[249 U.N.T.S. 215, signed on May 14, 1954, at The Hague]

. . .

Definition of Cultural Property

Article 1. 1. For the purposes of the present Convention, the term "cultural property" shall cover, irrespective of origin or ownership:

(a) movable or immovable property of great importance to the cultural heritage of every people, such as monuments of architecture, art or history, whether religious or secular; archaeological sites; groups of buildings which, as a whole, are of historical or artistic interest; works of art; manuscripts, books and other objects of artistic, historical or archaeological interest; as well as scientific collections and important collections of books or archives or of reproductions of the property defined above;

(b) buildings whose main and effective purpose is to preserve or exhibit the movable cultural property defined in sub-paragraph (a) such as museums, large libraries and depositories of archives, and refuges intended to shelter, in the event of armed conflict, the movable cultural property defined in sub-paragraph (a);

(c) centres containing a large amount of cultural property as defined in sub-paragraphs (a) and (b), to be known as "centres containing monuments".

Protection of Cultural Property

Article 2. For the purposes of the present Convention, the protection of cultural property shall comprise the safeguarding of and respect for such property.

Safeguarding of Cultural Property

Article 3. The High Contracting Parties undertake to prepare in time of peace for the safeguarding of cultural property situated within their own territory against the foreseeable effects of an armed conflict, by taking such measures as they consider appropriate.

Respect for Cultural Property

Article 4. 1. The High Contracting Parties undertake to respect cultural property situated within their own territory as well as within the territory of other High Contracting Parties by refraining from any use of the property and its immediate surroundings or of the appliances in use for its protection for purposes which are likely to expose it to destruction or damage in the event of armed conflict; and by refraining from any act of hostility directed against such property.

2. The obligations mentioned in paragraph 1 of the present Article may be waived only in cases where military necessity imperatively requires such a waiver.

3. The High Contracting Parties further undertake to prohibit, prevent and, if necessary, put a stop to any form of theft, pillage or misappropriation of, and any acts of vandalism directed against, cultural property. They shall refrain from requisitioning movable cultural property situated in the territory of another High Contracting Party.

4. They shall refrain from any act directed by way of reprisals against cultural property.

5. No High Contracting Party may evade the obligations incumbent upon it under the present Article, in respect of another High Contracting Party, by reason of the fact that the latter has not applied the measures of safeguard referred to in Article 3.

Occupation

Article 5. 1. Any High Contracting Party in occupation of the whole or part of the territory of another High Contracting Party shall as far as possible support the competent national authorities of the occupied country in safeguarding and preserving its cultural property.

2. Should it prove necessary to take measures to preserve cultural

property situated in occupied territory and damaged by military operations, and should the competent national authorities be unable to take such measures, the Occupying Power shall, as far as possible, and in close co-operation with such authorities, take the most necessary measures of preservation.

3. Any High Contracting Party whose government is considered their legitimate government by members of a resistance movement, shall, if possible, draw their attention to the obligation to comply with those provisions of the Convention dealing with respect for cultural property.

Distinctive Marking of Cultural Property

Article 6. In accordance with the provisions of Article 16, cultural property may bear a distinctive emblem so as to facilitate its recognition.

Military Measures

Article 7. 1. The High Contracting Parties undertake to introduce in time of peace into their military regulations or instructions such provisions as may ensure observance of the present Convention, and to foster in the members of their armed forces a spirit of respect for the culture and cultural property of all peoples.

2. The High Contracting Parties undertake to plan or establish in peacetime, within their armed forces, services or specialist personnel whose purpose will be to secure respect for cultural property and to cooperate with the civilian authorities responsible for safeguarding it.

. . .

Granting of Special Protection

Article 8. 1. There may be placed under special protection a limited number of refuges intended to shelter movable cultural property in the event of armed conflict, of centres containing monuments and other immovable cultural property of very great importance, provided that they:

(a) are situated at an adequate distance from any large industrial centre or from any important military objective constituting a vulnerable point, such as, for example, an aerodrome, broadcasting station, establishment engaged upon work of national defence, a port or railway station of relative importance or a main line of communication;

(b) are not used for military purposes.

2. A refuge for movable cultural property may also be placed under special protection, whatever its location, if it is so constructed that, in all probability, it will not be damaged by bombs.

3. A centre containing monuments shall be deemed to be used for military purposes whenever it is used for the movement of military personnel or material, even in transit. The same shall apply whenever activities directly connected with military operations, the stationing of military personnel, or the production of war material are carried on within the centre.

4. The guarding of cultural property mentioned in paragraph 1 above by armed custodians specially empowered to do so, or the presence, in the vicinity of such cultural property, of police forces normally responsible for the maintenance of public order shall not be deemed to be used for military purposes.

5. If any cultural property mentioned in paragraph 1 of the present Article is situated near an important military objective as defined in the said paragraph, it may nevertheless be placed under special protection if the High Contracting Party asking for that protection undertakes, in the event of armed conflict, to make no use of the objective and particularly, in the case of a port, railway station or aerodrome, to divert all traffic therefrom. In that event, such diversion shall be prepared in time of peace.

6. Special protection is granted to cultural property by its entry in the "International Register of Cultural Property under Special Protection". This entry shall only be made, in accordance with the provisions of the present Convention and under the conditions provided for in the Regulations [249 U.N.T.S. 270] for the executions of the Convention.

Immunity of Cultural Property under Special Protection

Article 9. The High Contracting Parties undertake to ensure the immunity of cultural property under special protection by refraining, from the time of entry in the International Register, from any act of hostility directed against such property and, except for the cases provided for in paragraph 5 of Article 8, from any use of such property or its surroundings for military purposes.

Identification and Control

Article 10. During an armed conflict, cultural property under special protection shall be marked with the distinctive emblem described in Article 16, and shall be open to international control as provided for in the Regulations for the execution of the Convention.

Withdrawal of Immunity

Article 11. 1. If one of the High Contracting Parties commits, in respect of any item of cultural property under special protection, a violation of the obligations under Article 9, the opposing Party shall, so long as this violation persists, be released from the obligation to ensure the immunity of the property concerned. Nevertheless, whenever possible, the latter Party shall first request the cessation of such violation within a reasonable time.

2. Apart from the case provided for in paragraph 1 of the present Article, immunity shall be withdrawn from cultural property under special protection only in exceptional cases of unavoidable military necessity, and only for such time as that necessity continues. Such necessity can be established only by the officer commanding a force the equivalent of a division in size or larger. Whenever circumstances permit, the opposing Party shall be notified, a reasonable time in advance, of the decision to withdraw immunity.

3. The Party withdrawing immunity shall, as soon as possible, so inform the Commissioner-General for cultural property provided for in the Regulations for the execution of the Convention, in writing, stating the reasons.

. . .

Transport under Special Protection

Article 12. 1. Transport exclusively engaged in the transfer of cultural property, whether within a territory or to another territory, may, at the request of the High Contracting Party concerned, take place under special protection in accordance with the conditions specified in the Regulations for the execution of the Convention.

2. Transport under special protection shall take place under the in-

ternational supervision provided for in the aforesaid Regulations and shall display the distinctive emblem described in Article 16.

3. The High Contracting Parties shall refrain from any act of hostility directed against transport under special protection.

Transport in Urgent Cases

Article 13. 1. If a High Contracting Party considers that the safety of certain cultural property requires its transfer and that the matter is of such urgency that the procedure laid down in Article 12 cannot be followed, especially at the beginning of an armed conflict, the transport may display the distinctive emblem described in Article 16, provided that an application for immunity referred to in Article 12 has not already been made and refused. As far as possible, notification of transfer should be made to the opposing Parties. Nevertheless, transport conveying cultural property to the territory of another country may not display the distinctive emblem unless immunity has been expressly granted to it.

2. The High Contracting Parties shall take, so far as possible, the necessary precautions to avoid acts of hostility directed against the transport described in paragraph 1 of the present Article and displaying the distinctive emblem.

Immunity from Seizure, Capture and Prize

Article 14. 1. Immunity from seizure, placing in prize, or capture shall be granted to:
  (a) cultural property enjoying the protection provided for in Article 12 or that provided for in Article 13;
  (b) the means of transport exclusively engaged in the transfer of such cultural property;
     2. Nothing in the present Article shall limit the right of visit and search.

. . . . .

Emblem of the Convention

Article 16. 1. The distinctive emblem of the Convention shall take the form of a shield, pointed below, per saltire blue and white (a shield consisting of a royal blue square, one of the angles of which forms the point of the shield, and of a royal-blue triangle above the square, the space on either side being taken up by a white triangle).

2. The emblem shall be used alone, or repeated three times in a triangular formation (one shield below), under the conditions provided for in Article 17.

Use of the Emblem

Article 17. 1. The distinctive emblem repeated three times may be used only as a means of identification of:
  (a) immovable cultural property under special protection;
  (b) the transport of cultural property under the conditions provided for in Articles 12 and 13;
  (c) improvised refuges, under the conditions provided for in the Regulations for the execution of the Convention.

2. The distinctive emblem may be used alone only as a means of identification of:
  (a) cultural property not under special protection;
  (b) the persons responsible for the duties of control in accordance with the Regulations for the execution of the Convention;
  (c) the personnel engaged in the protection of cultural property;
  (d) the identity cards mentioned in the Regulations for the execution of the Convention.

3. During an armed conflict, the use of the distinctive emblem in any other cases than those mentioned in the preceding paragraphs of the present Article, and the use for any purpose whatever of a sign resembling the distinctive emblem, shall be forbidden.

4. The distinctive emblem may not be placed on any immovable cultural property unless at the same time there is displayed an authorization duly dated and signed by the competent authority of the High Contracting Party.

. . .

Application of the Convention

Article 18. 1. Apart from the provisions which shall take effect in time of peace, the present Convention shall apply in the event of declared war or of any other armed conflict which may arise between two or more of the High Contracting Parties, even if the state of war is not recognized by one or more of them.

2. The Convention shall also apply to all cases of partial or total occupation of the territory of a High Contracting Party, even if the said occupation meets with no armed resistance.

3. If one of the Powers in conflict is not a Party to the present Convention, the Powers which are Parties thereto shall nevertheless remain bound by it in their mutual relations. They shall furthermore be bound by the Convention, in relation to the said Power, if the latter has declared that it accepts the provisions thereof and so long as it applies them.

Conflicts Not of an International Character

Article 19. 1. In the event of an armed conflict not of an international character occurring within the territory of one of the High Contracting Parties, each party to the conflict shall be bound to apply, as a minimum, the provisions of the present Convention which relate to respect for cultural property.

. . .

Relation to Previous Conventions

Article 36. 1. In the relations between Powers which are bound by the Conventions of The Hague concerning the Laws and Customs of War on Land (IV) and concerning Naval Bombardment in Time of War (IX), whether those of 29 July 1899 or those of 18 October 1907, and which are Parties to the present Convention, this last Convention shall be supplementary to the aforementioned Convention (IX) and to the Regulations annexed to the aforementioned Convention (IV) and shall substitute for the emblem described in Article 5 of the aforementioned Convention (IX) the emblem described in Article 16 of the present Convention, in cases in which the present Convention and the Regulations for its execution provide for the use of this distinctive emblem.

2. In the relations between Powers which are bound by the Washington Pact of 15 April, 1935 for the Protection of Artistic and Scientific Institutions and of Historic Monuments (Roerich Pact) and which are Parties to the present Convention, the latter Convention shall be supplementary to the Roerich Pact and shall substitute for the distinguishing flag described in Article III of the Pact the emblem defined in Article

16 of the present Convention, in cases in which the present Convention and the Regulations for its execution provide for the use of this distinctive emblem.

* * *

PROTOCOL I ADDITIONAL TO THE GENEVA CONVENTIONS OF 1949

[1125 U.N.T.S. 3, adopted on June 8, 1977, at Geneva]

* * *

CIVILIAN OBJECTS

* * *

Article 53—Protection of Cultural Objects and of Places of Worship
Without prejudice to the provisions of the Hague Convention for the Protection of Cultural Property in the Event of Armed Conflict of 14 May 1954, [footnote omitted] and of other relevant international instruments, it is prohibited:

(*a*) to commit any acts of hostility directed against the historic monuments, works of art or places of worship which constitute the cultural or spiritual heritage of peoples;
(*b*) to use such objects in support of the military effort;
(*c*) to make such objects the object of reprisals.

* * *

NOTE: We commenced this chapter with the obligation of states, under the law of war, to notify and instruct their soldiers of the law of war. The Eisenhower Memorandum is an example of such instruction. In contemporary practice, the detailed instructions that are given to forces in the field are referred to as "rules of engagement" (ROEs). Rules of engagement are drafted with strategic, tactical, and political implications in mind and often are extremely detailed, allowing relatively little discretion to commanders in the field. But they also are interesting in that they reflect operational conceptions of what is permissible under the law of war in different types of theaters.

Because ROEs would have great intelligence value for adversaries, they usually are classified. But in the wake of the Vietnam War, amidst general criticism of United States military action there—one side contending that the United States had violated the law of war, the other side that it had unduly restricted the military arm and increased losses while decreasing the chances of success—Senator Barry Goldwater read into the Congressional Record the rules of engagement that had been issued for United States forces in Vietnam. They warrant careful study precisely because they indicate the self-imposed limitations upon the United States military that reflect conceptions of what is the operational law of war. The more arcane military acronyms and abbreviations are deciphered in brackets.

TEXT OF VIETNAM RULES OF ENGAGEMENT

[131 Cong. Rec. S6261 (daily ed. Mar. 26, 1985)
(statement of Senator Goldwater)]

. . . I will place in the RECORD excerpts from the Joint Chiefs' bombing policy paper submitted by General Wheeler to the Clifford group in 1968. This was a senior group of advisors convened by Defense Secretary Clark Clifford from the State and Defense Departments, the CIA and the White House to review U.S. involvement in Vietnam. . . .

I ask that the paper written by the Joint Chiefs be included in the CONGRESSIONAL RECORD.

The excerpt follows:

EXCERPTS OF BOMBING POLICY

1. The air campaign against North Vietnam is now entering the fourth year of operations. Only during the latter part of the past favorable weather season of April through October 1967, however, has a significant weight of effort been applied against the major target systems. During this period, even though hampered by

continuous and temporarily imposed constraints, the air campaign made a marked impact on the capability of North Vietnam to prosecute the war. Unfortunately, this impact was rapidly overcome. The constraints on operations and the change in the monsoon weather provided North Vietnam with numerous opportunities to recuperate from the effects of the air strikes. Facilities were rebuilt and reconstituted and dispersal of the massive material aid from communist countries continued . . .

5. Targeting criteria for the effective accomplishment of a systematic air campaign would continue to preclude the attack of population as a target, but accept greater risks of civilian casualties in order to achieve the stated objective. The initial changes in operating authorities necessary to the initiation of an effective air campaign are:

a. Delete the 30/10NM [nautical mile] Hanoi Restricted/Prohibited Area and establish a 3NM Hanoi Control Area.

b. Delete the 10/4NM Haiphong Restricted/Prohibited Area and establish a 1.5NM Haiphong Control Area.

c. Delete the Special Northeast Coastal Armed Reconnaissance Area.

6. The present Restricted Areas around Hanoi and Haiphong have existed since 1965. The Prohibited Areas were created in December 1966 . . . [in original] A reduction of the control areas would expose approximately 140 additional miles of primary road, rail and waterway lines of communication to armed reconnaissance, as well as hundreds of miles of secondary lines of communication, dependent upon NVN [North Vietnam] reactions and usage. Additional military targets would automatically become authorized for air strikes under armed reconnaissance operating authorities. This would broaden the target base, spread the defenses, and thus add to the cumulative effects of the interdiction program as well as reducing risk of aircraft loss . . . [in original]

7. There have been repeated and reliable intelligence reports that indicate civilians not engaged in essential war supporting activities have been evacuated from the cities of Hanoi and Haiphong. Photographic intelligence, particularly of Haiphong, clearly shows that materials of war are stockpiled in all open storage areas and along the streets throughout almost one-half of the city. Rather than an area for urban living, the city has become an armed camp and a large logistics storage base. Consequently, air strikes in and around these cities endanger personnel primarily engaged directly or indirectly in support of the war effort.

8. The special coastal armed reconnaissance area in the Northeast has limited attacks on NVN craft to those within 3 NM of the NVN coast or coastal islands. This constraint has provided another sanctuary to assist NVN in accommodating to the interdiction effort . . . [in original]

Mr. GOLDWATER. Mr. President, in order to assist interest[ed] Members, the media, historians or individual citizens in better understanding the rules of engagement, I asked Secretary Weinberger to declassify them. Earlier this year he agreed and I am now able to insert in the RECORD for study the actual text of the rules of engag[e]ment covering South Vietnam. In the interest of comparison, I will first insert the rules applicable to air and surface operations in South Vietnam, dated June 28, 1966, with 1967 revisions, and the same rules as they appeared 5 years later on December 30, 1971. Also, I will insert directive 95-4, establishing procedures and responsibilities for command, control and coordination of U.S. military air operations in South Vietnam, both as it was issued on June 28, 1966[,] and as revised on August 15, 1970.

The rules governing bombing in North Vietnam were included in regular message traffic and were not in the form of directives. That message traffic was not retained and is no longer available.

. . . . .

RESTRICTIONS AND RULES OF ENGAGEMENT, RVN [REPUBLIC OF VIETNAM]

[ROEs applicable to air and surface operations in South Vietnam, dated June 28, 1966, with 1967 revisions]

1. (U) [Unclassified] Purpose. To define specific operational restrictions and rules of engagement for US aircraft in RVN.

2. (C) [Confidential] General.

a. All targets selected for an air strike will be approved by the Province Chief directly or through higher ARVN [Army of the Republic of Vietnam] authority.

b. All pilots will endeavor to minimize non-combatant casualties and civilian property damage. A strike will not be executed where identification of friendly forces is in doubt.

c. All pilots will have a knowledge of the disposition of friendly forces and/or civilians prior to conducting a strike. This information may come from ground or air briefing.

d. For purposes of this directive, references to the Forward Air Controller (FAC) also encompass and apply to the Marine Tactical Air Coordinator Airborne (TACA).

e. USAF [United States Air Force], USMC [United States Marine Corps], and USN [United States Navy] strike aircraft will normally be controlled by the following in the order of preference as listed:

  (1) US Air Force ALO [Air Liaison Officer]/FAC or Marine TACA.

  (2) VNAF [Republic of Vietnam Air Force] FAC/FAO [Forward Area Observer].

  (3) USAF MSQ-77 (SKY SPOT) or USMC TPQ-10. [MSQ-77 and TPQ-10 are acronyms for tracking systems]

f. In an emergency, when no qualified means of control is available, the following personnel may designate the target for strike aircraft:

  (1) The commander of a ground unit or US advisor engaged with the Viet Cong.

  (2) US pilot of an airplane or helicopter supporting a ground unit, who has radio contact with the ground unit involved and/or can identify friendly positions in relation to enemy positions.

  (3) US pilot of an airplane or helicopter required to operate within the vicinity of a hostile village or hamlet for the purpose of conducting a medical evacuation or supply mission, and where enemy fire presents an immediate threat to the lives of the helicopter or transport crew.

g. Close Air Support missions that involve strikes on hamlets or villages must always be controlled by a FAC. If the attack on a village or hamlet is deemed necessary and is executed in conjunction with a ground operation involving movement of ground forces through the area, the attack may be made without warning; however, appropriate US-GVN [Government of Vietnam]-RVNAF [Republic of Vietnam Armed Forces] approval is required, except in emergencies. If the attack on a village or hamlet is not in conjunction with any immediate ground operation, the inhabitants must be warned by leaflets and/or loudspeaker system prior to the attack and must be given sufficient time to evacuate the area.

3. (C) Specific instructions for close air support to include interdiction (day or night).

a. ALO/FAC will:

(1) Have thorough knowledge of the ground scheme of maneuver.

(2) Make every effort to secure a VNAF observer to assist in directing an air strike. If a VNAF observer is not available, an ALO/FAC is authorized to direct the air strike.

(3) Maintain reliable communications with ground unit and with strike aircraft.

(4) Make positive identification and mark the target.

(5) Insure that strike pilots are aware of friendly locations in relation to target, characteristics of target area, and local weather conditions.

(6) Use 1:50,000 scale maps of target area, and photographs when available.

b. Strike Pilots will:

(1) Always be under the control and have direct radio contact for a strike with a Forward Air Controller or designated control agency (airborne or ground).

(2) Have visual contact with target or target marker except as noted in paragraph (6), below.

(3) Always ascertain the position of friendly troops (or civilians, when applicable).

(4) Ascertain local conditions regarding weather, target area, and surrounding terrain characteristics.

(5) Defend themselves against ground fire providing:

(a) Source of fire can be visually identified.

(b) The strike can be positively oriented against the source.

(c) The fire is of such intensity that counter-action is necessary.

(6) Strike at night only with flares, unless under control of TPQ-10 or MSQ-77.

4. (C) Border restrictions for aircraft conducting assigned missions in RVN.

a. Aircraft will not cross the demilitarized zone or Cambodian border unless specifically authorized by COMUSMACV [Commander, United States Military Assistance Command Vietnam].

b. All FACs operating in the vicinity of the border will have a 1:50,000 map of the target area. Maps, mosaics, and photos will be made available to the pilots.

c. Joint operations-intelligence facilities will be established and complete prestrike briefings and poststrike debriefings will be conducted for strikes within 5000 meters of the border, when practical.

d. Cambodian border restrictions which are additional to the above:

(1) Strike aircraft within 5000 meters of the Cambodian border will be under positive control of a Forward Air Controller or MSQ-77/TPQ-10. The authority to waive this requirement is restricted to COMUSMACV or his designated representative.

(2) All organizations responsible for planning or execution of missions within 5 km of the border will have posted in operations a 1:250,000 or larger scale map on which the Cambodian border is distinctly marked, on the RVN side, to the depth of 5 km.

(3) Aircraft supporting border outposts (fire support, reconnaissance, supply, and transportation) are allowed to operate as necessary in the outpost area, but will neither cross nor fire across the border.

(4) Appropriate radar stations will flight follow aircraft on missions within 5 km of the border within equipment capability.

5. (C) Jettison.

a. Munitions will be jettisoned only in designated jettison areas.

b. During night or IFR [Instrument Flight Rules] conditions, aircraft will be under positive radar control while jettisoning.

c. During day VFR [Visual Flight Rules], drops will be monitored by radar whenever possible.

6. (C) US Armed Helicopters.

a. US Army and US Marine armed helicopters will be marked "US Army" or "US Marine," as appropriate, and may be manned with all-US crews at the unit commanders['] discretion.

b. If the target involves non-combatants, such as in a hamlet or village, whenever possible an RVNAF observer will be aboard the helicopter and US-GVN-RVNAF approval to fire must be obtained unless the situation clearly presents an immediate threat to the lives of the crew.

7. (C) USAF C-123 aircraft (Ranch Hand). Ranch Hand aircraft flying Trail Dust missions in RVN for the purpose of crop destruction will be flown under "Farmgate" rules which require Vietnamese markings on the aircraft and a Vietnamese observer aboard.

8. (C) Air reconnaissance and aerial surveillance missions.

a. Operational restrictions placed upon reconnaissance aircraft near the RVN/Cambodian border, for the purpose of insuring that inadvertent overflights do not occur, preclude aerial reconnaissance over large areas within RVN where significant enemy activity is known to be taking place. In order to eliminate the immunity of such areas to observation and photography, these restrictions may be waived on a case-by-case basis.

b. Reconnaissance requests for coverage in areas which present a danger of an overflight or border violation will be forwarded through normal reconnaissance request channels . . . Upon determination that a waiver is justified, the request will be executed. In the event of particularly sensitive complications, COMUSMACV will be the final determining authority.

c. US ARMY OV-1 aircraft may be armed with target marking ordnance while on surveillance missions.

9. (U) Air to air restrictions. Commander, 7th Air Force, prescribes Rules of [E]ngagement and Restrictions for air to air combat in RVN. These are published by that headquarters in Tactical Air Control Center (TACC) Operating Instructions (OI) No 55-33, 30 March 1966.

. . .

MILITARY OPERATIONS: RULES OF ENGAGEMENT FOR THE EMPLOYMENT OF FIREPOWER IN THE REPUBLIC OF VIETNAM (U)

[ROEs applicable to air and surface operations in South Vietnam, dated December 30, 1971]

1. (U) Purpose. This directive provides specific rules of engagement (ROE) for the conduct of the air and surface operations within the Republic of Vietnam (RVN).

2. (U) Applicability. This directive is applicable to all MACV [Mil-

itary Assistance Command Vietnam] staff agencies and subordinate commands.

3. (U) General.

a. The changing nature of operations in the RVN has necessitated a new approach to the ROE for the employment of firepower. The shift to predominantly Republic of Vietnam Armed Forces (RVNAF) operations supported and advised by US forces, coupled with a civilian populace that is less inclined to observe curfews and restricted areas, makes it imperative to ensure against the indiscriminate use of firepower. While the goal is maximum effectiveness in combat operations, every effort must be made to avoid civilian casualties, minimize the destruction of private property, and conserve diminishing resources. Accomplishment of these objectives requires that the ROE be adhered to by all friendly armed forces.

b. This directive will not be modified by subordinate commanders nor will directives modifying or interpreting substantive rules in this directive be published by subordinate commands. Unit commanders are authorized to issue instructions to users, provided such instructions do not circumvent the substantive rules contained in this directive.

c. This directive will serve as the basis for standing operating procedures for the conduct of all fires to include artillery, mortar, tank, riverine, strike aircraft, armed helicopters, air defense artillery, and naval gunfire.

d. It is not the intent of this directive to restrict any commander from exercising the inherent right and responsibility of self-defense of his forces. Commanders at all echelons must establish a balance between the force and weapons necessary to accomplish their mission yet ensure safety of noncombatants who are in the area.

4. (U) Responsibility.

a. Advisors will take all necessary advisory action to encourage RVNAF compliance with these ROE.

b. senior tactical commanders and senior advisors will:

(1) In coordination with their RVNAF counterparts, where applicable, insure that all units conduct operations in accordance with this directive, and develop positive, practical, and understandable target clearance procedures to preclude error or misunderstanding.

(2) Insure that all personnel engaged in fire support activities are

fully cognizant of the contents of this directive, with specific emphasis on procedures pertaining to clearance for fires and air strikes. Periodic testing of personnel on their knowledge of ROE is encouraged.

(3) Require advisory personnel to insure that US fire support resources provided in support of RVNAF operations are employed in accordance with this directive. If the request of a RVNAF unit falls outside the provisions of this directive, the advisor will take action to suspend the US fire support which is in violation of the ROE.

5. (U) Definitions.

. . .

g. Inhabited Area. Includes any dwelling or group of dwellings as well as established hamlets and villages that do not qualify as urban areas.

h. Military Clearance Authority. The U.S. military clearance authorities are the senior tactical commanders, senior advisors or their authorized representatives. The RVN military clearance authorities are the ARVN [Army of the Republic of Vietnam] corps commanders or their authorized representatives.

i. Political Clearance Authority. The RVN province chiefs, or their authorized representatives are the political clearance authority for their respective provinces.

. . .

k. Specified Strike Zones (SSZ). An area designated for a specific period of time by an ARVN corps commander in which there are no friendly forces or populace and in which targets may be attacked on the initiative of US, Free World Military Assistance Forces (FWMAF), or RVNAF commanders. SSZ will not be referred to as "free fire zones." Furthermore, the term "free fire zone" will not be used under any circumstances.

l. Strike Aircraft. Fixed wing aircraft of the fighter, bomber, and attack classification capable of conducting an air strike.

m. Troops In Contact (TIC). A unit is considered in contact when it is engaged with an enemy force, being fired upon, and returning fire. The supported unit commander is responsible for making the "in contact" determination.

n. Urban Area. Those areas depicted as built-up areas on an Army Map Service 1:50,000 scale map.

. . .

6. (C) General Rules.

a. All possible means will be employed to limit the risk to the lives and property of friendly forces and civilians. In this respect, a target must be clearly identified as hostile prior to making a decision to place fire on it.

b. Precautionary measures will be taken to avoid the violation of operational and national boundaries.

c. The enemy is known to take advantage of areas normally considered as non-military targets. Typical examples of non-military targets are places of religious or historical value and public or private buildings and dwellings. When the enemy has sheltered himself or installed defensive positions in such places, the responsible brigade or higher commander must positively identify the preparation for, or execution of, hostile enemy acts before ordering an attack. During the attack, weapons and forces used will be those which will insure prompt defeat of enemy forces with minimum damage to structures in the area.

d. The exception to the above policy is the palace compound in Hue Citadel. For this specific area, commanders will employ riot control agents and take all other possible actions to avoid damage to the compound.

e. The use of incendiary munitions in inhabited or urban areas will be avoided unless friendly survival is at stake or it is necessary for the accomplishment of the commander's mission.

f. Riot control agents (RCA) will be used to the maximum extent possible. RCA can be effectively employed in inhabited and urban area operations to flush enemy personnel from buildings and fortified positions, while reducing the unnecessary danger to civilians and the likelihood of destruction of civilian property.

g. The ARVN corps commander in each MR [Military Region] has the authority to designate, modify, suspend temporarily, or cancel a SSZ. Notification of SSZ designation, modification, temporary suspension, or cancellation will be disseminated by the ARVN corps commander to all commands operating in the MR with a minimum of 72 hours notification prior to the change becoming effective.

Notification of US and FWMAF will be through US command channels. Requests for SSZ changes will be submitted to the ARVN corps commander via appropriate command channels.

.   .   .

RULES OF ENGAGEMENT—SURFACE WEAPONS

1. (U) Purpose. This annex provides guidance for the control of organic weapons and the artillery, mortar, tank, naval, and riverine gunfire provided to the surface commander by US, FWMAF, and RVNAF.

2. (C) General.

a. These rules of engagement apply to the conduct of surface operations to include the employment of artillery, mortar, tank, naval, and riverine gunfire by US, FWMAF, and RVNAF in both offensive and defensive situations within the RVN. These rules also apply to the employment of US, FWMAF, and RVNAF fire support missions for all forces.

b. Artillery, mortar, tank, naval, and riverine gunfire requires that care and attention be exercised in the formulation of fire requests and the application of all gunnery techniques. The exercise of sound judgment on the part of all personnel involved in originating requests for fire, solving the gunnery problem, and exercising precise gunnery procedures will provide the best assurance against endangering friendly forces and noncombatants or destroying civilian property.

c. Procedures applicable to the conduct and control of naval gunfire are contained in the effective CTG 70.8 Operation Order 320. Market Time unites [*sic*] will comply with the provisions of COMCOSURVFOR [Commander Coastal Surveillance Forces Vietnam] Operation Order 201.

3. (C) Conduct of Fire.

a. Every effort will be made to observe fires regardless of the target location. Unobserved fires will be employed only where absolutely necessary for mission accomplishment and will be in accordance with the criteria outlined herein.

b. SSZ. Unobserved fire may be directed against all targets and target areas located within a SSZ after obtaining military clearance.

c. Uninhabited Areas Outside a SSZ.

(1) In uninhabited areas, fire may be directed against Viet Cong (VC)/North Vietnamese Army (NVA) forces in contact without obtaining military or political clearance.

(2) Observed fire may be directed against targets of opportunity which are clearly identified as hostile without obtaining military or political clearance.

(3) Unobserved fires may be directed at targets and target areas clearly identified as hostile, other than VC/NVA forces in contact, after obtaining military and political clearance.

d. Inhabited Areas. Fire missions directed against known or suspected VC-NVA targets in, or in the immediate vicinity of, inhabited areas will be conducted as follows:

(1) Inhabited areas from which hostile fire is received.

    (a) Surface commanders of units engaged in operations involving the maneuver of surface forces in or through inhabited areas may respond with direct fire without prior warning and without prior clearance if, in the judgment of the commander, his mission or troops would be jeopardized by such warning or delay. However, response should be designed for self-protection and directed only at the source of hostile fire.

    (b) Indirect fire missions will be controlled by an observer and may be executed after approval of the political and military clearance authority. The only exception to the clearance requirement would be a situation in which the hostile fire presents an immediate threat to friendly forces despite the employment of direct fire.

(2) Inhabited areas containing observed or suspected VC/NVA targets but from which hostile fire is not received.

    (a) Surface commanders may initiate direct fire against positively identified enemy targets after securing political and military clearance.

    (b) Indirect fire missions will be controlled by an observer and executed only after political and military clearance has been granted. Civilians will be given prior warning by leaflets, loudspeakers, or other appropriate means and given sufficient time to evacuate the area.

(3) Inhabited areas not immediately associated with the maneuver of surface forces will not be fired upon without prior warning by leaflets, loudspeakers, or other appropriate means, even

though fire is received therefrom. Should friendly troops be placed in jeopardy, the provisions of paragraph 3d(1), above, apply.

e. Urban Areas.

   (1) Fire missions directed against known or suspected VC/NVA targets in urban areas must preclude unnecessary danger to civilians and destruction of civilian property.

   (2) Fire support in urban areas will be governed by the following:

      (a) Approval by both the senior tactical commander and the ARVN corps commander is required to conduct fire missions in urban areas. This authority will not be delegated except for the built-up areas of Saigon, Cholon, and Gia Dinh City. CG [Commanding General], TRAC [Third Regional Assistance Command], is authorized to delegate authority to Commanding Officer, Capitol Military Assistance Team, for the employment of indirect fire in these areas. No further delegation is authorized.

      (b) All indirect fire missions will be controlled by an observer.

      (c) Direct fire, flat trajectory weapons are authorized in a direct fire role in urban areas at the discretion of a battalion or higher commander without the prior approval of the senior tactical commander, or, in the case of Saigon, Cholon, and Gia Dinh City, the Commanding Officer, Capit[o]l Military Assistance Team. Direct fire weapons will be used to the maximum in the elimination of enemy strong points or fortified structures in urban areas. All types of munitions, except incendiary, may be used in direct fire weapons including flechette (beehive), HEAT [High Explosive Anti-Tank], and canister rounds.

      (d) Maximum use will be made of helicopters to maneuver troops and heavy weapons to roofs of key buildings and other locations to expedite cordoning.

      (e) Prior to firing upon urban areas, leaflets, loudspeakers, or other appropriate means will be utilized to warn and secure the cooperation and support of the civilian populace even though fire is received from these areas.

f. Watercraft.

   (1) Fire will not be employed against waterborne craft in international or RVN territorial (coastal) waters unless the craft is positively identified as hostile and firing clearance is granted by the

appropriate coastal zone commander or coastal surveillance center.

(2) Return of fire when fired upon and firing in support of friendly forces receiving hostile fire in RVN territorial or international waters is authorized if the watercraft is positively identified as hostile.

(3) Illumination rounds are authorized over RVN territorial or international waters when specifically requested or cleared by a coastal surveillance center.

g. Vicinity of the RVN Border. Fire missions along or across the RVN border will be in accordance with current MACV border and cross-border authorities.

. . . .

RULES OF ENGAGEMENT—STRIKE AIRCRAFT OPERATIONS

. . .

2. (C) General.

a. All pilots will receive an air or ground briefing to determine the disposition of friendly forces and civilians prior to initiating an air to ground attack.

b. Pilots will endeavor to minimize civilian casualties and civilian property damage. Air attacks will not be executed where identification of friendly forces is in doubt.

c. US strike aircraft may be controlled by any of the following:

(1) US Forward Air Controller (FAC).

(2) VNAF FAC/Forward Air Observer (FAO).

(3) Flight leader control utilizing US Air Force LORAN or beacon-tracking, sensor-equipped aircraft.

(4) US Air Force MSQ-77 (SKY SPOT).

(5) US OV-10 aircraft commanders. In an emergency, US OV-10 aircraft commanders may mark a target for themselves and expend their own ordnance. They may also exercise FAC control of each other when operating in elements of two or more.

d. In an emergency, when compliance with the provisions of paragraph 2c, above, is not possible, the following personnel may designate the target for strike aircraft:

(1) The commander of a company or larger ground unit or US advisor of any unit engaged with enemy forces.

(2) The US, FWMAF, or RVNAF pilot of an aircraft supporting a ground unit, who has radio contact with the ground unit involved and can identify friendly and enemy positions.

(3) The US, FWMAF, or RVNAF pilot of an aircraft required to operate within the vicinity of a hostile inhabited area for the purpose of conducting medical evacuation or supply missions and where enemy fire presents an immediate threat to the lives of the aircraft crew.

e. Commanders of units assigned strike aircraft will ensure that records or ordnance expended are maintained a minimum of three months. Records will include as a minimum:

(1) Type and amount of ordnance expended on each target.

(2) Coordinates of target.

(3) Date and time of initial and final engagement of the target.

(4) Unit supported.

3. (C) Conduct of fire.

a. SSZ. Air attacks against targets or target areas in a SSZ, excluding the Demilitarized Zone, may be made under flight leader control after obtaining military clearance.

b. Uninhabited areas outside a SSZ. Military and political clearance are required for airstrikes against targets in uninhabited areas outside a SSZ except:

(1) When in close support of friendly troops in contact (paragraph 4, below).

(2) When returning ground fire (paragraph 4b(5), below).

c. Inhabited Areas. Fixed wing aircraft close air support missions that involve strikes in inhabited areas must be controlled by a FAC and be initiated only after political clearance has been obtained. The conduct of such air operations must be approved by the attacking battalion or higher commander.

(1) An attack deemed necessary on an inhabited area may be made without warning (prescribed in paragraph 3c(2), below) or delay provided all three of the following requirements are satisfied:

(a) Enemy fire is being received from the area.

(b) The attack is executed in conjunction with a ground operation involving the movement of ground forces through the area.

(c) In the judgment of the battalion or higher commander, his mission would be jeopardized by prior warning.

(2) If the attack on an inhabited area is not in conjunction with an immediate ground operation, the inhabitants must be warned by leaflets, loudspeakers, or other appropriate means prior to the attack, and given sufficient time to evacuate the area. Once the inhabitants of a target area have been adequately warned that the area has been selected as a target and given sufficient time to evacuate, the area may then be struck without further warning. An exception may be made for herbicide missions in cases where prior warning may jeopardize the safety of the spray aircraft (MACV Directive 525-216).

d. Urban Areas. Air attacks directed against known or suspected VC/NVA targets in urban areas must preclude unnecessary danger to civilians and destruction of civilian property, and by their nature require greater restrictions than the rules of engagement for less populated areas. Therefore, the following specific US, GVN, and RVNAF clearance procedures and restrictions must be strictly adhered to:

(1) Approval by both the senior tactical commander and the ARVN corps commander is required to conduct air attacks in urban areas including support of RVNAF. This authority will not be delegated except for the built-up areas of Saigon, Cholon, and Gia Dinh City. CG, TRAC, is authorized to delegate authority to Commanding Officer, Capitol Military Assistance Team, for the employment of US and FWMAF tactical air in these areas. No further delegation is authorized.

(2) Air attacks in urban areas will be controlled by a FAC.

(3) Prior to subjecting urban areas to an air attack, even when fire is being received from the area, the inhabitants must be warned by leaflets, loudspeakers, or other appropriate means prior to the attack and given sufficient time to evacuate the area.

e. Watercraft.

(1) Fixed wing aircraft are not authorized to engage watercraft of any description in international or RVN territorial (coastal) waters, except as authorized in paragraph 3e(3) below. This restriction does not deny aircraft commanders the right to return hostile fire in the exercise of self-defense.

(2) Watercraft on the inland waters may be engaged after being positively identified as hostile and with military and political clearance granted. During hours of announced curfews, any waterborne craft on inland waters may be presumed hostile and engaged after military and political clearance has been granted.

(3) Specific instructions for engagement of watercraft by fixed wing aircraft in the Tran Hung Dao Fifteen and Market Time tactical area of responsibility (TAOR):

    (a) Tran Hung Dao Fifteen and Market Time TAOR is defined as the water area off the coast of the RVN out to a distance of forty nautical miles. The northeastern boundary is 17 degrees North Latitude; and the northwestern boundary is the seaward extension of the RVN/GKR [Khmer Republic] border.

    (b) Fixed wing aircraft will not engage watercraft in this TAOR except in support of TRAN HUNG DAO FIFTEEN or MARKET TIME surface forces.

    (c) Surface craft must be positively identified as hostile and firing clearance must be granted by the appropriate coastal zone commander or coastal surveillance center except when firing is in support of a TRAN HUNG DAO FIFTEEN or MARKET TIME unit under actual attack.

4. (C) Specific Instructions for Close Air Support (Day or Night).

a. The FAC will:

(1) Have a thorough knowledge of the scheme of ground maneuver.

(2) Maintain reliable communications with the ground unit and strike aircraft.

(3) Make positive identification and mark the target.

(4) Insure that strike pilots are aware of friendly locations in relation to target, characteristics of target area, and local weather conditions.

(5) Use 1:50,000 or larger scale maps of target area and photographs when available.

b. During a strike, pilots of strike aircraft will:

(1) Always be under the control of, and in direct radio contact with, a FAC or designated control agency, airborne or ground, except in a SSZ when flight leader control is authorized (see paragraph 3a, above).

(2) Have visual contact with the target or target marker. During night strikes, the target must be visually identified through illumination, e.g., illumination flares, ground marking flares, fires, lunar illumination, etc. A waiver of this requirement is granted for aircraft equipped with night observation devices.

(3) Always ascertain the position of friendly forces (or civilians when applicable).

(4) Ascertain local conditions regarding weather, target area, and surrounding terrain characteristics.

(5) Defend themselves against ground fire provided:

    (a) The source of the fire can be visually identified.

    (b) The strike can be positively oriented against the source.

    (c) The fire is of such intensity that counteraction is necessary.

(6) Utilize LORAN or beacon-tracking sensor systems for instrument flight rules (IFR) deliveries. Aircrews making LORAN or beacon-tracking, sensor-directed strikes will be in direct radio contact with a designated control agency, airborne or ground, except in an SSZ.

5. (U) Air Interdiction. Air interdiction missions will be conducted and controlled in accordance with paragraphs 3 and 4, above.

6. (C) Vicinity of the RVN border.

a. US and FWMAF military fixed wing aircraft will not penetrate the DMZ [Demilitarized Zone], Laotian, or Khmer Republic airspace unless specifically authorized by COMUSMACV/DEP-COMUSMACV [Deputy Commander, United States Military Assistance Command Vietnam] for Air, 7th AF.

b. All FAC operating in the vicinity of the borders will have a 1:50,000 or larger scale map on the target area. Maps, mosaics, and photographs will be made available to the pilots whenever possible.

7. (C) Jettison.

a. Munitions will be jettisoned in designated jettison areas.

b. During night or IFR conditions, aircraft will be under positive radar control while jettisoning, except during emergencies as indicated in paragraph 7d, below.

c. During day visual flight rules (VFR), jettisons will be monitored by radar whenever possible.

d. Aircraft may jettison munitions in other than designated areas during emergencies when there is an immediate threat of injury to the crew or damage to the aircraft. Every effort will be made to insure that munitions are not jettisoned so that they impact into or near inhabited areas.

e. Emergency jettisoning of herbicides will be reported immediately to the MACV Command Center giving date-time, coordinates, agents, volume, and circumstances.

8. (C) Air Reconnaissance and Aerial Surveillance Missions. Aerial reconnaissance and surveillance missions conducted in the vicinity of the DMZ, Khmer Republic or Laotian border, and in Khmer Republic,

Laotian, or North Vietnamese airspace will be in accordance with authorities established by separate MACV directives.

9. (U) Air to Air Restrictions. 7th AF rules of engagement for air-to-air combat in the RVN are published in 7th AF OPORD [Air Force Operation Order] 71-7.

RULES OF ENGAGEMENT—ARMED HELICOPTER OPERATIONS

2. (C) General.

a. Ordnance delivery systems in armed helicopters will be fired only when authorized by the aircraft commander.

b. All pilots and gunners will receive an air or ground briefing to determine the disposition of friendly forces and civilians prior to initiating an air attack.

c. Pilots and gunners will endeavor to minimize civilian casualties and civilian property damage. Air attacks will not be executed where identification of friendly forces is in doubt.

d. Commanders of units assigned helicopters with an attached weapons system which is fired by the pilot or copilot will ensure that records of ordnance expended are maintained for a minimum of three months. Records will include as a minimum:

(1) Type and amount of ordnance expended on each target.

(2) Coordinates of each target.

(3) Date and time of initial and final engagement of the target.

(4) Unit supported.

e. Pilots of armed helicopters will:

(1) Fire only when all three of the following requirements are satisfied:

(a) They are under the control of, and in direct radio contact with the designated control agency, airborne or ground, except in a SSZ when a designated flight leader is authorized to control.

(b) The target or target marker can be visually identified.

(c) Friendly and civilian positions are positively identified.

(2) Ascertain local conditions regarding weather, target area, and surrounding terrain characteristics.

(3) Defend themselves against ground fire provided:

(a) The source of fire can be visually identified.

(b) The return fire can be positively oriented against the source.

f. The following personnel may designate targets for armed helicopters.

(1) The commander of a ground or VNN [Vietnamese Navy] surface unit or the US advisor of any unit in contact with enemy forces.

(2) The US, FWMAF, or RVNAF pilot of helicopter supporting a ground unit which has radio contact with the ground unit and can identify friendly positions in relation to enemy positions.

(3) The US, FWMAF, or RVNAF pilot of a helicopter required to operate in the vicinity of a hostile inhabited area for the purpose of conducting medical evacuation or supply missions, and where enemy fire presents an immediate threat to the lives of the helicopter crew.

g. Airborne test firing of weapons will be conducted only after obtaining military and political clearance.

h. When appropriate, US Army, US Air Force and US Navy armed helicopter operations will be coordinated within the operational area with controller aircraft of the other services.

3. (C) Conduct of fire.

a. SSZ. Armed helicopters may attack targets and target areas in a SSZ, excluding the DMZ, after obtaining a military clearance.

b. Uninhabited Areas Outside an SSZ. Military and political clearances are required to engage targets in uninhabited areas outside an SSZ except:

(1) When in close support of friendly troops in contact.

(2) When returning ground fire (paragraph 2f(3), above).

c. Inhabited Areas.

(1) Armed helicopters involved in air attacks on inhabited areas must receive the approval of, and always be in direct radio contact with, the designated control agency of the responsible ground commander. Attacks may be initiated after military and political clearances have been obtained.

(2) If the attack on an inhabited area from which enemy fire is being received is deemed necessary, the attack may be made without warning (as prescribed in paragraph 3c(3), below) or delay provided all three of the following requirements are satisfied.

(a) The enemy fire is being received from the area.

(b) The attack is executed in conjunction with a ground operation involving the movement of ground forces through the area.

(c) In the judgment of the commander, his mission would be jeopardized by prior warning.

(3) If the attack on an inhabited area is not in conjunction with an immediate ground operation, the inhabitants must be warned by leaflets, loudspeakers, or some other appropriate means prior to the attack and given sufficient time to evacuate the area. Once the inhabitants of a target area have been adequately warned that the area has been selected as a target and given sufficient time to evacuate, the area may then be attacked without further warning.

d. Urban Areas.

(1) Air attacks directed against known or suspected VC/NVA targets in urban areas must preclude unnecessary danger to civilians or destruction of civilian property, and by their nature require greater restrictions than the rules of engagement for less populated areas. Approval by both the senior tactical commander and the ARVN corps commander is required to conduct US and FWMAF air attacks in urban areas, including supporting RVNAF. This authority will not be delegated with the exception of the built-up areas of Saigon, Cholon, and Gia Dinh City. CG, TRAC, is authorized to delegate authority to Commanding Officer, Capit[o]l Military Assistance Team, for employment of armed helicopters in the built-up areas of Saigon, Cholon, and Gia Dinh City. No further delegation is authorized.

(2) Only point targets, e.g., a specific building, will be engaged and these targets must be positively identified to the pilot. The engagement of area targets in urban areas is prohibited.

(3) Prior to subjecting urban areas to air attack, even when fire is received from the area, the inhabitants must be warned by leaflets, loudspeakers, or some other appropriate means prior to the attack and given sufficient time to evacuate the area.

e. Watercraft.

(1) Helicopters are not authorized to engage watercraft of any description in international or RVN territorial (coastal) waters except as authorized in paragraph 3e(3), below. This restriction does not deny aircraft commanders the right to return hostile fire in the exercise of self-defense.

THE LAWS OF WAR

(2) Watercraft on inland waters may be engaged after being positively identified as hostile and with military and political clearance granted. During hours of announced curfews, any waterborne craft on inland waters may be presumed hostile and engaged after military and political clearances have been granted.

(3) Specific instructions for engagement of watercraft by helicopters in the Tran Hung Dao Fifteen and Market Time TAOR:

(a) Tran Hung Dao Fifteen and Market Time TAOR is defined as the water area off the coast of the RVN out to a distance of forty nautical miles. The northeastern boundary is 17 degrees North Latitude; and the northwestern boundary is the seaward extension of the RVN/GKR border.

(b) Helicopters will not engage watercraft in this T[AOR] except in support of Tran Hung Dao Fifteen or Market Time surface forces.

(c) Surface craft must be positively identified as hostile and firing clearance must be granted by the appropriate coastal zone commander or coastal surveillance center except when firing is in support of a Tran Hung Dao Fifteen or Market Time unit under actual attack.

4. (C) Jettison.

a. Munitions will be jettisoned in designated jettison ares.

b. During night or IFR conditions, aircraft will be under positive radar control while jettisoning, except during emergencies covered in paragraph 4c, below.

c. Aircraft may jettison munitions in other than designated areas during emergencies when there is an immediate threat of injury to crew or damage to the aircraft. Every effort will be made to ensure that munitions are not jettisoned so that they impact into or near inhabited areas.

d. Emergency jettisoning of herbicides will be reported immediately to the MACV Command Center giving date-time, coordinates, agent, volume, and circumstances.

5. (C) Vicinity of the RVN Border.

a. US and FWMAF military rotary wing aircraft will not penetrate the DMZ, Laotian, or Khmer Republic airspace unless specifically authorized by COMUSMACV/DEPCOMUSMACV for Air, 7th AF.

b. Aerial reconnaissance flights along or near the Cambodian or Laotian border are vital to the security of the RVN and US defense efforts. However, extreme care must be exercised in planning and executing in-country missions by reconnaissance aircraft of all services to ensure that inadvertent overflights do not occur. All aircraft involved in coordinating close air support and operating in the vicinity of the border will have a 1:50,000 or larger scale map of the target area. Maps, mosaics, and photographs will be made available to pilots whenever possible.

·   ·   ·

NOTE: In the United States invasion of Grenada in 1983, a card with the following rules of engagement was issued to all the United States troops.

RULES OF ENGAGEMENT

ALL ENEMY MILITARY PERSONNEL AND VEHICLES TRANS-PORTING THE ENEMY OR THEIR SUPPLIES MAY BE EN-GAGED SUBJECT TO THE FOLLOWING RESTRICTIONS:

A. When possible the enemy will be warned first and asked to surrender.

B. Armed force is the last resort.

C. Armed civilians will only be engaged in self-defense.

D. Civilian aircraft will not be engaged without approval from above Division level unless it is in self-defense.

E. Avoid harming civilians unless necessary to save U.S. lives. If possible, try to arrange for the evacuation of civilians prior to any U.S. attack.

F. If civilians are in the area, do not use artillery, mortars, armed helicopters, AC-130, lube or rocket-launched weapons, or M551 main guns against known or suspected targets without the permission of a ground maneuver Commander LTC [Lieutenant Colonel] or higher (for any of these weapons).

G. If civilians are in the area, all air attacks must also be controlled by a FAC [Forward Air Controller] or FO [Forward Observer].

H. If civilians are in the area, close air support (CAS), white phosphorus, and incendiary weapons are prohibited without approval from above Division level.

I. If civilians are in the area, Infantry does not shoot except at known enemy locations.

J. If civilians are not in the area, you can shoot at suspected enemy locations.

K. Public works such as power stations, water treatment plants, dams and/or other utilities may not be engaged without approval from above Division level.

L. Hospitals, Churches, Shrines, Schools, Museums, and any other historical or cultural site will not be engaged except in self-defense.

M. All indirect fire and air attacks must be observed.

N. Pilots must be briefed for each mission on the location of civilians and friendly forces.

O. No booby-traps. No mines except as approved by Division Commander. No riot control agents without approval from above Division level.

P. Avoid harming civilian property unless necessary to save U.S. lives.

Q. Treat all civilians and their property with respect and dignity. Before using privately owned property, check to see if any publicly owned property can substitute. No requisitioning of civilian property without permission of a company-level Commander and without giving a receipt. If an ordering officer can contract for the property, then do not requisition it. No looting. Do not kick down doors unless necessary. Do not sleep in their houses. If you must sleep in privately owned buildings, have an ordering officer contract for it.

R. Treat all prisoners humanely and with respect and dignity.

S. Annex R to the OPLAN [Operations Plan] provides more detail. Conflicts between this card and the OPLAN should be resolved in favor of the OPLAN.

DISTRIBUTION: 1 per every trooper deployed to include all ranks.

◆

CESSATION OF HOSTILITIES

HAGUE CONVENTION (IV) RESPECTING THE LAWS AND CUSTOMS OF WAR ON LAND, ANNEX TO THE CONVENTION

[1 Bevans 631, signed on October 18, 1907, at The Hague]

. . .

FLAGS OF TRUCE

Article 32. A person is regarded as bearing a flag of truce who has been authorized by one of the belligerents to enter into communication with the other, and who advances bearing a white flag. He has a right to inviolability, as well as the trumpeter, bugler or drummer, the flag-bearer and interpreter who may accompany him.

Article 33. The commander to whom a flag of truce is sent is not in all cases obliged to receive it.

He may take all the necessary steps to prevent the envoy taking advantage of his mission to obtain information.

In case of abuse, he has the right to detain the envoy temporarily.

Article 34. The envoy loses his rights of inviolability if it is proved in a clear and incontestable manner that he has taken advantage of his privileged position to provoke or commit an act of treachery.

. . .

CAPITULATIONS

Article 35. Capitulations agreed upon between the contracting parties must take into account the rules of military honour.

Once settled, they must be scrupulously observed by both parties.

. . .

ARMISTICES

Article 36. An armistice suspends military operations by mutual agreement between the belligerent parties. If its duration is not defined, the belligerent parties may resume operations at any time, provided always that the enemy is warned within the time agreed upon, in accordance with the terms of the armistice.

Article 37. An armistice may be general or local. The first suspends the military operations of the belligerent States everywhere; the second only between certain fractions of the belligerent armies and within a fixed radius.

Article 38. An armistice must be notified officially and in good time to the competent authorities and to the troops. Hostilities are suspended immediately after the notification, or on the date fixed.

Article 39. It rests with the contracting parties to settle, in the terms of the armistice, what communications may be held in the theatre of war with the inhabitants and between the inhabitants of one belligerent State and those of the other.

Article 40. Any serious violation of the armistice by one of the parties gives the other party the right of denouncing it, and even, in cases of urgency, of recommencing hostilities immediately.

Article 41. A violation of the terms of the armistice by private persons acting on their own initiative only entitles the injured party to demand the punishment of the offenders or, if necessary, compensation for the losses sustained.

. . .

ENDNOTES

1. In 1863 the United States attempted to codify the laws of war for Union forces fighting in the Civil War. Called the *Lieber Instructions,* they were prepared by Professor Francis Lieber of Columbia College, revised by a board of Army officers, and then issued by President Lincoln. As the first formal, fairly comprehensive codification of the laws of war, the *Lieber Instructions* had a significant impact upon future codifications.
2. The Convention is set out, in part, in this chapter.
3. The United States Army, *The Law of Land Warfare* (Field Manual [FM] 27-10 1956).
4. *Ibid.* at 3–4, 19.
5. Michael Bothe, Karl J. Partsch, and Waldemar A. Solf, *New Rules for Victims of Armed Conflicts: Commentary on the Two 1977 Protocols Additional to the Geneva Conventions of 1949* 119 (1982).
6. The law governing prisoners of war is set out in Chapter 4.

7. 29 I.L.M. 1582 (1990).
8. Article 2, common to all four of the 1949 Geneva Conventions, applies the Conventions to any case of armed conflict between the parties, even if it is not a declared war or if one of the states does not recognize it as such. Article 2 also applies the Conventions to all cases of partial or total occupation of territory of another party and obliges parties to the Convention to conform to it with regard to a nonparty that accepts and applies its provisions. Article 2 is set out below at p. 153. Article 1(4) of Protocol I of 1977 extends the application of that Protocol beyond the reach of common Article 2, to one species of civil war: the so-called wars of national liberation.
9. United States: Department of Defense Report to Congress on the Conduct of the Persian Gulf War—Appendix O on the Role of the Law of War (April 10, 1992), reprinted in 31 I.L.M. 612, 636–37 (1992).
10. *Ibid.* at 637.
11. Pertinent portions of this treaty are set out in Chapter 5 relating to the law of belligerent occupation.
12. 31 I.L.M. at 636.
13. Helsinki Watch, *War Crimes in Bosnia-Hercegovina* 1–2, 10 (1992).
14. *The Papers of Dwight David Eisenhower: The War Years*, vol. II (Chandler and Ambrose, eds., 1970), pp. 1890–91, reprinted in The United States Navy, *Annotated Supplement to the Commander's Handbook on the Law of Naval Operations* Section 8.28 (Naval Warfare Publication [NWP] 9 [Rev. A] 1989).

NEUTRALITY

The Industrial Revolution brought on expansion of world trade and increasing interdependence between states, and, consequently, it became harder and harder to isolate and contain wars between a few states. Even small wars began to threaten the commercial relationships upon which the rest of the international community depends. Nations like Switzerland and Belgium, which attempted to practice neutrality as a general policy, were particularly concerned to establish a protected status for themselves. Neutrality law was the response to all of these concerns.

This part of the law of war attempts to balance the conflicting interests of belligerents, who are interested in pursuing war against each other, and nonbelligerents, who are interested in continuing commercial contacts among themselves. It prescribes the rights and obligations of nonbelligerents and the competences of the belligerent parties with regard to neutral trade. Because today's belligerent is tomorrow's neutral and vice-versa, it has not been difficult for governments to see the utility of this part of the law, though belligerents in any conflict always chafe at the restraints it forces on them.

Neutrality law has been established at the international level and adapted, in different ways, in the national law of many states. In this chapter, we are concerned only with the international law dimension. United States neutrality law has figured importantly in our politics most recently as part of Irangate.

If limited military conflicts continue in the future, the laws of neutrality will continue to operate as part of the modern law of war. But when actions are directed by or under the authority of the United Nations to enforce its decisions against an aggressor, it is doubtful if any state that is a member of the United Nations can decide to "sit this one out" and claim neutral rights. There are, we might note, certain assurances in the UN Charter for states whose economic interests may be prejudiced in an enforcement action.

HAGUE CONVENTION (V) RESPECTING THE RIGHTS AND DUTIES OF NEUTRAL POWERS AND PERSONS IN CASE OF WAR ON LAND

[1 Bevans 654, signed on October 18, 1907, at The Hague]

. . .

THE RIGHTS AND DUTIES OF NEUTRAL POWERS

Article 1. The territory of neutral Powers is inviolable.

Article 2. Belligerents are forbidden to move troops or convoys of either munitions of war or supplies across the territory of a neutral Power.

Article 3. Belligerents are likewise forbidden to:

(a) Erect on the territory of a neutral Power a wireless telegraphy station or other apparatus for the purpose of communicating with belligerent forces on land or sea;

(b) Use any installation of this kind established by them before the war on the territory of a neutral Power for purely military purposes, and which has not been opened for the service of public messages.

Article 4. Corps of combatants cannot be formed nor recruiting agencies opened on the territory of a neutral Power to assist the belligerents.

Article 5. A neutral Power must not allow any of the acts referred to in Articles 2 to 4 to occur on its territory.

It is not called upon to punish acts in violation of its neutrality unless the said acts have been committed on its own territory.

Article 6. The responsibility of a neutral Power is not engaged by the fact of persons crossing the frontier separating [them] to offer their services to one of the belligerents.

Article 7. A neutral Power is not called upon to prevent the export or transport, on behalf of one or other of the belligerents, of arms, munitions of war, or, in general, of anything which can be of use to an army or a fleet.

Article 8. A neutral Power is not called upon to forbid or restrict the use on behalf of the belligerents of telegraph or telephone cables or of wireless telegraphy apparatus belonging to it or to Companies or private individuals.

Article 9. Every measure of restriction or prohibition taken by a neutral Power in regard to the matters referred to in Articles 7 and 8 must be impartially applied by it to both belligerents.

A neutral Power must see to the same obligation being observed by Companies or private individuals owning telegraph or telephone cables or wireless telegraphy apparatus.

Article 10. The fact of a neutral Power resisting, even by force, attempts to violate its neutrality cannot be regarded as a hostile act.

.   .   .

BELLIGERENTS INTERNED AND WOUNDED TENDED IN NEUTRAL TERRITORY

Article 11. A neutral Power which receives on its territory troops belonging to the belligerent armies shall intern them, as far as possible, at a distance from the theatre of war.

It may keep them in camps and even confine them in fortresses or in places set apart for this purpose.

It shall decide whether officers can be left at liberty on giving their parole not to leave the neutral territory without permission.

Article 12. In the absence of a special Convention to the contrary, the neutral Power shall supply the interned with the food, clothing, and relief required by humanity. At the conclusion of peace, the expenses caused by the internment shall be made good.

Article 13. A neutral Power which receives escaped prisoners of war shall leave them at liberty. If it allows them to remain in its territory it may assign them a place of residence.

The same rule applies to prisoners of war brought by troops taking refuge in the territory of a neutral Power.

Article 14. A neutral Power may authorize the passage into its territory of the sick and wounded belonging to the belligerent armies, on condition that the trains bringing them shall carry neither personnel [n]or war material. In such a case, the neutral Power is bound to take whatever measures of safety and control are necessary for the purpose.

The sick or wounded brought under these conditions into neutral territory by one of the belligerents, and belonging to the hostile party, must be guarded by the neutral Power so as to ensure their not taking part again in the military operations. The same duty shall devolve on the neutral State with regard to wounded or sick of the other army who may be committed to its care.

Article 15. The Geneva Convention [footnote omitted] applies to sick and wounded interned in neutral territory.

.   .   .

NEUTRAL PERSONS

Article 16. The nationals of a State which is not taking part in the war are considered as neutrals.

Article 17. A neutral cannot avail himself of his neutrality:
  (a) If he commits hostile acts against a belligerent;
  (b) If he commits acts in favor of a belligerent, particularly if he voluntarily enlists in the ranks of the armed force of one of the parties.

  In such a case, the neutral shall not be more severely treated by the belligerent as against whom he has abandoned his neutrality than a national of the other belligerent State could be for the same act.

Article 18. The following acts shall not be considered as committed in favour of one belligerent in the sense of Article 17, letter (b):
  (a) Supplies furnished or loans made to one of the belligerents, provided that the person who furnishes the supplies or who makes the loans lives neither in the territory of the other party nor in the territory occupied by him, and that the supplies do not come from these territories;
  (b) Services rendered in matters of police or civil administration.

.   .   .

Railway Material

Article 19. Railway material coming from the territory of neutral Powers, whether it be the property of the said Powers or of Companies or private persons, and recognizable as such, shall not be requisitioned or utilized by a belligerent except where and to the extent that it is absolutely necessary. It shall be sent back as soon as possible to the country of origin.

A neutral Power may likewise, in case of necessity, retain and utilize to an equal extent material coming from the territory of the belligerent Power.

Compensation shall be paid by one Party or the other in proportion to the material used, and to the period of usage.

. . . .

Final Provisions

Article 20. The provisions of the present Convention do not apply except between Contracting Powers, and then only if the belligerents are parties to the Convention.

Rights and Duties
of Neutral Powers in Naval War

[1 Bevans 723, signed on October 18, 1907, at The Hague]

. . . .

Article 1. Belligerents are bound to respect the sovereign rights of neutral Powers and to abstain, in neutral territory or neutral waters, from any act which would, if knowingly permitted by any Power, constitute a violation of neutrality.

Article 2. Any act of hostility, including capture and the exercise of the right of search, committed by belligerent war-ships in the territorial waters of a neutral Power, constitutes a violation of neutrality and is strictly forbidden.

Article 3. [footnote omitted] When a ship has been captured in the territorial waters of a neutral Power, this Power must employ, if the prize is still within its jurisdiction, the means at its disposal to release the prize with its officers and crew, and to intern the prize crew.

If the prize is not in the jurisdiction of the neutral Power, the captor Government, on the demand of that Power, must liberate the prize with its officers and crew.

Article 4. A Prize Court cannot be set up by a belligerent on neutral territory or on a vessel in neutral waters.

Article 5. Belligerents are forbidden to use neutral ports and waters as a base of naval operations against their adversaries, and in particular to erect wireless telegraphy stations or any apparatus for the purpose of communicating with the belligerent forces on land or sea.

Article 6. The supply, in any manner, directly or indirectly, by a neutral Power to a belligerent Power, of war-ships, ammunition, or war material of any kind whatever, is forbidden.

Article 7. A neutral Power is not bound to prevent the export or transit, for the use of either belligerent, of arms, ammunition, or, in general, of anything which would be of use to an army or fleet.

Article 8. A neutral Government is bound to employ the means at its disposal to prevent the fitting out or arming of any vessel within its jurisdiction which it has reason to believe is intended to cruise, or engage in hostile operations, against a Power with which that Government is at peace. It is also bound to display the same vigilance to prevent the departure from its jurisdiction of any vessel intended to cruise, or engage in hostile operations, which had been adapted entirely or partly within the said jurisdiction for use in war.

Article 9. A neutral Power must apply impartially to the two belligerents the conditions, restrictions, or prohibitions made by it in regard to the admission into its ports, roadsteads, or territorial waters, of belligerent war-ships or of their prizes.

Nevertheless, a neutral Power may forbid a belligerent vessel which has failed to conform to the orders and regulations made by it, or which has violated neutrality, to enter its ports or roadsteads.

Article 10. The neutrality of a Power is not affected by the mere passage through its territorial waters of war-ships or prizes belonging to belligerents.

Article 11. A neutral Power may allow belligerent war-ships to employ its licensed pilots.

Article 12. In the absence of special provisions to the contrary in the legislation of a neutral Power, belligerent war-ships are not permitted to remain in the ports, roadsteads, or territorial waters of the said Power for more than twenty-four hours, except in the cases covered by the present Convention.

Article 13. If a Power which has been informed of the outbreak of hostilities learns that a belligerent war-ship is in one of its ports or roadsteads, or in its territorial waters, it must notify the said ship to depart within twenty-four hours or within the time prescribed by local regulations.

Article 14. A belligerent war-ship may not prolong its stay in a neutral port beyond the permissible time except on account of damage or stress of weather. It must depart as soon as the cause of the delay is at an end.

The regulations as to the question of the length of time which these vessels may remain in neutral ports, roadsteads, or waters, do not apply to war-ships devoted exclusively to religious, scientific, or philanthropic purposes.

Article 15. In the absence of special provisions to the contrary in the legislation of a neutral Power, the maximum number of war-ships belonging to a belligerent which may be in one of the ports or roadsteads of that Power simultaneously shall be three.

Article 16. When war-ships belonging to both belligerents are present simultaneously in a neutral port or roadstead, a period of not less than twenty-four hours must elapse between the departure of the ship belonging to one belligerent and the departure of the ship belonging to the other.

The order of departure is determined by the order of arrival, unless the ship which arrived first is so circumstanced that an extension of its stay is permissible.

A belligerent war-ship may not leave a neutral port or roadstead until twenty-four hours after the departure of a merchant-ship flying the flag of its adversary.

Article 17. In neutral ports and roadsteads belligerent war-ships may only carry out such repairs as are absolutely necessary to render them seaworthy, and may not add in any manner whatsoever to their fighting force. The local authorities of the neutral Power shall decide what repairs are necessary, and these must be carried out with the least possible delay.

Article 18. Belligerent war-ships may not make use of neutral ports, roadsteads, or territorial waters for replenishing or increasing their supplies of war material or their armament, or for completing their crews.

Article 19. Belligerent war-ships may only revictual in neutral ports or roadsteads to bring up their supplies to the peace standard.

Similarly these vessels may only ship sufficient fuel to enable them to reach the nearest port in their own country. They may, on the other hand, fill up their bunkers built to carry fuel, when in neutral countries which have adopted this method of determining the amount of fuel to be supplied.

If, in accordance with the law of the neutral Power, the ships are not supplied with coal within twenty-four hours of their arrival, the permissible duration of their stay is extended by twenty-four hours.

Article 20. Belligerent war-ships which have shipped fuel in a port belonging to a neutral Power may not within the succeeding three months replenish their supply in a port of the same Power.

Article 21. A prize may only be brought into a neutral port on account of unseaworthiness, stress of weather, or want of fuel or provisions.

It must leave as soon as the circumstances which justified its entry are at an end. If it does not, the neutral Power must order it to leave at once; should it fail to obey, the neutral Power must employ the means at its disposal to release it with its officers and crew and to intern the prize crew.

Article 22. A neutral Power must, similarly, release a prize brought into one of its ports under circumstances other than those referred to in Article 21.

Article 23. [footnote omitted] A neutral Power may allow prizes to enter its ports and roadsteads, whether under convoy or not, when they are brought there to be sequestrated pending the decision of a Prize Court. It may have the prize taken to another of its ports.

If the prize is convoyed by a war-ship, the prize crew may go on board the convoying ship.

If the prize is not under convoy, the prize crew are left at liberty.

Article 24. If, notwithstanding the notification of the neutral Power, a belligerent ship of war does not leave a port where it is not entitled to remain, the neutral Power is entitled to take such measures as it considers necessary to render the ship incapable of taking the sea during the war, and the commanding officer of the ship must facilitate the execution of such measures.

When a belligerent ship is detained by a neutral Power, the officers and crew are likewise detained.

The officers and crew thus detained may be left in the ship or kept either on another vessel or on land, and may be subjected to the measures of restriction which it may appear necessary to impose upon them. A sufficient number of men for looking after the vessel must, however, be always left on board.

The officers may be left at liberty on giving their word not to quit the neutral territory without permission.

.   .   .

CONVENTION ON CONTACT MINES 1907

[1 Bevans 669, signed on October 18, 1907, at The Hague]

. . .

Article 4. Neutral Powers which lay automatic contact mines off their coasts must observe the same rules and take the same precautions as are imposed on belligerents.

The Neutral Power must inform ship-owners, by a notice issued in advance, where automatic contact mines have been laid. This notice must be communicated at once to the Governments through the diplomatic channel.

. . .

HAGUE RULES OF AËRIAL WARFARE

[32 A.J.I.L. (Supp.) 12 (1938), signed on February 19, 1923, at The Hague; not in force]

. . .

BELLIGERENT DUTIES TOWARDS NEUTRAL STATES AND NEUTRAL DUTIES TOWARDS BELLIGERENT STATES

Article 39. Belligerent aircraft are bound to respect the rights of neutral Powers and to abstain within the jurisdiction of a neutral state from the commission of any act which it is the duty of that state to prevent.

. . .

Article 40. Belligerent military aircraft are forbidden to enter the jurisdiction of a neutral state.

. . .

Article 41. Aircraft on board vessels of war, including aircraft-carriers, shall be regarded as part of such vessels.

. . .

Article 42. A neutral government must use the means at its disposal to prevent the entry within its jurisdiction of belligerent military aircraft and to compel them to alight if they have entered such jurisdiction.

A neutral government shall use the means at its disposal to intern any belligerent military aircraft which is within its jurisdiction after having alighted for any reason whatsoever, together with its crew and the passengers, if any.

. . .

Article 43. The personnel of a disabled belligerent military aircraft rescued outside neutral waters and brought into the jurisdiction of a neutral state by a neutral military aircraft and there landed shall be interned.

. . .

Article 44. The supply in any manner, directly or indirectly, by a neutral government to a belligerent Power of aircraft, parts of aircraft, or material, supplies or munitions required for aircraft is forbidden.

. . .

Article 45. Subject to the provisions of Article 46, a neutral Power is not bound to prevent the export or transit on behalf of a belligerent of aircraft, parts of aircraft, or material, supplies or munitions for aircraft.

. . .

Article 46. A neutral government is bound to use the means at its disposal:
(1) To prevent the departure from its jurisdiction of an aircraft in a condition to make a hostile attack against a belligerent Power, or carrying or accompanied by appliances or materials the mounting or utilization of which would enable it to make a hostile attack, if there is reason to believe that such aircraft is destined for use against a belligerent Power;
(2) To prevent the departure of an aircraft the crew of which includes any member of the combatant forces of a belligerent Power;
(3) To prevent work upon an aircraft designed to prepare it to depart in contravention of the purposes of this article.

On the departure by air of any aircraft despatched by persons or companies in neutral jurisdiction to the order of a belligerent Power, the neutral government must prescribe for such aircraft a route avoiding the neighborhood of the military operations of the opposing belligerent, and must exact whatever guarantees may be required to ensure that the aircraft follows the route prescribed.

. . .

Article 47. A neutral state is bound to take such steps as the means at its disposal permit to prevent within its jurisdiction aërial observation of the movements, operations or defenses of one belligerent, with the intention of informing the other belligerent.

. . .

This provision applies equally to a belligerent military aircraft on board a vessel of war.

. . .

Article 48. The action of a neutral Power in using force or other means at its disposal in the exercise of its rights or duties under these Rules cannot be regarded as a hostile act.

. . .

MARITIME NEUTRALITY (INTER-AMERICAN)

[2 Bevans 721, signed on February 20, 1928, at Havana]

. . .

FREEDOM OF COMMERCE IN TIME OF WAR

Article 1. The following rules shall govern commerce in time of war:
(1) Warships of the belligerents have the right to stop and visit on the high seas and in territorial waters that are not neutral any merchant ship with the object of ascertaining its character and nationality and of verifying whether it conveys cargo prohibited by international law or has committed any violation of blockade. If the merchant ship does not heed the signal to stop, it may be pursued by the warship and stopped by force; outside of such a case the ship cannot be attacked unless, after being hailed, it fails to observe the instructions given it.

·The ship shall not be rendered incapable of navigation before the crew and passengers have been placed in safety.

(2) Belligerent submarines are subject to the foregoing rules. If the submarine cannot capture the ship while observing these rules, it shall not have the right to continue to attack or to destroy the ship.

Article 2. Both the detention of the vessel and its crew for violation of neutrality shall be made in accordance with the procedure which best suits the state effecting it and at the expense of the transgressing ship. Said state, except in the case of grave fault on its part, is not responsible for damages which the vessel may suffer.

. . .

Duties and Rights of Belligerents

Article 3. Belligerent states are obligated to refrain from performing acts of war in neutral waters or other acts which may constitute on the part of the state that tolerates them, a violation of neutrality.

Article 4. Under the terms of the preceding article, a belligerent state is forbidden:

(a) To make use of neutral waters as a base of naval operations against the enemy, or to renew or augment military supplies or the armament of its ships, or to complete the equipment of the latter;

(b) To install in neutral waters radio-telegraph stations or any other apparatus which may serve as a means of communication with its military forces, or to make use of installations of this kind it may have established before the war and which may not have been opened to the public.

Article 5. Belligerent warships are forbidden to remain in the ports or waters of a neutral state more than twenty-four hours. This provision will be communicated to the ship as soon as it arrives in port or in the territorial waters, and if already there at the time of the declaration of war, as soon as the neutral state becomes aware of this declaration.

Vessels used exclusively for scientific, religious, or philanthropic purposes are exempted from the foregoing provisions.

A ship may extend its stay in port more than twenty-four hours in case of damage or bad conditions at sea, but must depart as soon as the cause of the delay has ceased.

When, according to the domestic law of the neutral state, the ship may not receive fuel until twenty-four hours after its arrival in port, the period of its stay may be extended an equal length of time.

Article 6. The ship which does not conform to the foregoing rules may be interned by order of the neutral government.

A ship shall be considered as interned from the moment it receives notice to that effect from the local neutral authority, even though a petition for reconsideration of the order has been interposed by the transgressing vessel, which shall remain under custody from the moment it receives the order.

Article 7. In the absence of a special provision of the local legislation, the maximum number of ships of war of a belligerent which may be in a neutral port at the same time shall be three.

Article 8. A ship of war may not depart from a neutral port within less than twenty-four hours after the departure of an enemy warship. The one entering first shall depart first, unless it is in such condition as to warrant extending its stay. In any case the ship which arrived later has the right to notify the other through the competent local authority that within twenty-four hours it will leave the port, the one first entering, however, having the right to depart within that time. If it leaves, the notifying ship must observe the interval which is above stipulated.

Article 9. Damaged belligerent ships shall not be permitted to make repairs in neutral ports beyond those that are essential to the continuance of the voyage and which in no degree constitute an increase in its military strength.

Damages which are found to have been produced by the enemy's fire shall in no case be repaired.

The neutral state shall ascertain the nature of the repairs to be made and will see that they are made as rapidly as possible.

Article 10. Belligerent warships may supply themselves with fuel and stores in neutral ports, under the conditions especially established by the local authority and in case there are no special provisions to that effect, they may supply themselves in the manner prescribed for provisioning in time of peace.

Article 11. Warships which obtain fuel in a neutral port cannot renew their supply in the same state until a period of three months has elapsed.

Article 12. Where the sojourn, supplying, and provisioning of belligerent ships in the ports and jurisdictional waters of neutrals are concerned, the provisions relative to ships of war shall apply equally;

(1) To ordinary auxiliary ships;

(2) To merchant ships transformed into warships, in accordance with Convention VII of The Hague of 1907.

The neutral vessel shall be seized and in general subjected to the same treatment as enemy merchantmen:

(a) When taking a direct part in the hostilities;

(b) When at the orders or under the direction of an agent placed on board by an enemy government;

(c) When entirely freight-loaded by an enemy government;

(d) When actually and exclusively destined for transporting enemy troops or for the transmission of information on behalf of the enemy.

In the cases dealt with in this article, merchandise belonging to the owner of the vessel or ship shall also be liable to seizure.

(3) To armed merchantmen. [footnote omitted]

Article 13. Auxiliary ships of belligerents, converted anew into merchantmen, shall be admitted as such in neutral ports subject to the following conditions:

(1) That the transformed vessel has not violated the neutrality of the country where it arrives;

(2) That the transformation has been made in the ports or jurisdictional waters of the country to which the vessel belongs, or in the ports of its allies;

(3) That the transformation be genuine, namely, that the vessel show neither in its crew nor in its equipment that it can serve the armed fleet of its country as an auxiliary, as it did before;

(4) That the government of the country to which the ship belongs communicate to the state the names of auxiliary craft which have lost such character in order to recover that of merchantmen; and

(5) That the same government obligate itself that said ships shall not again be used as auxiliaries to the war fleet.

Article 14. The airships of belligerents shall not fly above the territorial waters of neutrals if it is not in conformity with the regulations of the latter.

. . .

RIGHTS AND DUTIES OF NEUTRALS

Article 15. Of the acts of assistance coming from the neutral states, and the acts of commerce on the part of individuals, only the first are contrary to neutrality.

Article 16. The neutral state is forbidden:
  (a) To deliver to the belligerent, directly or indirectly, or for any reason whatever, ships of war, munitions or any other war material;
  (b) To grant it loans, or to open credits for it during the duration of war.

Credits that a neutral state may give to facilitate the sale or exportation of its food products and raw materials are not included in this prohibition.

Article 17. Prizes cannot be taken to a neutral port except in case of unseaworthiness, stress of weather, or want of fuel or provisions. When the cause has disappeared, the prizes must leave immediately; if none of the indicated conditions exist, the state shall suggest to them that they depart, and if not obeyed shall have recourse to the means at its disposal to disarm them with their officers and crew, or to intern the prize crew placed on board by the captor.

Article 18. Outside of the cases provided for in Article 17, the neutral state must release the prizes which may have been brought into its territorial waters.

Article 19. When a ship transporting merchandise is to be interned in a neutral state, cargo intended for said country shall be unloaded and that destined for others shall be transhipped.

Article 20. The merchantman supplied with fuel or other stores in a neutral state which repeatedly delivers the whole or part of its supplies to a belligerent vessel, shall not again receive stores and fuel in the same state.

Article 21. Should it be found that a merchantman flying a belligerent flag, by its preparations or other circumstances, can supply to warships of a state the stores which they need, the local authority may refuse it supplies or demand of the agent of the company a guaranty that the said ship will not aid or assist any belligerent vessel.

Article 22. Neutral states are not obligated to prevent the export or transit at the expense of any one of the belligerents of arms, munitions and in general of anything which may be useful to their military forces.

Transit shall be permitted when, in the event of a war between two American nations, one of the belligerents is a Mediterranean country, having no other means of supplying itself, provided the vital interests of the country through which transit is requested do not suffer by the granting thereof.

Article 23. Neutral states shall not oppose the voluntary departure of nationals of belligerent states even though they leave simultaneously in great numbers; but they may oppose the voluntary departure of their own nationals going to enlist in the armed forces.

Article 24. The use by the belligerents of the means of communication of neutral states or which cross or touch their territory is subject to the measures dictated by the local authority.

Article 25. If as the result of naval operations beyond the territorial waters of neutral states there should be dead or wounded on board belligerent vessels, said states may send hospital ships under the vigilance of the neutral government to the scene of the disaster. These ships shall enjoy complete immunity during the discharge of their mission.

Article 26. Neutral states are bound to exert all the vigilance within their power in order to prevent in their ports or territorial waters any violation of the foregoing provisions.

NOTE: Neutrality law came under great stress during the Iran-Iraq War of 1979–1988. Both Iran and Iraq interfered with the maritime traffic of nationals from neutral states. The United States and other nations ultimately tried to protect neutral traffic through a significant naval presence that accompanied Kuwaiti vessels, some of which were reflagged as American.

The introduction of over-the-horizon weapons, some of which may be launched from ships that are not clearly marked as military vessels, has made it increasingly impractical and dangerous for naval vessels of belligerents in war zones to try to distinguish neutral or nonmilitary vessels from military threats. Hence the practice of closing substantial areas of the high seas to all traffic with notice to all vessels that they enter the zone at their own risk is on the rise. When safe sea-lanes for neutral traffic are still maintained, this new practice of creating a "maritime exclusion zone" may be an adequate contemporary accommodation of the conflicting interests that give rise to neutrality law. But if no neutral commercial traffic is allowed, one would expect the major maritime powers in the international system to reject such belligerent claims.

PRISONERS OF WAR

Prisoners of war are combatants who have surrendered or, due to injury, are unable to continue to fight and come into the control of their adversary. As long as there have been wars, combatants have grappled with the question of how to treat prisoners of war: spare their lives or provide no quarter? The second option was (and, alas, is) especially likely to be chosen when religious, racial, or cultural hatred was a factor in the conflict.

Treatment of prisoners of war began to change in the Renaissance. As one noted scholar on the history of the treatment of prisoners has written:

> The breakdown of feudalism, the increased use of mercenaries, and the rise of nationalism . . . contributed to an evolution in fundamental concepts which began to make its appearance during the seventeenth century. . . . By the end of the Thirty Years' War (1648), a prisoner of war had come to be considered as being in the custody of the enemy State, rather than of the individual captor. There was by then a better than even chance that he would not be killed or enslaved, but he still had little or no protection against other types of maltreatment. This basic change in concept did, however, serve as a foundation upon which the principle of humanitarian treatment of prisoners of war could be

erected. . . . During the eighteenth and nineteenth centuries the practice of exchanging prisoners of war, both during and after the cessation of hostilities, became firmly established as a norm of international law. . . .[1]

Beginning with the 1785 Treaty of Amity and Commerce between Prussia and the United States, there has been an international movement to improve the treatment of prisoners of war. This movement, encompassing the codifying attempts of Dr. Francis Lieber during the U.S. Civil War and the Institute of International Law's 1880 *Oxford Manual*, provided the foundation for the widely accepted Second Hague Convention of 1899—which was updated with few revisions in the Fourth Hague Convention of 1907—extracts of which follow.

HAGUE CONVENTION (IV) RESPECTING THE LAWS AND CUSTOMS OF WAR ON LAND, ANNEX TO THE CONVENTION

[1 Bevans 631, signed on October 18, 1907, at The Hague]

.   .   .

Article 4. Prisoners of war are in the power of the hostile Government, but not of the individuals or corps who capture them.

They must be humanely treated.

All their personal belongings, except arms, horses, and military papers, remain their property.

Article 5. Prisoners of war may be interned in a town, fortress, camp, or other place, and bound not to go beyond certain fixed limits; but they cannot be confined except as in indispensable measure of safety *and only while the circumstances which necessitate the measure continue to exist.* [emphasis supplied]

Article 6. The State may utilize the labour of prisoners of war according to their rank and aptitude, *officers excepted.* The tasks shall not be excessive and shall have no connection with the operations of the war. [emphasis supplied] . . .

Article 7. The Government into whose hands prisoners of war have fallen is charged with their maintenance.

In the absence of a special agreement between the belligerents, prisoners of war shall be treated as regards board, lodging, and clothing on the same footing as the troops of the Government who captured them.

Article 8. Prisoners of war shall be subject to the laws, regulations, and orders in force in the army of the State in whose power they are. Any act of insubordination justifies the adoption towards them of such measures of severity as may be considered necessary.

Escaped prisoners who are retaken before being able to rejoin their own army or before leaving the territory occupied by the army which captured them are liable to disciplinary punishment.

Prisoners who after succeeding in escaping, are again taken prisoners, are not liable to any punishment on account of the previous flight.

Article 9. Every prisoner of war is bound to give, if he is questioned on the subject, his true name and rank, and if he infringes this rule, he is liable to have the advantages given to prisoners of his class curtailed.

Article 10. Prisoners of war may be set at liberty on parole if the laws of their country allow, and, in such cases, they are bound, on their personal honour, scrupulously to fulfil, both towards their own Government and the Government by whom they were made prisoners, the engagements they have contracted.

In such cases their own Government is bound neither to require of nor accept from them any service incompatible with the parole given.

Article 11. A prisoner of war cannot be compelled to accept his liberty on parole; similarly the hostile Government is not obliged to accede to the request of the prisoner to be set at liberty on parole.

Article 12. Prisoners of war liberated on parole and recaptured bearing arms against the Government to whom they had pledged their honour, or against the allies of that Government, forfeit their right to be treated as prisoners of war, and can be brought before the courts.

NOTE: The Hague Convention's system proved inadequate in World War I. The International Committee of the Red Cross (ICRC) initiated the drafting of a new agreement, the 1929 Geneva Convention relative to the Treatment of Prisoners of War, that was rather widely accepted and provided the legal basis for treatment of POWs during World War II. But that treaty, too, proved unsatisfactory, and the ICRC convened another conference after the war that resulted in the four Geneva Conventions of 1949. The first three Geneva Conventions dealing, respectively, with the amelioration of the condition of the wounded and sick in armed forces in the field (I); the amelioration of the condition of wounded, sick and shipwrecked members of the armed forces at sea (II); and the treatment of prisoners of war (III) are concerned with combatants who have surrendered or, due to injury or circumstances, are unable to continue to fight and come into the control of the adversary. The Conventions aspire to establish a detailed, humane regime governing the treatment of these enemy combatants who have been captured.

An overwhelming majority of states have ratified or acceded to these conventions. But the actual treatment that prisoners of war have received has been mixed. Sometimes the regime prescribed by the Geneva Conventions has been substantially followed; for example, the United States has a particularly good record of compliance. Other times, the regime has been substantially disregarded—by Korea in its war with the United States and by both Iran and Iraq in their conflict. In the early phases of the Gulf War, the coalition forces allowed the ICRC to operate, but Iraq did not.

Because many of the provisions in the three Conventions are virtually identical, the excerpts that follow have been selected to provide the reader with a picture of the regimes common to all three.

The 1977 Protocol I to the Geneva Conventions of 1949 generally recodified the existing requirements of the 1949 Conventions. However, in at least two ways, it attempted to make major changes, both expanding and contracting the categories of individuals that may be considered combatants and thus entitled to the protections of the 1949 Conventions. Protocol I attempts to include as combatants those individuals who do not wear uniforms to distinguish themselves as combatants, on the condition that they carry their arms openly during each military engagement and are visible to the adversary while they are engaged in a military deployment (Article 43(3)). Second, for the first time in codified form, the international law of war attempts to place mercenaries outside the protective umbrella of the regime of protection of prisoners of war (Article 47).

GENEVA CONVENTION (II) FOR THE AMELIORATION OF THE CONDITION OF WOUNDED, SICK AND SHIPWRECKED MEMBERS OF ARMED FORCES AT SEA

[6 U.S.T. 3219, signed on August 12, 1949, at Geneva]

. . .

GENERAL PROVISIONS

Article 1. The High Contracting Parties undertake to respect and to ensure respect for the present Convention in all circumstances.

Article 2. In addition to the provisions which shall be implemented in peacetime, the present Convention shall apply to all cases of declared war or of any other armed conflict which may arise between two or more of the High Contracting Parties, even if the state of war is not recognized by one of them.

The Convention shall also apply to all cases of partial or total occupation of the territory of a High Contracting Party, even if the said occupation meets with no armed resistance.

Although one of the Powers in conflict may not be a Party to the present Convention, the Powers who are parties thereto shall remain bound by it in their mutual relations. They shall furthermore be bound by the Convention in relation to the said Power, if the latter accepts and applies the provisions thereof.

Article 3. In the case of armed conflict not of an international character occurring in the territory of one of the High Contracting Parties, each Party to the conflict shall be bound to apply, as a minimum, the following provisions:

(1) Persons taking no active part in the hostilities, including members of armed forces who have laid down their arms and those placed *hors de combat* by sickness, wounds, detention, or any other cause, shall in all circumstances be treated humanely, without any adverse distinction founded on race, colour, religion or faith, sex, birth or wealth, or any other similar criteria.

   To this end, the following acts are and shall remain prohibited at any time and in any place whatsoever with respect to the above-mentioned persons:

   (a) violence to life and person, in particular murder of all kinds, mutilation, cruel treatment and torture;

(b) taking of hostages;

(c) outrages upon personal dignity, in particular, humiliating and degrading treatment;

(d) the passing of sentences and the carrying out of executions without previous judgment pronounced by a regularly constituted court, affording all the judicial guarantees which are recognized as indispensable by civilized peoples.

(2) The wounded, sick and shipwrecked shall be collected and cared for.

An impartial humanitarian body, such as the International Committee of the Red Cross, may offer its services to the Parties to the conflict.

The Parties to the conflict should further endeavour to bring into force, by means of special agreements, all or part of the other provisions of the present Convention . . . .

Article 4. In case of hostilities between land and naval forces of Parties to the conflict, the provisions of the present Convention shall apply only to forces on board ship.

Forces put ashore shall immediately become subject to the provisions of the Geneva Convention for the Amelioration of the Condition of the Wounded and Sick in Armed Forces in the Field of 12 August 1949.

Article 5. Neutral Powers shall apply by analogy the provisions of the present Convention to the wounded, sick and shipwrecked, and to members of the medical personnel and to chaplains of the armed forces of the Parties to the conflict received or interned in their territory, as well as to dead persons found.

Article 6. In addition to the agreements expressly provided for in Articles 10, 18, 31, 38, 39, 40, 43 and 53, the High Contracting Parties may conclude other special agreements for all matters concerning which they may deem it suitable to make separate provision. No special agreement shall adversely affect the situation of wounded, sick and shipwrecked persons, of members of the medical personnel or of chaplains, as defined by the present Convention, nor restrict the rights which it confers upon them.

Wounded, sick and shipwrecked persons, as well as medical personnel and chaplains, shall continue to have the benefit of such agreements as long as the Convention is applicable to them, except where express provisions to the contrary are contained in the aforesaid or in subsequent agreements, or where more favourable measures have been taken with regard to them by one or other of the Parties to the conflict.

Article 7. Wounded, sick and shipwrecked persons, as well as members of the medical personnel and chaplains, may in no circumstances re-nounce in part or in entirety the rights secured to them by the present Convention, and by the special agreements referred to in the foregoing Article, if such there be.

Article 8. The present Convention shall be applied with the cooperation and under the scrutiny of the Protecting Powers whose duty it is to safeguard the interests of the Parties to the conflict. For this purpose, the Protecting Powers may appoint, apart from their diplomatic or consular staff, delegates from amongst their own nationals or the nationals of other neutral Powers. The said delegates shall be subject to the approval of the Power with which they are to carry out their duties.

The Parties to the conflict shall facilitate to the greatest extent possible the task of the representatives or delegates of the Protecting Powers.

The representatives or delegates of the Protecting Powers shall not in any case exceed their mission under the present Convention. They shall, in particular, take account of the imperative necessities of security of the State wherein they carry out their duties. Their activities shall only be restricted as an exceptional and temporary measure when this is rendered necessary by imperative military necessities.

Article 9. The provisions of the present Convention constitute no ob-stacle to the humanitarian activities which the International Committee of the Red Cross or any other impartial humanitarian organization may, subject to the consent of the Parties to the conflict concerned, undertake for the protection of wounded, sick and shipwrecked persons, medical personnel and chaplains, and for their relief.

Article 10. The High Contracting Parties may at any time agree to entrust to an organization which offers all guarantees of impartiality and efficacy the duties incumbent on the Protecting Powers by virtue of the present Convention.

When wounded, sick and shipwrecked, or medical personnel and chaplains do not benefit or cease to benefit, no matter for what reason, by the activities of a Protecting Power or of an organization provided for in the first paragraph above, the Detaining Power shall request a neutral State, or such an organization, to undertake the functions performed under the present Convention by a Protecting Power designated by the Parties to a conflict.

If protection cannot be arranged accordingly, the Detaining Power shall request or shall accept, subject to the provisions of this Article, the offer of the services of a humanitarian organization, such as the Inter-national Committee of the Red Cross, to assume the humanitarian functions performed by Protecting Powers under the present Convention.

Any neutral Power, or any organization invited by the Power concerned or offering itself for these purposes, shall be required to act with a sense of responsibility towards the Party to the conflict on which persons protected by the present Convention depend, and shall be required to furnish sufficient assurances that it is in a position to undertake the appropriate functions and to discharge them impartially.

No derogation from the preceding provisions shall be made by special agreements between Powers one of which is restricted, even temporarily, in its freedom to negotiate with the other Power or its allies by reason of military events, more particularly where the whole, or a substantial part, of the territory of the said Power is occupied.

Whenever, in the present Convention, mention is made of a Protecting Power, such mention also applies to substitute organizations in the sense of the present Article.

Article 11. In cases where they deem it advisable in the interest of protected persons, particularly in cases of disagreement between the Parties to the conflict as to the application or interpretation of the provisions of the present Convention, the Protecting Powers shall lend their good offices with a view to settling the disagreement.

For this purpose, each of the Protecting Powers may, either at the invitation of one Party or on its own initiative, propose to the Parties to the conflict a meeting of their representatives, in particular of the authorities responsible for the wounded, sick and shipwrecked, medical personnel and chaplains, possibly on neutral territory suitably chosen. The Parties to the conflict shall be bound to give effect to the proposals made to them for this purpose. The Protecting Powers may, if necessary, propose for approval by the Parties to the conflict, a person belonging to a neutral Power or delegated by the International Committee of the Red Cross, who shall be invited to take part in such a meeting.

. . .

WOUNDED, SICK AND SHIPWRECKED

Article 12. Members of the armed forces and other persons mentioned in the following Article, who are at sea and who are wounded, sick or shipwrecked, shall be respected and protected in all circumstances, it being understood that the term "shipwrecked" means shipwreck from any cause and includes forced landings at sea by or from aircraft.

Such persons shall be treated humanely and cared for by the Parties to the conflict in whose power they may be, without any adverse distinction founded on sex, race, nationality, religion, political opinions, or any other similar criteria. Any attempts upon their lives, or violence to their persons, shall be strictly prohibited; in particular, they shall not be murdered or exterminated, subjected to torture or to biological experiments; they shall not wilfully be left without medical assistance and care, nor shall conditions exposing them to contagion or infection be created.

Only urgent medical reasons will authorize priority in the order of treatment to be administered.

Women shall be treated with all consideration due to their sex.

Article 13. The present Convention shall apply to the wounded, sick and shipwrecked at sea belonging to the following categories:

(1) Members of the armed forces of a Party to the conflict, as well as members of militias or volunteer corps forming part of such armed forces.

(2) Members of other militias and members of other volunteer corps, including those of organized resistance movements, belonging to a Party to the conflict and operating in or outside their own territory, even if this territory is occupied, provided that such militias or volunteer corps, including such organized resistance movements, fulfil the following conditions:

    (a) that of being commanded by a person responsible for his subordinates;

    (b) that of having a fixed distinctive sign recognizable at a distance;

    (c) that of carrying arms openly;

    (d) that of conducting their operations in accordance with the laws and customs of war.

(3) Members of regular armed forces who profess allegiance to a Government or an authority not recognized by the Detaining Power.

(4) Persons who accompany the armed forces without actually being members thereof, such as civilian members of military aircraft crews, war correspondents, supply contractors, members of labour units or of services responsible for the welfare of the armed forces, provided that they have received authorization from the armed forces which they accompany.

(5) Members of crews, including masters, pilots and apprentices, of the merchant marine and the crews of civil aircraft of the Parties to the conflict, who do not benefit by more favourable treatment under any other provisions of international law.

(6) Inhabitants of a non-occupied territory who, on the approach of the enemy, spontaneously take up arms to resist the invading forces, without having had time to form themselves into regular armed units, provided they carry arms openly and respect the laws and customs of war.

Article 14. All warships of a belligerent Party shall have the right to demand that the wounded, sick or shipwrecked on board military hospital ships, and hospital ships belonging to relief societies or to private individuals, as well as merchant vessels, yachts and other craft shall be surrendered, whatever their nationality, provided that the wounded and sick are in a fit state to be moved and that the warship can provide adequate facilities for necessary medical treatment.

Article 15. If wounded, sick or shipwrecked persons are taken on board a neutral warship or a neutral military aircraft, it shall be ensured, where so required by international law, that they can take no further part in operations of war.

Article 16. Subject to the provisions of Article 12, the wounded, sick and shipwrecked of a belligerent who fall into enemy hands shall be prisoners of war, and the provisions of international law concerning prisoners of war shall apply to them. The captor may decide, according to circumstances, whether it is expedient to hold them, or to convey them to a port in the captor's own country, to a neutral port or even to a port in enemy territory. In the last case, prisoners of war thus returned to their home country may not serve for the duration of the war.

Article 17. Wounded, sick or shipwrecked persons who are landed in neutral ports with the consent of the local authorities, shall, failing arrangements to the contrary between the neutral and the belligerent Powers, be so guarded by the neutral Power, where so required by international law, that the said persons cannot again take part in operations of war.

The costs of hospital accommodation and internment shall be borne by the Power on whom the wounded, sick or shipwrecked persons depend.

Article 18. After each engagement, Parties to the conflict shall, without delay, take all possible measures to search for and collect the shipwrecked, wounded and sick, to protect them against pillage and ill-treatment, to ensure their adequate care, and to search for the dead and prevent their being despoiled.

Whenever circumstances permit, the Parties to the conflict shall conclude local arrangements for the removal of the wounded and sick by sea from a besieged or encircled area and for the passage of medical and religious personnel and equipment on their way to that area.

Article 19. The Parties to the conflict shall record as soon as possible, in respect of each shipwrecked, wounded, sick or dead person of the adverse Party falling into their hands, any particulars which may assist in his identification. These records should if possible include:

(a) designation of the Power on which he depends;

(b) army, regimental, personal or serial number;

(c) surname;

(d) first name or names;

(e) date of birth;

(f) any other particulars shown on his identity card or disc;

(g) date and place of capture or death;

(h) particulars concerning wounds or illness, or cause of death.

As soon as possible the above-mentioned information shall be forwarded to the information bureau described in Article 122 of the Geneva Convention relative to the Treatment of Prisoners of War of 12 August, 1949, which shall transmit this information to the Power on which these persons depend through the intermediary of the Protecting Power and of the Central Prisoners of War Agency.

Parties to the conflict shall prepare and forward to each other through the same bureau, certificates of death or duly authenticated lists of the dead. They shall likewise collect and forward through the same bureau one half of the double identity disc, or the identity disc itself if it is a single disc, last wills or other documents of importance to the next of kin, money and in general all articles of an intrinsic or sentimental value, which are found on the dead. These articles, together with unidentified articles, shall be sent in sealed packets, accompanied by statements giving all particulars necessary for the identification of the deceased owners, as well as by a complete list of the contents of the parcel.

Article 20. Parties to the conflict shall ensure that burial at sea of the dead, carried out individually as far as circumstances permit, is preceded by a careful examination, if possible by a medical examination, of the bodies, with a view to confirming death, establishing identity and enabling a report to be made. Where a double identity disc is used, one half of the disc should remain on the body.

If dead persons are landed, the provisions of the Geneva Convention for the Amelioration of the Condition of the Wounded and Sick in Armed Forces in the Field of 12 August, 1949, shall be applicable.

Article 21. The Parties to the conflict may appeal to the charity of commanders of neutral merchant vessels, yachts or other craft, to take on board and care for wounded, sick or shipwrecked persons, and to collect the dead.

Vessels of any kind responding to this appeal, and those having of their own accord collected wounded, sick or shipwrecked persons, shall enjoy special protection and facilities to carry out such assistance.

They may, in no case, be captured on account of any such transport; but, in the absence of any promise to the contrary, they shall remain liable to capture for any violations of neutrality they may have committed.

. . .

HOSPITAL SHIPS

Article 22. Military hospital ships, that is to say, ships built or equipped by the Powers specially and solely with a view to assisting the wounded, sick and shipwrecked, to treating them and to transporting them, may in no circumstances be attacked or captured, but shall at all times be respected and protected, on condition that their names and descriptions have been notified to the Parties to the conflict ten days before those ships are employed.

The characteristics which must appear in the notification shall include registered gross tonnage, the length from stem to stern and the number of masts and funnels.

Article 23. Establishments ashore entitled to the protection of the Geneva Convention for the Amelioration of the Condition of the Wounded and Sick in Armed Forces in the Field of August 12, 1949, shall be protected from bombardment or attack from the sea.

Article 24. Hospital ships utilized by National Red Cross Societies, by officially recognized relief societies or by private persons shall have the same protection as military hospital ships and shall be exempt from capture, if the Party to the conflict on which they depend has given them an official commission and in so far as the provisions of Article 22 concerning notification have been complied with.

These ships must be provided with certificates from the responsible authorities, stating that the vessels have been under their control while fitting out and on departure.

Article 25. Hospital ships utilized by National Red Cross Societies, officially recognized relief societies, or private persons of neutral countries shall have the same protection as military hospital ships and shall be exempt from capture, on condition that they have placed themselves under the control of one of the Parties to the conflict, with the previous consent of their own governments and with the authorization of the Party to the conflict concerned, in so far as the provisions of Article 22 concerning notification have been complied with.

Article 26. The protection mentioned in Articles 22, 24 [and] 25 shall apply to hospital ships of any tonnage and to their lifeboats, wherever they are operating. Nevertheless, to ensure the maximum comfort and security, the Parties to the conflict shall endeavour to utilize, for the transport of wounded, sick and shipwrecked over long distances and on the high seas, only hospital ships of over 2,000 tons gross.

Article 27. Under the same conditions as those provided for in Articles 22 and 24, small craft employed by the State or by the officially recognized lifeboat institutions for coastal rescue operations, shall also be respected and protected, so far as operational requirements permit.

The same shall apply so far as possible to fixed coastal installations used exclusively by these craft for their humanitarian missions.

Article 28. Should fighting occur on board a warship, the sick-bays shall be respected and spared as far as possible. Sick-bays and their equipment shall remain subject to the laws of warfare, but may not be diverted from their purpose so long as they are required for the wounded and sick. Nevertheless, the commander into whose power they have fallen may, after ensuring the proper care of the wounded and sick who are accommodated therein, apply them to other purposes in case of urgent military necessity.

Article 29. Any hospital ship in a port which falls into the hands of the enemy shall be authorized to leave the said port.

Article 30. The vessels described in Articles 22, 24, 25 and 27 shall afford relief and assistance to the wounded, sick and shipwrecked without distinction of nationality.

The High Contracting Parties undertake not to use these vessels for any military purpose.

Such vessels shall in no wise hamper the movements of the combatants.

During and after an engagement, they will act at their own risk.

Article 31. The Parties to the conflict shall have the right to control and search the vessels mentioned in Articles 22, 24, 25 and 27. They can refuse assistance from these vessels, order them off, make them take a certain course, control the use of their wireless and other means of communication, and even detain them for a period not exceeding seven days from the time of interception, if the gravity of the circumstances so requires.

They may put a commissioner temporarily on board whose sole task shall be to see that orders given in virtue of the provisions of the preceding paragraph are carried out.

As far as possible, the Parties to the conflict shall enter in the log of the hospital ship, in a language he can understand, the orders they have given the captain of the vessel.

Parties to the conflict may, either unilaterally or by particular agreements, put on board their ships neutral observers who shall verify the strict observation of the provisions contained in the present Convention.

Article 32. Vessels described in Articles 22, 24, 25 and 27 are not classed as warships as regards their stay in a neutral port.

Article 33. Merchant vessels which have been transformed into hospital ships cannot be put to any other use throughout the duration of hostilities.

Article 34. The protection to which hospital ships and sick-bays are entitled shall not cease unless they are used to commit, outside their humanitarian duties, acts harmful to the enemy. Protection may, however, cease only after due warning has been given, naming in all appropriate cases a reasonable time limit, and after such warning has remained unheeded.

In particular, hospital ships may not possess or use a secret code for their wireless or other means of communication.

Article 35. The following conditions shall not be considered as depriving hospital ships or sick-bays of vessels of the protection due to them:

(1) The fact that the crews of ships or sick-bays are armed for the maintenance of order, for their own defence or that of the sick and wounded.

(2) The presence on board of apparatus exclusively intended to facilitate navigation or communication.

(3) The discovery on board hospital ships or in sick-bays of portable arms and ammunition taken from the wounded, sick and shipwrecked and not yet handed to the proper service.

(4) The fact that the humanitarian activities of hospital ships and sick-bays of vessels or of the crews extend to the care of wounded, sick or shipwrecked civilians.

(5) The transport of equipment and of personnel intended exclusively for medical duties, over and above the normal requirements.

·   ·   ·

PERSONNEL

Article 36. The religious, medical and hospital personnel of hospital ships and their crews shall be respected and protected; they may not be captured during the time they are in the service of the hospital ship, whether or not there are wounded and sick on board.

Article 37. The religious, medical and hospital personnel assigned to the medical or spiritual care of the persons designated in Articles 12 and 13 shall, if they fall into the hands of the enemy, be respected and protected; they may continue to carry out their duties as long as this is necessary for the care of the wounded and sick. They shall afterwards be sent back as soon as the Commander-in-Chief, under whose authority they are, considers it practicable. They may take with them, on leaving the ship, their personal property.

If, however, it prove[s] necessary to retain some of this personnel owing to the medical or spiritual needs of prisoners of war, everything possible shall be done for their earliest possible landing.

Retained personnel shall be subject, on landing, to the provisions of the Geneva Convention for the Amelioration of the Condition of the Wounded and Sick in Armed Forces in the Field of August 12, 1949.

.   .   .

MEDICAL TRANSPORTS

Article 38. Ships chartered for that purpose shall be authorized to transport equipment exclusively intended for the treatment of wounded and sick members of armed forces or for the prevention of disease, provided that the particulars regarding their voyage have been notified to the adverse Power and approved by the latter. The adverse Power shall preserve the right to board the carrier ships, but not to capture them or seize the equipment carried.

By agreement amongst the Parties to the conflict, neutral observers may be placed on board such ships to verify the equipment carried. For this purpose, free access to the equipment shall be given.

Article 39. Medical aircraft, that is to say, aircraft exclusively employed for the removal of the wounded, sick and shipwrecked, and for the transport of medical personnel and equipment, may not be the object of attack, but shall be respected by the Parties to the conflict, while flying at heights, at times and on routes specifically agreed upon between the Parties to the conflict concerned.

They shall be clearly marked with the distinctive emblem prescribed in Article 41, together with their national colours, on their lower, upper and lateral surfaces. They shall be provided with any other markings or means of identification which may be agreed upon between the Parties to the conflict upon the outbreak or during the course of hostilities.

Unless agreed otherwise, flights over enemy or enemy-occupied territory are prohibited.

Medical aircraft shall obey every summons to alight on land or water. In the event of having thus to alight, the aircraft with its occupants may continue its flight after examination, if any.

In the event of alighting involuntarily on land or water in enemy or enemy-occupied territory, the wounded, sick and shipwrecked, as well as the crew of the aircraft shall be prisoners of war. The medical personnel shall be treated according to Articles 36 and 37.

Article 40. Subject to the provisions of the second paragraph, medical aircraft of Parties to the conflict may fly over the territory of neutral Powers, land thereon in case of necessity, or use it as a port of call. They shall give neutral Powers prior notice of their passage over the said territory, and obey every summons to alight, on land or water. They will be immune from attack only when flying on routes, at heights and at times specifically agreed upon between the Parties to the conflict and the neutral Power concerned.

The neutral Powers may, however, place conditions or restrictions on the passage or landing of medical aircraft on their territory. Such possible conditions or restrictions shall be applied equally to all Parties to the conflict.

Unless otherwise agreed between the neutral Powers and the Parties to the conflict, the wounded, sick or shipwrecked who are disembarked with the consent of the local authorities on neutral territory by medical aircraft shall be detained by the neutral Power, where so required by international law, in such a manner that they cannot again take part in operations of war. The cost of their accommodation and internment shall be borne by the Power on which they depend.

·   ·   ·

THE DISTINCTIVE EMBLEM

Article 41. Under the direction of the competent military authority, the emblem of the red cross on a white ground shall be displayed on the flags, armlets and on all equipment employed in the Medical Service.

Nevertheless, in the case of countries which already use as emblem, in place of the red cross, the red crescent or the red lion and sun on a white ground, these emblems are also recognized by the terms of the present Convention.

Article 42. The personnel designated in Articles 36 and 37 shall wear, affixed to the left arm, a water-resistant armlet bearing the distinctive emblem, issued and stamped by the military authority.

Such personnel in addition to wearing the identity disc mentioned in Article 19, shall also carry a special identity card bearing the distinctive emblem. This card shall be water-resistant and of such size that it can be carried in the pocket. It shall be worded in the national language, shall mention at least the surname and first names, the date of birth, the rank and the service number of the bearer, and shall state in what capacity he is entitled to the protection of the present Convention. The card shall bear the photograph of the owner and also either his signature or his fingerprints or both. It shall be embossed with the stamp of the military authority.

The identity card shall be uniform throughout the same armed forces and, as far as possible, of a similar type in the armed forces of the High Contracting Parties. The Parties to the conflict may be guided by the model which is annexed, by way of example, to the present Convention. They shall inform each other, at the outbreak of hostilities, of the model they are using. Identity cards should be made out, if possible, at least in duplicate, one copy being kept by the home country.

In no circumstances may the said personnel be deprived of their insignia or identity cards nor the right to wear the armlet. In case of loss they shall be entitled to receive duplicates of the cards and to have the insignia replaced.

Article 43. The ships designated in Articles 22, 24, 25 and 27 shall be distinctively marked as follows:

(a) All exterior surfaces shall be white.
(b) One or more dark red crosses, as large as possible, shall be painted and displayed on each side of the hull and on the horizontal surfaces, so placed as to afford the greatest possible visibility from the sea and from the air.

All hospital ships shall make themselves known by hoisting their national flag and further, if they belong to a neutral state, the flag of the Party to the conflict whose direction they have accepted. A white flag with a red cross shall be flown at the mainmast as high as possible.

Lifeboats of hospital ships, coastal lifeboats and all small craft used by the Medical Service shall be painted white with dark red crosses prominently displayed and shall, in general, comply with the identification system prescribed above for hospital ships.

The above-mentioned ships and craft, which may wish to ensure by night and in times of reduced visibility the protection to which they are entitled, must, subject to the assent of the Party to the conflict under whose power they are, take the necessary measures to render their painting and distinctive emblems sufficiently apparent.

Hospital ships which, in accordance with Article 31 are provisionally detained by the enemy, must haul down the flag of the Party to the conflict in whose service they are or whose direction they have accepted.

Coastal lifeboats, if they continue to operate with the consent of the Occupying Power from a base which is occupied, may be allowed, when away from their base, to continue to fly their own national colours along with a flag carrying a red cross on a white ground, subject to prior notification to all the Parties to the conflict concerned.

All the provisions in this Article relating to the red cross shall apply equally to the other emblems mentioned in Article 41.

Parties to the conflict shall at all times endeavour to conclude mutual agreements in order to use the most modern methods available to facilitate the identification of hospital ships.

Article 44. The distinguishing signs referred to in Article 43 can only be used, whether in time of peace or war, for indicating or protecting the ships therein mentioned, except as may be provided in any other international Convention or by agreement between all the Parties to the conflict concerned.

.   .   .

Execution of the Convention

.   .   .

Article 47. Reprisals against the wounded, sick and shipwrecked persons, the personnel, the vessels or the equipment protected by the Convention are prohibited.

Article 48. The High Contracting Parties undertake, in time of peace as in time of war, to disseminate the text of the present Convention as widely as possible in their respective countries, and, in particular, to include the study thereof in their programmes of military and, if possible, civil instruction, so that the principles thereof may become known to the entire population, in particular to the armed fighting forces, the medical personnel and the chaplains.

. . .

REPRESSION OF ABUSES AND INFRACTIONS

Article 50. The High Contracting Parties undertake to enact any legislation necessary to provide effective penal sanctions for persons committing, or ordering to be committed, any of the grave breaches of the present Convention defined in the following Article.

Each High Contracting Party shall be under the obligation to search for persons alleged to have committed, or to have ordered to be committed, such grave breaches, and shall bring such persons, regardless of their nationality, before its own courts. It may also, if it prefers, and in accordance with the provisions of its own legislation, hand such persons over for trial to another High Contracting Party concerned, provided such High Contracting Party has made out a *prima facie* case.

Each High Contracting Party shall take measures necessary for the suppression of all acts contrary to the provisions of the present Convention other than the grave breaches defined in the following Article.

In all circumstances, the accused persons shall benefit by safeguards of proper trial and defence, which shall not be less favourable than those provided by Article 105 and those following of the Geneva Convention relative to the Treatment of Prisoners of War of August 12, 1949.

Article 51. Grave breaches to which the preceding Article relates shall be those involving any of the following acts, if committed against persons or property protected by the Convention: wilful killing, torture or inhuman treatment, including biological experiments, wilfully causing great suffering or serious injury to body or health, and extensive destruction and appropriation of property, not justified by military necessity and carried out unlawfully and wantonly.

Article 52. No High Contracting Party shall be allowed to absolve itself or any other High Contracting Party of any liability incurred by itself or by another High Contracting Party in respect of breaches referred to in the preceding Article.

Article 53. At the request of a Party to the conflict, an enquiry shall be instituted, in a manner to be decided between the interested Parties, concerning any alleged violation of the Convention.

If agreement has not been reached concerning the procedure for the enquiry, the Parties should agree on the choice of an umpire, who will decide upon the procedure to be followed.

Once the violation has been established, the Parties to the conflict shall put an end to it and shall repress it with the least possible delay.

·   ·   ·

GENEVA CONVENTION (I) FOR THE AMELIORATION OF THE CONDITION OF THE WOUNDED AND SICK IN ARMED FORCES IN THE FIELD

[6 U.S.T. 3115, signed on August 12, 1949, at Geneva]

·   ·   ·

Article 5. For the protected persons who have fallen into the hands of the enemy, the present Convention shall apply until their final repatriation.

·   ·   ·

WOUNDED AND SICK

Article 12.   . . . The Party to the conflict which is compelled to abandon wounded or sick to the enemy shall, as far as military considerations permit, leave with them a part of its medical personnel and material to assist in their care.

·   ·   ·

Article 14. Subject to the provisions of Article 12, the wounded and sick of a belligerent who fall into enemy hands shall be prisoners of war, and the provisions of international law concerning prisoners of war shall apply to them.

Article 15. At all times, and particularly after an engagement, Parties to the conflict shall, without delay, take all possible measures to search for and collect the wounded and sick, to protect them against pillage and ill-treatment, to ensure their adequate care, and to search for the dead and prevent their being despoiled.

Whenever circumstances permit, an armistice or a suspension of fire shall be arranged, or local arrangements made, to permit the removal, exchange and transport of the wounded left on the battlefield.

Likewise, local arrangements may be concluded between Parties to the conflict for the removal or exchange of wounded and sick from a besieged or encircled area, and for the passage of medical and religious personnel and equipment on their way to that area.

. . .

Article 17. Parties to the conflict shall ensure that burial or cremation of the dead, carried out individually as far as circumstances permit, is preceded by a careful examination, if possible by a medical examination, of the bodies, with a view to confirming death, establishing identity and enabling a report to be made. One half of the double identity disc, or the identity disc itself if it is a single disc, should remain on the body.

Bodies shall not be cremated except for imperative reasons of hygiene or for motives based on the religion of the deceased. In case of cremation, the circumstances and reasons for cremation shall be stated in detail in the death certificate or on the authenticated list of the dead.

They shall further ensure that the dead are honourably interred, if possible according to the rites of the religion to which they belonged, that their graves are respected, grouped if possible according to the nationality of the deceased, properly maintained and marked so that they may always be found. For this purpose, they shall organize at the commencement of hostilities an Official Graves Registration Service, to allow subsequent exhumations and to ensure the identification of bodies, whatever the site of the graves, and the possible transportation to the home country. These provisions shall likewise apply to the ashes, which shall be kept by the Graves Registration Service until proper disposal thereof in accordance with the wishes of the home country.

As soon as circumstances permit, and at latest at the end of hostilities, these Services shall exchange, through the Information Bureau mentioned in the second paragraph of Article 16,[2] lists showing the exact location and markings of the graves, together with particulars of the dead interred therein.

Article 18. The military authorities may appeal to the charity of the inhabitants voluntarily to collect and care for, under their direction, the wounded and sick, granting persons who have responded to this appeal the necessary protection and facilities. Should the adverse Party take or retake control of the area, he shall likewise grant these persons the same protection and the same facilities.

The military authorities shall permit the inhabitants and relief societies, even in invaded or occupied areas, spontaneously to collect and care for wounded or sick of whatever nationality. The civilian population shall respect these wounded and sick, and in particular abstain from offering them violence.

No one may ever be molested or convicted for having nursed the wounded or sick.

The provisions of the present Article do not relieve the occupying Power of its obligation to give both physical and moral care to the wounded and sick.

.   .   .

MEDICAL UNITS AND ESTABLISHMENTS

Article 19. Fixed establishments and mobile medical units of the Medical Service may in no circumstances be attacked, but shall at all times be respected and protected by the Parties to the conflict. Should they fall into the hands of the adverse Party, their personnel shall be free to pursue their duties, as long as the capturing Power has not itself ensured the necessary care of the wounded and sick found in such establishments and units.

The responsible authorities shall ensure that the said medical establishments and units are, as far as possible, situated in such a manner that attacks against military objectives cannot imperil their safety.

Article 20. Hospital ships entitled to the protection of the Geneva Convention for the Amelioration of the Condition of Wounded, Sick and Shipwrecked Members of Armed Forces at Sea of August 12, 1949, shall not be attacked from the land.

Article 21. The protection to which fixed establishments and mobile medical units of the Medical Service are entitled shall not cease unless they are used to commit, outside their humanitarian duties, acts harmful to the enemy. Protection may, however, cease only after a due warning has been given, naming, in all appropriate cases, a reasonable time limit, and after such warning has remained unheeded.

Article 22. The following conditions shall not be considered as depriving a medical unit or establishment of the protection guaranteed by Article 19:

(1) That the personnel of the unit or establishment are armed, and

that they use the arms in their own defence, or in that of the wounded and sick in their charge.

(2) That in the absence of armed orderlies, the unit or establishment is protected by a picket or by sentries or by an escort.

(3) That small arms and ammunition taken from the wounded and sick and not yet handed to the proper service, are found in the unit or establishment.

(4) That personnel and material of the veterinary service are found in the unit or establishment, without forming an integral part thereof.

(5) That the humanitarian activities of medical units and establishments or of their personnel extend to the care of civilian wounded or sick.

Article 23. In time of peace, the High Contracting Parties and, after the outbreak of hostilities, the Parties thereto, may establish in their own territory and, if the need arises, in occupied areas, hospital zones and localities so organized as to protect the wounded and sick from the effects of war, as well as the personnel entrusted with the organization and administration of these zones and localities and with the care of the persons therein assembled.

Upon the outbreak and during the course of hostilities, the Parties concerned may conclude agreements on mutual recognition of the hospital zones and localities they have created. They may for this purpose implement the provisions of the Draft Agreement annexed to the present Convention, with such amendments as they may consider necessary.

The Protecting Powers and the International Committee of the Red Cross are invited to lend their good offices in order to facilitate the institution and recognition of these hospital zones and localities.

· · ·

PERSONNEL

Article 24. Medical personnel exclusively engaged in the search for, or the collection, transport or treatment of the wounded or sick, or in the prevention of disease, staff exclusively engaged in the administration of medical units and establishments, as well as chaplains attached to the armed forces, shall be respected and protected in all circumstances.

Article 25. Members of the armed forces specially trained for employment, should the need arise, as hospital orderlies, nurses or auxiliary stretcher-bearers, in the search for or the collection, transport or treatment of the wounded and sick shall likewise be respected and protected if they are carrying out these duties at the time when they come into contact with the enemy or fall into his hands.

Article 26. The staff of National Red Cross Societies and that of other Voluntary Aid Societies, duly recognized and authorized by their Governments, who may be employed on the same duties as the personnel named in Article 24, are placed on the same footing as the personnel named in the said Article, provided that the staff of such societies are subject to military laws and regulations.

Each High Contracting Party shall notify to the other, either in time of peace or at the commencement of or during hostilities, but in any case before actually employing them, the names of the societies which it has authorized, under its responsibility, to render assistance to the regular medical service of its armed forces.

Article 27. A recognized Society of a neutral country can only lend the assistance of its medical personnel and units to a Party to the conflict with the previous consent of its own Government and the authorization of the Party to the conflict concerned. That personnel and those units shall be placed under the control of that Party to the conflict.

The neutral Government shall notify this consent to the adversary of the State which accepts such assistance. The Party to the conflict who accepts such assistance is bound to notify the adverse Party thereof before making any use of it.

In no circumstances shall this assistance be considered as interference in the conflict.

The members of the personnel named in the first paragraph shall be duly furnished with the identity cards provided for in Article 40 before leaving the neutral country to which they belong.

Article 28. Personnel designated in Articles 24 and 26 who fall into the hands of the adverse Party, shall be retained only in so far as the state of health, the spiritual needs and the number of prisoners of war require.

Personnel thus retained shall not be deemed prisoners of war. Nevertheless they shall at least benefit by all the provisions of the Geneva Convention relative to the Treatment of Prisoners of War of August 12, 1949. Within the framework of the military laws and regulations of the Detaining Power, and under the authority of its competent service, they shall continue to carry out, in accordance with their professional ethics, their medical and spiritual duties on behalf of prisoners of war, preferably those of the armed forces to which they themselves belong. They shall further enjoy the following facilities for carrying out their medical or spiritual duties:

(a) They shall be authorized to visit periodically the prisoners of war in labour units or hospitals outside the camp. The Detaining Power shall put at their disposal the means of transport required.

(b) In each camp the senior medical officer of the highest rank shall be responsible to the military authorities of the camp for the professional activity of the retained medical personnel. For this purpose, from the outbreak of hostilities, the Parties to the conflict shall agree regarding the corresponding seniority of the ranks of their medical personnel, including those of the societies designated in Article 26. In all questions arising out of their duties, this medical officer, and the chaplains, shall have direct access to the military and medical authorities of the camp who shall grant them the facilities they may require for correspondence relating to these questions.

(c) Although retained personnel in a camp shall be subject to its internal discipline, they shall not, however, be required to perform any work outside their medical or religious duties.

During hostilities the Parties to the conflict shall make arrangements for relieving where possible retained personnel, and shall settle the procedure of such relief.

None of the preceding provisions shall relieve the Detaining Power of the obligations imposed upon it with regard to the medical and spiritual welfare of the prisoners of war

Article 29. Members of the personnel designated in Article 25 who have fallen into the hands of the enemy, shall be prisoners of war, but shall be employed on their medical duties in so far as the need arises.

Article 30. Personnel whose retention is not indispensable by virtue of the provisions of Article 28 shall be returned to the Party to the conflict to whom they belong, as soon as a road is open for their return and military requirements permit.

Pending their return, they shall not be deemed prisoners of war. Nevertheless they shall at least benefit by all the provisions of the Geneva Convention relative to the Treatment of Prisoners of War of August 12, 1949. They shall continue to fulfil their duties under the orders of the adverse Party and shall preferably be engaged in the care of the wounded and sick of the Party to the conflict to which they themselves belong.

On their departure, they shall take with them the effects, personal belongings, valuables and instruments belonging to them.

Article 31. The selection of personnel for return under Article 30 shall be made irrespective of any consideration of race, religion or political opinion, but preferably according to the chronological order of their capture and their state of health.

As from the outbreak of hostilities, Parties to the conflict may determine by special agreement the percentage of personnel to be retained, in proportion to the number of prisoners and the distribution of the said personnel in the camps.

Article 32. Persons designated in Article 27 who have fallen into the hands of the adverse Party may not be detained.

Unless otherwise agreed, they shall have permission to return to their country, or if this is not possible, to the territory of the Party to the conflict in whose service they were, as soon as a route for their return is open and military considerations permit.

Pending their release, they shall continue their work under the direction of the adverse Party; they shall preferably be engaged in the care of the wounded and sick of the Party to the conflict in whose service they were.

On their departure, they shall take with them their effects, personal articles and valuables and the instruments, arms and if possible the means of transport belonging to them.

The Parties to the conflict shall secure to this personnel, while in their power, the same food, lodging, allowances and pay as are granted to the corresponding personnel of their armed forces. The food shall in any case be sufficient as regards quantity, quality and variety to keep the said personnel in a normal state of health.

Article 33. The material of mobile medical units of the armed forces which fall into the hands of the enemy, shall be reserved for the care of wounded and sick.

The buildings, material and stores of fixed medical establishments of the armed forces shall remain subject to the laws of war, but may not be diverted from their purpose as long as they are required for the care of wounded and sick. Nevertheless, the commanders of forces in the field may make use of them, in case of urgent military necessity, provided that they make previous arrangements for the welfare of the wounded and sick who are nursed in them.

The material and stores defined in the present Article shall not be intentionally destroyed.

Article 34. The real and personal property of aid societies which are admitted to the privileges of the Convention shall be regarded as private property.

The right of requisition recognized for belligerents by the laws and customs of war shall not be exercised except in case of urgent necessity, and only after the welfare of the wounded and sick has been ensured.

. . .

MEDICAL TRANSPORTS

Article 35. Transports of wounded and sick or of medical equipment shall be respected and protected in the same way as mobile medical units.

Should such transports or vehicles fall into the hands of the adverse Party, they shall be subject to the laws of war, on condition that the Party to the conflict who captures them shall in all cases ensure the care of the wounded and sick they contain

The civilian personnel and all means of transport obtained by requisition shall be subject to the general rules of international law.

. . .

Article 41. The personnel designated in Article 25 shall wear, but only while carrying out medical duties, a white armlet bearing in its centre the distinctive sign in miniature; the armlet shall be issued and stamped by the military authority.

Military identity documents to be carried by this type of personnel shall specify what special training they have received, the temporary character of the duties they are engaged upon, and their authority for wearing the armlet.

Article 42. The distinctive flag of the Convention shall be hoisted only over such medical units and establishments as are entitled to be respected under the Convention, and only with the consent of the military authorities.

In mobile units, as in fixed establishments, it may be accompanied by the national flag of the Party to the conflict to which the unit or establishment belongs. . . .

EXECUTION OF THE CONVENTION

. . .

Article 46. Reprisals against the wounded, sick, personnel, buildings or equipment protected by the Convention are prohibited.

Article 47. The High Contracting Parties undertake, in time of peace as in time of war, to disseminate the text of the present Convention as widely as possible in their respective countries, and, in particular, to include the study thereof in their programmes of military and, if possible, civil instruction, so that the principles thereof may become known to the entire population, in particular to the armed fighting forces, the medical personnel and the chaplains.

. . .

REPRESSION OF ABUSES AND INFRACTIONS

Article 49. The High Contracting Parties undertake to enact any legislation necessary to provide effective penal sanctions for persons committing, or ordering to be committed, any of the grave breaches of the present Convention defined in the following Article.

Each High Contracting Party shall be under the obligation to search for persons alleged to have committed, or to have ordered to be committed, such grave breaches, and shall bring such persons, regardless of their nationality, before its own courts. It may also, if it prefers, and in accordance with the provisions of its own legislation, hand such persons over for trial to another High Contracting Party concerned, provided such High Contracting Party has made out a *prima facie* case.

Each High Contracting Party shall take measures necessary for the suppression of all acts contrary to the provisions of the present Convention other than the grave breaches defined in the following Article.

In all circumstances, the accused persons shall benefit by safeguards of proper trial and defence, which shall not be less favourable than those provided by Article 105 and those following of the Geneva Convention relative to the Treatment of Prisoners of War of August 12, 1949.

Article 50. Grave breaches to which the preceding Article relates shall be those involving any of the following acts, if committed against persons or property protected by the Convention: wilful killing, torture or inhuman treatment, including biological experiments, wilfully causing great suffering or serious injury to body or health, and extensive destruction and appropriation of property, not justified by military necessity and carried out unlawfully and wantonly.

Article 51. No High Contracting Party shall be allowed to absolve itself or any other High Contracting Party of any liability incurred by itself or by another High Contracting Party in respect of breaches referred to in the preceding Article.

Article 52. At the request of a Party to the conflict, an enquiry shall be instituted, in a manner to be decided between the interested Parties, concerning any alleged violation of the Convention.

If agreement has not been reached concerning the procedure for the enquiry, the Parties should agree on the choice of an umpire who will decide upon the procedure to be followed.

Once the violation has been established, the Parties to the conflict shall put an end to it and shall repress it with the least possible delay.

· · ·

ANNEX 1
DRAFT AGREEMENT RELATING TO HOSPITAL ZONES AND LOCALITIES

Article 1. Hospital zones shall be strictly reserved for the persons named in Article 23 of the Geneva Convention for the Amelioration of the Condition of the Wounded and Sick in Armed Forces in the Field of August 12, 1949, and for the personnel entrusted with the organization and administration of these zones and localities and with the care of the persons therein assembled.

Nevertheless, persons whose permanent residence is within such zones shall have the right to stay there.

Article 2. No persons residing, in whatever capacity, in a hospital zone shall perform any work, either within or without the zone, directly connected with military operations or the production of war material.

Article 3. The Power establishing a hospital zone shall take all necessary measures to prohibit access to all persons who have no right of residence or entry therein.

Article 4. Hospital zones shall fulfil the following conditions:

(a) They shall comprise only a small part of the territory governed by the Power which has established them.

(b) They shall be thinly populated in relation to the possibilities of accommodation.

(c) They shall be far removed and free from all military objectives, or large industrial or administrative establishments.

(d) They shall not be situated in areas which, according to every probability, may become important for the conduct of the war.

Article 5. Hospital zones shall be subject to the following obligations:

(a) The lines of communication and means of transport which they possess shall not be used for the transport of military personnel or material, even in transit.

(b) They shall in no case be defended by military means.

Article 6. Hospital zones shall be marked by means of red crosses (red crescents, red lions and suns) on a white background placed on the outer precincts and on the buildings. They may be similarly marked at night by means of appropriate illumination.

Article 7. The Powers shall communicate to all the High Contracting Parties in peacetime or on the outbreak of hostilities, a list of the hospital zones in the territories governed by them. They shall also give notice of any new zones set up during hostilities.

As soon as the adverse Party has received the above-mentioned notification, the zone shall be regularly constituted.

If, however, the adverse Party considers that the conditions of the present agreement have not been fulfilled, it may refuse to recognize the zone by giving immediate notice thereof to the Party responsible for the said zone, or may make its recognition of such zone dependent upon the institution of the control provided for in Article 8.

Article 8. Any Power having recognized one or several hospital zones instituted by the adverse Party shall be entitled to demand control by one or more Special Commissions, for the purpose of ascertaining if the zones fulfil the conditions and obligations stipulated in the present agreement.

For this purpose, the members of the Special Commissions shall at all times have free access to the various zones and may even reside there permanently. They shall be given all facilities for their duties of inspection.

Article 9. Should the Special Commissions note any facts which they consider contrary to the stipulations of the present agreement, they shall at once draw the attention of the Power governing the said zone to these facts, and shall fix a time limit of five days within which the matter should be rectified. They shall duly notify the Power who has recognized the zone.

If, when the time limit has expired, the Power governing the zone has not complied with the warning, the adverse Party may declare that it is no longer bound by the present agreement in respect of the said zone.

Article 10. Any Power setting up one or more hospital zones and localities, and the adverse Parties to whom their existence has been notified, shall nominate or have nominated by neutral Powers, the persons who shall be members of the Special Commissions mentioned in Articles 8 and 9.

Article 11. In no circumstances may hospital zones be the object of attack. They shall be protected and respected at all times by the Parties to the conflict.

Article 12. In the case of occupation of a territory, the hospital zones therein shall continue to be respected and utilized as such.

Their purpose may, however, be modified by the Occupying Power, on condition that all measures are taken to ensure the safety of the persons accommodated.

Article 13. The present agreement shall also apply to localities which the Powers may utilize for the same purposes as hospital zones.

.   .   .

GENEVA CONVENTION (III) RELATIVE TO THE TREATMENT OF PRISONERS OF WAR

[6 U.S.T. 3317, signed on August 12, 1949, at Geneva]

.   .   .

Article 4. A. Prisoners of war, in the sense of the present Convention, are persons belonging to one of the following categories, who have fallen into the power of the enemy:

(1) Members of the armed forces of a Party to the conflict, as well as members of militias or volunteer corps forming part of such armed forces.

(2) Members of other militias and members of other volunteer corps, including those of organized resistance movements, belonging to a Party to the conflict and operating in or outside their own territory, even if this territory is occupied, provided that such militias or volunteer corps, including such organized resistance movements, fulfil the following conditions:

    (a) that of being commanded by a person responsible for his subordinates;

    (b) that of having a fixed distinctive sign recognizable at a distance;

    (c) that of carrying arms openly;

    (d) that of conducting their operations in accordance with the laws and customs of war.

(3) Members of regular armed forces who profess allegiance to a government or an authority not recognized by the Detaining Power.

(4) Persons who accompany the armed forces without actually being members thereof, such as civilian members of military aircraft crews, war correspondents, supply contractors, members of labour units or of services responsible for the welfare of the armed forces, provided that they have received authorization from the armed forces which they accompany, who shall provide them for that purpose with an identity card similar to the annexed model.

(5) Members of crews, including masters, pilots and apprentices, of the merchant marine and the crews of civil aircraft of the Parties to the conflict, who do not benefit by more favourable treatment under any other provisions of international law.

(6) Inhabitants of a non-occupied territory, who on the approach of the enemy spontaneously take up arms to resist the invading forces, without having had time to form themselves into regular armed units, provided they carry arms openly and respect the laws and customs of war.

B. The following shall likewise be treated as prisoners of war under the present Convention:

(1) Persons belonging, or having belonged, to the armed forces of the occupied country, if the occupying Power considers it necessary by reason of such allegiance to intern them, even though it has originally liberated them while hostilities were going on outside the territory it occupies, in particular where such persons have made an unsuccessful attempt to rejoin the armed forces to which they belong and which are engaged in combat, or where they fail to comply with a summons made to them with a view to internment.

(2) The persons belonging to one of the categories enumerated in the present Article, who have been received by neutral or non-belligerent Powers on their territory and whom these Powers are required to intern under international law, without prejudice to any more favourable treatment which these Powers may choose to give and with the exception of Articles 8, 10, 15, 30, fifth paragraph, 58–67, 92, 126 and, where diplomatic relations exist between the Parties to the conflict and the neutral or non-belligerent Power concerned, those Articles concerning the Protecting Power. Where such diplomatic relations exist, the Parties to a conflict on whom these persons depend shall be allowed to perform towards them the functions of a Protecting Power as provided in the present Convention, without prejudice to the functions which these Parties normally exercise in conformity with diplomatic and consular usage and treaties.

C. This Article shall in no way affect the status of medical personnel and chaplains as provided for in Article 33 of the present Convention.

Article 5. The present Convention shall apply to the persons referred to in Article 4 from the time they fall into the power of the enemy and until their final release and repatriation.

Should any doubt arise as to whether persons, having committed a belligerent act and having fallen into the hands of the enemy, belong to any of the categories enumerated in Article 4, such persons shall enjoy the protection of the present Convention until such time as their status has been determined by a competent tribunal.

. . .

Article 7. Prisoners of war may in no circumstance renounce in part or in entirely the rights secured to them by the present Convention, and by the special agreements referred to in the foregoing Article, if such there be.

. . .

Article 9. The provisions of the present Convention constitute no obstacle to the humanitarian activities which the International Committee of the Red Cross or any other impartial humanitarian organization may, subject to the consent of the Parties to the conflict concerned, undertake for the protection of prisoners of war and for their relief.

Article 10. The High Contracting Parties may at any time agree to entrust to an organization which offers all guarantees of impartiality and efficacy the duties incumbent on the Protecting Powers by virtue of the present Convention.

When prisoners of war do not benefit or cease to benefit, no matter for what reason, by the activities of a Protecting Power or of an organization provided for in the first paragraph above, the Detaining Power shall request a neutral State, or such an organization, to undertake the functions performed under the present Convention by a Protecting Power designated by the Parties to a conflict.

If protection cannot be arranged accordingly, the Detaining Power shall request or shall accept, subject to the provisions of this Article, the offer of the services of a humanitarian organization, such as the International Committee of the Red Cross, to assume the humanitarian functions performed by Protecting Powers under the present Convention.

Any neutral Power or any organization invited by the Power concerned or offering itself for these purposes, shall be required to act with a sense of responsibility towards the Party to the conflict on which persons protected by the present Convention depend, and shall be required to furnish sufficient assurances that it is in a position to undertake the appropriate functions and to discharge them impartially.

. . . .

GENERAL PROTECTION OF PRISONERS OF WAR

Article 12. Prisoners of war are in the hands of the enemy Power, but not of the individuals or military units who have captured them. Irrespective of the individual responsibilities that may exist, the Detaining Power is responsible for the treatment given them.

Prisoners of war may only be transferred by the Detaining Power to a Power which is a party to the Convention and after the Detaining Power has satisfied itself of the willingness and ability of such transferee Power to apply the Convention. When prisoners of war are transferred under such circumstances, responsibility for the application of the Convention rests on the Power accepting them while they are in its custody.

Nevertheless, if that Power fails to carry out the provisions of the Convention in any important respect, the Power by whom the prisoners of war were transferred shall, upon being notified by the Protecting Power, take effective measures to correct the situation or shall request the return of the prisoners of war. Such requests must be complied with.

Article 13. Prisoners of war must at all times be humanely treated. Any unlawful act or omission by the Detaining Power causing death or seriously endangering the health of a prisoner of war in its custody is prohibited, and will be regarded as a serious breach of the present Convention. In particular, no prisoner of war may be subjected to physical mutilation or to medical or scientific experiments of any kind which are not justified by the medical, dental or hospital treatment of the prisoner concerned and carried out in his interest.

Likewise, prisoners of war must at all times be protected, particularly against acts of violence or intimidation and against insults and public curiosity. Measures of reprisal against prisoners of war are prohibited.

Article 14. Prisoners of war are entitled in all circumstances to respect for their persons and their honour.

Women shall be treated with all the regard due to their sex and shall in all cases benefit by treatment as favourable as that granted to men.

Prisoners of war shall retain the full civil capacity which they enjoyed at the time of their capture. The Detaining Power may not restrict the exercise, either within or without its own territory, of the rights such capacity confers except in so far as the captivity requires.

Article 15. The Power detaining prisoners of war shall be bound to provide free of charge for their maintenance and for the medical attention required by their state of health.

Article 16. Taking into consideration the provisions of the present Convention relating to rank and sex, and subject to any privileged treatment which may be accorded to them by reason of their state of health, age or professional qualifications, all prisoners of war shall be treated alike by the Detaining Power, without any adverse distinction based on race, nationality, religious belief or political opinions, or any other distinction founded on similar criteria.

BEGINNING OF CAPTIVITY

Article 17. Every prisoner of war, when questioned on the subject, is bound to give only his surname, first names and rank, date of birth, and army, regimental, personal or serial number, or failing this, equivalent information.

If he wilfully infringes this rule, he may render himself liable to a restriction of the privileges accorded to his rank or status.

Each Party to a conflict is required to furnish the persons under its jurisdiction who are liable to become prisoners of war, with an identity card showing the owner's surname, first names, rank, army, regimental, personal or serial number or equivalent information, and date of birth. The identity card may, furthermore, bear the signature or the fingerprints, or both, of the owner, and may bear, as well, any other information the Party to the conflict may wish to add concerning persons belonging to its armed forces. As far as possible the card shall measure 6.5 x 10 cm. and shall be issued in duplicate. The identity card shall be shown by the prisoner of war upon demand, but may in no case be taken away from him.

No physical or mental torture, nor any other form of coercion, may be inflicted on prisoners of war to secure from them information of any kind whatever. Prisoners of war who refuse to answer may not be threatened, insulted, or exposed to unpleasant or disadvantageous treatment of any kind.

Prisoners of war who, owing to their physical or mental condition, are unable to state their identity, shall be handed over to the medical service. The identity of such prisoners shall be established by all possible means, subject to the provisions of the preceding paragraph.

The questioning of prisoners of war shall be carried out in a language which they understand.

Article 18. All effects and articles of personal use, except arms, horses, military equipment and military documents, shall remain in the possession of prisoners of war, likewise their metal helmets and gas masks and like articles issued for personal protection. Effects and articles used for their clothing or feeding shall likewise remain in their possession, even if such effects and articles belong to their regulation military equipment.

At no time should prisoners of war be without identity documents. The Detaining Power shall supply such documents to prisoners of war who possess none.

Badges of rank and nationality, decorations and articles having above all a personal or sentimental value may not be taken from prisoners of war.

Sums of money carried by prisoners of war may not be taken away from them except by order of an officer, and after the amount and particulars of the owner have been recorded in a special register and an itemized receipt has been given, legibly inscribed with the name, rank and unit of the person issuing the said receipt. Sums in the currency of the Detaining Power, or which are changed into such currency at the prisoner's request, shall be placed to the credit of the prisoner's account.

The Detaining Power may withdraw articles of value from prisoners of war only for reasons of security; when such articles are withdrawn, the procedure laid down for sums of money impounded shall apply.

Such objects, likewise sums taken away in any currency other than that of the Detaining Power and the conversion of which has not been asked for by the owners, shall be kept in the custody of the Detaining Power and shall be returned in their initial shape to prisoners of war at the end of their captivity.

Article 19. Prisoners of war shall be evacuated, as soon as possible after their capture, to camps situated in an area far enough from the combat zone for them to be out of danger.

Only those prisoners of war who, owing to wounds or sickness, would run greater risks by being evacuated than by remaining where they are, may be temporarily kept back in a danger zone.

Prisoners of war shall not be unnecessarily exposed to danger while awaiting evacuation from a fighting zone.

Article 20. The evacuation of prisoners of war shall always be effected humanely and in conditions similar to those for the forces of the Detaining Power in their changes of station.

The Detaining Power shall supply prisoners of war who are being evacuated with sufficient food and potable water, and with the necessary clothing and medical attention. The Detaining Power shall take all suitable precautions to ensure their safety during evacuation, and shall establish as soon as possible a list of the prisoners of war who are evacuated.

If prisoners of war must, during evacuation, pass through transit camps, their stay in such camps shall be as brief as possible.

.　　.　　.

INTERNMENT OF PRISONERS OF WAR

.　　.　　.

GENERAL OBSERVATIONS

Article 21. The Detaining Power may subject prisoners of war to internment. It may impose on them the obligation of not leaving, beyond certain limits, the camp where they are interned, or if the said camp is fenced in, of not going outside its perimeter. Subject to the provisions of the present Convention relative to penal and disciplinary sanctions, prisoners of war may not be held in close confinement except where necessary to safeguard their health and then only during the continuation of the circumstances which make such confinement necessary.

Prisoners of war may be partially or wholly released on parole or promise, in so far as is allowed by the laws of the Power on which they depend. Such measures shall be taken particularly in cases where this may contribute to the improvement of their state of health. No prisoner of war shall be compelled to accept liberty on parole or promise.

Upon the outbreak of hostilities, each Party to the conflict shall notify the adverse Party of the laws and regulations allowing or forbidding its own nationals to accept liberty on parole or promise. Prisoners of war who are paroled or who have given their promise in conformity with the laws and regulations so notified, are bound on their personal honour scrupulously to fulfil, both towards the Power which they depend and towards the Power on which has captured them, the engagements of their paroles or promises. In such cases, the Power on which they depend is bound neither to require nor to accept from them any service incompatible with the parole or promise given.

Article 22. Prisoners of war may be interned only in premises located on land and affording every guarantee of hygiene and healthfulness. Except in particular cases which are justified by the interest of the prisoners themselves, they shall not be interned in penitentiaries.

Prisoners of war interned in unhealthy areas, or where the climate is injurious for them, shall be removed as soon as possible to a more favourable climate.

The Detaining Power shall assemble prisoners of war in camps or camp compounds according to their nationality, language and customs, provided that such prisoners shall not be separated from prisoners of war belonging to the armed forces with which they were serving at the time of their capture, except with their consent.

Article 23. No prisoner of war may at any time be sent to, or detained in areas where he may be exposed to the fire of the combat zone, nor may his presence be used to render certain points or areas immune from military operations.

Prisoners of war shall have shelters against air bombardment and other hazards of war, to the same extent as the local civilian population. With the exception of those engaged in the protection of their quarters against the aforesaid hazards, they may enter such shelters as soon as possible after the giving of the alarm. Any other protective measure taken in favour of the population shall also apply to them.

Detaining Powers shall give the Powers concerned, through the intermediary of the Protecting Powers, all useful information regarding the geographical location of prisoner of war camps.

Whenever military considerations permit, prisoner of war camps shall be indicated in the day-time by the letters PW or PG, placed so as to be clearly visible from the air. The Powers concerned may, however, agree upon any other system of marking. Only prisoner of war camps shall be marked as such.

Article 24. Transit or screening camps of a permanent kind shall be fitted out under conditions similar to those described in the present Section, and the prisoners therein shall have the same treatment as in other camps.

. . .

QUARTERS, FOOD AND CLOTHING
OF PRISONERS OF WAR

Article 25. Prisoners of war shall be quartered under conditions as favourable as those for the forces of the Detaining Power who are billeted in the same area. The said conditions shall make allowance for the habits and customs of the prisoners and shall in no case be prejudicial to their health.

The foregoing provisions shall apply in particular to the dormitories of prisoners of war as regards both total surface and minimum cubic space, and the general installations, bedding and blankets.

The premises provided for the use of prisoners of war individually or collectively, shall be entirely protected from dampness and adequately heated and lighted, in particular between dusk and lights out. All precautions must be taken against the danger of fire.

In any camps in which women prisoners of war, as well as men, are accommodated, separate dormitories shall be provided for them.

Article 26. The basic daily food rations shall be sufficient in quantity, quality and variety to keep prisoners of war in good health and to prevent loss of weight or the development of nutritional deficiencies. Account shall also be taken of the habitual diet of the prisoners.

The Detaining Power shall supply prisoners of war who work with such additional rations as are necessary for the labour on which they are employed.

Sufficient drinking water shall be supplied to prisoners of war. The use of tobacco shall be permitted.

Prisoners of war shall, as far as possible, be associated with the preparation of their meals; they may be employed for that purpose in the kitchens. Furthermore, they shall be given the means of preparing, themselves, the additional food in their possession.

Adequate premises shall be provided for messing.

Collective disciplinary measures affecting food are prohibited.

Article 27. Clothing, underwear and footwear shall be supplied to prisoners of war in sufficient quantities by the Detaining Power, which shall make allowance for the climate of the region where the prisoners are detained. Uniforms of enemy armed forces captured by the Detaining Power should, if suitable for the climate, be made available to clothe prisoners of war.

The regular replacement and repair of the above articles shall be assured by the Detaining Power. In addition, prisoners of war who work shall receive appropriate clothing, wherever the nature of the work demands.

Article 28. Canteens shall be installed in all camps, where prisoners of war may procure foodstuffs, soap and tobacco and ordinary articles in daily use. The tariff shall never be in excess of local market prices . . . .

HYGIENE AND MEDICAL ATTENTION

Article 29. The Detaining Power shall be bound to take all sanitary measures necessary to ensure the cleanliness and healthfulness of camps and to prevent epidemics.

Prisoners of war shall have for their use, day and night, conveniences which conform to the rules of hygiene and are maintained in a constant state of cleanliness. In any camps in which women prisoners of war are accommodated, separate conveniences shall be provided for them . . . .

Article 30. Every camp shall have an adequate infirmary where prisoners of war may have the attention they require, as well as appropriate diet. Isolation wards shall, if necessary, be set aside for cases of contagious or mental disease.

Prisoners of war suffering from serious disease, or whose condition necessitates special treatment, a surgical operation or hospital care, must be admitted to any military or civil medical unit where such treatment can be given, even if their repatriation is contemplated in the near future. Special facilities shall be afforded for the care to be given to the disabled, in particular to the blind, and for their rehabilitation, pending repatriation.

Prisoners of war shall have the attention, preferably, of medical personnel of the Power on which they depend and, if possible, of their nationality.

. . . .

The costs of treatment, including those of any apparatus necessary for the maintenance of prisoners of war in good health, particularly dentures and other artificial appliances, and spectacles, shall be borne by the Detaining Power.

Article 31. Medical inspections of prisoners of war shall be held at least once a month. They shall include the checking and the recording of the weight of each prisoner of war. Their purpose shall be, in particular, to supervise the general state of health, nutrition and cleanliness of prisoners and to detect contagious diseases, especially tuberculosis, malaria and venereal disease. For this purpose the most efficient methods available shall be employed, e.g.[,] periodic mass miniature radiography for the early detection of tuberculosis.

Article 32. Prisoners of war who, though not attached to the medical service of their armed forces, are physicians, surgeons, dentists, nurses or medical orderlies, may be required by the Detaining Power to exercise their medical functions in the interests of prisoners of war dependent on the same Power. In that case they shall continue to be prisoners of war, but shall receive the same treatment as corresponding medical personnel retained by the Detaining Power. They shall be exempted from any other work under Article 49.

. . .

MEDICAL PERSONNEL AND CHAPLAINS
RETAINED TO ASSIST PRISONERS OF WAR

Article 33. Members of the medical personnel and chaplains while retained by the Detaining Power with a view to assisting prisoners of war, shall not be considered as prisoners of war. They shall, however, receive as a minimum the benefits and protection of the present Convention, and shall also be granted all facilities necessary to provide for the medical care of, and religious ministration to prisoners of war.

They shall continue to exercise their medical and spiritual functions for the benefit of prisoners of war, preferably those belonging to the armed forces upon which they depend, within the scope of the military laws and regulations of the Detaining Power and under the control of its competent services, in accordance with their professional etiquette. They shall also benefit by the following facilities in the exercise of their medical or spiritual functions:

(a) They shall be authorized to visit periodically prisoners of war situated in working detachments or in hospitals outside the camp. For this purpose, the Detaining Power shall place at their disposal the necessary means of transport.

(b) The senior medical officer in each camp shall be responsible to the camp military authorities for everything connected with the activities of retained medical personnel. For this purpose, Parties to the conflict shall agree at the outbreak of hostilities on the subject of the corresponding ranks of the medical personnel, including that of societies mentioned in Article 26 of the Geneva Convention for the Amelioration of the Condition of the Wounded and Sick in Armed Forces in the Field of August 12, 1949. This senior medical officer, as well as chaplains, shall have the right to deal with the competent authorities of the camp on all questions relating to their duties. Such authorities shall afford them all necessary facilities for correspondence relating to these questions.

(c) Although they shall be subject to the internal discipline of the camp in which they are retained, such personnel may not be compelled to carry out any work other than that concerned with their medical or religious duties.

. . .

RELIGIOUS, INTELLECTUAL AND PHYSICAL ACTIVITIES

Article 34. Prisoners of war shall enjoy complete latitude in the exercise of their religious duties, including attendance at the service of their faith, on condition that they comply with the disciplinary routine prescribed by the military authorities.

Adequate premises shall be provided where religious services may be held.

Article 35. Chaplains who fall into the hands of the enemy Power and who remain or are retained with a view to assisting prisoners of war, shall be allowed to minister to them and to exercise freely their ministry amongst prisoners of war of the same religion, in accordance with their religious conscience. They shall be allocated among the various camps and labour detachments containing prisoners of war belonging to the same forces, speaking the same language or practising the same religion. They shall enjoy the necessary facilities, including the means of transport provided for in Article 33, for visiting the prisoners of war outside their camp . . . .

Article 36. Prisoners of war who are ministers of religion, without having officiated as chaplains to their own forces, shall be at liberty, whatever their denomination, to minister freely to the members of their community. For this purpose, they shall receive the same treatment as the chaplains retained by the Detaining Power. They shall not be obliged to do any other work.

. . .

DISCIPLINE

Article 39. Every prisoner of war camp shall be put under the immediate authority of a responsible commissioned officer belonging to the regular armed forces of the Detaining Power. Such officer shall have in his possession a copy of the present Convention; he shall ensure that its provisions are known to the camp staff and the guard and shall be responsible, under the direction of his government, for its application.

Prisoners of war, with the exception of officers, must salute and show to all officers of the Detaining Power the external marks of respect provided for by the regulations applying in their own forces.

Officer prisoners of war are bound to salute only officers of a higher rank of the Detaining Power; they must, however, salute the camp commander regardless of his rank.

Article 40. The wearing of badges of rank and nationality, as well as of decorations, shall be permitted.

Article 41. In every camp the text of the present Convention and its Annexes and the contents of any special agreement provided for in Article 6, shall be posted, in the prisoners' own language in places where all may read them. Copies shall be supplied, on request, to the prisoners who cannot have access to the copy which has been posted.

Regulations, orders, notices and publications of every kind relating to the conduct of prisoners of war shall be issued to them in a language which they understand. Such regulations, orders and publications shall be posted in the manner described above and copies shall be handed to the prisoners' representative. Every order and command addressed to prisoners of war individually must likewise be given in a language which they understand.

Article 42. The use of weapons against prisoners of war, especially against those who are escaping or attempting to escape, shall constitute an extreme measure, which shall always be preceded by warnings appropriate to the circumstances.

. . .

RANK OF PRISONERS OF WAR

Article 43. Upon the outbreak of hostilities, the Parties to the conflict shall communicate to one another the titles and ranks of all the persons mentioned in Article 4 of the present Convention, in order to ensure equality of treatment between prisoners of equivalent rank. Titles and ranks which are subsequently created shall form the subject of similar communications.

The Detaining Power shall recognize promotions in rank which have been accorded to prisoners of war and which have been duly notified by the Power on which these prisoners depend.

Article 44. Officers and prisoners of equivalent status shall be treated with the regard due to their rank and age.

In order to ensure service in officers' camps, other ranks of the same armed forces who, as far as possible, speak the same language, shall be assigned in sufficient numbers, account being taken of the rank of officers and prisoners of equivalent status. Such orderlies shall not be required to perform any other work.

Supervision of the mess by the officers themselves shall be facilitated in every way.

Article 45. Prisoners of war other than officers and prisoners of equivalent status shall be treated with the regard due to their rank and age.

Supervision of the mess by the prisoners themselves shall be facilitated in every way.

. . . .

Article 47. Sick or wounded prisoners of war shall not be transferred as long as their recovery may be endangered by the journey, unless their safety imperatively demands it . . . .

LABOUR OF PRISONERS OF WAR

Article 49. The Detaining Power may utilize the labour of prisoners of war who are physically fit, taking into account their age, sex, rank and physical aptitude, and with a view particularly to maintaining them in a good state of physical and mental health.

Non-commissioned officers who are prisoners of war shall only be required to do supervisory work. Those not so required may ask for other suitable work which shall, so far as possible, be found for them.

If officers or persons of equivalent status ask for suitable work, it shall be found for them, so far as possible, but they may in no circumstances be compelled to work.

Article 50. Besides work connected with camp administration, installation or maintenance, prisoners of war may be compelled to do only such work as is included in the following classes:

(a) agriculture;
(b) industries connected with the production or the extraction of raw materials, and manufacturing industries, with the exception of met-

allurgical, machinery and chemical industries; public works and building operations which have no military character or purpose;

(c) transport and handling of stores which are not military in character or purpose;

(d) commercial business, and arts and crafts;

(e) domestic service;

(f) public utility services having no military character or purpose.

Should the above provisions be infringed, prisoners of war shall be allowed to exercise their right of complaint, in conformity with Article 78.

Article 51. Prisoners of war must be granted suitable working conditions, especially as regards accommodation, food, clothing and equipment; such conditions shall not be inferior to those enjoyed by nationals of the Detaining Power employed in similar work; account shall also be taken of climatic conditions.

The Detaining Power, in utilizing the labour of prisoners of war, shall ensure that in areas in which such prisoners are employed, the national legislation concerning the protection of labour, and, more particularly, the regulations for the safety of workers, are duly applied. . . .

Article 52. Unless he be a volunteer, no prisoner of war may be employed on labour which is of an unhealthy or dangerous nature.

No prisoner of war shall be assigned to labour which would be looked upon as humiliating for a member of the Detaining Power's own forces.

The removal of mines or similar devices shall be considered as dangerous labour.

Article 53. The duration of the daily labour of prisoners of war, including the time of the journey to and fro, shall not be excessive, and must in no case exceed that permitted for civilian workers in the district, who are nationals of the Detaining Power and employed on the same work.

Prisoners of war must be allowed, in the middle of the day's work, a rest of not less than one hour. This rest will be the same as that to which workers of the Detaining Power are entitled, if the latter is of longer duration. They shall be allowed in addition a rest of twenty-four consecutive hours every week, preferably on Sunday or the day of rest in their country of origin. Furthermore, every prisoner who has worked for one year shall be granted a rest of eight consecutive days, during which his working pay shall be paid him. . . .

Article 58. Upon the outbreak of hostilities, and pending an arrangement on this matter with the Protecting Power, the Detaining Power may determine the maximum amount of money in cash or in any similar form, that prisoners may have in their possession. Any amount in excess, which was properly in their possession and which has been taken or withheld from them, shall be placed to their account, together with any monies deposited by them, and shall not be converted into any other currency without their consent.

If prisoners of war are permitted to purchase services or commodities outside the camp against payment in cash, such payments shall be made by the prisoner himself or by the camp administration who will charge them to the accounts of the prisoners concerned. The Detaining Power will establish the necessary rules in this respect.

.   .   .

Article 60. The Detaining Power shall grant all prisoners of war a monthly advance of pay, the amount of which shall be fixed by conversion, into the currency of the said Power, of the following amounts:

Category I: Prisoners ranking below sergeants: eight Swiss francs.

Category II: Sergeants and other non-commissioned officers, or prisoners of equivalent rank: twelve Swiss francs.

Category III: Warrant officers and commissioned officers below the rank of major or prisoners of equivalent rank: fifty Swiss francs.

Category IV: Majors, lieutenant-colonels, colonels or prisoners of equivalent rank: sixty Swiss francs.

Category V: General officers or prisoners of war of equivalent rank: seventy-five Swiss francs.

However, the Parties to the conflict concerned may by special agreement modify the amount of advances of pay due to prisoners of the preceding categories. . . .

Article 61. The Detaining Power shall accept for distribution as supplementary pay to prisoners of war sums which the Power on which the prisoners depend may forward to them, on condition that the sums to be paid shall be the same for each prisoner of the same category, shall be payable to all prisoners of that category depending on that Power, and shall be placed in their separate accounts, at the earliest opportunity; . . . Such supplementary pay shall not relieve the Detaining Power of any obligation under this Convention.

Article 62. Prisoners of war shall be paid fair working rate of pay by the detaining authorities direct. The rate shall be fixed by the said authorities, but shall at no time be less than one-fourth of one Swiss franc for a full working day. The Detaining Power shall inform prisoners of war, as well as the Power on which they depend, through the intermediary of the Protecting Power, of the rate of daily working pay that it has fixed. . . .

Article 63. Prisoners of war shall be permitted to receive remittances of money addressed to them individually or collectively.

. . . .

Article 66. On the termination of captivity, through the release of a prisoner of war or his repatriation, the Detaining Power shall give him a statement, signed by an authorized officer of that Power, showing the credit balance then due to him. . . .

. . . .

RELATIONS OF PRISONERS OF WAR WITH THE EXTERIOR

Article 69. Immediately upon prisoners of war falling into its power, the Detaining Power shall inform them and the Powers on which they depend, through the Protecting Power, of the measures taken to carry out the provisions of the present Section. They shall likewise inform the parties concerned of any subsequent modifications of such measures.

Article 70. Immediately upon capture, or not more than one week after arrival at a camp, even if it is a transit camp, likewise in case of sickness or transfer to hospital or to another camp, every prisoner of war shall be enabled to write direct to his family, on the one hand, and to the Central Prisoners of War Agency provided for in Article 123, on the other hand, a card similar, if possible, to the model annexed to the present Convention, informing his relatives of his capture, address and state of health. The said cards shall be forwarded as rapidly as possible and may not be delayed in any manner.

Article 71. Prisoners of war shall be allowed to send and receive letters and cards. If the Detaining Power deems it necessary to limit the number of letters and cards sent by each prisoner of war, the said number shall not be less than two letters and four cards monthly, exclusive of the capture cards provided for in Article 70, and conforming as closely as possible to the models annexed to the present Convention. Further limitations may be imposed only if the Protecting Power is satisfied that it would be in the interests of the prisoners of war concerned to do so owing to difficulties of translation caused by the Detaining Power's inability to find sufficient qualified linguists to carry out the necessary censorship. If limitations must be placed on the correspondence addressed to prisoners of war, they may be ordered only by the Power on which the prisoners depend, possibly at the request of the Detaining Power. Such letters and cards must be conveyed by the most rapid method at the disposal of the Detaining Power; they may not be delayed or retained for disciplinary reasons.

Prisoners of war who have been without news for a long period, or who are unable to receive news from their next of kin or to give them news by the ordinary postal route, as well as those who are at a great distance from their homes, shall be permitted to send telegrams, the fees being charged against the prisoner of war's accounts with the Detaining Power or paid in the currency at their disposal. They shall likewise benefit by this measure in cases of urgency.

As a general rule, the correspondence of prisoners of war shall be written in their native language. The Parties to the conflict may allow correspondence in other languages. . . .

Article 72. Prisoners of war shall be allowed to receive by post or by any other means individual parcels or collective shipments containing, in particular, foodstuffs, clothing, medical supplies and articles of a religious, educational or recreational character which may meet their needs, including books, devotional articles, scientific equipment, examination papers, musical instruments, sports outfits and materials allowing prisoners of war to pursue their studies or their cultural activities.

Such shipments shall in no way free the Detaining Power from the obligations imposed upon it by virtue of the present Convention.

The only limits which may be placed on these shipments shall be those proposed by the Protecting Power in the interest of the prisoners themselves, or by the International Committee of the Red Cross or any other organization giving assistance to the prisoners, in respect of their own shipments only, on account of exceptional strain on transport or communications.

The conditions for the sending of individual parcels and collective relief shall, if necessary, be the subject of special agreements between the Powers concerned, which may in no case delay the receipt by the prisoners of relief supplies. Books may not be included in parcels of clothing and foodstuffs. Medical supplies shall, as a rule, be sent in collective parcels.

.   .   .

Article 74. All relief shipments for prisoners of war shall be exempt from import, customs and other dues.

Correspondence, relief shipments and authorized remittances of money addressed to prisoners of war or despatched by them through the post office, either direct or through the Information Bureaux provided for in Article 122 and the Central Prisoners of War Agency provided for in Article 123, shall be exempt from any postal dues, both in the countries of origin and destination, and in intermediate countries. . . .

Article 76. The censoring of correspondence addressed to prisoners of war or despatched by them shall be done as quickly as possible. Mail shall be censored only by the despatching State and the receiving State, and once only by each.

The examination of consignments intended for prisoners of war shall not be carried out under conditions that will expose the goods contained in them to deterioration; except in the case of written or printed matter, it shall be done in the presence of the addressee, or of a fellow-prisoner duly delegated by him. The delivery to prisoners of individual or collective consignments shall not be delayed under the pretext of difficulties of censorship.

Any prohibition of correspondence ordered by Parties to the conflict, either for military or political reasons, shall be only temporary and its duration shall be as short as possible. . . .

.   .   .

RELATIONS BETWEEN PRISONERS OF WAR AND THE AUTHORITIES

COMPLAINTS OF PRISONERS OF WAR RESPECTING THE CONDITIONS OF CAPTIVITY

Article 78. Prisoners of war shall have the right to make known to the military authorities in whose power they are, their requests regarding the conditions of captivity to which they are subjected.

They shall also have the unrestricted right to apply to the representatives of the Protecting Powers either through their prisoners' representative or, if they consider it necessary, direct, in order to draw their attention to any points on which they may have complaints to make regarding their conditions of captivity.

These requests and complaints shall not be limited nor considered to be a part of the correspondence quota referred to in Article 71. They must be transmitted immediately. Even if they are recognized to be unfounded, they may not give rise to any punishment.

Prisoners' representatives may send periodic reports on the situation in the camps and the needs of the prisoners of war to the representatives of the Protection Powers. ...

PRISONERS OF WAR REPRESENTATIVES

Article 79. In all places where there are prisoners of war, except in those where there are officers, the prisoners shall freely elect by secret ballot, every six months, and also in case of vacancies, prisoners' representatives entrusted with representing them before the military authorities, the Protecting Powers, the International Committee of the Red Cross and any other organization which may assist them. These prisoners' representatives shall be eligible for re-election.

In camps for officers and persons of equivalent status or in mixed camps, the senior officer among the prisoners of war shall be recognized as the camp prisoners' representative. In camps for officers, he shall be assisted by one or more advisers chosen by the officers; in mixed camps, his assistants shall be chosen from among the prisoners of war who are not officers and shall be elected by them.

Officer prisoners of war of the same nationality shall be stationed in labour camps for prisoners of war, for the purpose of carrying out the camp administration duties for which the prisoners of war are responsible. These officers may be elected as prisoners' representatives under the first paragraph of this Article. In such a case the assistants to the prisoners' representatives shall be chosen from among those prisoners of war who are not officers.

Every representative elected must be approved by the Detaining Power before he has the right to commence his duties. Where the Detaining Power refuses to approve a prisoner of war elected by his fellow prisoners of war, it must inform the Protecting Power of the reason for such refusal.

In all cases the prisoners' representative must have the same nationality, language and customs as the prisoners of war whom he represents. Thus, prisoners of war distributed in different sections of a camp, according to their nationality, language or customs, shall have for each section their own prisoners' representative, in accordance with the foregoing paragraphs.

Article 80. Prisoners' representatives shall further the physical, spiritual and intellectual well-being of prisoners of war.

In particular, where the prisoners decide to organize amongst themselves a system of mutual assistance, this organization will be within the province of the prisoners' representative, in addition to the special duties entrusted to him by other provisions of the present Convention.

Prisoners' representatives shall not be held responsible, simply by reason of their duties, for any offences committed by prisoners of war.

Article 81. Prisoners' representatives shall not be required to perform any other work, if the accomplishment of their duties is thereby made more difficult.

Prisoners' representatives may appoint from amongst the prisoners such assistants as they may require. All material facilities shall be granted them, particularly a certain freedom of movement necessary for the accomplishment of their duties (inspections of labour detachments, receipt of supplies, etc.).

Prisoners' representatives shall be permitted to visit premises where prisoners of war are detained, and every prisoner of war shall have the right to consult freely his prisoners' representative.

All facilities shall likewise be accorded to the prisoners' representatives for communication by post and telegraph with the detaining authorities, the Protecting Powers, the International Committee of the Red Cross and their delegates, the Mixed Medical Commissions and the bodies which give assistance to prisoners of war. Prisoners' representatives of labour detachments shall enjoy the same facilities for communication with the prisoners' representatives of the principal camp. Such communications shall not be restricted, nor considered as forming a part of the quota mentioned in Article 71.

Prisoners' representatives who are transferred shall be allowed a reasonable time to acquaint their successors with current affairs.

In case of dismissal, the reasons therefore shall be communicated to the Protecting Power.

. . . .

PENAL AND DISCIPLINARY SANCTIONS

I. GENERAL PROVISIONS

Article 82. A prisoner of war shall be subject to the laws, regulations and orders in force in the armed forces of the Detaining Power; the Detaining Power shall be justified in taking judicial or disciplinary measures in respect of any offence committed by a prisoner of war against such laws, regulations or orders. However, no proceedings or punishments contrary to the provisions of this Chapter shall be allowed.

If any law, regulation or order of the Detaining Power shall declare acts committed by a prisoner of war to be punishable, whereas the same acts would not be punishable if committed by a member of the forces of the Detaining Power, such acts shall entail disciplinary punishments only.

Article 83. In deciding whether proceedings in respect of an offence alleged to have been committed by a prisoner of war shall be judicial or disciplinary, the Detaining Power shall ensure that the competent authorities exercise the greatest leniency and adopt, wherever possible, disciplinary rather than judicial measures.

Article 84. A prisoner of war shall be tried only by a military court, unless the existing laws of the Detaining Power expressly permit the civil courts to try a member of the armed forces of the Detaining Power in respect of the particular offence alleged to have been committed by the prisoner of war.

In no circumstances whatever shall a prisoner of war be tried by a court of any kind which does not offer the essential guarantees of independence and impartiality as generally recognized, and, in particular, the procedure of which does not afford the accused the rights and means of defence provided for in Article 105.

Article 85. Prisoners of war prosecuted under the laws of the Detaining Power for acts committed prior to capture shall retain, even if convicted, the benefits of the present Convention.

Article 86. No prisoner of war may be punished more than once for the same act or on the same charge.

Article 87. Prisoners of war may not be sentenced by the military authorities and courts of the Detaining Power to any penalties except those provided for in respect of members of the armed forces of the said Power who have committed the same acts.

When fixing the penalty, the courts or authorities of the Detaining Power shall take into consideration, to the widest extent possible, the fact that the accused, not being a national of the Detaining Power, is not bound to it by any duty of allegiance, and that he is in its power as a result of circumstances independent of his own will. The said courts or authorities shall be at liberty to reduce the penalty provided for the violation of which the prisoner of war is accused, and shall therefore not be bound to apply the minimum penalty prescribed.

Collective punishment for individual acts, corporal punishment, imprisonment in premises without daylight and, in general, any form of torture or cruelty, are forbidden.

No prisoner of war may be deprived of his rank by the Detaining Power, or prevented from wearing his badges.

Article 88. Officers, non-commissioned officers and men who are prisoners of war undergoing a disciplinary or judicial punishment, shall not be subjected to more severe treatment than that applied in respect of the same punishment to members of the armed forces of the Detaining Power of equivalent rank.

A woman prisoner of war shall not be awarded or sentenced to a punishment more severe, or treated whilst undergoing punishment more severely, than a woman member of the armed forces of the Detaining Power dealt with for a similar offence.

In no case may a woman prisoner of war be awarded or sentenced to a punishment more severe, or treated whilst undergoing punishment more severely, than a male member of the armed forces of the Detaining Power dealt with for a similar offence.

Prisoners of war who have served disciplinary or judicial sentences may not be treated differently from other prisoners of war.

II. DISCIPLINARY SANCTIONS

Article 89. The disciplinary punishments applicable to prisoners of war are the following:

(1) A fine which shall not exceed 50 per cent of the advances of pay and working pay which the prisoner of war would otherwise receive under the provisions of Articles 60 and 62 during a period of not more than thirty days.

(2) Discontinuance of privileges granted over and above the treatment provided for by the present Convention.

(3) Fatigue duties not exceeding two hours daily.

(4) Confinement.

The punishment referred to under (3) shall not be applied to officers.

In no case shall disciplinary punishments be inhuman, brutal or dangerous to the health of prisoners of war.

Article 90. The duration of any single punishment shall in no case exceed thirty days. Any period of confinement awaiting the hearing of a disciplinary offence or the award of disciplinary punishment shall be deducted from an award pronounced against a prisoner of war.

The maximum of thirty days provided above may not be exceeded, even if the prisoner of war is answerable for several acts at the same time when he is awarded punishment, whether such acts are related or not.

The period between the pronouncing of an award of disciplinary punishment and its execution shall not exceed one month.

When a prisoner of war is awarded a further disciplinary punishment, a period of at least three days shall elapse between the execution of any two of the punishments, if the duration of one of these is ten days or more.

Article 91. The escape of a prisoner of war shall be deemed to have succeeded when:

(1) he has joined the armed forces of the Power on which he depends, or those of an allied Power;

(2) he has left the territory under the control of the Detaining Power, or of an ally of the said Power;

(3) he has joined a ship flying the flag of the Power on which he depends, or of an allied Power, in the territorial waters of the Detaining Power, the said ship not being under the control of the last named Power.

Prisoners of war wh[o] have made good their escape in the sense of this Article and who are recaptured, shall not be liable to any punishment in respect of their previous escape.

Article 92. A prisoner of war who attempts to escape and is recaptured before having made good his escape in the sense of Article 91 shall be liable only to a disciplinary punishment in respect of this act, even if it is a repeated offence.

A prisoner of war who is recaptured shall be handed over without delay to the competent military authority.

Article 88, fourth paragraph, notwithstanding, prisoners of war punished as a result of an unsuccessful escape may be subjected to special surveillance. Such surveillance must not affect the state of their health, must be undergone in a prisoner of war camp, and must not entail the suppression of any of the safeguards granted them by the present Convention.

Article 93. Escape or attempt to escape, even if it is a repeated offence, shall not be deemed an aggravating circumstance if the prisoner of war is subjected to trial by judicial proceedings in respect of an offence committed during his escape or attempt to escape.

In conformity with the principle stated in Article 83, offences committed by prisoners of war with the sole intention of facilitating their escape and which do not entail any violence against life or limb, such as offences against public property, theft without intention of self-enrichment, the drawing up or use of false papers, or the wearing of civilian clothing, shall occasion disciplinary punishment only.

Prisoners of war who aid or abet an escape or an attempt to escape shall be liable on this count to disciplinary punishment only.

Article 94. If an escaped prisoner of war is recaptured, the Power on which he depends shall be notified thereof in the manner defined in Article 122, provided notification of his escape has been made.

Article 95. A prisoner of war accused of an offence against discipline shall not be kept in confinement pending the hearing unless a member of the armed forces of the Detaining Power would be so kept if he were accused of a similar offence, or if it is essential in the interests of camp order and discipline.

Any period spent by a prisoner of war in confinement awaiting the disposal of an offence against discipline shall be reduced to an absolute minimum and shall not exceed fourteen days.

The provisions of Articles 97 and 98 of this Chapter shall apply to prisoners of war who are in confinement awaiting the disposal of offences against discipline.

Article 96. Acts which constitute offences against discipline shall be investigated immediately.

Without prejudice to the competence of courts and superior military authorities, disciplinary punishment may be ordered only by an officer having disciplinary powers in his capacity as camp commander, or by a responsible officer who replaces him or to whom he has delegated his disciplinary powers.

In no case may such powers be delegated to a prisoner of war or be exercised by a prisoner of war.

Before any disciplinary award is pronounced, the accused shall be given precise information regarding the offences of which he is accused, and given an opportunity of explaining his conduct and of defending himself. He shall be permitted, in particular, to call witnesses and to have recourse, if necessary, to the services of a qualified interpreter. The decision shall be announced to the accused prisoner of war and to the prisoners' representative.

A record of disciplinary punishments shall be maintained by the camp commander and shall be open to inspection by representatives of the Protecting Power.

Article 97. Prisoners of war shall not in any case be transferred to penitentiary establishments (prisons, penitentiaries, convict prisons, etc.) to undergo disciplinary punishment therein.

All premises in which disciplinary punishments are undergone shall conform to the sanitary requirements set forth in Article 25. A prisoner of war undergoing punishment shall be enabled to keep himself in a state of cleanliness, in conformity with Article 29.

Officers and persons of equivalent status shall not be lodged in the same quarters as non-commissioned officers or men.

Women prisoners of war undergoing disciplinary punishment shall be confined in separate quarters from male prisoners of war and shall be under the immediate supervision of women.

Article 98. A prisoner of war undergoing confinement as a disciplinary punishment, shall continue to enjoy the benefits of the provisions of this Convention except in so far as these are necessarily rendered inapplicable by the mere fact that he is confined. In no case may he be deprived of the benefits of the provisions of Articles 78 and 126.

A prisoner of war awarded disciplinary punishment may not be deprived of the prerogatives attached to his rank.

Prisoners of war awarded disciplinary punishment shall be allowed to exercise and to stay in the open air at least two hours daily.

They shall be allowed, on their request, to be present at the daily medical inspections. They shall receive the attention which their state of health requires and, if necessary, shall be removed to the camp infirmary or to a hospital.

They shall have permission to read and write, likewise to send and receive letters. Parcels and remittances of money however, may be withheld from them until the completion of the punishment; they shall meanwhile be entrusted to the prisoners' representative, who will hand over to the infirmary the perishable goods contained in such parcels.

Article 99. No prisoner of war may be tried or sentenced for an act which is not forbidden by the law of the Detaining Power or by International Law, in force at the time the said act was committed.

No moral or physical coercion may be exerted on a prisoner of war in order to induce him to admit himself guilty of the act of which he is accused.

No prisoner of war may be convicted without having had an opportunity to present his defence and the assistance of a qualified advocate or counsel.

Article 100. Prisoners of war and the Protecting Powers shall be informed as soon as possible of the offences which are punishable by the death sentence under the laws of the Detaining Power.

Other offences shall not thereafter be made punishable by the death penalty without the concurrence of the Power on which the prisoners of war depend.

The death sentence cannot be pronounced on a prisoner of war unless the attention of the court has, in accordance with Article 87, second paragraph, been particularly called to the fact that since the accused is not a national of the Detaining Power, he is not bound to it by any duty of allegiance, and that he is in its power as the result of circumstances independent of his own will.

Article 101. If the death penalty is pronounced on a prisoner of war, the sentence shall not be executed before the expiration of a period of at least six months from the date when the Protecting Power receives, at an indicated address, the detailed communication provided for in Article 107.

Article 102. A prisoner of war can be validly sentenced only if the sentence has been pronounced by the same courts according to the same procedure as in the case of members of the armed forces of the Detaining Power, and if, furthermore, the provisions of the present Chapter have been observed.

Article 103. Judicial investigations relating to a prisoner of war shall be conducted as rapidly as circumstances permit and so that his trial shall take place as soon as possible. A prisoner of war shall not be confined while awaiting trial unless a member of the armed forces of the Detaining Power would be so confined if he were accused of a similar offence, or if it is essential to do so in the interests of national security. In no circumstances shall this confinement exceed three months.

Any period spent by a prisoner of war in confinement awaiting trial shall be deducted from any sentence of imprisonment passed upon him and taken into account in fixing any penalty.

The provisions of Articles 97 and 98 of this Chapter shall apply to a prisoner of war whilst in confinement awaiting trial.

Article 104. In any case in which the Detaining Power has decided to institute judicial proceedings against a prisoner of war, it shall notify the Protecting Power as soon as possible and at least three weeks before the opening of the trial. This period of three weeks shall run as from the day on which such notification reaches the Protecting Power at the address previously indicated by the latter to the Detaining Power.

The said notification shall contain the following information:

(1) Surname and first names of the prisoner of war, his rank, his army, regimental, personal or serial number, his date of birth, and his profession or trade, if any;

(2) Place of internment or confinement;

(3) Specification of the charge or charges on which the prisoner of war is to be arraigned, giving the legal provisions applicable;

(4) Designation of the court which will try the case, likewise the date and place fixed for the opening of the trial.

The same communication shall be made by the Detaining Power to the prisoners' representative.

If no evidence is submitted, at the opening of a trial, that the notification referred to above was received by the Protecting Power, by the prisoner of war and by the prisoners' representative concerned, at least three weeks before the opening of the trial, then the latter cannot take place and must be adjourned.

Article 105. The prisoner of war shall be entitled to assistance by one of his prisoner comrades, to defence by a qualified advocate or counsel of his own choice, to the calling of witnesses and, if he deems necessary, to the services of a competent interpreter. He shall be advised of these rights by the Detaining Power in due time before the trial.

Failing a choice by the prisoner of war, the protecting Power shall find him an advocate or counsel, and shall have at least one week at its disposal for the purpose. The Detaining Power shall deliver to the said Power, on request, a list of persons qualified to present the defence. Failing a choice of an advocate or counsel by the prisoner of war or the Protecting Power, the Detaining Power shall appoint a competent advocate or counsel to conduct the defence.

The advocate or counsel conducting the defence on behalf of the prisoner of war shall have at his disposal a period of two weeks at least before the opening of the trial, as well as the necessary facilities to prepare the defence of the accused. He may, in particular, freely visit the accused and interview him in private. He may also confer with any witnesses for the defence, including prisoners of war. He shall have the benefit of these facilities until the term of appeal or petition has expired.

Particulars of the charge or charges on which the prisoner of war is to be arraigned, as well as the documents which are generally communicated to the accused by virtue of the laws in force in the armed forces of the Detaining Power, shall be communicated to the accused prisoner of war in a language which he understands, and in good time before the opening of the trial. The same communication in the same circumstances shall be made to the advocate or counsel conducting the defence on behalf of the prisoner of war.

The representatives of the Protecting Power shall be entitled to attend the trial of the case, unless, exceptionally, this is held *in camera* in the interest of State security. In such a case the Detaining Power shall advise the Protecting Power accordingly.

Article 106. Every prisoner of war shall have, in the same manner as the members of the armed forces of the Detaining Power, the right of appeal or petition from any sentence pronounced upon him, with a view to the quashing or revising of the sentence or the re-opening of the trial. He shall be fully informed of his right to appeal or petition and of the time limit within which he may do so.

Article 107. Any judgment and sentence pronounced upon a prisoner of war shall be immediately reported to the Protecting Power in the form of a summary communication, which shall also indicate whether he has the right of appeal with a view to the quashing of the sentence or the reopening of the trial. This communication shall likewise be sent to the prisoners' representative concerned. It shall also be sent to the accused prisoner of war in a language he understands, if the sentence was not pronounced in his presence. The Detaining Power shall also immediately communicate to the Protecting Power the decision of the prisoner of war to use or to waive his right of appeal.

Furthermore, if a prisoner of war is finally convicted or if a sentence pronounced on a prisoner of war in the first instance is a death sentence, the Detaining Power shall as soon as possible address to the Protecting Power a detailed communication containing:

(1) the precise wording of the finding and sentence;
(2) a summarized report of any preliminary investigation and of the trial, emphasizing in particular the elements of the prosecution and the defence;
(3) notification, where applicable, of the establishment where the sentence will be served.

The communications provided for in the foregoing sub-paragraphs shall be sent to the Protecting Power at the address previously made known to the Detaining Power.

Article 108. Sentences pronounced on prisoners of war after a conviction has become duly enforceable, shall be served in the same establishments and under the same conditions as in the case of members of the armed forces of the Detaining Power. These conditions shall in all cases conform to the requirements of health and humanity.

A woman prisoner of war on whom such a sentence has been pronounced shall be confined in separate quarters and shall be under the supervision of women.

In any case, prisoners of war sentenced to a penalty depriving them of their liberty shall retain the benefit of the provisions of Articles 78 and 126 of the present Convention. Furthermore, they shall be entitled to receive and despatch correspondence, to receive at least one relief parcel monthly, to take regular exercise in the open air, to have the medical care required by their state of health, and the spiritual assistance they may desire. Penalties to which they may be subjected shall be in accordance with the provisions of Article 87, third paragraph.

PART IV
TERMINATION OF CAPTIVITY

SECTION I
DIRECT REPATRIATION AND ACCOMMODATION IN NEUTRAL COUNTRIES

Article 109. Subject to the provisions of the third paragraph of this Article, Parties to the conflict are bound to send back to their own country, regardless of number or rank, seriously wounded and seriously sick prisoners of war, after having cared for them until they are fit to travel, in accordance with the first paragraph of the following Article.

Throughout the duration of hostilities, Parties to the conflict shall endeavour, with the cooperation of the neutral Powers concerned, to make arrangements for the accommodation in neutral countries of the sick and wounded prisoners of war referred to in the second paragraph of the following Article. They may, in addition, conclude agreements with a view to the direct repatriation or internment in a neutral country of able-bodied prisoners of war who have undergone a long period of captivity.

No sick or injured prisoner of war who is eligible for repatriation under the first paragraph of this Article, may be repatriated against his will during hostilities.

Article 110. The following shall be repatriated direct:

(1) Incurably wounded and sick whose mental or physical fitness seems to have been gravely diminished.

(2) Wounded and sick who, according to medical opinion, are not likely to recover within one year, whose condition requires treatment and whose mental or physical fitness seems to have been gravely diminished.

(3) Wounded and sick who have recovered, but whose mental or physical fitness seems to have gravely and permanently diminished.

The following may be accommodated in a neutral country:

(1) Wounded and sick whose recovery may be expected within one year of the date of the wound or the beginning of the illness, if treatment in a neutral country might increase the prospects of a more certain and speedy recovery.

(2) Prisoners of war whose mental or physical health, according to medical opinion, is seriously threatened by continued captivity, but whose accommodation in a neutral country might remove such a threat.

The conditions which prisoners of war accommodated in a neutral country must fulfil in order to permit their repatriation shall be fixed, as shall likewise their status, by agreement between the Powers concerned. In general, prisoners of war who have been accommodated in a neutral country, and who belong to the following categories, should be repatriated:

(1) Those whose state of health has deteriorated so as to fulfil the conditions laid down for direct repatriation;

(2) Those whose mental or physical powers remain, even after treatment, considerably impaired.

If no special agreements are concluded between the Parties to the conflict concerned, to determine the cases of disablement or sickness entailing direct repatriation or accommodation in a neutral country, such cases shall be settled in accordance with the principles laid down in the Model Agreement concerning direct repatriation and accommodation in neutral countries of wounded and sick prisoners of war and in the Regulations concerning Mixed Medical Commissions annexed to the present Convention.

Article 111. The Detaining Power, the Power on which the prisoners of war depend, and a neutral Power agreed upon by these two Powers, shall endeavour to conclude agreements which will enable prisoners of war to be interned in the territory of the said neutral Power until the close of hostilities.

Article 112. Upon the outbreak of hostilities, Mixed Medical Commissions shall be appointed to examine sick and wounded prisoners of war, and to make all appropriate decisions regarding them. The appointment, duties and functioning of these Commissions shall be in conformity with the provisions of the Regulations annexed to the present Convention.

However, prisoners of war who, in the opinion of the medical authorities of the Detaining Power, are manifestly seriously injured or seriously sick, may be repatriated without having to be examined by a Mixed Medical Commission.

Article 113. Besides those who are designated by the medical authorities of the Detaining Power, wounded or sick prisoners of war belonging to the categories listed below shall be entitled to present themselves for examination by the Mixed Medical Commissions provided for in the foregoing Article:

(1) Wounded and sick proposed by a physician or surgeon who is of the same nationality, or a national of a Party to the conflict allied with the Power on which the said prisoners depend, and who exercises his functions in the camp.

(2) Wounded and sick proposed by their prisoners' representative.

(3) Wounded and sick proposed by the Power on which they depend, or by an organization duly recognized by the said Power and giving assistance to the prisoners.

Prisoners of war who do not belong to one of the three foregoing categories may nevertheless present themselves for examination by Mixed Medical Commissions, but shall be examined only after those belonging to the said categories.

The physician or surgeon of the same nationality as the prisoners who present themselves for examination by the Mixed Medical Commission, likewise the prisoners' representative of the said prisoners, shall have permission to be present at the examination.

Article 114. Prisoners of war who meet with accidents shall, unless the injury is self-inflicted, have the benefit of the provisions of this Convention as regards repatriation or accommodation in a neutral country.

Article 115. No prisoner of war on whom a disciplinary punishment has been imposed and who is eligible for repatriation or for accommodation in a neutral country, may be kept back on the plea that he has not undergone his punishment.

Prisoners of war detained in connection with a judicial prosecution or conviction and who are designated for repatriation or accommodation in a neutral country, may benefit by such measures before the end of the proceedings or the completion of the punishment, if the Detaining Power consents.

Parties to the conflict shall communicate to each other the names of those who will be detained until the end of the proceedings or the completion of the punishment.

Article 116. The costs of repatriating prisoners of war or of transporting them to a neutral country shall be borne, from the frontiers of the Detaining Power, by the Power on which the said prisoners depend.

Article 117. No repatriated person may be employed on active military service.

· · ·

RELEASE AND REPATRIATION OF PRISONERS OF WAR AT THE CLOSE OF HOSTILITIES

Article 118. Prisoners of war shall be released and repatriated without delay after the cessation of active hostilities.

In the absence of stipulations to the above effect in any agreement concluded between the Parties to the conflict with a view to the cessation of hostilities, or failing any such agreement, each of the Detaining Powers shall itself establish and execute without delay a plan of repatriation in conformity with the principle laid down in the foregoing paragraph.

In either case, the measures adopted shall be brought to the knowledge of the prisoners of war.

The costs of repatriation of prisoners of war shall in all cases be equitably apportioned between the Detaining Power and the Power on which the prisoners depend. This apportionment shall be carried out on the following basis:

(a) If the two Powers are contiguous, the Power on which the prisoners of war depend shall bear the costs of repatriation from the frontiers of the Detaining Power.

(b) If the two Powers are not contiguous, the Detaining Power shall bear the costs of transport of prisoners of war over its own territory as far as its frontier or its port of embarkation nearest to the territory of the Power on which the prisoners of war depend. The Parties concerned shall agree between themselves as to the equitable apportionment of the remaining costs of the repatriation. The conclusion of this agreement shall in no circumstances justify any delay in the repatriation of the prisoners of war.

Article 119. Repatriation shall be effected in conditions similar to those laid down in [. . .] the present Convention for the transfer of prisoners of war, having regard to the provisions of Article 118 and to those of the following paragraphs.

On repatriation, any articles of value impounded from prisoners of war under Article 18, and any foreign currency which has not been converted into the currency of the Detaining Power, shall be restored to them. Articles of value and foreign currency which, for any reason whatever, are not restored to prisoners of war on repatriation, shall be despatched to the Information Bureau set up under Article 122.

Prisoners of war shall be allowed to take with them their personal effects, and any correspondence and parcels which have arrived for them. The weight of such baggage may be limited, if the conditions of repatriation so require, to what each prisoner can reasonably carry. Each prisoner shall in all cases be authorized to carry at least twenty-five kilogrammes.

The other personal effects of the repatriated prisoner shall be left in the charge of the Detaining Power which shall have them forwarded to him as soon as it has concluded an agreement to this effect, regulating the conditions of transport and the payment of the costs involved, with the Power on which the prisoner depends.

Prisoners of war against whom criminal proceedings for an indictable offence are pending may be detained until the end of such proceedings, and, if necessary, until the completion of the punishment. The same shall apply to prisoners of war already convicted for an indictable offence.

Parties to the conflict shall communicate to each other the names of any prisoners of war who are detained until the end of the proceedings or until punishment has been completed.

By agreement between the Parties to the conflict, commissions shall be established for the purpose of searching for dispersed prisoners of war and of assuring their repatriation with the least possible delay.

. . .

DEATH OF PRISONERS OF WAR

Article 120. Wills of prisoners of war shall be drawn up so as to satisfy the conditions of validity required by the legislation of their country of origin, which will take steps to inform the Detaining Power of its requirements in this respect. At the request of the prisoner of war and, in all cases, after death, the will shall be transmitted without delay to the Protecting Power; a certified copy shall be sent to the Central Agency.

Death certificates, in the form annexed to the present Convention, or lists certified by a responsible officer, of all persons who die as prisoners of war shall be forwarded as rapidly as possible to the Prisoner of War Information Bureau established in accordance with Article 122. The death certificates or certified lists shall show particulars of identity as set out in the third paragraph of Article 17, and also the date and place of death, the cause of death, the date and place of burial and all particulars necessary to identify the graves.

The burial or cremation of a prisoner of war shall be preceded by a medical examination of the body with a view to confirming death and enabling a report to be made and, where necessary, establishing identity.

The detaining authorities shall ensure that prisoners of war who have died in captivity are honourably buried, if possible according to the rites of the religion to which they belonged, and that their graves are respected, suitably maintained and marked so as to be found at any time. Wherever possible, deceased prisoners of war who depended on the same Power shall be interred in the same place.

Deceased prisoners of war shall be buried in individual graves unless unavoidable circumstances require the use of collective graves. Bodies may be cremated only for imperative reasons of hygiene, on account of the religion of the deceased or in accordance with his express wish to this effect. In case of cremation, the fact shall be stated and the reasons given in the death certificate of the deceased.

In order that graves may always be found, all particulars of burials and graves shall be recorded with a Graves Registration Service established by the Detaining Power. Lists of graves and particulars of the prisoners of war interred in cemeteries and elsewhere shall be transmitted to the Power on which such prisoners of war depended. Responsibility for the care of these graves and for records of any subsequent moves of the bodies shall rest on the Power controlling the territory, if a Party to the present Convention. These provisions shall also apply to the ashes, which shall be kept by the Graves Registration Service until proper disposal thereof in accordance with the wishes of the home country.

Article 121. Every death or serious injury of a prisoner of war caused or suspected to have been caused by a sentry, another prisoner of war, or any other person, as well as any death the cause of which is unknown, shall be immediately followed by an official enquiry by the Detaining Power.

A communication on this subject shall be sent immediately to the Protecting Power. Statements shall be taken from witnesses, especially from those who are prisoners of war, and a report including such statements shall be forwarded to the Protecting Power.

If the enquiry indicates the guilt of one or more persons, the Detaining Power shall take all measures for the prosecution of the person or persons responsible.

.   .   .

INFORMATION BUREAUX AND RELIEF SOCIETIES FOR PRISONERS OF WAR

Article 122. Upon the outbreak of a conflict and in all cases of occupation, each of the Parties to the conflict shall institute an official Information Bureau for prisoners of war who are in its power. Neutral or non-belligerent Powers who may have received within their territory persons belonging to one of the categories referred to in Article 4, shall take the same action with respect to such persons. The Power concerned shall ensure that the Prisoners of War Information Bureau is provided with the necessary accommodation, equipment and staff to ensure its efficient working. It shall be at liberty to employ prisoners of war in such a Bureau under the conditions laid down in the Section of the Present Convention dealing with work by prisoners of war.

Within the shortest possible period, each of the Parties to the conflict shall give its Bureau the information referred to in the fourth, fifth and sixth paragraphs of this Article regarding any enemy persons belonging to one of the categories referred to in Article 4, who has fallen into its power. Neutral or non-belligerent Powers shall take the same action with regard to persons belonging to such categories whom they have received within their territory.

The Bureau shall immediately forward such information by the most rapid means to the Powers concerned, through the intermediary of the Protecting Powers and likewise of the Central Agency provided for in Article 123.

This information shall make it possible quickly to advise the next of kin concerned. Subject to the provisions of Article 17, the information shall include, in so far as available to the Information Bureau, in respect of each prisoner of war, his surname, first names, rank, army, regimental, personal or serial number, place and full date of birth, indication of the Power on which he depends, first name of the father and maiden name of the mother, name and address of the person to be informed and the address to which correspondence for the prisoner may be sent.

The Information Bureau shall receive from the various departments concerned information regarding transfers, releases, repatriations, escapes, admissions to hospital, and deaths, and shall transmit such information in the manner described in the third paragraph above.

Likewise, information regarding the state of health of prisoners of war who are seriously ill or seriously wounded shall be supplied regularly, every week if possible.

The Information Bureau shall also be responsible for replying to all enquiries sent to it concerning prisoners of war, including those who have died in captivity; it will make any enquiries necessary to obtain the information which is asked for if this is not in its possession.

All written communications made by the Bureau shall be authenticated by a signature or a seal.

The Information Bureau shall furthermore be charged with collecting all personal valuables, including sums in currencies other than that of the Detaining Power and documents of importance to the next of kin, left by prisoners of war who have been repatriated or released, or who have escaped or died, and shall forward the said valuables to the Powers concerned. Such articles shall be sent by the Bureau in sealed packets which shall be accompanied by statements giving clear and full particulars of the identity of the person to whom the articles belonged, and by a complete list of the contents of the parcel. Other personal effects of such prisoners of war shall be transmitted under arrangements agreed upon between the Parties to the conflict concerned.

Article 123. A Central Prisoners of War Information Agency shall be created in a neutral country. The International Committee of the Red Cross shall, if it deems necessary, propose to the Powers concerned the organization of such an Agency.

The function of the Agency shall be to collect all the information it may obtain through official or private channels respecting prisoners of war, and to transmit it as rapidly as possible to the country of origin of the prisoners of war or to the Power on which they depend. It shall receive from the Parties to the conflict all facilities for effecting such transmissions.

The High Contracting Parties, and in particular those whose nationals benefit by the services of the Central Agency, are requested to give the said Agency the financial aid it may require.

The foregoing provisions shall in no way be interpreted as restricting the humanitarian activities of the International Committee of the Red Cross, or of the relief societies provided for in Article 125.

Article 124. The national Information Bureaux and the Central Information Agency shall enjoy free postage for mail, likewise all the exemptions provided for in Article 74, and further, so far as possible, exemption from telegraphic charges or, at least, greatly reduced rates.

Article 125. Subject to the measures which the Detaining Powers may consider essential to ensure their security or to meet any other reasonable need, the representatives of religious organizations, relief societies, or any other organization assisting prisoners of war, shall receive from the said Powers, for themselves and their duly accredited agents, all necessary facilities for visiting the prisoners, for distributing relief supplies and material, from any source, intended for religious, educational or recreative purposes, and for assisting them in organizing their leisure time within the camps. Such societies or organizations may be constituted in the territory of the Detaining Power or in any other country, or they may have an international character.

The Detaining Power may limit the number of societies and organizations whose delegates are allowed to carry out their activities in its territory and under its supervision, on condition, however, that such limitation shall not hinder the effective operation of adequate relief to all prisoners of war.

The special position of the International Committee of the Red Cross in this field shall be recognized and respected at all times.

As soon as relief supplies or material intended for the above-mentioned purposes are handed over to prisoners of war, or very shortly afterwards, receipts for each consignment, signed by the prisoners' representative, shall be forwarded to the relief society or organization making the shipment. At the same time, receipts for these consignments shall be supplied by the administrative authorities responsible for guarding the prisoners.

. . .

Article 126. Representatives or delegates of the Protecting Powers shall have permission to go to all places where prisoners of war may be, particularly to places of internment, imprisonment and labour, and shall have access to all premises occupied by prisoners of war; they shall also be allowed to go to the places of departure, passage and arrival of prisoners who are being transferred. They shall be able to interview the prisoners, and in particular the prisoners' representatives, without witnesses, either personally or through an interpreter.

Representatives and delegates of the Protecting Power shall have full liberty to select the places they wish to visit. The duration and frequency of these visits shall not be restricted. Visits may not be prohibited except for reasons of imperative military necessity, and then only as an exceptional and temporary measure.

The Detaining Power and the Power on which the said prisoners of war depend may agree, if necessary, that compatriots of these prisoners of war be permitted to participate in the visits.

The delegates of the International Committee of the Red Cross shall enjoy the same prerogatives. The appointment of such delegates shall be submitted to the approval of the Power detaining the prisoners of war to be visited.

Article 127. The High Contracting Parties undertake, in time of peace as in time of war, to disseminate the text of the present Convention as widely as possible in their respective countries, and, in particular, to include the study thereof in their programmes of military and, if possible, civil instruction, so that the principles thereof may become known to all their armed forces and to the entire population.

Any military or other authorities, who in time of war assume responsibilities in respect of prisoners of war, must possess the text of the Convention and be specially instructed as to its provisions.

Article 128. The High Contracting Parties shall communicate to one another through the Swiss Federal Council and, during hostilities, through the Protecting Powers, the official translations of the present Convention, as well as the laws and regulations which they may adopt to ensure the application thereof.

Article 129. The High Contracting Parties undertake to enact any legislation necessary to provide effective penal sanctions for persons committing, or ordering to be committed, any of the grave breaches of the present Convention defined in the following Article.

Each High Contracting Party shall be under the obligation to search for persons alleged to have committed, or to have ordered to be committed, such grave breaches, and shall bring such persons, regardless of their nationality, before its own courts. It may also, if it prefers, and in accordance with the provisions of its own legislation, hand such persons over for trial to another High Contracting Party concerned, provided such High Contracting Party has made out a *prima facie* case.

Each High Contracting Party shall take measures necessary for the suppression of all acts contrary to the provisions of the present Convention other than the grave breaches defined in the following Article.

In all circumstances, the accused persons shall benefit by safeguards of proper trial and defence, which shall not be less favourable than those provided by Article 105 and those following of the present Convention.

Article 130. Grave breaches to which the preceding Article relates shall be those involving any of the following act, if committed against persons or property protected by the Convention: wilful killing, torture or in-human treatment, including biological experiments, wilfully causing great suffering or serious injury to body or health, compelling a prisoner of war to serve in the forces of the hostile Power, or wilfully depriving a prisoner of war of the rights of fair and regular trial prescribed in this Convention.

Article 131. No High Contracting Party shall be allowed to absolve itself or any other High Contracting Party of any liability incurred by itself or by another High Contracting Party in respect of breaches referred to in the preceding Article.

Article 132. At the request of a Party to the conflict, an enquiry shall be instituted, in a manner to be decided between the interested Parties, concerning any alleged violation of the Convention.

If Agreement has not been reached concerning the procedure for the enquiry, the Parties should agree on the choice of an umpire who will decide upon the procedure to be followed.

Once the violation has been established, the Parties to the conflict shall put an end to it and shall repress it with the least possible delay.

.   .   .

Article 134. The Present Convention replaces the Convention of July 27, 1929, in relations between the High Contracting Parties.

Article 135. In the relations between the Powers which are bound by the Hague Convention respecting the Laws and Customs of War on Land, whether that of July 29, 1899, or that of October 18, 1907, and which are parties to the present Convention, this last Convention shall be complementary to Chapter II of the Regulations annexed to the above-mentioned Conventions of the Hague.

.   .   .

NOTE: Since 1954, when the Conventions went into force, the International Committee of the Red Cross has been engaged in numerous wars in which prisoners of war were taken. In a large number of cases, the belligerents did not allow ICRC representatives to visit POW camps. In other cases, serious restrictions on visits were imposed. Treatment of POWs in some modern wars has been barbaric.

The dynamic that enforces this part of the law of war is complex but often effective. In 1991, when Saddam Hussein paraded captured American flyers before television cameras and forced some of the POWs, who then appeared to have been maltreated, to make statements, the international condemnation was sufficiently strong to lead the Iraqi government to change its policy and to assure the world that it would not continue the practice. Journalistic accounts and then public protest of harsh POW treatment in the wars in the former Yugoslavia led to some amelioration. Alas, in wars in which the indignation of public opinion could not be engaged or sustained, for example, the Iran-Iraq War, the poor treatment of POWs was unrelieved.

A federal district court recently had occasion, in the context of the criminal charges brought by the United States against General Manuel Noriega, to consider certain provisions of the Geneva Convention relative to the Treatment of Prisoners of War. The court held, among other things, that General Noriega is a prisoner of war, and, in so holding, provided an informative overview of the Convention.

[808 F.Supp. 791 (S.D. Fla. 1992)]

.   .   .

Because of the unique nature of this case and the presence of important questions of international law, the Court afforded the parties an opportunity to file post-sentencing memoranda. Having considered the memoranda submitted, the argument of counsel, and all other materials relevant to this inquiry, the Court has concluded that it lacks the authority to order the Bureau of Prisons ("BOP") to place General Noriega in any particular facility. However, as with all sentencing proceedings, it is clearly the right—and perhaps the duty—of this Court to make a recommendation that the BOP place Noriega in a facility or type of facility the Court finds most appropriate given the circumstances of the case. The Court takes this responsibility quite seriously, especially in the novel situation presented here where the defendant is both a convicted felon and a prisoner of war. This dual status implicates important and previously unaddressed questions of international law that the Court must explore if it hopes to make a fair and reasoned recommendation on the type of facility in which the General should serve his sentence.

II. APPLICABILITY OF GENEVA III

Before examining in detail the various provisions of Geneva III, the Court must address whether the treaty has any application to the case at bar. Geneva III is an international treaty designed to protect prisoners of war from inhumane treatment at the hands of their captors. Regardless of whether it is legally enforceable under the present circumstances, the treaty is undoubtedly a valid international agreement and "the law of the land" in the United States. As such, Geneva III applies to any POW captured and detained by the United States, and the U.S. government has—at minimum—an international obligation to uphold the treaty. In addition, this Court believes Geneva III is self-executing and provides General Noriega with a right of action in a U.S. court for violation of its provisions.

A. Noriega's Prisoner of War Status

The government has thus far obviated the need for a formal determination of General Noriega's status. On a number of occasions as the case developed, counsel for the government advised that General Noriega was being and would continue to be afforded all of the benefits of the Geneva Convention. At no time was it agreed that he was, in fact, a prisoner of war. [footnote omitted]

The government's position provides no assurances that the government will not at some point in the future decide that Noriega is *not* a POW, and therefore not entitled to the protections of Geneva III. [footnote omitted] This would seem to be just the type of situation Geneva III was designed to protect against. Because of the issues presented in connection with the General's further confinement and treatment, it seems appropriate—even necessary—to address the issue of Defendant's status. Articles 2, 4, and 5 of Geneva III establish the standard for determining who is a POW. Must this determination await some kind of formal complaint by Defendant or a lawsuit presented on his behalf? In view of the issues presently raised by Defendant, the Court thinks not.

> ARTICLE 2
> [T]he present Convention shall apply to all cases of declared war or of *any other armed conflict which may arise between two or more of the High Contracting Parties, even if the state of war is not recognized by one of them*. [Italics supplied by court.]
>
> The Convention shall also apply to all cases of partial or total occupation of the territory of a High Contracting Party . . .

The Convention applies to an incredibly broad spectrum of events. The government has characterized the deployment of U.S. Armed Forces to Panama on December 20, 1989 as the "hostilities" in Panama. . . . However the government wishes to label it, what occurred in late 1989–early 1990 was clearly an "armed conflict" within the meaning of Article 2. Armed troops intervened in a conflict between two parties to the treaty. While the text of Article 2 itself does not define "armed conflict," the Red Cross Commentary to the Geneva Conventions of 1949[3] states that:

> Any difference arising between two states and leading to the intervention of members of the armed forces is an armed conflict within the meaning of Article 2. . . . [in original] It makes no difference how long the conflict lasts, how much slaughter takes place, or

how numerous are the participating forces; it suffices for the armed forces of one Power to have captured adversaries falling within the scope of Article 4.

Commentary at 23 (footnote omitted).

In addition, the government has professed a policy of liberally interpreting Article 2:

> The United States is a firm supporter of the four Geneva Conventions of 1949 . . . [in original] As a nation, we have a strong desire to promote respect for the laws of armed conflict and to secure maximum legal protection for captured members of the U.S. Armed Forces. Consequently, the United States has a policy of applying the Geneva Conventions of 1949 whenever armed hostilities occur with regular foreign armed forces, even if arguments could be made that the threshold standards for the applicability of the Conventions contained in common Article 2 are not met. In this respect, we share the views of the International Committee of the Red Cross that Article 2 of the Conventions should be construed liberally.

Letter from the State Dept. to the Attorney General of the United States, Jan. 31, 1990 at 1–2.

ARTICLE 4

A. Prisoners of war, in the sense of the present Convention, are persons belonging to one of the following categories, who have fallen into the power of the enemy:

(1) Members of the armed forces of a Party to the conflict. . . . [in original]

Geneva III's definition of a POW is easily broad enough to encompass General Noriega. It is not disputed that he was the head of the PDF, and that he has "fallen into the power of the enemy." Subsection 3 of Article 4 states that captured military personnel are POWs even if they "profess allegiance to a government or an authority not recognized by the Detaining Power."

ARTICLE 5

The present Convention shall apply to the persons referred to in Article 4 from the time they fall into the power of the enemy and until their final release and repatriation.

> Should any doubt arise as to whether persons, having committed a belligerent act and having fallen into the hands of the enemy, belong to any of the categories enumerated in Article 4, such persons shall enjoy the protection of the present Convention until such time as their status has been determined by a competent tribunal.

An important issue raised by the last two words of Article 5 is, of course, what *is* a "competent tribunal"? . . .

During the Geneva III drafting process, the phrase "military tribunal" was considered in place of "competent tribunal." The drafter rejected this suggestion, however, feeling that "to bring a person before a military tribunal might have more serious consequences than a decision to deprive him of the benefits afforded by the Convention" *Commentary* at 77 (citing II-A Final Record of the Diplomatic Conference of Geneva of 1949, at 388). Clearly, there was concern on the part of the drafters that whatever entity was to make determinations about POW status would be fair, competent, and impartial.

. . . .

The Court does suggest that where the Court is properly presented with the problem it is, under the law, a "competent tribunal" which can decide the issue. With that in mind, the Court finds that General Noriega is in fact a prisoner of war as defined by Geneva III, and as such must be afforded the protections established by the treaty, regardless of the type of facility in which the Bureau of Prisons chooses to incarcerate him.

B. "Law of the Land"

The Geneva Convention applies to this case because it has been incorporated into the domestic law of the United States. A treaty becomes the "supreme law of the land" upon ratification by the United States Senate. U.S. Const. art. VI, cl. 2. Geneva III was ratified by a unanimous Senate vote on July 6, 1955. 101 Cong. Rec. 8537 (daily ed. July 6, 1955). Thus, Geneva III is a properly ratified treaty which the United States must uphold. The government acknowledges that Geneva III is "the law of the land," but questions whether that law is binding and enforceable in U.S. courts.

C. Enforcement

If the BOP fails to treat Noriega according to the standard established for prisoners of war in Geneva III, what can he do to force the government to comply with the mandates of the treaty?

1. Article 78 Right of Protest

There are potentially two enforcement avenues available to a POW who feels his rights under the Geneva Convention have been violated. The first is the right to complain about the conditions of confinement to the military authorities of the Detaining Power or to representatives of the Protecting Power or humanitarian organizations. This right is established in Article 78 of Geneva III, and cannot be renounced by the POW or revoked or unnecessarily limited by the Detaining Power. *See* Articles 5, 7, 78, 85.

> ARTICLE 78
>
> Prisoners of war shall have the right to make known to the military authorities in whose power they are, their requests regarding the conditions of captivity to which they are subjected.
>
> They shall also have the unrestricted right to apply to the representatives of the Protecting Powers either through their prisoners' representative or, if they consider it necessary, direct, in order to draw their attention to any points on which they may have complaints to make regarding their conditions of captivity.

. . .

In theory, by calling attention to violations of the Convention the prisoner of war will embarrass the government into rectifying any unacceptable conditions to which he is being subjected. However, the obvious weakness of this complaint procedure is that it has no real teeth. Incentive for the government to comply with the treaty stems from its eagerness to be looked upon favorably by others, and, it is hoped, from its desire simply to do what is proper under the circumstances. However, if we truly believe in the goals of the Convention, a more substantial and dependable method must also be available, if necessary, to protect the POW's rights. Recourse to the courts of the Detaining Power seems an appropriate measure, where available.

2. Legal Action a [*sic*] in U.S. Court

A second method of enforcing the Convention would be a legal action in federal court. The government has maintained that if General Noriega feels that the conditions in any facility in which BOP imprisons him do not meet the Geneva III requirements, he can file a *habeas corpus* action under 28 U.S.C. § 2255. However, the government also argues that Geneva III is not self-executing, and thus does not provide an individual the right to bring an action in a U.S. court. Considered together, these two arguments lead to the conclusion that what the government is offering General Noriega is a hollow right. According to the government's position, Noriega could file a § 2255 claim, but any attempt to base it on violations of the Geneva Convention would be rejected because the General would not have standing to invoke the treaty.

The doctrine of self-execution has been called "one of the most confounding" issues in treaty law. . . . It is complex and not particularly well understood. . . . [G]iven the opportunity to address this issue in the context of a live controversy, the Court would almost certainly hold that the majority of provisions of Geneva III are, in fact, self-executing. [footnote omitted]

Essentially, a self-executing treaty is one that becomes domestic law of the signatory nation without implementing legislation, and provides a private right of action to individuals alleging a breach of its provisions. . . . Thus, even though Geneva III is undoubtedly "the law of the land," [it] is not necessarily binding on domestic courts if the treaty requires implementing legislation or does not provide an individual right of action. . . .

While the courts have generally presumed treaties to be nonself-executing in the absence of express language to the contrary, the Restatement would find treaties to be self-executing *unless* the agreement itself explicitly requires special implementing legislation, the Senate requires implementing legislation as a condition to ratification, or implementing legislation is constitutionally required. Restatement (Third) of Foreign Relations Law of the United States § 111(4)(1986). Most of the scholarly commentators agree, and make a compelling argument for finding treaties designed to protect individual rights, like Geneva III, to be self-executing. [footnote omitted]

.   .   .

Finally, the Court considered a number of other international treaties, and found that none were self-executing. . . . A determination that the U.N. Charter, the O.A.S. Charter, and the Hague Convention are not self-executing does not affect whether or not Geneva III is self-executing because the self-execution issue is individual to each treaty. The language of those other agreements is of a broad and general nature and is clearly not intended to impart on an individual the right to bring a legal action to force compliance with the treaty.

In the case of Geneva III, however, it is inconsistent with both the language and spirit of the treaty and with our professed support of its purpose to find that the rights established therein cannot be enforced by the individual POW in a court of law. After all, the ultimate goal of Geneva III is to ensure humane treatment of POWs—not to create some amorphous, unenforceable code of honor among the signatory nations. "It must not be forgotten that the Conventions have been drawn up first and foremost to protect individuals, and not to serve State interests." *Commentary* at 23.

The Court can envision numerous situations in which the Article 78 right of protest may not adequately protect a POW who is not being afforded all of the applicable safeguards of Geneva III. [footnote omitted] If in fact the United States holds Geneva III in the high regard that it claims, it must ensure that its provisions are enforceable by the POW entitled to its protections. Were this Court in a position to decide the matter, it would almost certainly find that Geneva III is self-executing and that general Noriega could invoke its provisions in a federal court action challenging the conditions of his confinement. Even if Geneva III is not self-executing, though, the United States is still obligated to honor its international commitment.

III. Controlling Provisions of Geneva III

The Court's final task is to determine which provisions of Geneva III are relevant to an individual who is both a prisoner of war and a convicted felon. . . .

The essential dispute between Noriega and the government is whether to rely on Articles 21 and 22 or on Article 108 in determining where to place the General. The defense argues that Articles 21 and 22, which explicitly prohibit placing POWs in penitentiaries, apply to General Noriega. The government contends that Article 108 controls, and allows the BOP to incarcerate a POW serving a criminal sentence anywhere U.S. military personnel convicted of similar offenses could be confined, including penitentiaries.

Some concern has been expressed about the potential inconsistency between these provisions. However, a careful reading of the various Articles in their proper context proves that no inconsistency exists. Simply stated, Articles 21 and 22 do not apply to POWs convicted of common crimes against the Detaining Power. The Convention clearly sets POWs convicted of crimes apart from other prisoners of war, making special provision for them in Articles 82–108 on "penal and disciplinary sanctions."

.   .   .

Articles 21 and 22 appear at the beginning of Chapter I—"General Observations"—of Section II—"Internment of Prisoners of War." This chapter of Geneva III deals with the internment of POWs who have not been convicted of crimes, and is thus inapplicable to General Noriega. Defendant's reliance on these Articles is misplaced; if anything, they make clear that POWs convicted of crimes are subject to a different set of rules than other prisoners of war. Article 22's general prohibition against internment of POWs in penitentiaries is limited by Article 21's acknowledgement that all general requirements regarding the treatment of POWs are "subject to the provisions of the present Convention relative to penal and disciplinary sanctions." This reference to Articles 82–108 shows that the Articles in Section II, Chapter I do *not* apply to POWs serving judicial sentences.

Further support for this argument is the use of the term "internment" throughout Section II, Chapter I, as opposed to the terms "detention," "confinement," or "imprisonment" used in the penal sanctions Articles. The Commentary elaborates on this point.

> The concept of internment should not be confused with that of detention. Internment involves the obligation not to leave the town, village, or piece of land, whether or not fenced in, on which the camp installations are situated, but it does not necessarily mean that a prisoner of war may be confined to a cell or room. *Such confinement may only be imposed in execution of penal or disciplinary sanctions, for which express provision is made in Section VI, Chapter III.*

Commentary at 178 . . . Thus, Article 22 prohibits *internment*—but not *imprisonment*—of POWs in penitentiaries.

For these reasons, it is the opinion of this Court that Articles 21 and 22 do not apply to General Noriega.

B. Article 108

The government has argued that the Geneva Convention "explicitly and unambiguously" authorizes the BOP to incarcerate Noriega in a penitentiary, so long as he is not treated more harshly than would be a member of the U.S. armed forces convicted of a similar offense.

Pursuant to 18 U.S.C. § 3231, federal district courts have concurrent jurisdiction with military courts over all violations of the laws of the United States committed by military personnel. *Noriega*, 746 F.Supp. at 1525. Ten U.S.C. § 814 and 32 CFR § 503.2(a) instruct the military authorities to deliver the alleged offender to the civil authorities for trial just like any other individual accused of a crime. Once that individual is convicted and sentenced by a civil court, he or she is also incarcerated in a civil facility, including a federal penitentiary, just like any other convicted criminal.

Paragraph one of Article 108 reads:

> Sentences announced on prisoners of war after a con-
> viction has become duly enforceable, shall be served in
> the same establishments and under the same conditions
> as in the case of members of the armed forces of the
> Detaining Power. These conditions shall in all cases con-
> form to the requirements of health and humanity.

Pursuant, then, to paragraph one it appears that General Noriega could technically be incarcerated in a federal penitentiary without violating the Geneva Convention. However, this should not be the end of the inquiry. The real issue is whether federal penitentiaries in general or any particular federal penitentiary can afford a prisoner of war the various protections due him under the Geneva Convention.[4]

Article 108 requires that the conditions in any facility in which a POW serves his sentence "shall in all cases conform to the requirements of health and humanity." Interpreting the language of these provisions is not always easy. The Commentary to Article 108 says reference should be made to Articles 25 and 29, [footnote omitted] which lay down minimum standards of accommodation for POWs. *Commentary* at 502.

.   .   .

This Court finds that, at a minimum, all of the Articles contained in Section I, General Provisions, should apply to General Noriega, as well as any provisions relating to health. By their own terms, Articles 82–88 (the General Provisions section of the Penal and Disciplinary Sanctions chapter) and 99–108 (Judicial Proceedings subsection) apply.

. . .

IV. CONCLUSION

. . . Noriega is plainly a prisoner of war under the Geneva Convention III. He is, and will be, entitled to the full range of rights under the treaty, which has been incorporated into U.S. law. Nonetheless, he can serve his sentence in a civilian prison to be designated by the Attorney General or the Bureau of Prisons (this is a pre-guidelines case) so long as he is afforded the full benefits of the Convention.

Whether or not those rights can be fully provided in a maximum security penitentiary setting is open to serious question. For the time being, however, that question must be answered by those who will determine Defendant's place and type of confinement. In this determination, those charged with that responsibility must keep in mind the importance to our own troops of faithful and, indeed, liberal adherence to the mandates of Geneva III. Regardless of how the government views the Defendant as a person, the implications of a failure to adhere to the Convention are too great to justify departures.

. . .

ENDNOTES

1. Howard S. Levie, *International Law Studies*, vol. 59: *Prisoners of War in International Armed Conflict* 5 (1977).
2. Article 122 of the Third Geneva Convention, which is set out at pp. 214–15, obliges each party to a conflict to establish a Prisoners of War Information Bureau and to give it information about every prisoner who comes under its control. The Bureau is then to forward that information to the other state. Article 16 of the First Geneva Convention refers to Article 122.
3. International Committee of the Red Cross, Commentary on the Geneva Conventions, (J. Pictet, ed., 1960) (hereinafter "Commentary"). While the Red Cross Commentary is not part of the treaty and is not binding law, it is widely recognized as a respected authority on interpretation of the Geneva Conventions. The authors of the Commentary were primarily individuals intimately involved with the revision of the Convention of 1929 and the drafting of the present Conventions. . . . [footnote 6 in original]

4. The government has argued that because all federal penal facilities must satisfy the Eighth Amendment prohibition on cruel and unusual punishment, any facility is at least theoretically "humane." This misses the point, however, that the Geneva III standard of humane treatment is not the same as the Constitutional standard embodied in the Eighth Amendment. The Eighth Amendment establishes a minimum level of treatment. As long as the BOP meets that minimum standard, it can operate within the confines of the Eighth Amendment. The Geneva Convention, on the other hand, delineates some fairly specific benefits for POWs which may not always be required by the Eighth Amendment. [footnote 15 in original]

BELLIGERENT OCCUPATION

5

In the course of a war, the military forces of one state may come into possession of some of the territory of another. As a matter of international law, that territory is deemed to continue to belong to the state that has been ousted, but it may be ruled by the occupiers under a special regime called "belligerent occupation." The law of belligerent occupation establishes the rights and duties of the occupier, the duties of the civilian population of the occupied lands, the limitations on exercises of power against the civilian population, and the continuing property rights of the ousted sovereign.

Like the law of war in general, belligerent occupation law is an application of the principles of necessity and proportionality. It acknowledges the needs of the belligerent occupant to maintain military efficiency and its own security while restricting the means of fulfilling those needs to tests of proportionality that benefit the civilian population of the territory. The law of belligerent occupation is a continuing exercise in finding an appropriate balance between these two competitive interests.

Situations of belligerent occupation have existed in the West Bank, the Gaza Strip, the Golan Heights, and Jerusalem since the Arab-Israeli War of 1967; in those areas held by Syrian forces in Lebanon; in Kuwait, as long as that country was held by Iraqi forces; in Grenada and Panama after the U.S. invasions; and also in those parts of Iraq subject to the control of the coalition forces at the time of the cease-fire. Thus the law of belligerent occupation is a frequently tested part of the modern law of war.

Not infrequently, a state that seizes control of territory it claims to have "liberated," and which it asserts always belonged to it, will insist that the law of belligerent occupation does not apply. Hence Israel resisted the notion that the law of belligerent occupation might be relevant to Jerusalem and also questions its application to the West Bank. Iraq did not apply the law of belligerent occupation to Kuwait, insisting that it was the nineteenth province of Iraq.

HAGUE CONVENTION (IV) RESPECTING THE LAWS AND CUSTOMS OF WAR ON LAND, ANNEX TO THE CONVENTION

[1 Bevans 631, signed on October 18, 1907, at The Hague]

. . .

MILITARY AUTHORITY OVER THE TERRITORY OF THE HOSTILE STATE

Article 42. Territory is considered occupied when it is actually placed under the authority of the hostile army.

The occupation extends only to the territory where such authority has been established and can be exercised.

Article 43. The authority of the legitimate power having in fact passed into the hands of the occupant, the latter shall take all the measures in his power to restore, and ensure, as far as possible, public order and safety, while respecting, unless absolutely prevented, the laws in force in the country.

Article 44. A belligerent is forbidden to force the inhabitants of territory occupied by it to furnish information about the army of the other belligerent, or about its means of defence.

Article 45. It is forbidden to compel the inhabitants of occupied territory to swear allegiance to the hostile Power.

Article 46. Family honour and rights, the lives of persons, and private

vate property, as well as religious convictions and practice, must be respected.

Private property cannot be confiscated.

Article 47. Pillage is formally forbidden.

. . .

Article 50. No general penalty, pecuniary or otherwise, shall be inflicted upon the population on account of the acts of individuals for which they cannot be regarded as jointly and severally responsible.

. . .

NOTE: The experience of Axis belligerent occupation during World War II made it clear that more precise standards and enforcement mechanisms were necessary for the security of civilians and their property in occupied territories. The Fourth Geneva Convention of 1949 is primarily concerned with this problem.

GENEVA CONVENTION (IV) RELATIVE TO THE PROTECTION OF CIVILIAN PERSONS IN TIME OF WAR

[6 U.S.T. 3516, signed on August 12, 1949, at Geneva]

. . .

PART I

. . .

Article 4. Persons protected by the Convention are those who, at a given moment and in any manner whatsoever, find themselves, in case of a conflict or occupation, in the hands of a Party to the conflict or Occupying Power of which they are not nationals.

Nationals of a State which is not bound by the Convention are not protected by it. Nationals of a neutral State who find themselves in the territory of a belligerent State, and nationals of a co-belligerent State, shall not be regarded as protected persons while the State of which they are nationals has normal diplomatic representation in the State in whose hands they are.

The provisions of Part II are, however, wider in application, as defined in Article 13.

Persons protected by the Geneva Convention for the Amelioration of the Condition of the Wounded and Sick in Armed Forces in the Field of August 12, 1949, or by the Geneva Convention for the Amelioration of the Condition of Wounded, Sick and Shipwrecked Members of Armed Forces at Sea of August 12, 1949, or by the Geneva Convention relative to the Treatment of Prisoners of War of August 12, 1949, shall not be considered as protected persons within the meaning of the present Convention.

Article 5. Where, in the territory of a Party to the conflict, the latter is satisfied that an individual protected person is definitely suspected of or engaged in activities hostile to the security of the State, such individual person shall not be entitled to claim such rights and privileges under the present Convention as would, if exercised in the favour of such individual person, be prejudicial to the security of such State.

Where in occupied territory an individual protected person is detained as a spy or saboteur, or as a person under definite suspicion of activity hostile to the security of the Occupying Power, such person shall, in those cases where absolute military security so requires, be regarded as having forfeited rights of communication under the present Convention.

In each case, such persons shall nevertheless be treated with humanity, and in case of trial, shall not be deprived of the rights of fair and regular trial prescribed by the present Convention. They shall also be granted the full rights and privileges of a protected person under the present Convention at the earliest date consistent with the security of the State or Occupying Power, as the case may be.

Article 6. The present Convention shall apply from the outset of any conflict or occupation mentioned in Article 2.[1]

In the territory of Parties to the conflict, the application of the present Convention shall cease on the general close of military operations.

In the case of occupied territory, the application of the present Convention shall cease one year after the general close of military operations; however, the Occupying Power shall be bound, for the duration of the occupation, to the extent that such Power exercises the functions of government in such territory, by the provisions of the following Articles of the present Convention: 1 to 12, 27, 29 to 34, 47, 49, 51, 52[,] 53, 59, 61 to 77, 143.

Protected persons whose release, repatriation or re-establishment may take place after such dates shall meanwhile continue to benefit by the present Convention.

Article 7. In addition to the agreements expressly provided for in Articles 11, 14, 15, 17, 36, 108, 109, 132, 133 and 149, the High Contracting Parties may conclude other special agreements for all matters concerning which they may deem it suitable to make separate provision. No special agreement shall adversely affect the situation of protected persons, as defined by the present Convention, nor restrict the rights which it confers upon them.

Protected persons shall continue to have the benefit of such agreements as long as the Convention is applicable to them, except where express provisions to the contrary are contained in the aforesaid or in subsequent agreements, or where more favourable measures have been taken with regard to them by one or other of the Parties to the conflict.

Article 8. Protected persons may in no circumstances renounce in part or in entirety the rights secured to them by the present Convention, and by the special agreements referred to in the foregoing Article, if such there be.

. . . .

PART II
GENERAL PROTECTION OF POPULATIONS AGAINST CERTAIN CONSEQUENCES OF WAR

Article 13. The provisions of Part II cover the whole of the populations of the countries in conflict, without any adverse distinction based, in particular, on race, nationality, religion or political opinion, and are intended to alleviate the sufferings caused by war.

Article 14. In time of peace, the High Contracting Parties and, after the outbreak of hostilities, the Parties thereto, may establish in their own territory and, if the need arises, in occupied areas, hospital and safety zones and localities so organized as to protect from the effects of war, wounded, sick and aged persons, children under fifteen, expectant mothers and mothers of children under seven.

Upon the outbreak and during the course of hostilities, the Parties concerned may conclude agreements on mutual recognition of the zones and localities they have created. They may for this purpose implement the provisions of the Draft Agreement annexed to the present Convention, with such amendments as they may consider necessary.

The Protecting Powers and the International Committee of the Red

Cross are invited to lend their good offices in order to facilitate the institution and recognition of these hospital and safety zones and localities.

Article 15. Any Party to the conflict may, either directly or through a neutral State or some humanitarian organization, propose to the adverse Party to establish, in the regions where fighting is taking place, neutralized zones intended to shelter from the effects of war the following persons, without distinction:

(a) wounded and sick combatants or non-combatants;

(b) civilian persons who take no part in hostilities, and who, while they reside in the zones, perform no work of a military character.

When the Parties concerned have agreed upon the geographical position, administration, food supply and supervision of the proposed neutralized zone, a written agreement shall be concluded and signed by the representatives of the Parties to the conflict. The agreement shall fix the beginning and the duration of the neutralization of the zone.

Article 16. The wounded and sick, as well as the infirm, and expectant mothers, shall be the object of particular protection and respect.

As far as military considerations allow, each Party to the conflict shall facilitate the steps taken to search for the killed and wounded, to assist the shipwrecked and other persons exposed to grave danger, and to protect them against pillage and ill-treatment.

Article 17. The Parties to the conflict shall endeavour to conclude local agreements for the removal from besieged or encircled areas, of wounded, sick, infirm, and aged persons, children and maternity cases, and for the passage of ministers of all religions, medical personnel and medical equipment on their way to such areas.

Article 18. Civilian hospitals organized to give care to the wounded and sick, the infirm and maternity cases, may in no circumstances be the object of attack, but shall at all times be respected and protected by the Parties to the conflict.

States which are Parties to a conflict shall provide all civilian hospitals with certificates showing that they are civilian hospitals and that the buildings which they occupy are not used for any purpose which would deprive these hospitals of protection in accordance with Article 19.

Civilian hospitals shall be marked by means of the emblem provided for in Article 38 of the Geneva Convention for the Amelioration of the Condition of the Wounded and Sick in Armed Forces in the Field of August 12, 1949, but only if so authorized by the State.

The Parties to the conflict shall, in so far as military considerations permit, take the necessary steps to make the distinctive emblems indicating civilian hospitals clearly visible to the enemy land, air and naval forces in order to obviate the possibility of any hostile action.

In view of the dangers to which hospitals may be exposed by being close to military objectives, it is recommended that such hospitals be situated as far as possible from such objectives.

Article 19. The protection to which civilian hospitals are entitled shall not cease unless they are used to commit, outside their humanitarian duties, acts harmful to the enemy. Protection may, however, cease only after due warning has been given, naming, in all appropriate cases, a reasonable time limit, and after such warning has remained unheeded.

The fact that sick or wounded members of the armed forces are nursed in these hospitals, or the presence of small arms and ammunition taken from such combatants and not yet handed to the proper service, shall not be considered to be acts harmful to the enemy.

Article 20. Persons regularly and solely engaged in the operation and administration of civilian hospitals, including the personnel engaged in the search for, removal and transporting of and caring for wounded and sick civilians, the infirm and maternity cases, shall be respected and protected.

In occupied territory and in zones of military operations, the above personnel shall be recognizable by means of an identity card certifying their status, bearing the photograph of the holder and embossed with the stamp of the responsible authority, and also by means of a stamped, water-resistant armlet which they shall wear on the left arm while carrying out their duties. This armlet shall be issued by the State and shall bear the emblem provided for in Article 38 of the Geneva Convention for the Amelioration of the Condition of the Wounded and Sick in Armed Forces in the Field of August 12, 1949.

Other personnel who are engaged in the operation and administration of civilian hospitals shall be entitled to respect and protection and to wear the armlet, as provided in and under the conditions prescribed in this Article, while they are employed on such duties. The identity card shall state the duties on which they are employed.

The management of each hospital shall at all times hold at the disposal of the competent national or occupying authorities an up-to-date list of such personnel.

Article 21. Convoys of vehicles or hospital trains on land or specially provided vessels on sea, conveying wounded and sick civilians, the infirm and maternity cases, shall be respected and protected in the same manner as the hospitals provided for in Article 18, and shall be marked, with the consent of the State, by the display of the distinctive emblem provided for in Article 38 of the Geneva Convention for the Amelioration of the Condition of the Wounded and Sick in Armed Forces in the Field of August 12, 1949[.]

Article 22. Aircraft exclusively employed for the removal of wounded and sick civilians, the infirm and maternity cases, or for the transport of medical personnel and equipment, shall not be attacked, but shall be respected while flying at heights, times and on routes specifically agreed upon between all the Parties to the conflict concerned.

They may be marked with the distinctive emblem provided for in Article 38 of the Geneva Convention for the Amelioration of the Condition of the Wounded and Sick in Armed Forces in the Field of August 12, 1949.

Unless agreed otherwise, flights over enemy or enemy-occupied territory are prohibited.

Such aircraft shall obey every summons to land. In the event of a landing thus imposed, the aircraft with its occupants may continue its flight after examination, if any.

Article 23. Each High Contracting Party shall allow the free passage of all consignments of medical and hospital stores and objects necessary for religious worship intended only for civilians of another High Contracting Party, even if the latter is its adversary. It shall likewise permit the free passage of all consignments of essential foodstuffs, clothing and tonics intended for children under fifteen, expectant mothers and maternity cases.

The obligation of a High Contracting Party to allow the free passage of the consignments indicated in the preceding paragraph is subject to the condition that this Party is satisfied that there are no serious reasons for fearing:

(a) that the consignments may be diverted from their destination,

(b) that the control may not be effective, or

(c) that a definite advantage may accrue to the military efforts or economy of the enemy through the substitution of the above-mentioned consignments for goods which would otherwise be provided or produced by the enemy or through the release of such material, services or facilities as would otherwise be required for the production of such goods.

The Power which allows the passage of the consignments indicated in the first paragraph of this Article may make such permission conditional on the distribution to the persons benefited thereby being made under the local supervision of the Protecting Powers.

Such consignments shall be forwarded as rapidly as possible, and the Power which permits their free passage shall have the right to prescribe the technical arrangements under which such passage is allowed.

Article 24 The Parties to the conflict shall take the necessary measures to ensure that children under fifteen, who are orphaned or are separated from their families as a result of the war, are not left to their own resources, and that their maintenance, the exercise of their religion and their education are facilitated in all circumstances. Their education shall, as far as possible, be entrusted to persons of a similar cultural tradition.

The Parties to the conflict shall facilitate the reception of such children in a neutral country for the duration of the conflict with the consent of the Protecting Power, if any, and under due safeguards for the observance of the principles stated in the first paragraph.

They shall, furthermore, endeavour to arrange for all children under twelve to be identified by the wearing of identity discs, or by some other means.

Article 25. All persons in the territory of a Party to the conflict, or in a territory occupied by it, shall be enabled to give news of a strictly personal nature to members of their families, wherever they may be, and to receive news from them. This correspondence shall be forwarded speedily and without undue delay.

If, as a result of circumstances, it becomes difficult or impossible to exchange family correspondence by the ordinary post, the Parties to the conflict concerned shall apply to a neutral intermediary, such as the Central Agency provided for in Article 140, and shall decide in consultation with it how to ensure the fulfilment of their obligations under the best possible conditions, in particular with the cooperation of the National Red Cross (Red Crescent, Red Lion and Sun) Societies.

If the Parties to the conflict deem it necessary to restrict family correspondence, such restrictions shall be confined to the compulsory use of standard forms containing twenty-five freely chosen words, and to the limitation of the number of these forms despatched to one each month.

Article 26. Each Party to the conflict shall facilitate enquiries made by members of families dispersed owing to the war, with the object of renewing contact with one another and of meeting, if possible. It shall encourage, in particular, the work of organizations engaged on this task provided they are acceptable to it and conform to its security regulations.

PART III
STATUS AND TREATMENT OF PROTECTED PERSONS

SECTION I
PROVISIONS COMMON TO THE TERRITORIES
OF THE PARTIES TO THE CONFLICT
AND TO OCCUPIED TERRITORIES

Article 27. Protected persons are entitled, in all circumstances, to respect for their persons, their honour, their family rights, their religious convictions and practices, and their manners and customs. They shall at all times be humanely treated, and shall be protected especially against all acts of violence or threats thereof and against insults and public curiosity.

Women shall be especially protected against any attack on their honour, in particular against rape, enforced prostitution, or any form of indecent assault.

Without prejudice to the provisions relating to their state of health, age and sex, all protected persons shall be treated with the same consideration by the Party to the conflict in whose power they are, without any adverse distinction based, in particular, on race, religion or political opinion.

However, the Parties to the conflict may take such measures of control and security in regard to protected persons as may be necessary as a result of the war.

Article 28. The presence of a protected person may not be used to render certain points or areas immune from military operations.

Article 29. The Party to the conflict in whose hands protected persons may be, is responsible for the treatment accorded to them by its agents, irrespective of any individual responsibility which may be incurred.

Article 30. Protected persons shall have every facility for making application to the Protecting Powers, the International Committee of the Red Cross, the National Red Cross (Red Crescent, Red Lion and Sun) Society of the country where they may be, as well as to any organization that might assist them.

These several organizations shall be granted all facilities for that purpose by the authorities, within the bounds set by military or security considerations.

Apart from the visits of the delegates of the Protecting Powers and of the International Committee of the Red Cross, provided for by Article 143, the Detaining or Occupying Powers shall facilitate as much as possible, visits to protected persons by the representatives of other organizations whose object is to give spiritual aid or material relief to such persons.

Article 31. No physical or moral coercion shall be exercised against protected persons, in particular to obtain information from them or from third parties.

Article 32. The High Contracting Parties specifically agree that each of them is prohibited from taking any measure of such a character as to cause the physical suffering or extermination of protected persons in their hands. This prohibition applies not only to murder, torture, corporal punishment, mutilation and medical or scientific experiments not necessitated by the medical treatment of a protected person, but also to any other measures of brutality whether applied by civilian or military agents.

Article 33. No protected person may be punished for an offence he or she has not personally committed. Collective penalties and likewise all measures of intimidation or of terrorism are prohibited.

Pillage is prohibited.

Reprisals against protected persons and their property are prohibited.

Article 34. The taking of hostages is prohibited.

SECTION II
ALIENS IN THE TERRITORY OF A PARTY TO THE CONFLICT

Article 35. All protected persons who may desire to leave the territory at the outset of, or during a conflict, shall be entitled to do so, unless their departure is contrary to the national interests of the State. The applications of such persons to leave shall be decided in accordance with regularly established procedures and the decision shall be taken as rapidly as possible. Those persons permitted to leave may provide themselves with the necessary funds for their journey and take with them a reasonable amount of their effects and articles of personal use.

If any such person is refused permission to leave the territory, he shall be entitled to have such refusal reconsidered as soon as possible by an appropriate court or administrative board designated by the Detaining Power for that purpose.

Upon request, representatives of the Protecting Power shall, unless reasons of security prevent it, or the persons concerned object, be furnished with the reasons for refusal of any request for permission to leave the territory and be given, as expeditiously as possible, the names of all persons who have been denied permission to leave.

Article 36. Departures permitted under the foregoing Article shall be carried out in satisfactory conditions as regards safety, hygiene, sanitation and food. All costs in connection therewith, from the point of exit in the territory of the Detaining Power, shall be borne by the country of destination, or, in the case of accommodation in a neutral country, by the Power whose nationals are benefited. The practical details of such movements may, if necessary, be settled by special agreements between the Powers concerned.

The foregoing shall not prejudice such special agreements as may be concluded between Parties to the conflict concerning the exchange and repatriation of their nationals in enemy hands.

Article 37. Protected persons who are confined pending proceedings or serving a sentence involving loss of liberty, shall during their confinement be humanely treated.

As soon as they are released, they may ask to leave the territory in conformity with the foregoing Articles.

Article 38. With the exception of special measures authorized by the present Convention, in particular by Articles 27 and 41 thereof, the situation of protected persons shall continue to be regulated, in principle, by the provisions concerning aliens in time of peace. In any case, the following rights shall be granted to them:

(1) they shall be enabled to receive the individual or collective relief that may be sent to them.

(2) they shall, if their state of health so requires, receive medical attention and hospital treatment to the same extent as the nationals of the State concerned.

(3) they shall be allowed to practise their religion and to receive spiritual assistance from ministers of their faith.

(4) if they reside in an area particularly exposed to the dangers of war, they shall be authorized to move from that area to the same extent as the nationals of the State concerned.

(5) children under fifteen years, pregnant women and mothers of children under seven years shall benefit by any preferential treatment to the same extent as the nationals of the State concerned.

Article 39. Protected persons who, as a result of the war, have lost their gainful employment, shall be granted the opportunity to find paid employment. That opportunity shall, subject to security considerations and to the provisions of Article 40, be equal to that enjoyed by the nationals of the Power in whose territory they are.

Where a Party to the conflict applies to a protected person methods of control which result in his being unable to support himself, and especially if such a person is prevented for reasons of security from finding paid employment on reasonable conditions, the said Party shall ensure his support and that of his dependents.

Protected persons may in any case receive allowances from their home country, the Protecting Power, or the relief societies referred to in Article 30.

Article 40. Protected persons may be compelled to work only to the same extent as nationals of the Party to the conflict in whose territory they are.

If protected persons are of enemy nationality, they may only be compelled to do work which is normally necessary to ensure the feeding, sheltering, clothing, transport and health of human beings and which is not directly related to the conduct of military operations

In the cases mentioned in the two preceding paragraphs, protected persons compelled to work shall have the benefit of the same working conditions and of the same safeguards as national workers, in particular as regards wages, hours of labour, clothing and equipment, previous training and compensation for occupational accidents and diseases.

If the above provisions are infringed, protected persons shall be allowed to exercise their right of complaint in accordance with Article 30.

Article 41. Should the Power in whose hands protected persons may be consider the measures of control mentioned in the present Convention to be inadequate, it may not have recourse to any other measure of control more severe than that of assigned residence or internment, in accordance with the provisions of Articles 42 and 43.

In applying the provisions of Article 39, second paragraph, to the cases of persons required to leave their usual places of residence by virtue of a decision placing them in assigned residence elsewhere, the Detaining Power shall be guided as closely as possible by the standards of welfare set forth in Part III, Section IV of this Convention.

Article 42. The internment or placing in assigned residence of protected persons may be ordered only if the security of the Detaining Power makes it absolutely necessary.

If any person, acting through the representatives of the Protecting Power, voluntarily demands internment, and if his situation renders this step necessary, he shall be interned by the Power in whose hands he may be.

Article 43. Any protected person who has been interned or placed in assigned residence shall be entitled to have such action reconsidered as soon as possible by an appropriate court or administrative board designated by the Detaining Power for that purpose. If the [i]nternment or placing in assigned residence is maintained, the court or administrativ,e [*sic*] iboard [*sic*] shall periodically, and at least twice yearly, give consideration to his or her case with a view to the favourable amendment of the initial decision, if circumstances permit.

Unless the protected persons concerned object, the Detaining Power shall, as rapidly as possible, give the Protecting Power the names of any protected persons who have been interned or subjected to assigned residence, or who have been released from internment or assigned residence. The decisions of the courts or boards mentioned in the first paragraph of the present Article shall also, subject to the same conditions, be notified as rapidly as possible to the Protecting Power.

Article 44. In applying the measures of control mentioned in the present Convention, the Detaining Power shall not treat as enemy aliens exclusively on the basis of their nationality *de jure* of an enemy State, refugees who do not, in fact, enjoy the protection of any government.

Article 45. Protected persons shall not be transferred to a Power which is not a party to the Convention.

This provision shall in no way constitute an obstacle to the repatriation of protected persons, or to their return to their country of residence after the cessation of hostilities.

Protected persons may be transferred by the Detaining Power only to a Power which is a party to the present Convention and after the Detaining Power has satisfied itself of the willingness and ability of such transferee Power to apply the present Convention. If protected persons are transferred under such circumstances, responsibility for the application of the present Convention rests on the Power accepting them, while they are in its custody. Nevertheless, if that Power fails to carry out the provisions of the present Convention in any important respect, the Power by which the protected persons were transferred shall, upon being so notified by the Protecting Power, take effective measures to correct the situation or shall request the return of the protected persons. Such request must be complied with.

In no circumstances shall a protected person be transferred to a country where he or she may have reason to fear persecution for his or her political opinions or religious beliefs.

The provisions of this Article do not constitute an obstacle to the extradition, in pursuance of extradition treaties concluded before the outbreak of hostilities, of protected persons accused of offences against ordinary criminal law.

Article 46. In so far as they have not been previously withdrawn, restrictive measures taken regarding protected persons shall be cancelled as soon as possible after the close of hostilities.

Restrictive measures affecting their property shall be cancelled, in accordance with the law of the Detaining Power, as soon as possible after the close of hostilities.

SECTION III
OCCUPIED TERRITORIES

Article 47. Protected persons who are in occupied territory shall not be deprived, in any case or in any manner whatsoever, of the benefits of the present Convention by any change introduced, as the result of the occupation of a territory, into the institutions or government of the said territory, nor by any agreement concluded between the authorities of the occupied territories and the Occupying Power, nor by any annexation by the latter of the whole or part of the occupied territory.

Article 48. Protected persons who are not nationals of the Power whose territory is occupied, may avail themselves of the right to leave the territory subject to the provisions of Article 35, and decisions thereon shall be taken according to the procedure which the Occupying Power shall establish in accordance with the said Article.

Article 49. Individual or mass forcible transfers, as well as deportations of protected persons from occupied territory to the territory of the Occupying Power or to that of any other country, occupied or not, are prohibited, regardless of their motive.

Nevertheless, the Occupying Power may undertake total or partial evacuation of a given area if the security of the population or imperative military reasons so demand. Such evacuations may not involve the displacement of protected persons outside the bounds of the occupied territory except when for material reasons it is impossible to avoid such displacement. Persons thus evacuated shall be transferred back to their homes as soon as hostilities in the area in question have ceased.

The Occupying Power undertaking such transfers or evacuations shall ensure, to the greatest practicable extent, that proper accommodation is provided to receive the protected persons, that the removals are effected in satisfactory conditions of hygiene, health, safety and nutrition, and that members of the same family are not separated.

The Protecting Power shall be informed of any transfers and evacuations as soon as they have taken place.

The Occupying Power shall not detain protected persons in an area particularly exposed to the dangers of war unless the security of the population or imperative military reasons so demand.

The Occupying Power shall not deport or transfer parts of its own civilian population into the territory it occupies.

Article 50. The Occupying Power shall, with the cooperation of the national and local authorities, facilitate the proper working of all institutions devoted to the care and education of children.

The Occupying Power shall take all necessary steps to facilitate the identification of children and the registration of their parentage. It may not, in any case, change their personal status, nor enlist them in formations or organizations subordinate to it.

Should the local institutions be inadequate for the purpose, the Occupying Power shall make arrangements for the maintenance and education, if possible by persons of their own nationality, language and religion, of children who are orphaned or separated from their parents as a result of the war and who cannot be adequately cared for by a near relative or friend.

A special section of the Bureau set up in accordance with Article 136 shall be responsible for taking all necessary steps to identify children whose identity is in doubt. Particulars of their parents or other near relatives should always be recorded if available.

The Occupying Power shall not hinder the application of any preferential measures in regard to food, medical care and protection against the effects of war, which may have been adopted prior to the occupation in favour of children under fifteen years, expectant mothers, and mothers of children under seven years.

Article 51. The Occupying Power may not compel protected persons to serve in its armed or auxiliary forces. No pressure or propaganda which aims at securing voluntary enlistment is permitted.

The Occupying Power may not compel protected persons to work unless they are over eighteen years of age, and then only on work which is necessary either for the needs of the army of occupation, or for the public utility services, or for the feeding, sheltering, clothing, transportation or health of the population of the occupied country. Protected persons may not be compelled to undertake any work which would involve them in the obligation of taking part in military operations. The Occupying Power may not compel protected persons to employ forcible means to ensure the security of the installations where they are performing compulsory labour.

The work shall be carried out only in the occupied territory where the persons whose services have been requisitioned are. Every such person shall, so far as possible, be kept in his usual place of employment. Workers shall be paid a fair wage and the work shall be proportionate to their physical and intellectual capacities. The legislation in force in the occupied country concerning working conditions, and safeguards as regards, in particular, such matters as wages, hours of work, equipment, preliminary training and compensation for occupational accidents and diseases, shall be applicable to the protected persons assigned to the work referred to in this Article.

In no case shall requisition of labour lead to a mobilization of workers in an organization of a military or semi-military character.

Article 52. No contract, agreement or regulation shall impair the right of any worker, whether voluntary or not and wherever he may be, to apply to the representatives of the Protecting Power in order to request the said Power's intervention.

All measures aiming at creating unemployment or at restricting the opportunities offered to workers in an occupied territory, in order to induce them to work for the Occupying Power, are prohibited.

Article 53. Any destruction by the Occupying Power of real or personal property belonging individually or collectively to private persons, or to the State, or to other public authorities, or to social or cooperative organizations, is prohibited, except where such destruction is rendered absolutely necessary by military operations.

Article 54. The Occupying Power may not alter the status of public officials or judges in the occupied territories, or in any way apply sanctions to or take any measures of coercion or discrimination against them, should they abstain from fulfilling their functions for reasons of conscience.

This prohibition does not prejudice the application of the second paragraph of Article 51. It does not affect the right of the Occupying Power to remove public officials from their posts.

Article 55. To the fullest extent of the means available to it, the Occupying Power has the duty of ensuring the food and medical supplies of the population; it should, in particular, bring in the necessary foodstuffs, medical stores and other articles if the resources of the occupied territory are inadequate.

The Occupying Power may not requisition foodstuffs, articles or medical supplies available in the occupied territory, except for use by the occupation forces and administration personnel, and then only if the requirements of the civilian population have been taken into account. Subject to the provisions of other international Conventions, the Occupying Power shall make arrangements to ensure that fair value is paid for any requisitioned goods.

The Protecting Power shall, at any time, be at liberty to verify the state of the food and medical supplies in occupied territories, except where temporary restrictions are made necessary by imperative military requirements.
Article 56. To the fullest extent of the means available to it, the Occupying Power has the duty of ensuring and maintaining, with the cooperation of national and local authorities, the medical and hospital establishments and services, public health and hygiene in the occupied territory, with particular reference to the adoption and application of the prophylactic and preventive measures necessary to combat the spread of contagious diseases and epidemics. Medical personnel of all categories shall be allowed to carry out their duties.

If new hospitals are set up in occupied territory and if the competent organs of the occupied State are not operating there, the occupying authorities shall, if necessary, grant them the recognition provided for in Article 18. In similar circumstances, the occupying authorities shall also grant recognition to hospital personnel and transport vehicles under the provisions of Articles 20 and 21.

In adopting measures of health and hygiene and in their implementation, the Occupying Power shall take into consideration the moral and ethical susceptibilities of the population of the occupied territory.
Article 57. The Occupying Power may requisition civilian hospitals only temporarily and only in cases of urgent necessity for the care of military wounded and sick, and then on condition that suitable arrangements are made in due time for the care and treatment of the patients and for the needs of the civilian population for hospital accommodation.

The material and stores of civilian hospitals cannot be requisitioned so long as they are necessary for the needs of the civilian population.
Article 58. The Occupying Power shall permit ministers of religion to give spiritual assistance to the members of their religious communities.

The Occupying Power shall also accept consignments of books and articles required for religious needs and shall facilitate their distribution in occupied territory.

Article 59. If the whole or part of the population of an occupied territory is inadequately supplied, the Occupying Power shall agree to relief schemes on behalf of the said population, and shall facilitate them by all the means at its disposal.

Such schemes, which may be undertaken either by States or by impartial humanitarian organizations such as the International Committee of the Red Cross, shall consist, in particular, of the provision of consignments of foodstuffs, medical supplies and clothing.

All Contracting Parties shall permit the free passage of these consignments and shall guarantee their protection.

A Power granting free passage to consignments on their way to territory occupied by an adverse Party to the conflict shall, however, have the right to search the consignments, to regulate their passage according to prescribed times and routes, and to be reasonably satisfied through the Protecting Power that these consignments are to be used for the relief of the needy population and are not to be used for the benefit of the Occupying Power.

Article 60. Relief consignments shall in no way relieve the Occupying Power of any of its responsibilities under Articles 55, 56 and 59. The Occupying Power shall in no way whatsoever divert relief consignments from the purpose for which they are intended, except in cases of urgent necessity, in the interests of the population of the occupied territory and with the consent of the Protecting Power.

Article 61. The distribution of the relief consignments referred to in the foregoing Articles shall be carried out with the cooperation and under the supervision of the Protecting Power. This duty may also be delegated, by agreement between the Occupying Power and the Protecting Power, to a neutral Power, to the International Committee of the Red Cross or to any other impartial humanitarian body.

Such consignments shall be exempt in occupied territory from all charges, taxes or customs duties unless these are necessary in the interests of the economy of the territory. The Occupying Power shall facilitate the rapid distribution of these consignments.

All Contracting Parties shall endeavour to permit the transit and transport, free of charge, of such relief consignments on their way to occupied territories.

Article 62. Subject to imperative reasons of security, protected persons in occupied territories shall be permitted to receive the individual relief consignments sent to them.

Article 63. Subject to temporary and exceptional measures imposed for urgent reasons of security by the Occupying Power:

(a) recognized National Red Cross (Red Crescent, Red Lion and Sun) Societies shall be able to pursue their activities in accordance with Red Cross principles, as defined by the International Red Cross Conferences. Other relief societies shall be permitted to continue their humanitarian activities under similar conditions;

(b) the Occupying Power may not require any changes in the personnel or structure of these societies, which would prejudice the aforesaid activities.

The same principles shall apply to the activities and personnel of special organizations of a non-military character, which already exist or which may be established, for the purpose of ensuring the living conditions of the civilian population by the maintenance of the essential public utility services, by the distribution of relief and by the organization of rescues.

Article 64. The penal laws of the occupied territory shall remain in force, with the exception that they may be repealed or suspended by the Occupying Power in cases where they constitute a threat to its security or an obstacle to the application of the present Convention. Subject to the latter consideration and to the necessity for ensuring the effective administration of justice, the tribunals of the occupied territory shall continue to function in respect of all offences covered by the said laws.

The Occupying Power may, however, subject the population of the occupied territory to provisions which are essential to enable the Occupying Power to fulfil its obligations under the present Convention, to maintain the orderly government of the territory, and to ensure the security of the Occupying Power, of the members and property of the occupying forces or administration, and likewise of the establishments and lines of communication used by them.

Article 65. The penal provisions enacted by the Occupying Power shall not come into force before they have been published and brought to the knowledge of the inhabitants in their own language. The effect of these penal provisions shall not be retroactive.

Article 66. In case of a breach of the penal provisions promulgated by it by virtue of the second paragraph of Article 64 the Occupying Power may hand over the accused to its properly constituted, non-political military courts, on condition that the said courts sit in the occupied country. Courts of appeal shall preferably sit in the occupied country.

Article 67. The courts shall apply only those provisions of law which were applicable prior to the offence, and which are in accordance with general principles of law, in particular the principle that the penalty shall be proportionate to the offence. They shall take into consideration the fact the accused is not a national of the Occupying Power.

Article 68. Protected persons who commit an offence which is solely intended to harm the Occupying Power, but which does not constitute an attempt on the life or limb of members of the occupying forces or administration, nor a grave collective danger, nor seriously damage the property of the occupying forces or administration or the installations used by them, shall be liable to internment or simple imprisonment, provided the duration of such internment or imprisonment is proportionate to the offence committed. Furthermore, internment or imprisonment shall, for such offences, be the only measure adopted for depriving protected persons of liberty. The courts provided for under Article 66 of the present Convention may at their discretion convert a sentence of imprisonment to one of internment for the same period.

The penal provisions promulgated by the Occupying Power in accordance with Articles 64 and 65 may impose the death penalty on a protected person only in cases where the person is guilty of espionage, of serious acts of sabotage against the military installations of the Occupying Power or of intentional offences which have caused the death of one or more persons, provided that such offences were punishable by death under the law of the occupied territory in force before the occupation began.

The death penalty may not be pronounced against a protected person unless the attention of the court has been particularly called to the fact that since the accused is not a national of the Occupying Power, he is not bound to it by any duty of allegiance.

In any case, the death penalty may not be pronounced against a protected person who was under eighteen years of age at the time of the offence.

Article 69. In all cases, the duration of the period during which a protected person accused of an offence is under arrest awaiting trial or punishment shall be deducted from any period of imprisonment awarded.

Article 70. Protected persons shall not be arrested, prosecuted or convicted by the Occupying Power for acts committed or for opinions expressed before the occupation, or during a temporary interruption thereof, with the exception of breaches of the laws and customs of war.

Nationals of the [O]ccupying Power who, before the outbreak of hostilities, have sought refuge in the territory of the occupied State, shall not be arrested, prosecuted, convicted or deported from the occupied territory, except for offences committed after the outbreak of hostilities, or for offences under common law committed before the outbreak of hostilities which, according to the law of the occupied State, would have justified extradition in time of peace.

Article 71. No sentence shall be pronounced by the competent courts of the Occupying Power except after a regular trial.

Accused persons who are prosecuted by the Occupying Power shall be promptly informed, in writing, in a language which they understand, of the particulars of the charges preferred against them, and shall be brought to trial as rapidly as possible. The Protecting Power shall be informed of all proceedings instituted by the Occupying Power against protected persons in respect of charges involving the death penalty or imprisonment for two years or more; it shall be enabled, at any time, to obtain information regarding the state of such proceedings. Furthermore, the Protecting Power shall be entitled, on request, to be furnished with all particulars of these and of any other proceedings instituted by the Occupying Power against protected persons.

The notification to the Protecting Power, as provided for in the second paragraph above, shall be sent immediately, and shall in any case reach the Protecting Power three weeks before the date of the first hearing. Unless, at the opening of the trial, evidence is submitted that the provisions of this Article are fully complied with, the trial shall not proceed. The notification shall include the following particulars:

 (a) description of the accused;
 (b) place of residence or detention;
 (c) specification of the charge or charges (with mention of the penal provisions under which it is brought);
 (d) designation of the court which will hear the case;
 (e) place and date of the first hearing.

Article 72. Accused persons shall have the right to present evidence necessary to their defence and may, in particular, call witnesses. They shall have the right to be assisted by a qualified advocate or counsel of their own choice, who shall be able to visit them freely and shall enjoy the necessary facilities for preparing the defence.

Failing a choice by the accused, the Protecting Power may provide him with an advocate or counsel. When an accused person has to meet a serious charge and the Protecting Power is not functioning, the Occupying Power, subject to the consent of the accused, shall provide an advocate or counsel.

Accused persons shall, unless they freely waive such assistance, be aided by an interpreter, both during preliminary investigation and during the hearing in court. They shall have the right at any time to object to the interpreter and to ask for his replacement.

Article 73. A convicted person shall have the right of appeal provided for by the laws applied by the court. He shall be fully informed of his right to appeal or petition and of the time limit within which he may do so.

The penal procedure provided in the present Section shall apply, as far as it is applicable, to appeals. Where the laws applied by the Court make no provision for appeals, the convicted person shall have the right to petition against the finding and sentence to the competent authority of the Occupying Power.

Article 74. Representatives of the Protecting Power shall have the right to attend the trial of any protected person, unless the hearing has, as an exceptional measure, to be held *in camera* in the interests of the security of the Occupying Power, which shall then notify the Protecting Power. A notification in respect of the date and place of trial shall be sent to the Protecting Power.

Any judgment involving a sentence of death, or imprisonment for two years or more, shall be communicated, with the relevant grounds, as rapidly as possible to the Protecting Power. The notification shall contain a reference to the notification made under Article 71, and, in the case of sentences of imprisonment, the name of the place where the sentence is to be served. A record of judgments other than those referred to above shall be kept by the court and shall be open to inspection by representatives of the Protecting Power. Any period allowed for appeal in the case of sentences involving the death penalty, or imprisonment of two years or more, shall not run until notification of judgment has been received by the Protecting Power.

Article 75. In no case shall persons condemned to death be deprived of the right of petition for pardon or reprieve.

No death sentence shall be carried out before the expiration of a period of at least six months from the date of receipt by the Protecting Power of the notification of the final judgment confirming such death sentence, or of an order denying pardon or reprieve.

The six months period of suspension of the death sentence herein prescribed may be reduced in individual cases in circumstances of grave emergency involving an organized threat to the security of the Occupying Power or its forces, provided always that the Protecting Power is notified of such reduction and is given reasonable time and opportunity to make representations to the competent occupying authorities in respect of such death sentences.

Article 76. Protected persons accused of offences shall be detained in the occupied country, and if convicted they shall serve their sentences therein. They shall, if possible, be separated from other detainees and shall enjoy conditions of food and hygiene which will be sufficient to keep them in good health, and which will be at least equal to those obtaining in prisons in the occupied country.

They shall receive the medical attention required by their state of health.

They shall also have the right to receive any spiritual assistance which they may require.

Women shall be confined in separate quarters and shall be under the direct supervision of women.

Proper regard shall be paid to the special treatment due to minors.

Protected persons who are detained shall have the right to be visited by delegates of the Protecting Power and of the International Committee of the Red Cross, in accordance with the provisions of Article 143.

Such persons shall have the right to receive at least one relief parcel monthly.

Article 77. Protected persons who have been accused of offences or convicted by the courts in occupied territory, shall be handed over at the close of occupation, with the relevant records, to the authorities of the liberated territory.

Article 78. If the Occupying Power considers it necessary, for imperative reasons of security, to take safety measures concerning protected persons, it may, at the most, subject them to assigned residence or to internment.

Decisions regarding such assigned residence or internment shall be made according to a regular procedure to be prescribed by the Occupying Power in accordance with the provisions of the present Convention. This procedure shall include the right of appeal for the parties concerned. Appeals shall be decided with the least possible delay. In the event of the decision being upheld, it shall be subject to periodical review, if possible every six months, by a competent body set up by the said Power.

Protected persons made subject to assigned residence and thus required to leave their homes shall enjoy the full benefit of Article 39 of the present Convention.

.   .   .   .

SECTION IV
REGULATIONS FOR THE TREATMENT
OF INTERNEES

Chapter I
General Provisions

Article 79. The Parties to the conflict shall not intern protected persons, except in accordance with the provisions of Articles 41, 42, 43, 68 and 78.

Article 80. Internees shall retain their full civil capacity and shall exercise such attendant rights as may be compatible with their status.

Article 81. Parties to the conflict who intern protected persons shall be bound to provide free of charge for their maintenance, and to grant them also the medical attention required by their state of health.

No deduction from the allowances, salaries or credits due to the internees shall be made for the repayment of these costs.

The Detaining Power shall provide for the support of those dependent on the internees, if such dependents are without adequate means of support or are unable to earn a living.

Article 82. The Detaining Power shall, as far as possible, accommodate the internees according to their nationality, language and customs. Internees who are nationals of the same country shall not be separated merely because they have different languages.

Throughout the duration of their internment, members of the same family, and in particular parents and children, shall be lodged together in the same place of internment, except when separation of a temporary nature is necessitated for reasons of employment or health or for the purposes of enforcement of the provisions of Chapter IX of the present Section. Internees may request that their children who are left at liberty without parental care shall be interned with them.

Wherever possible, interned members of the same family shall be housed in the same premises and given separate accommodation from other internees, together with facilities for leading a proper family life.

Chapter II
Places of Internment

Article 83. The Detaining Power shall not set up places of internment in areas particularly exposed to the dangers of war.

The Detaining Power shall give the enemy Powers, through the intermediary of the Protecting Powers, all useful information regarding the geographical location of places of internment.

Whenever military considerations permit, internment camps shall be indicated by the letters IC, placed so as to be clearly visible in the daytime from the air. The Powers concerned may, however, agree upon any other system of marking. No place other than an internment camp shall be marked as such.

Article 84. Internees shall be accommodated and administered separately from prisoners of war and from persons deprived of liberty for any other reason.

Article 85. The Detaining Power is bound to take all necessary and possible measures to ensure that protected persons shall, from the outset of their internment, be accommodated in buildings or quarters which afford every possible safeguard as regards hygiene and health, and provide efficient protection against the rigours of the climate and the effects of the war. In no case shall permanent places of internment be situated in unhealthy areas, or in districts the climate of which is injurious to the internees. In all cases where the district, in which a protected person is temporarily interned, is in an unhealthy area or has a climate which is harmful to his health, he shall be removed to a more suitable place of internment as rapidly as circumstances permit.

The premises shall be fully protected from dampness, adequately heated and lighted, in particular between dusk and lights out. The sleeping quarters shall be sufficiently spacious and well ventilated, and the internees shall have suitable bedding and sufficient blankets, account being taken of the climate, and the age, sex, and state of health of the internees.

Internees shall have for their use, day and night, sanitary conveniences which conform to the rules of hygiene and are constantly maintained in a state of cleanliness. They shall be provided with sufficient water and soap for their daily personal toilet and for washing their personal laundry; installations and facilities necessary for this purpose shall be granted to them. Showers or baths shall also be available. The necessary time shall be set aside for washing and for cleaning.

Whenever it is necessary, as an exceptional and temporary measure, to accommodate women internees who are not members of a family unit in the same place of internment as men, the provision of separate sleeping quarters and sanitary conveniences for the use of such women internees shall be obligatory.

Article 86. The Detaining Power shall place at the disposal of interned persons, of whatever denomination, premises suitable for the holding of their religious services.

Article 87. Canteens shall be installed in every place of internment, except where other suitable facilities are available. Their purpose shall be to enable internees to make purchases, at prices not higher than local market prices, of foodstuffs and articles of everyday use, including soap and tobacco, such as would increase their personal well-being and comfort.

Profits made by canteens shall be credited to a welfare fund to be set up for each place of internment, and administered for the benefit of the internees attached to such place of internment. The Internee Committee provided for in Article 102 shall have the right to check the management of the canteen and of the said fund.

When a place of internment is closed down, the balance of the welfare fund shall be transferred to the welfare fund of a place of internment for internees of the same nationality, or, if such a place does not exist, to a central welfare fund which shall be administered for the benefit of all internees remaining in the custody of the Detaining Power. In case of a general release, the said profits shall be kept by the Detaining Power, subject to any agreement to the contrary between the Powers concerned.

Article 88. In all places of internment exposed to air raids and other hazards of war, shelters adequate in number and structure to ensure the necessary protection shall be installed. In case of alarms, the internees shall be free to enter such shelters as quickly as possible, excepting those who remain for the protection of their quarters against the aforesaid hazards. Any protective measures taken in favour of the population shall also apply to them.

All due precautions must be taken in places of internment against the danger of fire.

Chapter III
Food and Clothing

Article 89. Daily food rations for internees shall be sufficient in quantity, quality and variety to keep internees in a good state of health and prevent the development of nutritional deficiencies. Account shall also be taken of the customary diet of the internees.

Internees shall also be given the means by which they can prepare for themselves any additional food in their possession.

Sufficient drinking water shall be supplied to internees. The use of tobacco shall be permitted.

Internees who work shall receive additional rations in proportion to the kind of labour which they perform.

Expectant and nursing mothers, and children under fifteen years of age, shall be given additional food, in proportion to their physiological needs.

Article 90. When taken into custody, internees shall be given all facilities to provide themselves with the necessary clothing, footwear and change of underwear, and later on, to procure further supplies if required. Should any internees not have sufficient clothing, account being taken of the climate, and be unable to procure any, it shall be provided free of charge to them by the Detaining Power.

The clothing supplied by the Detaining Power to internees and the outward markings placed on their own clothes shall not be ignominious nor expose them to ridicule.

Workers shall receive suitable working outfits, including protective clothing, whenever the nature of their work so requires.

Chapter IV
Hygiene and Medical Attention

Article 91. Every place of internment shall have an adequate infirmary, under the direction of a qualified doctor, where internees may have the attention they require, as well as appropriate diet. Isolation wards shall be set aside for cases of contagious or mental diseases.

Maternity cases and internees suffering from serious diseases, or whose condition requires special treatment, a surgical operation or hospital care, must be admitted to any institution where adequate treatment can be given and shall receive care not inferior to that provided for the general population.

Internees shall, for preference, have the attention of medical personnel of their own nationality.

Internees may not be prevented from presenting themselves to the medical authorities for examination. The medical authorities of the Detaining Power shall, upon request, issue to every internee who has undergone treatment an official certificate showing the nature of his illness or injury, and the duration and nature of the treatment given. A duplicate of this certificate shall be forwarded to the Central Agency provided for in Article 140.

Treatment, including the provision of any apparatus necessary for the maintenance of internees in good health, particularly dentures and other artificial appliances and spectacles, shall be free of charge to the internee.

Article 92. Medical inspections of internees shall be made at least once a month. Their purpose shall be, in particular, to supervise the general state of health, nutrition and cleanliness of internees, and to detect contagious diseases, especially tuberculosis, malaria, and venereal diseases. Such inspections shall include, in particular, the checking of weight of each internee and, at least once a year, radioscopic examination.

Chapter V
Religious, Intellectual and Physical Activities

Article 93. Internees shall enjoy complete latitude in the exercise of their religious duties, including attendance at the services of their faith, on condition that they comply with the disciplinary routine prescribed by the detaining authorities.

Ministers of religion who are interned shall be allowed to minister freely to the members of their community. For this purpose the Detaining Power shall ensure their equitable allocation amongst the various places of internment in which there are internees speaking the same language and belonging to the same religion. Should such ministers be too few in number, the Detaining Power shall provide them with the necessary facilities, including means of transport, for moving from one place to another, and they shall be authorized to visit any internees who are in hospital. Ministers of religion shall be at liberty to correspond on matters concerning their ministry with the religious authorities in the country of detention and, as far as possible, with the international religious organizations of their faith. Such correspondence shall not be considered as forming a part of the quota mentioned in Article 107. It shall, however, be subject to the provisions of Article 112.

When internees do not have at their disposal the assistance of ministers of their faith, or should these latter be too few in number, the local religious authorities of the same faith may appoint, in agreement with the Detaining Power, a minister of the internees' faith or, if such a course is feasible from a denominational point of view, a minister of similar religion or a qualified layman. The latter shall enjoy the facilities granted to the ministry he has assumed. Persons so appointed shall comply with all regulations laid down by the Detaining Power in the interests of discipline and security.

Article 94. The Detaining Power shall encourage intellectual, educational and recreational pursuits, sports and games amongst internees, whilst leaving them free to take part in them or not. It shall take all practicable measures to ensure the exercise thereof, in particular by providing suitable premises.

All possible facilities shall be granted to internees to continue their studies or to take up new subjects. The education of children and young people shall be ensured; they shall be allowed to attend schools either within the place of internment or outside.

Internees shall be given opportunities for physical exercise, sports and outdoor games. For this purpose, sufficient open spaces shall be set aside in all places of internment. Special playgrounds shall be reserved for children and young people.

Article 95. The Detaining Power shall not employ internees as workers, unless they so desire. Employment which, if undertaken under compulsion by a protected person not in internment, would involve a breach of Articles 40 or 51 of the present Convention, and employment on work which is of a degrading or humiliating character are in any case prohibited.

After a working period of six weeks, internees shall be free to give up work at any moment, subject to eight days' notice.

These provisions constitute no obstacle to the right of the Detaining Power to employ interned doctors, dentists and other medical personnel in their professional capacity on behalf of their fellow internees, or to employ internees for administrative and maintenance work in places of internment and to detail such persons for work in the kitchens or for other domestic tasks, or to require such persons to undertake duties connected with the protection of internees against aerial bombardment or other war risks. No internee may, however, be required to perform tasks for which he is, in the opinion of a medical officer, physically unsuited.

The Detaining Power shall take entire responsibility for all working conditions, for medical attention, for the payment of wages, and for ensuring that all employed internees receive compensation for occupational accidents and diseases. The standards prescribed for the said working conditions and for compensation shall be in accordance with the national laws and regulations, and with the existing practice; they shall in no case be inferior to those obtaining for work of the same nature in the same district. Wages for work done shall be determined on an equitable basis by special agreements between the internees, the Detaining Power, and, if the case arises, employers other than the Detaining Power, due regard being paid to the obligation of the Detaining Power to provide for free maintenance of internees and for the medical attention which their state of health may require. Internees permanently detailed for categories of work mentioned in the third paragraph of this Article, shall be paid fair wages by the Detaining Power. The working conditions and the scale of compensation for occupational accidents and diseases to internees thus detailed, shall not be inferior to those applicable to work of the same nature in the same district.

Article 96. All labour detachments shall remain part of and dependent upon a place of internment. The competent authorities of the Detaining Power and the commandant of a place of internment shall be responsible for the observance in a labour detachment of the provisions of the present Convention. The commandant shall keep an up-to-date list of the labour detachments subordinate to him and shall communicate it to the delegates of the Protecting Power, of the International Committee of the Red Cross and of other humanitarian organizations who may visit the places of internment.

Chapter VI
Personal Property and Financial Resources

Article 97. Internees shall be permitted to retain articles of personal use. Monies, cheques, bonds, etc., and valuables in their possession may not be taken from them except in accordance with established procedure. Detailed receipts shall be given thereof.

The amounts shall be paid into the account of every internee as provided for in Article 98. Such amounts may not be converted into any other currency unless legislation in force in the territory in which the owner is interned so requires or the internee gives his consent.

Articles which have above all a personal or sentimental value may not be taken away.

A woman internee shall not be searched except by a woman.

On release or repatriation, internees shall be given all articles, monies or other valuables taken from them during internment and shall receive in currency the balance of any credit to their accounts kept in accordance with Article 98, with the exception of any articles or amounts withheld by the Detaining Power by virtue of its legislation in force. If the property of an internee is so withheld, the owner shall receive a detailed receipt.

Family or identity documents in the possession of internees may not be taken away without a receipt being given. At no time shall internees be left without identity documents. If they have none, they shall be issued with special documents drawn up by the detaining authorities, which will serve as their identity papers until the end of their internment.

Internees may keep on their persons a certain amount of money, in cash or in the shape of purchase coupons, to enable them to make purchases.

Article 98. All internees shall receive regular allowances, sufficient to enable them to purchase goods and articles, such as tobacco, toilet requisites, etc. Such allowances may take the form of credits or purchase coupons.

Furthermore, internees may receive allowances from the Power to which they owe allegiance, the Protecting Powers, the organizations which may assist them, or their families, as well as the income on their property in accordance with the law of the Detaining Power. The amount of allowances granted by the Power to which they owe allegiance shall be the same for each category of internees (infirm, sick, pregnant women, etc.) but may not be allocated by that Power or distributed by the Detaining Power on the basis of discriminations between internees which are prohibited by Article 27 of the present Convention.

The Detaining Power shall open a regular account for every internee, to which shall be credited the allowances named in the present Article, the wages earned and the remittances received, together with such sums taken from him as may be available under the legislation in force in the territory in which he is interned. Internees shall be granted all facilities consistent with the legislation in force in such territory to make remittances to their families and to other dependents. They may draw from their accounts the amounts necessary for their personal expenses, within the limits fixed by the Detaining Power. They shall at all times be afforded reasonable facilities for consulting and obtaining copies of their accounts. A statement of accounts shall be furnished to the Protecting Power on request, and shall accompany the internee in case of transfer.

Chapter VII
Administration and Discipline

Article 99. Every place of internment shall be put under the authority of a responsible officer, chosen from the regular military forces or the regular civil administration of the Detaining Power. The officer in charge of the place of internment must have in his possession a copy of the present Convention in the official language, or one of the official languages, of his country and shall be responsible for its application. The staff in control of internees shall be instructed in the provisions of the present Convention and of the administrative measures adopted to ensure its application.

The text of the present Convention and the texts of special agreements concluded under the said Convention shall be posted inside the place of internment, in a language which the internees understand, or shall be in the possession of the Internee Committee.

Regulations, orders, notices and publications of every kind shall be communicated to the internees and posted inside the places of internment, in a language which they understand.

Every order and command addressed to internees individually, must likewise, be given in a language which they understand.

Article 100. The disciplinary regime in places of internment shall be consistent with humanitarian principles, and shall in no circumstances include regulations imposing on internees any physical exertion dangerous to their health or involving physical or moral victimization. Identification by tattooing or imprinting signs or markings on the body, is prohibited.

In particular, prolonged standing and roll-calls, punishment drill, military drill and manoeuvres, or the reduction of food rations, are prohibited.

Article 101. Internees shall have the right to present to the authorities in whose power they are, any petition with regard to the conditions of internment to which they are subjected.

They shall also have the right to apply without restriction through the Internee Committee or, if they consider it necessary, direct to the representatives of the Protecting Power, in order to indicate to them any points on which they may have complaints to make with regard to the conditions of internment.

Such petitions and complaints shall be transmitted forthwith and without alteration, and even if the latter are recognized to be unfounded, they may not occasion any punishment.

Periodic reports on the situation in places of internment and as to the needs of the internees, may be sent by the Internee Committees to the representatives of the Protecting Powers.

Article 102. In every place of internment, the internees shall freely elect by secret ballot every six months, the members of a Committee empowered to represent them before the Detaining and the Protecting Powers, the International Committee of the Red Cross and any other organization which may assist them. The members of the Committee shall be eligible for re-election.

Internees so elected shall enter upon their duties after their election has been approved by the detaining authorities. The reasons for any refusals or dismissals shall be communicated to the Protecting Powers concerned.

Article 103. The Internee Committees shall further the physical, spiritual and intellectual well-being of the internees.

In case the internees decide, in particular, to organize a system of mutual assistance amongst themselves, this organization would be within the competence of the Committees in addition to the special duties entrusted to them under other provisions of the present Convention.

Article 104. Members of Internee Committees shall not be required to perform any other work, if the accomplishment of their duties is rendered more difficult thereby.

Members of Internee Committees may appoint from amongst the internees such assistants as they may require. All material facilities shall be granted to them, particularly a certain freedom of movement necessary for the accomplishment of their duties (visits to labour detachments, receipt of supplies, etc.).

All facilities shall likewise be accorded to members of Internee Committees for communication by post and telegraph with the detaining authorities, the Protecting Powers, the International Committee of the Red Cross and their delegates, and with the organizations which give assistance to internees. Committee members in labour detachments shall enjoy similar facilities for communication with their Internee Committee in the principal place of internment. Such communications shall not be limited, nor considered as forming a part of the quota mentioned in Article 107.

Members of Internee Committees who are transferred shall be allowed a reasonable time to acquaint their successors with current affairs.

Chapter VIII
Relations with the Exterior

Article 105. Immediately upon interning protected persons, the Detaining Powers shall inform them, the Power to which they owe allegiance and their Protecting Power of the measures taken for executing the provisions of the present Chapter. The Detaining Powers shall likewise inform the Parties concerned of any subsequent modifications of such measures.

Article 106. As soon as he is interned, or at the latest not more than one week after his arrival in a place of internment, and likewise in cases of sickness or transfer to another place of internment or to a hospital, every internee shall be enabled to send direct to his family, on the one hand, and to the Central Agency provided for by Article 140, on the other, an internment card similar, if possible, to the model annexed to the present Convention, informing his relatives of his detention, address and state of health. The said cards shall be forwarded as rapidly as possible and may not be delayed in any way.

Article 107. Internees shall be allowed to send and receive letters and cards. If the Detaining Power deems it necessary to limit the number of letters and cards sent by each internee, the said number shall not be less than two letters and four cards monthly; these shall be drawn up so as to conform as closely as possible to the models annexed to the present Convention. If limitations must be placed on the correspondence addressed to internees, they may be ordered only by the Power to which such internees owe allegiance, possibly at the request of the Detaining Power. Such letters and cards must be conveyed with reasonable despatch; they may not be delayed or retained for disciplinary reasons.

Internees who have been a long time without news, or who find it impossible to receive news from their relatives, or to give them news by the ordinary postal route, as well as those who are at a considerable distance from their homes, shall be allowed to send telegrams, the charges being paid by them in the currency at their disposal. They shall likewise benefit by this provision in cases which are recognized to be urgent.

As a rule, internees' mail shall be written in their own language. The Parties to the conflict may authorize correspondence in other languages.

Article 108. Internees shall be allowed to receive, by post or by any other means, individual parcels or collective shipments containing in particular foodstuffs, clothing, medical supplies, as well as books and objects of a devotional, educational or recreational character which may meet their needs. Such shipments shall in no way free the Detaining Power from the obligations imposed upon it by virtue of the present Convention.

Should military necessity require the quantity of such shipments to be limited, due notice thereof shall be given to the Protecting Power and to the International Committee of the Red Cross, or to any other organization giving assistance to the internees and responsible for the forwarding of such shipments.

The conditions for the sending of individual parcels and collective shipments shall, if necessary, be the subject of special agreements between the Powers concerned, which may in no case delay the receipt by the internees of relief supplies. Parcels of clothing and foodstuffs may not include books. Medical relief supplies shall, as a rule, be sent in collective parcels.

Article 109. In the absence of special agreements between Parties to the conflict regarding the conditions for the receipt and distribution of collective relief shipments, the regulations concerning collective relief which are annexed to the present Convention shall be applied.

The special agreements provided for above shall in no case restrict the right of Internee Committees to take possession of collective relief shipments intended for internees, to undertake their distribution and to dispose of them in the interests of the recipients.

Nor shall such agreements restrict the right of representatives of the Protecting Powers, the International Committee of the Red Cross, or any other organization giving assistance to internees and responsible for the forwarding of collective shipments, to supervise their distribution to the recipients.

Article 110. All relief shipments for internees shall be exempt from import, customs and other dues.

All matter sent by mail, including relief parcels sent by parcel post and remittances of money, addressed from other countries to internees or despatched by them through the post office, either direct or through the Information Bureaux provided for in Article 136 and the Central Information Agency provided for in Article 140, shall be exempt from all postal dues both in the countries of origin and destination and in intermediate countries. To this end, in particular, the exemption provided by the Universal Postal Convention of 1947 and by the agreements of the Universal Postal Union in favour of civilians of enemy nationality detained in camps or civilian prisons, shall be extended to the other interned persons protected by the present Convention. The countries not signatory to the above-mentioned agreements shall be bound to grant freedom from charges in the same circumstances.

The cost of transporting relief shipments which are intended for internees and which, by reason of their weight or any other cause, cannot be sent through the post office, shall be borne by the Detaining Power in all the territories under its control. Other Powers which are Parties to the present Convention shall bear the cost of transport in their respective territories.

Costs connected with the transport of such shipments, which are not covered by the above paragraphs, shall be charged to the senders.

The High Contracting Parties shall endeavour to reduce, so far as possible, the charges for telegrams sent by internees, or addressed to them.

Article 111. Should military operations prevent the Powers concerned from fulfilling their obligation to ensure the conveyance of the mail and relief shipments provided for in Articles 106, 107, 108 and 113, the Protecting Powers concerned, the International Committee of the Red Cross or any other organization duly approved by the Parties to the conflict may undertake the conveyance of such shipments by suitable means (rail, motor vehicles, vessels or aircraft, etc.). For this purpose, the High Contracting Parties shall endeavour to supply them with such transport, and to allow its circulation, especially by granting the necessary safe-conducts.

Such transport may also be used to convey:

(a) correspondence, lists and reports exchanged between the Central Information Agency referred to in Article 140 and the National Bureaux referred to in Article 136;

(b) correspondence and reports relating to internees which the Protecting Powers, the International Committee of the Red Cross or any other organization assisting the internees exchange either with their own delegates or with the Parties to the conflict.

These provisions in no way detract from the right of any Party to the conflict to arrange other means of transport if it should so prefer, nor preclude the granting of safe-conducts, under mutually agreed conditions, to such means of transport.

The costs occasioned by the use of such means of transport shall be borne, in proportion to the importance of the shipments, by the Parties to the conflict whose nationals are benefited thereby.

Article 112. The censoring of correspondence addressed to internees or despatched by them shall be done as quickly as possible.

The examination of consignments intended for internees shall not be carried out under conditions that will expose the goods contained in them to deterioration. It shall be done in the presence of the addressee, or of a fellow-internee duly delegated by him. The delivery to internees of individual or collective consignments shall not be delayed under the pretext of difficulties of censorship.

Any prohibition of correspondence ordered by the Parties to the conflict either for military or political reasons, shall be only temporary and its duration shall be as short as possible.

Article 113. The Detaining Powers shall provide all reasonable facilities for the transmission, through the Protecting Power or the Central Agency provided for in Article 140, or as otherwise required, of wills, powers of attorney, letters of authority, or any other documents intended for internees or despatched by them.

In all cases the Detaining Powers shall facilitate the execution and authentication in due legal form of such documents on behalf of internees, in particular by allowing them to consult a lawyer.

Article 114. The Detaining Power shall afford internees all facilities to enable them to manage their property, provided this is not incompatible with the conditions of internment and the law which is applicable. For this purpose, the said Power may give them permission to leave the place of internment in urgent cases and if circumstances allow.

Article 115. In all cases where an internee is a party to proceedings in any court, the Detaining Power shall, if he so requests, cause the court to be informed of his detention and shall, within legal limits, ensure that all necessary steps are taken to prevent him from being in any way prejudiced, by reason of his internment, as regards the preparation and conduct of his case or as regards the execution of any judgment of the court.

Article 116. Every internee shall be allowed to receive visitors, especially near relatives, at regular intervals and as frequently as possible.

As far as is possible, internees shall be permitted to visit their homes in urgent cases, particularly in cases of death or serious illness of relatives.

Chapter IX
Penal and Disciplinary Sanctions

Article 117. Subject to the provisions of the present Charter, the laws in force in the territory in which they are detained will continue to apply to internees who commit offences during internment.

If general laws, regulations or orders declare acts committed by internees to be punishable, whereas the same acts are not punishable when committed by persons who are not internees, such acts shall entail disciplinary punishments only.

No internee may be punished more than once for the same act, or on the same count.

Article 118. The courts or authorities shall in passing sentence take as far as possible into account the fact that the defendant is not a national of the Detaining Power. They shall be free to reduce the penalty prescribed for the offence with which the internee is charged and shall not be obliged, to this end, to apply the minimum sentence prescribed.

Imprisonment in premises without daylight and, in general, all forms of cruelty without exception are forbidden.

Internees who have served disciplinary or judicial sentences shall not be treated differently from other internees.

The duration of preventive detention undergone by an internee shall be deducted from any disciplinary or judicial penalty involving confinement to which he may be sentenced.

Internee Committees shall be informed of all judicial proceedings instituted against internees whom they represent, and of their result.

Article 119. The disciplinary punishments applicable to internees shall be the following:

(1) a fine which shall not exceed 50 per cent of the wages which the internee would otherwise receive under the provisions of Article 95 during a period of not more than thirty days.

(2) discontinuance of privileges granted over and above the treatment provided for by the present Convention.

(3) fatigue duties, not exceeding two hours daily, in connection with the maintenance of the place of internment.

(4) confinement.

In no case shall disciplinary penalties be inhuman, brutal or dangerous for the health of internees. Account shall be taken of the internee's age, sex and state of health.

The duration of any single punishment shall in no case exceed a maximum of thirty consecutive days, even if the internee is answerable for several breaches of discipline when his case is dealt with, whether such breaches are connected or not.

Article 120. Internees who are recaptured after having escaped or when attempting to escape, shall be liable only to disciplinary punishment in respect of this act, even if it is a repeated offence.

Article 118, paragraph 3, notwithstanding, internees punished as a result of escape or attempt to escape, may be subjected to special surveillance, on condition that such surveillance does not affect the state of their health, that it is exercised in a place of internment and that it does not entail the abolition of any of the safeguards granted by the present Convention.

Internees who aid and abet an escape or attempt to escape, shall be liable on this count to disciplinary punishment only.

Article 121. Escape, or attempt to escape, even if it is a repeated offence, shall not be deemed an aggravating circumstance in cases where an internee is prosecuted for offences committed during his escape.

The Parties to the conflict shall ensure that the competent authorities exercise leniency in deciding whether punishment inflicted for an offence shall be of a disciplinary or judicial nature, especially in respect of acts committed in connection with an escape, whether successful or not.

Article 122. Acts which constitute offences against discipline shall be investigated immediately. This rule shall be applied, in particular, in cases of escape or attempt to escape. Recaptured internees shall be handed over to the competent authorities as soon as possible.

In case of offences against discipline, confinement awaiting trial shall be reduced to an absolute minimum for all internees, and shall not exceed fourteen days. Its duration shall in any case be deducted from any sentence of confinement.

The provisions of Articles 124 and 125 shall apply to internees who are in confinement awaiting trial for offences against discipline.

Article 123. Without prejudice to the competence of courts and higher authorities, disciplinary punishment may be ordered only by the commandant of the place of internment, or by a responsible officer or official who replaces him, or to whom he has delegated his disciplinary powers.

Before any disciplinary punishment is awarded, the accused internee shall be given precise information regarding the offences of which he is accused, and given an opportunity of explaining his conduct and of defending himself. He shall be permitted, in particular, to call witnesses and to have recourse, if necessary, to the services of a qualified interpreter. The decision shall be announced in the presence of the accused and of a member of the Internee Committee.

The period elapsing between the time of award of a disciplinary punishment and its execution shall not exceed one month.

When an internee is awarded a further disciplinary punishment, a period of at least three days shall elapse between the execution of any two of the punishments, if the duration of one of these is ten days or more.

A record of disciplinary punishments shall be maintained by the commandant of the place of internment and shall be open to inspection by representatives of the Protecting Power.

Article 124. Internees shall not in any case be transferred to penitentiary establishments (prisons, penitentiaries, convict prisons, etc.) to undergo disciplinary punishment therein.

The premises in which disciplinary punishments are undergone shall conform to sanitary requirements; they shall in particular be provided with adequate bedding. Internees undergoing punishment shall be enabled to keep themselves in a state of cleanliness.

Women internees undergoing disciplinary punishment shall be confined in separate quarters from male internees and shall be under the immediate supervision of women.

Article 125. Internees awarded disciplinary punishment shall be allowed to exercise and to stay in the open air at least two hours daily.

They shall be allowed, if they so request, to be present at the daily medical inspections. They shall receive the attention which their state of health requires and, if necessary, shall be removed to the infirmary of the place of internment or to a hospital.

They shall have permission to read and write, likewise to send and receive letters. Parcels and remittances of money, however, may be withheld from them until the completion of their punishment; such consignments shall meanwhile be entrusted to the Internee Committee, who will hand over to the infirmary the perishable goods contained in the parcels.

No internee given a disciplinary punishment may be deprived of the benefit of the provisions of Articles 107 and 143 of the present Convention.

Article 126. The provisions of Articles 71 to 76 inclusive shall apply, by analogy, to proceedings against internees who are in the national territory of the Detaining Power.

Chapter X
Transfers of Internees

Article 127. The transfer of internees shall always be effected humanely. As a general rule, it shall be carried out by rail or other means of transport, and under conditions at least equal to those obtaining for the forces of the Detaining Power in their changes of station. If, as an exceptional measure, such removals have to be effected on foot, they may not take place unless the internees are in a fit state of health, and may not in any case expose them to excessive fatigue.

The Detaining Power shall supply internees during transfer with drinking water and food sufficient in quantity, quality and variety to maintain them in good health, and also with the necessary clothing, adequate shelter and the necessary medical attention. The Detaining Power shall take all suitable precautions to ensure their safety during transfer, and shall establish before their departure a complete list of all internees transferred.

Sick, wounded or infirm internees and maternity cases shall not be transferred if the journey would be seriously detrimental to them, unless their safety imperatively so demands.

If the combat zone draws close to a place of internment, the internees in the said place shall not be transferred unless their removal can be carried out in adequate conditions of safety, or unless they are exposed to greater risks by remaining on the spot than by being transferred.

When making decisions regarding the transfer of internees, the Detaining Power shall take their interests into account and, in particular, shall not do anything to increase the difficulties of repatriating them or returning them to their own homes.

Article 128. In the event of transfer, internees shall be officially advised of their departure and of their new postal address. Such notification shall be given in time for them to pack their luggage and inform their next of kin.

They shall be allowed to take with them their personal effects, and the correspondence and parcels which have arrived for them. The weight of such baggage may be limited if the conditions of transfer so require, but in no case to less than twenty-five kilogrammes per internee.

Mail and parcels addressed to their former place of internment shall be forwarded to them without delay.

The commandant of the place of internment shall take, in agreement with the Internee Committee, any measures needed to ensure the transport of the internees' community property and of the luggage the internees are unable to take with them in consequence of restrictions imposed by virtue of the second paragraph.

Chapter XI
Deaths

Article 129. The wills of internees shall be received for safe-keeping by the responsible authorities; and in the event of the death of an internee his will shall be transmitted without delay to a person whom he has previously designated.

Deaths of internees shall be certified in every case by a doctor, and a death certificate shall be made out, showing the causes of death and the conditions under which it occurred.

An official record of the death, duly registered, shall be drawn up in accordance with the procedure relating thereto in force in the territory where the place of interment is situated, and a duly certified copy of such record shall be transmitted without delay to the Protecting Power as well as to the Central Agency referred to in Article 140.

Article 130. The detaining authorities shall ensure that internees who die while interned are honourably buried, if possible according to the rites of the religion to which they belonged and that their graves are respected, properly maintained, and marked in such a way that they can always be recognized.

Deceased internees shall be buried in individual graves unless unavoidable circumstances require the use of collective graves. Bodies may be cremated only for imperative reasons of hygiene, on account of the religion of the deceased or in accordance with his expressed wish to this effect. In case of cremation, the fact shall be stated and the reasons given in the death certificate of the deceased. The ashes shall be retained for safe-keeping by the detaining authorities and shall be transferred as soon as possible to the next of kin on their request.

As soon as circumstances permit, and not later than the close of hostilities, the Detaining Power shall forward lists of graves of deceased internees to the Powers on whom the deceased internees depended, through the Information Bureaux provided for in Article 136. Such lists shall include all particulars necessary for the identification of the deceased internees, as well as the exact location of their graves.

Article 131. Every death or serious injury of an internee, caused or suspected to have been caused by a sentry, another internee or any other person, as well as any death the cause of which is unknown, shall be immediately followed by an official enquiry by the Detaining Power.

A communication on this subject shall be sent immediately to the Protecting Power. The evidence of any witnesses shall be taken, and a report including such evidence shall be prepared and forwarded to the said Protecting Power.

If the enquiry indicates the guilt of one or more persons, the Detaining Power shall take all necessary steps to ensure the prosecution of the person or persons responsible.

Chapter XII
Release, Repatriation and Accommodation in Neutral Countries

Article 132. Each interned person shall be released by the Detaining Power as soon as the reasons which necessitated his internment no longer exist.

The Parties to the conflict shall, moreover, endeavour during the course of hostilities, to conclude agreements for the release, the repatriation, the return to places of residence or the accommodation in a neutral country of certain classes of internees, in particular children, pregnant women and mothers with infants and young children, wounded and sick, and internees who have been detained for a long time.

Article 133. Internment shall cease as soon as possible after the close of hostilities.

Internees in the territory of a Party to the conflict against whom penal proceedings are pending for offences not exclusively subject to disciplinary penalties, may be detained until the close of such proceedings and, if circumstances require, until the completion of the penalty. The same shall apply to internees who have been previously sentenced to a punishment depriving them of liberty.

By agreement between the Detaining Power and the Powers concerned, committees may be set up after the close of hostilities, or of the occupation of territories, to search for dispersed internees.

Article 134. The High Contracting Parties shall endeavour, upon the close of hostilities or occupation, to ensure the return of all internees to their last place of residence, or to facilitate their repatriation.

Article 135. The Detaining Power shall bear the expense of returning released internees to the places where they were residing when interned, or, if it took them into custody while they were in transit or on the high seas, the cost of completing their journey or of their return to their point of departure.

Where a Detaining Power refuses permission to reside in its territory to a released internee who previously had his permanent domicile therein, such Detaining Power shall pay the cost of the said internee's repatriation. If, however, the internee elects to return to his country on his own responsibility or in obedience to the Government of the Power to which he owes allegiance, the Detaining Power need not pay the expenses of his journey beyond the point of his departure from its territory. The Detaining Power need not pay the cost of repatriation of an internee who was interned at his own request.

If internees are transferred in accordance with Article 45, the transferring and receiving Powers shall agree on the portion of the above costs to be borne by each.

The foregoing shall not prejudice such special agreements as may be concluded between Parties to the conflict concerning the exchange and repatriation of their nationals in enemy hands.

SECTION V
INFORMATION BUREAUX AND CENTRAL AGENCY

Article 136. Upon the outbreak of a conflict and in all cases of occupation, each of the Parties to the conflict shall establish an official Information Bureau responsible for receiving and transmitting information in respect of the protected persons who are in its power.

Each of the Parties to the conflict shall, within the shortest possible period, give its Bureau information of any measure taken by it concerning any protected persons who are kept in custody for more than two weeks, who are subjected to assigned residence or who are interned. It shall, furthermore, require its various departments concerned with such matters to provide the aforesaid Bureau promptly with information concerning all changes pertaining to these protected persons, as, for example, transfers, releases, repatriations, escapes, admittances to hospitals, births and deaths.

Article 137. Each national Bureau shall immediately forward information concerning protected persons by the most rapid means to the Powers of whom the aforesaid persons are nationals, or to Powers in whose territory they resided, through the intermediary of the Protecting Powers and likewise through the Central Agency provided for in Article 140. The Bureaux shall also reply to all enquiries which may be received regarding protected persons.

Information Bureaux shall transmit information concerning a protected person unless its transmission might be detrimental to the person concerned or to his or her relatives. Even in such a case, the information may not be withheld from the Central Agency which, upon being notified of the circumstances, will take the necessary precautions indicated in Article 140.

All communications in writing made by any Bureau shall be authenticated by a signature or a seal.

Article 138. The information received by the national Bureau and transmitted by it shall be of such a character as to make it possible to identify the protected person exactly and to advise his next of kin quickly. The information in respect of each person shall include at least his surname, first names, place and date of birth, nationality, last residence and distinguishing characteristics, the first name of the father and the maiden name of the mother, the date, place and nature of the action taken with regard to the individual, the address at which correspondence may be sent to him and the name and address of the person to be informed.

Likewise, information regarding the state of health of internees who are seriously ill or seriously wounded shall be supplied regularly and if possible every week.

Article 139. Each national Information Bureau shall, furthermore, be responsible for collecting all personal valuables left by protected persons mentioned in Article 136, in particular those who have been repatriated or released, or who have escaped or died; it shall forward the said valuables to those concerned, either direct, or, if necessary, through the Central Agency. Such articles shall be sent by the Bureau in sealed packets which shall be accompanied by statements giving clear and full identity particulars of the person to whom the articles belonged, and by a complete list of the contents of the parcel. Detailed records shall be maintained of the receipt and despatch of all such valuables.

Article 140. A Central Information Agency for protected persons, in particular for internees, shall be created in a neutral country. The International Committee of the Red Cross shall, if it deems necessary, propose to the Powers concerned the organization of such an Agency, which may be the same as that provided for in Article 123 of the Geneva Convention relative to the Treatment of Prisoners of War of August 12, 1949. ʼ

The function of the Agency shall be to collect all information of the type set forth in Article 136 which it may obtain through official or private channels and to transmit it as rapidly as possible to the countries of origin or of residence of the persons concerned, except in cases where such transmissions might be detrimental to the persons whom the said information concerns, or to their relatives. It shall receive from the Parties to the conflict all reasonable facilities for effecting such transmissions.

The High Contracting Parties, and in particular those whose nationals benefit by the services of the Central Agency, are requested to give the said Agency the financial aid it may require.

The foregoing provisions shall in no way be interpreted as restricting the humanitarian activities of the International Committee of the Red Cross and of the relief societies described in Article 142.

Article 141. The national Information Bureaux and the Central Information Agency shall enjoy free postage for all mail, likewise the exemptions provided for in Article 110, and further, so far as possible, exemption from telegraphic charges or, at least, greatly reduced rates.

PART IV
EXECUTION OF THE CONVENTION

SECTION I
GENERAL PROVISIONS

Article 142. Subject to the measures which the Detaining Powers may consider essential to ensure their security or to meet any other reasonable need, the representatives of religious organizations, relief societies, or any other organizations assisting the protected persons, shall receive from these Powers, for themselves or their duly accredited agents, all facilities for visiting the protected persons, for distributing relief supplies and material from any source, intended for educational, recreational or religious purposes, or for assisting them in organizing their leisure time within the places of internment. Such societies or organizations may be constituted in the territory of the Detaining Power, or in any other country, or they may have an international character.

The Detaining Power may limit the number of societies and organizations whose delegates are allowed to carry out their activities in its territory and under its supervision, on condition, however, that such limitation shall not hinder the supply of effective and adequate relief to all protected persons.

The special position of the International Committee of the Red Cross in this field shall be recognized and respected at all times.

Article 143. Representatives or delegates of the Protecting Powers shall have permission to go to all places where protected persons are, particularly to places of internment, detention and work.

They shall have access to all premises occupied by protected persons and shall be able to interview the latter without witnesses, personally or through an interpreter.

Such visits may not be prohibited except for reasons of imperative military necessity, and then only as an exceptional and temporary measure. Their duration and frequency shall not be restricted.

Such representatives and delegates shall have full liberty to select the places they wish to visit. The Detaining or Occupying Power, the Protecting Power and when occasion arises the Power of origin of the persons to be visited, may agree that compatriots of the internees shall be permitted to participate in the visits.

The delegates of the International Committee of the Red Cross shall also enjoy the above prerogatives. The appointment of such delegates shall be submitted to the approval of the Power governing the territories where they will carry out their duties.

Article 144. The High Contracting Parties undertake, in time of peace as in time of war, to disseminate the text of the present Convention as widely as possible in their respective countries, and, in particular, to include the study thereof in their programmes of military and, if possible, civil instruction, so that the principles thereof may become known to the entire population.

Any civilian, military, police or other authorities, who in time of war assume responsibilities in respect of protected persons, must possess the text of the Convention and be specially instructed as to its provisions.

Article 145. The High Contracting Parties shall communicate to one another through the Swiss Federal Council and, during hostilities, through the Protecting Powers, the official translations of the present Convention, as well as the laws and regulations which they may adopt to ensure the application thereof.

Article 146. The High Contracting Parties undertake to enact any legislation necessary to provide effective penal sanctions for persons committing, or ordering to be committed, any of the grave breaches of the present Convention defined in the following Article.

Each High Contracting Party shall be under the obligation to search for persons alleged to have committed, or to have ordered to be committed, such grave breaches, and shall bring such persons, regardless of their nationality, before its own courts. It may also, if it prefers, and in accordance with the provisions of its own legislation, hand such persons over for trial to another High Contracting Party concerned, provided such High Contracting Party has made out a *prima facie* case.

Each High Contracting Party shall take measures necessary for the suppression of all acts contrary to the provisions of the present Convention other than the grave breaches defined in the following Article.

In all circumstances, the accused persons shall benefit by safeguards of proper trial and defence, which shall not be less favourable than those provided by Article 105 and those following of the Geneva Convention relative to the Treatment of Prisoners of War of August 12, 1949.

Article 147. Grave breaches to which the preceding Article relates shall be those involving any of the following acts, if committed against persons or property protected by the present Convention: wilful killing, torture or inhuman treatment, including biological experiments, wilfully causing great suffering or serious injury to body or health, unlawful deportation or transfer or unlawful confinement of a protected person, compelling a protected person to serve in the forces of a hostile Power, or wilfully depriving a protected person of the rights of fair and regular trial prescribed in the present Convention, taking of hostages and extensive destruction and appropriation of property, not justified by military necessity and carried out unlawfully and wantonly.

Article 148. No High Contracting Party shall be allowed to absolve itself or any other High Contracting Party of any liability incurred by itself or by another High Contracting Party in respect of breaches referred to in the preceding Article.

Article 149. At the request of a Party to the conflict, an enquiry shall be instituted, in a manner to be decided between the interested Parties, concerning any alleged violation of the Convention.

If agreement has not been reached concerning the procedure for the enquiry, the Parties should agree on the choice of an umpire who will decide upon the procedure to be followed.

Once the violation has been established, the Parties to the conflict shall put an end to it and shall repress it with the least possible delay.

. . .

ANNEX I
DRAFT AGREEMENT RELATING TO HOSPITAL AND SAFETY ZONES AND LOCALITIES

Article 1. Hospital and safety zones shall be strictly reserved for the persons mentioned in Article 23 of the Geneva Convention for the Amelioration of the Condition of the Wounded and Sick in Armed Forces in the Field of August 12, 1949, and in Article 14 of the Geneva Convention relative to the Protection of Civilian Persons in Time of War of August 12, 1949, and for the personnel entrusted with the organization and administration of these zones and localities and with the care of the persons therein assembled.

Nevertheless, persons whose permanent residence is within such zones shall have the right to stay there.

Article 2. No persons residing, in whatever capacity, in a hospital and safety zone shall perform any work, either within or without the zone, directly connected with military operations or the production of war material.

Article 3. The Power establishing a hospital and safety zone shall take all necessary measures to prohibit access to all persons who have no right of residence or entry therein.

Article 4. Hospital and safety zones shall fulfil the following conditions:

(a) They shall comprise only a small part of the territory governed by the Power which has established them.

(b) They shall be thinly populated in relation to the possibilities of accommodation.

(c) They shall be far removed and free from all military objectives, or large industrial or administrative establishments.

(d) They shall not be situated in areas which, according to every probability, may become important for the conduct of the war.

Article 5. Hospital and safety zones shall be subject to the following obligations:

(a) The lines of communication and means of transport which they possess shall not be used for the transport of military personnel or material, even in transit.

(b) They shall in no case be defended by military means.

Article 6. Hospital and safety zones shall be marked by means of oblique red bands on a white ground, placed on the buildings and outer precincts.

Zones reserved exclusively for the wounded and sick may be marked by means of the Red Cross (Red Crescent, Red Lion and Sun) emblem on a white ground.

They may be similarly marked at night by means of appropriate illumination.

Article 7. The Powers shall communicate to all the High Contracting Parties in peacetime or on the outbreak of hostilities, a list of the hospital and safety zones in the territories governed by them. They shall also give notice of any new zones set up during hostilities.

As soon as the adverse Party has received the above-mentioned notification, the zone shall be regularly established.

If, however, the adverse Party considers that the conditions of the present agreement have not been fulfilled, it may refuse to recognize the zone by giving immediate notice thereof to the Party responsible for the said zone, or may make its recognition of such zone dependent upon the institution of the control provided for in Article 8.

Article 8. Any Power having recognized one or several hospital and safety zones instituted by the adverse Party shall be entitled to demand control by one or more Special Commissions, for the purpose of ascertaining if the zones fulfil the conditions and obligations stipulated in the present agreement.

For this purpose, members of the Special Commissions shall at all times have free access to the various zones and may even reside there permanently. They shall be given all facilities for their duties of inspection.

Article 9. Should the Special Commissions note any facts which they consider contrary to the stipulations of the present agreement, they shall at once draw the attention of the Power governing the said zone to these facts, and shall fix a time limit of five days within which the matter should be rectified. They shall duly notify the Power who has recognized the zone.

If, when the time limit has expired, the Power governing the zone has not complied with the warning, the adverse Party may declare that it is no longer bound by the present agreement in respect of the said zone.

Article 10. Any Power setting up one or more hospital and safety zones, and the adverse Parties to whom their existence has been notified, shall nominate or have nominated by the Protecting Powers or by other neutral Powers, persons eligible to be members of the Special Commissions mentioned in Articles 8 and 9.

Article 11. In no circumstances may hospital and safety zones be the object of attack. They shall be protected and respected at all times by the Parties to the conflict.

Article 12. In the case of occupation of a territory, the hospital and safety zones therein shall continue to be respected and utilized as such.

Their purpose may, however, be modified by the Occupying Power, on condition that all measures are taken to ensure the safety of the persons accommodated.

Article 13. The present agreement shall also apply to localities which the Powers may utilize for the same purposes as hospital and safety zones.

ANNEX II
DRAFT REGULATIONS CONCERNING COLLECTIVE RELIEF

Article 1. The Internee Committees shall be allowed to distribute collective relief shipments for which they are responsible to all internees who are dependent for administration on the said Committee's place of internment, including those internees who are in hospitals, or in prisons or other penitentiary establishments.

Article 2. The distribution of collective relief shipments shall be effected in accordance with the instructions of the donors and with a plan drawn up by the Internee Committees. The issue of medical stores shall, however, be made for preference in agreement with the senior medical officers, and the latter may, in hospitals and infirmaries, waive the said instructions, if the needs of their patients so demand. Within the limits thus defined, the distribution shall always be carried out equitably.

Article 3. Members of Internee Committees shall be allowed to go to the railway stations or other points of arrival of relief supplies near their places of internment so as to enable them to verify the quantity as well as the quality of the goods received and to make out detailed reports thereon for the donors.

Article 4. Internee Committees shall be given the facilities necessary for verifying whether the distribution of collective relief in all subdivisions and annexes of their places of internment has been carried out in accordance with their instructions.

Article 5. Internee Committees shall be allowed to complete, and to cause to be completed by members of the Internee Committees in labour detachments or by the senior medical officers of infirmaries and hospitals, forms or questionnaires intended for the donors, relating to collective relief supplies (distribution, requirements, quantities, etc.). Such forms and questionnaires, duly completed, shall be forwarded to the donors without delay.

Article 6. In order to secure the regular distribution of collective relief supplies to the internees in their place of internment, and to meet any needs that may arise through the arrival of fresh parties of internees, the Internee Committees shall be allowed to create and maintain sufficient reserve stocks of collective relief. For this purpose, they shall have suitable warehouses at their disposal; each warehouse shall be provided with two locks, the Internee Committee holding the keys of one lock, and the commandant of the place of internment the keys of the other.

Article 7. The High Contracting Parties, and the Detaining Powers in particular, shall, so far as is in any way possible and subject to the regulations governing the food supply of the population, authorize purchases of goods to be made in their territories for the distribution of collective relief to the internees. They shall likewise facilitate the transfer of funds and other financial measures of a technical or administrative nature taken for the purpose of making such purchases.

Article 8. The foregoing provisions shall not constitute an obstacle to the right of internees to receive collective relief before their arrival in a place of internment or in the course of their transfer, nor to the possibility of representatives of the Protecting Power, or of the International Committee of the Red Cross or any other humanitarian organization giving assistance to internees and responsible for forwarding such supplies, ensuring the distribution thereof to the recipients by any other means they may deem suitable.

. . .

NOTE: Among the few judicial applications of the Fourth Geneva Convention, Israeli courts, since 1967, have had occasion to consider the Convention and customary international law regarding belligerent occupation. One of the more important and controversial decisions involved the interpretation of the prohibition on individual and mass forcible transfers of the population from occupied territory under Article 49 of the Fourth Geneva Convention.

AL AFFO AND THE ASSOCIATION FOR CIVIL RIGHTS IN ISRAEL v. COMMANDER OF THE ISRAEL DEFENSE FORCES IN THE WEST BANK

[April 10, 1988]
[29 I.L.M. 139 (1990); the Judgment is commonly
referred to as the "Affo Judgment"]

. . .

JUDGMENT

Shamgar P.:

1. These three petitions, which we have heard together, concern deportation orders under Regulation 112 of the Defence (Emergency) Regulations, 1945, which were issued with respect to each of the petitioners by the Commander of I.D.F. [Israel Defense Forces] Forces in his region. . . .

On 13 March 1988 we decided to dismiss the petitions . . .

3. (a) The petitioners raised, as a central reason for their petitions, the argument that Article 49 of the Geneva Convention relative to the Protection of Civilian Persons in Time of War, 1949 (hereinafter: the Fourth Geneva Convention) forbids the deportation of any of the petitioners from Judea, Samaria or the Gaza Strip, as the case may be. According to the argument, an absolute prohibition exists, with regard to a resident of one of the territories occupied by the I.D.F., against the application of Article 112 of the Defence (Emergency) Regulations, 1945[,] or of any other legal provision (if such exists) whose subject is deportation. This is due to the provisions of the above-mentioned international convention which, according to the contention, should be seen as a rule of public international law, binding upon the State of Israel and the Military Government bodies acting on its behalf and granting those injured the right of access to this Court. . . .

(d) *The accepted interpretation in our law:* We accept that the interpretive rules applied in a given legal system are peculiar to that system and are not necessarily identical with those applied in another legal system. . . .

The method of interpretation which our courts have applied for quite some time is that which attributes to the wording of the law the meaning which realizes its purpose; this is the interpretative method based on the legislative purpose. . .

In other words, language does not govern the purpose, rather it serves it. The law is an instrument for realizing legal policy, and therefore interpretation needs to aim toward emancipating the wording from its semantic bonds, were these to distance it from the legislative purpose which the words are intended to realize. . . .

In a nutshell, what has been said until now may be summarized thus: We have referred to the guidelines used in establishing the relation between the literal meaning of the written word and the correct legal interpretation, as far as this applies to our legal system. Interpretation in this sector seeks, as was said, to pave the way to a revelation of the legislative purpose. Setting the purpose in this form is directed to the sources which one may turn to in order to ascertain the purpose. It is customary in this matter to examine more than the text and, *inter alia*, also the legislative history; the legal and substantive context, and the meanings stemming from the structure of the legislation. . . .

(g) *Article 49 of the Fourth Geneva Convention:* What is the dispute regarding the interpretation of the above-mentioned Article 49. The relevant portions of the Article state:

> "Individual or mass forcible transfers, as well as deportations of protected persons from occupied territory to the territory of the Occupying Power or to that of any other country, occupied or not, are prohibited, regardless of their motive.
>
> Nevertheless, the Occupying Power may undertake total or partial evacuation of a given area if the security of the population or imperative military reasons so demand. . . . [in original]
>
> The Occupying Power shall not deport or transfer parts of its own civilian population into the territory it occupies.". . .

(h) *What were the considerations guiding the draftsmen of the Convention:*

. . . .

The Convention draftsmen referred to deportations "as those that took place during the last war" . . . [T]he purpose which the draftsmen of the Convention had in mind was the protection of the civilian population, which had become a principal victim of modern-day wars, and the adoption of rules which would ensure that civilians would not serve as a target for arbitrary acts and inhuman exploitation. What guided the draftsmen of the Convention were the mass deportations for purposes of extermination, mass population transfers for political or ethnic reasons or for forced labour. This is the "legislative purpose" and this is the material context.

It is reasonable to conclude that the reference to mass and individual deportations in the text of the Article was inserted in reaction also to the Nazi methods of operation used in World War II, in which mass transfers were conducted, sometimes on the basis of common ethnic identity, or by rounding up people in Ghettos, in streets or houses, at times on the basis of individual summonses through lists of names. Summons by name was done for the purpose of sending a person to death, to internment in a concentration camp, or for recruitment for slave labour in the factories of the occupier or in agriculture. Moreover, it seems that the summons to slave labour was always on an individual basis.

(i) The gist of the petitioners' argument is that the first paragraph prohibits any transfer of a person from the territory against his will.

The implications of this thesis are that Article 49 does not refer only to deportations, evacuations and transfers of civilian populations, as they were commonly defined in the period of the last war, but also to the removal of any person from the territory under any circumstances, whether after a legitimate judicial proceeding (e.g.[,] an extradition request), or after proving that the residence was unlawful and without permission . . . or for any other legal reason, based upon the internal law of the occupied territory.

According to the said argument, from the commencement of military rule over the territory there is a total freeze on the removal of persons, and whosoever is found in a territory under military rule cannot be removed for any reason whatsoever, as long as the military rule continues. In this matter there would be no difference between one dwelling lawfully or unlawfully in the territory, since Article 49 extends its protection to anyone termed "protected persons", and this expression embraces, according to Article 4 of the Convention, all persons found in the territory, whether or not they are citizens or permanent residents thereof and even if they are there illegally as infiltrators (including armed infiltrators), . . .

The petitioners' submission rests essentially on one portion of the first paragraph of the Article, i.e.[,] on the words ". . . transfers . . . deportations . . . regardless of their motive". [in original] That is, according to this thesis, the reason or legal basis for the deportation is no longer relevant. Although the petitioners would agree that the background to the wording of Article 49 is that described above, the Article must now be interpreted according to them in its *literal and simple* meaning, thus including any forced removal from the territory.

(j) I do not accept the thesis described for a number of reasons:

It is appropriate to present the implications of this argument in all its aspects. In this respect we should again detail what is liable to happen, according to the said argument, and what is the proper application of Article 49 in the personal sense and in the material sense.

. . .

The acceptance of the argument that the prohibition in Article 49 applies, whatever the motive for its personal application, means that if someone arrives in the territory for a visit of a limited period, or as a result of being shipwrecked on the Gaza coast, or even *as an infiltrator for the purpose of spying or sabotage* (and even if he is not a resident or national of the territory, for that is not a requirement of Article 4), it is prohibited to deport him so long as the territory is under military rule. In other words, the literal, simple and all-inclusive definition of Article 49, when read together with Article 4, leads to the conclusion that the legality of a person's presence in the territory is not relevant, for his physical presence in the territory is sufficient to provide him with absolute immunity from deportation. . . .

(k) From here we shall proceed to the essence of the concept "deportation", used in the Article. It is my opinion that, in accordance with the applicable rules of interpretation, one should not view the content of Article 49 as anything but a reference to those arbitrary deportations of groups of nationals as were carried out during World War II for purposes of subjugation, extermination and for similarly cruel reasons.

If, on the other hand, one accepts the proposed interpretation of the petitioners, according to which deportation means any physical removal from the territory, then the above would apply, for instance, to deportation for the purposes of extradition of the protected person, for this too requires removing a person from the territory. Laws, judicial decisions and legal literature use, in the context of extradition, the term deportation to refer to the stage of carrying out the extradition or the rendition. A murderer who escaped to the occupied territory would have a safe haven, which would preclude his transfer to the authorized jurisdiction. . . .

(m) To summarize, this Court had the authority to choose the interpretation that rests upon the principles explained above over the literal interpretation urged by the petitioners.

. . .

4. (a) This Court has indicated in its judgments that the above-mentioned Article 49 is within the realm of conventional international law. In consequence of this determination, the petitioners have now raised a new thesis . . .

(b) The petitioners submit that not only does customary international law automatically become part of the country's laws (barring any contradictory law), but that there are also parts of conventional international law which are automatically incorporated, without the need for adoption by way of legislation as a substantive part of Israeli municipal law. These are those parts of conventional international law which are within the realm of "law-making treaties". . . .

5. (d) . . . [A]ccording to the law applying in Israel, an international treaty does not become part of Israeli law unless—

(1) Its provisions are adopted by way of legislation and to the extent that they are so adopted, or,

(2) The provisions of the treaty are but a repetition or declaration of existing customary international law, namely, the codification of existing custom.

This is the way that Israel has approached the provisions of international treaties, which are indicative of "law-making treaties [*sic*]", such as in the enactment of the Crime of Genocide (Prevention and Punishment) Law, 5710-1950, which was passed pursuant to the Convention on the Prevention and Punishment of the Crime of Genocide; the Air Navigation (Security in Civil Aviation) Law, 5737-1977, which was passed pursuant to the 1970 Hague Conventions against the seizure of aircrafts and the 1971 Montreal Convention for the Suppression of Unlawful Acts Against the Safety of Civil Aviation; . . .

(e) If we apply what was said above to the issue before us, we must remember that Article 49 has been categorized in our judgments as conventional law which does not express customary international law. . . .

Bach J.:

1. I concur in the final conclusion that my esteemed colleague, the President, has reached regarding these petitions; however, on one point of principal importance I must dissent from his opinion . . . [in original]

The issue concerns the proper interpretation of Article 49 of the Fourth Geneva Convention (hereinafter "The Convention"). . . .

5. . . . I tend to accept the position of the petitioners on this matter, and my reasons are as follows:

a) The language of Article 49 is unequivocal and explicit. The combination of the words "*Individual or mass forcible tra[n]sfers as well as deportations*" in conjunction with the phrase "*regardless of their motive*" (emphasis added—g.b.), admits in my opinion no room to doubt, that the Article applies not only to mass deportations but to the deportation of individuals as well, and that the prohibition was intended to be total, sweeping and unconditional—"regardless of their motive."

b) I accept the approach, which found expression in Sussman P.'s judgment in *H.C. 97/79*, namely that the Convention was framed in the wake of the Hitler period in Germany, and in face of the crimes which were perpetrated against the civilian population by the Nazis during World War II. Similarly, I would subscribe to the opinion that one may consider the historical facts accompanying the making of a convention and the purpose for its framing in order to find a suitable interpretation for the articles of the convention. Even the Vienna Convention, upon which Professor Kretzmer relied in this context, does not refute this possibility, for Article 31 of the Convention establishes the following:

> "A treaty shall be interpreted in good faith in accordance with the ordinary meaning to be given to the terms of the treaty in their context and in the light of its object and purpose."

On this issue I do not dissent at all from the opinion of the esteemed President and most of the authorities cited in his opinion are acceptable to me as well.

However, I find no contradiction between this "historical approach" and the possibility of giving a broad interpretation to the Article in question.

. . . .

The text of the Article, both in terms of its context and against the backdrop of the treaty in its entirety, cannot admit in my opinion the interpretation, that it is directed solely towards preventing actions such as those that were committed by the Nazis for racial, ethnic or national reasons.

We must not deviate by way of interpretation from the clear and simple meaning of the words of an enactment when the language of the Article is unequivocal and when the linguistic interpretation does not contradict the legislative purpose and does not lead to illogical and absurd conclusions.

. . . .

6. . . . My esteemed colleague, the President, also relies on the argument that, in light of the sweeping formulation of Article 4 of the Convention which includes a definition of the term "protected persons" under the Convention, a literal interpretation of Article 49 would lead to the conclusion that one could not even deport terrorists who illegally infiltrate into the territory during the occupation, and similarly that it would not be possible to extradite criminals from the territories to other states in accordance with extradition treaties.

The question regarding infiltrators could arise because of a certain difficulty in the interpretation of Article 4 of the Convention, which is not free of ambiguity. Thus when that same Article 4 states that "Persons protected by the Convention are those who *find themselves* in case of a conflict or occupation in the hands of a Party to the conflict or an Occupying Power. . ." (emphasis added—g.b.) [in original] then there is perhaps room to argue that the reference is to people who due to an armed conflict or belligerence between states, have fallen into a situation where against their will they *find themselves* in the hands of one of the parties to the conflict or in the hands of the occupying power; whereas people who subsequently penetrate into that territory with malicious intent are not included in that definition. If and when this problem arises in an actual case, there will be a need to resolve it through an appropriate interpretation of Article 4 of the Convention, but this does not suffice, in my opinion, to raise doubts concerning the interpretation of Article 49. In the matter before us, the aforesaid difficulty is in any case non-existent, since the petitioners are, by all opinions, permanent residents of the territories controlled by the I.D.F.; and if the Convention under discussion applies to those territories, then they are undoubtedly included in the definition of "protected persons".

The same applies to the problem of extraditing criminals. The question of to what extent an extradition treaty between states is feasible, when it concerns people who are located in territories occupied by countries which are parties to the treaty, is thorny and complicated in itself; and whatever may be the answer to this question, one can not draw inferences from this regarding the interpretation of Article 49. In any case, should it be established that it is indeed possible to extradite persons who are residents of occupied territories on the basis of the Extradition Law, 5714-1954[,] and the treaties that were signed in accordance with it, then regarding the possibility of actually extraditing the persons concerned, I would arrive at the same ultimate conclusion as I do regarding the petitioners against whom the deportation orders were issued under Regulation 112 of the Defence (Emergency) Regulations, as will be detailed below.

7. Despite the aforesaid I concur with the opinion of my esteemed colleague, the President, that these petitions should be dismissed. I do indeed see a need to dissent from the rule established in *H.C.* 97/79 regarding the interpretation of Article 49 of the Convention. On the other hand, I do not see any grounds for deviating from the rule that was established and upheld in an appreciable number of judgments under which Article 49 of the Convention is solely a provision of conventional international law as opposed to a provision of customary international

law. Such a provision does not constitute binding law and cannot serve as a basis for petitions to the courts by individuals.

. . .

NOTE: On December 17, 1992, Israel deported 415 Palestinians (ten of whom were deemed a week later to have been wrongly deported and thus permitted to return) from the occupied West Bank and Gaza Strip to the buffer zone Israel established in southern Lebanon. The mass deportation was the largest undertaken by Israel since the period just after the 1967 Arab-Israeli War and relied upon the same Emergency Defence Regulations, dating from the British mandate in Palestine, that were at issue in the *Affo Judgment*. The expulsions were in response to violence emanating from several Islamic fundamentalist groups, the most recent of which were the fatal shootings of four Israeli soldiers and the slaying of an Israeli border policeman, for which the Islamic group Hamas claimed responsibility. The Israeli government asserted that those deported were members either of Hamas or another group, Islamic Holy War, and, consequently, Israel was justified, for security reasons, in deporting them en masse. The deportations were to last for two years.

International condemnation of the mass expulsions was swift and uniform. Commentators claimed that the deportations violated Article 49 of the Fourth Geneva Convention and represented a grave breach of the Convention. The Security Council of the United Nations was no less unequivocal. The Security Council unanimously approved a resolution condemning Israel for the deportations and demanding that those expelled be permitted to return forthwith.

The Israeli High Court of Justice upheld the mass deportation on January 28, 1993, in an opinion consistent with previous High Court rulings in deportation cases, such as the *Affo Judgment*. The court held, among other things, that Article 49 envisages deportations of entire peoples as were conducted by the Nazis in World War II, not deportations of specific individuals considered to be security threats. But the court said that the expulsions had not been processed individually, as required, and hence were reviewable on a case-by-case basis at the initiative of the expelled parties. This, obviously, presented certain logistical problems.

Notwithstanding the High Court's ruling, the Israeli government later modified its position. Succumbing to international pressures and, perhaps, a wish to facilitate progress in the Middle East peace negotiations, Israel offered in February 1993 to permit most of the Palestinians to return, but not all at the same time. The deportees rejected this piecemeal plan. After the Israel-P.L.O. peace accord of 1993, Israel permitted the remaining 415 expellees to return.

ENDNOTE

1. Article 2 is identical in all four of the Geneva Conventions of 1949 and is usually referred to as "common Article 2." It is set out above at p. 153.

TERRORISM

Terrorism has come to mean the intentional use of violence against civilian and military targets generally outside of an acknowledged war zone by private groups or groups that appear to be private but have some measure of covert state sponsorship. Given the ease and rapidity of international transportation and the relative miniaturization of weapons of great destructive power, the opportunities for terrorism have increased dramatically in recent years. As we saw in Chapter 1, the support of the General Assembly of the United Nations for so-called wars of national liberation led to a number of provisions in some legal instruments that characterized certain examples of this form of coercion as lawful or even heroic.

The tide appears to have turned. In general, the international community now condemns terrorism. But the reaction is not uniform. The taking of hostages for political or extortionary purposes, for example, widely practiced in Lebanon, is condemned in Western Europe and North America. Reactions in the Middle East are more equivocal. Whatever purpose terrorism claims to serve, it violates the law of war. It does not discriminate between combatants and noncombatants but, rather, intentionally targets civilians. It violates the principles of proportionality and necessity and extends the arena of conflict.

A number of international instruments seek to establish ways of prosecuting and deterring certain terrorist practices deemed especially noxious to international life.

AVIATION: OFFENCES AND CERTAIN OTHER ACTS COMMITTED ON BOARD AIRCRAFT

[20 U.S.T. 2941, convention done on September 14, 1963, at Tokyo; entered into force for United States on December 4, 1969]

. . .

Article 11

1. When a person on board has unlawfully committed by force or threat thereof an act of interference, seizure, or other wrongful exercise of control of an aircraft in flight or when such an act is about to be committed, Contracting States shall take all appropriate measures to restore control of the aircraft to its lawful commander or to preserve his control of the aircraft.

. . .

Article 16

1. Offences committed on aircraft registered in a Contracting State shall be treated, for the purpose of extradition, as if they had been committed not only in the place in which they have occurred but also in the territory of the State of registration of the aircraft.

2. Without prejudice to the provisions of the preceding paragraph, nothing in this Convention shall be deemed to create an obligation to grant extradition.

. . .

SUPPRESSION OF UNLAWFUL SEIZURE OF AIRCRAFT (HIJACKING)

[22 U.S.T. 1641, convention done on December 16, 1970, at The Hague; entered into force for the United States on October 14, 1971]

. . .

Article 1

Any person who on board an aircraft in flight:
(a) unlawfully, by force or threat thereof, or by any other form of intimidation, seizes, or exercises control of, that aircraft, or attempts to perform any such act, or

(b) is an accomplice of a person who performs or attempts to perform any such act commits an offence (hereinafter referred to as "the offence").

Article 2

Each Contracting State undertakes to make the offence punishable by severe penalties.

.   .   .

Article 7

The Contracting State in the territory of which the alleged offender is found shall, if it does not extradite him, be obliged, without exception whatsoever and whether or not the offence was committed in its territory, to submit the case to its competent authorities for the purpose of prosecution.

Those authorities shall take their decision in the same manner as in the case of any ordinary offence of a serious nature under the law of that State.

Article 8

1. The offence shall be deemed to be included as an extraditable offence in any extradition treaty existing between Contracting States. Contracting States undertake to include the offence as an extraditable offence in every extradition treaty to be concluded between them.

.   .   .

Article 9

1. When any of the acts mentioned in Article 1(a) has occurred or is about to occur, Contracting States shall take all appropriate measures to restore control of the aircraft to its lawful commander or to preserve his control of the aircraft.

.   .   .

Article 12

1. Any dispute between two or more Contracting States concerning the interpretation or application of this Convention which cannot be settled through negotiation, shall, at the request of one of them, be submitted to arbitration. If within six months from the date of the request for arbitration the Parties are unable to agree on the organization of the arbitration, any one of those Parties may refer the dispute to the Inter-

national Court of Justice by request in conformity with the Statute of the Court.

. . .

CONVENTION FOR THE SUPPRESSION OF UNLAWFUL ACTS AGAINST THE SAFETY OF CIVIL AVIATION

[24 U.S.T. 565, done on September 23, 1971, at Montreal; entered into force for United States on January 26, 1973]

. . .

Article 1

1. Any person commits an offence if he unlawfully and intentionally:
(a) performs an act of violence against a person on board an aircraft in flight if that act is likely to endanger the safety of that aircraft; or
(b) destroys an aircraft in service or causes damage to such an aircraft which renders it incapable of flight or which is likely to endanger its safety in flight; or
(c) places or causes to be placed on an aircraft in service, by any means whatsoever, a device or substance which is likely to destroy that aircraft, or to cause damage to it which renders it incapable of flight, or to cause damage to it which is likely to endanger its safety in flight; or
(d) destroys or damages air navigation facilities or interferes with their operation, if any such act is likely to endanger the safety of aircraft in flight; or
(e) communicates information which he knows to be false, thereby endangering the safety of an aircraft in flight.
2. Any person also commits an offence if he:
(a) attempts to commit any of the offences mentioned in paragraph 1 of this Article; or
(b) is an accomplice of a person who commits or attempts to commit any such offence.

. . .

Article 3

Each Contracting State undertakes to make the offences mentioned in Article 1 punishable by severe penalties.

Article 4

1. This Convention shall not apply to aircraft used in military, customs or police services.

2. In the cases contemplated in subparagraphs (a), (b), (c) and (e) of paragraph 1 of Article 1, this Convention shall apply, irrespective of whether the aircraft is engaged in an international or domestic flight, only if:

 (a) the place of take-off or landing, actual or intended, of the aircraft is situated outside the territory of the State of registration of that aircraft; or

 (b) the offence is committed in the territory of a State other than the State of registration of the aircraft.

3. Notwithstanding paragraph 2 of this Article, in the cases contemplated in subparagraphs (a), (b), (c) and (e) of paragraph 1 of Article 1, this Convention shall also apply if the offender or the alleged offender is found in the territory of a State other than the State of registration of the aircraft.

4. With respect to the States mentioned in Article 9 and in the cases mentioned in subparagraphs (a), (b), (c) and (e) of paragraph 1 of Article 1, this Convention shall not apply if the places referred to in subparagraph (a) of paragraph 2 of this Article are situated within the territory of the same State where that State is one of those referred to in Article 9, unless the offence is committed or the offender or alleged offender is found in the territory of a State other than that State.

5. In the cases contemplated in subparagraph (d) of paragraph 1 of Article 1, this Convention shall apply only if the air navigation facilities are used in international air navigation.

6. The provisions of paragraphs 2, 3, 4 and 5 of this Article shall also apply in the cases contemplated in paragraph 2 of Article 1.

. . .

Article 7

The Contracting State in the territory of which the alleged offender is found shall, if it does not extradite him, be obliged, without exception whatsoever and whether or not the offence was committed in its territory, to submit the case to its competent authorities for the purpose of prosecution. Those authorities shall take their decision in the same manner as in the case of any ordinary offence of a serious nature under the law of that State.

Article 8

1. The offences shall be deemed to be included as extraditable offences in any extradition treaty existing between Contracting States. Contracting States undertake to include the offences as extraditable offences in every extradition treaty to be concluded between them.

Article 9

The Contracting States which establish joint air transport operating organizations or international operating agencies, which operate aircraft which are subject to joint or international registration shall, by appropriate means, designate for each aircraft the State among them which shall exercise the jurisdiction and have the attributes of the State of registration for the purpose of this Convention and shall give notice thereof to the International Civil Aviation Organization which shall communicate the notice to all States Parties to this Convention.

. . .

Article 14

1. Any dispute between two or more Contracting States concerning the interpretation or application of this Convention which cannot be settled through negotiation, shall, at the request of one of them, be submitted to arbitration. If within six months from the date of the request for arbitration the Parties are unable to agree on the organization of the arbitration, any one of those Parties may refer the dispute to the International Court of Justice by request in conformity with the Statute of the Court.

. . .

◆

INTERNATIONAL TERRORISM

PREVENTION AND PUNISHMENT OF CRIMES AGAINST INTERNATIONALLY PROTECTED PERSONS, INCLUDING DIPLOMATIC AGENTS

[28 U.S.T. 1975, convention adopted by the General Assembly of the United Nations on December 14, 1973, at New York; entered into force for the United States on February 20, 1977]

. . .

Article 1

For the purposes of this Convention:
1. "[I]nternationally protected person" means:
   (a) a Head of State, including any member of a collegial body performing the functions of a Head of State under the constitution of the State concerned, a Head of Government or a Minister for Foreign Affairs, whenever any such person is in a foreign State, as well as members of his family who accompany him;
   (b) any representative or official of a State or any official or other agent of an international organization of an intergovernmental character who, at the time when and in the place where a crime against him, his official premises, his private accommodation or his means of transport is committed, is entitled pursuant to international law to special protection from any attack on his person, freedom or dignity, as well as members of his family forming part of his household;
2. "[A]lleged offender" means a person as to whom there is sufficient evidence to determine *prima facie* that he has committed or participated in one or more of the crimes set forth in article 2.

Article 2

1. The intentional commission of:
   (a) a murder, kidnapping or other attack upon the person or liberty of an internationally protected person;
   (b) a violent attack upon the official premises, the private accommodation or the means of transport of an internationally protected person likely to endanger his person or liberty;

(c) a threat to commit any such attack;

(d) an attempt to commit any such attack; and

(e) an act constituting participation as an accomplice in any such attack shall be made by each State Party a crime under its internal law.

2. Each State Party shall make these crimes punishable by appropriate penalties which take into account their grave nature.

3. Paragraphs 1 and 2 of this article in no way derogate from the obligations of States Parties under international law to take all appropriate measures to prevent other attacks on the person, freedom or dignity of an internationally protected person.

.   .   .

Article 7

The State Party in whose territory the alleged offender is present shall, if it does not extradite him, submit, without exception whatsoever and without undue delay, the case to its competent authorities for the purpose of prosecution, through proceedings in accordance with the laws of that State.

Article 8

1. To the extent that the crimes set forth in article 2 are not listed as extraditable offences in any extradition treaty existing between States Parties, they shall be deemed to be included as such therein. States Parties undertake to include those crimes as extraditable offences in every future extradition treaty to be concluded between them.

.   .   .

INTERNATIONAL CONVENTION AGAINST THE TAKING OF HOSTAGES

[G.A. Res. 146, U.N. GAOR, 34th Sess., Supp. No. 46, at 245, U.N. Doc. A/34/46 (1980), adopted by the General Assembly of the United Nations on December 17, 1979, at New York]

.   .   .

Article 1

1. Any person who seizes or detains and threatens to kill, to injure or to continue to detain another person (hereinafter referred to as the

"hostage") in order to compel a third party, namely, a State, an international intergovernmental organization, a natural or juridical person, or a group of persons, to do or abstain from doing any act as an explicit or implicit condition for the release of the hostage commits the offence of taking of hostages ("hostage-taking") within the meaning of this Convention.

2. Any person who:

(a) attempts to commit an act of hostage-taking, or

(b) participates as an accomplice of anyone who commits or attempts to commit an act of hostage-taking

likewise commits an offence for the purpose of this Convention.

Article 2

Each State Party shall make the offences set forth in article 1 punishable by appropriate penalties which take into account the grave nature of those offences.

Article 3

1. The State Party in the territory of which the hostage is held by the offender shall take all measures it considers appropriate to ease the situation of the hostage, in particular, to secure his release and, after his release, to facilitate, when relevant, his departure.

2. If any object which the offender has obtained as a result of the taking of hostages comes into the custody of a State Party, that State Party shall return it as soon as possible to the hostage or the third party referred to in article 1, as the case may be, or to the appropriate authorities thereof.

.   .   .

Article 8

1. The State Party in the territory of which the alleged offender is found shall, if it does not extradite him, be obliged, without exception whatsoever and whether or not the offence was committed in its territory, to submit the case to its competent authorities for the purpose of prosecution, through proceedings in accordance with the laws of that State. Those authorities shall take their decision in the same manner as in the case of any ordinary offence of a grave nature under the law of that State.

2. Any person regarding whom proceedings are being carried out in connexion with any of the offences set forth in article 1 shall be guar-

anteed fair treatment at all stages of the proceedings, including enjoyment of all the rights and guarantees provided by the law of the State in the territory of which he is present.

. . .

Article 12

In so far as the Geneva Conventions of 1949 for the protection of war victims [footnote omitted] or the Protocols Additional to those Conventions are applicable to a particular act of hostage-taking, and in so far as States Parties to this Convention are bound under those conventions to prosecute or hand over the hostage-taker, the present Convention shall not apply to an act of hostage-taking committed in the course of armed conflicts as defined in the Geneva Conventions of 1949 and the Protocols thereto, including armed conflicts, mentioned in article 1, paragraph 4, of Additional Protocol I of 1977, [footnote omitted] in which peoples are fighting against colonial domination and alien occupation and against racist régimes in the exercise of their right of self-determination, as enshrined in the Charter of the United Nations and the Declaration on Principles of International Law concerning Friendly Relations and Cooperation among States in accordance with the Charter of the United Nations.

. . .

NOTE: There also have been regional efforts. In 1971, the Organization of American States enacted a convention to prevent and punish acts of terrorism that are of international significance. It largely tracks the international conventions already reproduced here. In 1977, the Council of Europe enacted the European Convention on the Suppression of Terrorism that established a regime for members of the council to deal with terrorism. On December 4, 1979, the European Community concluded an additional agreement, concerning the application of the European Convention on the Suppression of Terrorism among the member states.

During the last decade, a growing consensus within the international community has developed about the condemnation of international terrorism. This consensus is evidenced by, among other things, two United Nations resolutions condemning terrorism, a Group of Seven statement condemning terrorism, and a recent convention concerning the marking of plastic explosives (as a means to increase the detectability of such explosives), extracts from each of which follow.

RESOLUTION ADOPTED BY THE UNITED NATIONS GENERAL ASSEMBLY TO PREVENT INTERNATIONAL TERRORISM

[G.A. Res. 61, U.N. GAOR, 40th Sess., Supp. No. 53, at 301, U.N. Doc. A/40/53 (1986), adopted December 9, 1985]

The General Assembly,

. . .

1. *Unequivocally condemns*, as criminal, all acts, methods and practices of terrorism wherever and by whomever committed, including those which jeopardize friendly relations among States and their security;

2. *Deeply deplores* the loss of innocent human lives which results from such acts of terrorism;

3. *Also deplores* the pernicious impact of acts of international terrorism on relations of co-operation among States, including co-operation for development;

4. *Appeals* to all States that have not yet done so to consider becoming party to the existing international conventions relating to various aspects of international terrorism;

5. *Invites* all States to take all appropriate measures at the national level with a view to the speedy and final elimination of the problem of international terrorism, such as the harmonization of domestic legislation with existing international conventions, the fulfilment of assumed international obligations, and the prevention of the preparation and organization in their respective territories of acts directed against other States;

6. *Calls upon* all States to fulfil their obligations under international law to refrain from organizing, instigating, assisting or participating in terrorist acts in other States, or acquiescing in activities within their territory directed towards the commission of such acts;

. . .

Resolution Adopted by the United Nations Security Council Condemning Hostage-Taking and Abduction

[S.C. Res. 579, U.N. SCOR, 40th Sess., 2637th mtg., at 24, U.N. Doc. S/INF/41 (1986), adopted December 18, 1985]

The Security Council,

Deeply disturbed at the prevalence of incidents of hostage-taking and abduction, several of which are of protracted duration and have included loss of life,

Considering that the taking of hostages and abductions are offences of grave concern to the international community, having severe adverse consequences for the rights of the victims and for the promotion of friendly relations and co-operation among States.

. . .

1. *Condemns unequivocally* all acts of hostage-taking and abduction;
2. *Calls for* the immediate safe release of all hostages and abducted persons wherever and by whomever they are being held;
3. *Affirms* the obligation of all States in whose territory hostages or abducted persons are held urgently to take all appropriate measures to secure their safe release and to prevent the commission of acts of hostage-taking and abduction in the future;

. . .

Texts of the Statements Adopted by Leaders of Seven Industrial Democracies [At the Tokyo Summit Meeting, Concerning Terrorism]

[Statement on International Terrorism, Adopted by Leaders of Seven Industrial Democracies at the Tokyo Summit, May 5, 1986, Weekly Compilation of Presidential Documents, Volume 22, Number 19, at 583.]

. . .

We, the heads of state or government of seven major democracies and the representatives of the European Community, assembled here in

Tokyo, strongly reaffirm our condemnation of international terrorism in all its forms, of its accomplices and of those, including governments, who sponsor or support it. We abhor the increase in the level of such terrorism since our last meeting, and in particular its blatant and cynical use as an instrument of government policy. Terrorism has no justification. It spreads only by the use of contemptible means, ignoring the values of human life, freedom and dignity. It must be fought relentlessly and without compromise.

Recognizing that the continuing fight against terrorism is a task which the international community as a whole has to undertake, we pledge ourselves to make maximum efforts to fight against the scourge. Terrorism must be fought effectively through determined tenacious, discreet and patient action combining national measures with international cooperation. Therefore, we urge all like-minded nations to collaborate with us, particularly in such international fora as the United Nations, the International Civil Aviation Organization and the International Maritime Organization, drawing on their expertise to improve and extend countermeasures against terrorism and those who sponsor or support it.

We, the heads of state or government, agree to intensify the exchange of information in relevant fora on threats and potential threats emanating from terrorist activities and those who support and sponsor them, and on ways to prevent them.

We specify the following as measures open to any government concerned to deny to international terrorists the opportunity and the means to carry out their aims, and to identify and deter those who perpetrate such terrorism. We have decided to apply these measures within the framework of international law and in our own jurisdictions in respect of any state which is clearly involved in sponsoring or supporting international terrorism, and in particular of Libya, until such time as the state concerned abandons its complicity in, or support for, such terrorism. These measures are:

Refusal to export arms to states which sponsor or support terrorism.

Strict limits on the size of the diplomatic and consular missions and other official bodies abroad of states which engage in such activities, control of travel of members of such missions and bodies, and, where appropriate, radical reductions in, or even the closure of, such missions and bodies.

Denial of entry to all persons, including diplomatic personnel, who have been expelled or excluded from one of our states on suspicion of involvement in international terrorism or who have been convicted of such a terrorist offense.

Improved extradition procedures within due process of domestic law for bringing to trial those who have perpetrated such acts of terrorism.

Stricter immigration and visa requirements and procedures in respect of nationals of states which sponsor or support terrorism.

The closest possible bilateral and multilateral cooperation between police and security organizations and other relevant authorities in the fight against terrorism.

CONVENTION ON THE MARKING OF PLASTIC EXPLOSIVES FOR THE PURPOSE OF DETECTION

[30 I.L.M. 721 (1991), done on March 1, 1991, at Montreal]

THE STATES PARTIES TO THIS CONVENTION,

CONSCIOUS of the implications of acts of terrorism for international security;

EXPRESSING deep concern regarding terrorist acts aimed at destruction of aircraft, other means of transportation and other targets;

CONCERNED that plastic explosives have been used for such terrorist acts;

CONSIDERING that the marking of such explosives for the purpose of detection would contribute significantly to the prevention of such unlawful acts;

RECOGNIZING that for the purpose of deterring such unlawful acts there is an urgent need for an international instrument obliging States to adopt appropriate measures to ensure that plastic explosives are duly marked;

CONSIDERING United Nations Security Council Resolution 635 of 14 June 1989, and United Nations General Assembly Resolution 44/29 of 4 December 1989 urging the International Civil Aviation Organization to intensify its work on devising an international regime for the marking of plastic or sheet explosives for the purpose of detection;

. . .

HAVE AGREED AS FOLLOWS:

Article I

For the purpose of this Convention:

1. "Explosives" mean explosive products, commonly known as "plastic explosives", including explosives in flexible or elastic sheet form, as described in the Technical Annex to this Convention.

2. "Detection agent" means a substance as described in the Technical Annex to this Convention which is introduced into an explosive to render it detectable.

3. "Marking" means introducing into an explosive a detection agent in accordance with the Technical Annex to this Convention.

4. "Manufacture" means any process, including reprocessing, that produces explosives.

5. "Duly authorized military devices" include, but are not restricted to, shells, bombs, projectiles, mines, missiles, rockets, shaped charges, grenades and perforators manufactured exclusively for military or police purposes according to the laws and regulations of the State Party concerned.

6. "Producer State" means any State in whose territory explosives are manufactured.

Article II

Each State Party shall take the necessary and effective measures to prohibit and prevent the manufacture in its territory of unmarked explosives.

Article III

1. Each State Party shall take the necessary and effective measures to prohibit and prevent the movement into or out of its territory of unmarked explosives.

2. The preceding paragraph shall not apply in respect of movements for purposes not inconsistent with the objectives of this Convention, by authorities of a State Party performing military or police functions, of unmarked explosives under the control of that State Party in accordance with paragraph 1 of Article IV.

Article IV

1. Each State Party shall take the necessary measures to exercise strict and effective control over the possession and transfer of possession of

unmarked explosives which have been manufactured in or brought into its territory prior to the entry into force of this Convention in respect of that State, so as to prevent their diversion or use for purposes inconsistent with the objectives of this Convention.

2. Each State Party shall take the necessary measures to ensure that all stocks of those explosives referred to in paragraph 1 of this Article not held by its authorities performing military or police functions are destroyed or consumed for purposes not inconsistent with the objectives of this Convention, marked or rendered permanently ineffective, within a period of three years from the entry into force of this Convention in respect of that State.

3. Each State Party shall take the necessary measures to ensure that all stocks of those explosives referred to in paragraph 1 of this Article held by its authorities performing military or police functions and that are not incorporated as an integral part of duly authorized military devices are destroyed or consumed for purposes not inconsistent with the objectives of this Convention, marked or rendered permanently ineffective, within a period of fifteen years from the entry into force of this Convention in respect of that State.

4. Each State Party shall take the necessary measures to ensure the destruction, as soon as possible, in its territory of unmarked explosives which may be discovered therein and which are not referred to in the preceding paragraphs of this Article, other than stocks of unmarked explosives held by its authorities performing military or police functions and incorporated as an integral part of duly authorized military devices at the date of the entry into force of this Convention in respect of that State.

5. Each State Party shall take the necessary measures to exercise strict and effective control over the possession and transfer of possession of the explosives referred to in paragraph II of Part 1 of the Technical Annex to this Convention so as to prevent their diversion or use for purposes inconsistent with the objectives of this Convention.

6. Each State Party shall take the necessary measures to ensure the destruction, as soon as possible, in its territory of unmarked explosives manufactured since the coming into force of this Convention in respect of that State that are not incorporated as specified in paragraph II d) of Part 1 of the Technical Annex to this Convention and of unmarked explosives which no longer fall within the scope of any other subparagraphs of the said paragraph II.

Article V

1. There is established by this Convention an International Explosives Technical Commission (hereinafter referred to as "the Commission") consisting of not less than fifteen nor more than nineteen members appointed by the Council of the International Civil Aviation Organization (hereinafter referred to as "the Council") from among persons nominated by States Parties to this Convention.

2. The members of the Commission shall be experts having direct and substantial experience in matters relating to the manufacture or detection of, or research in, explosives.

3. Members of the Commission shall serve for a period of three years and shall be eligible for re-appointment.

4. Sessions of the Commission shall be convened, at least once a year at the Headquarters of the International Civil Aviation Organization, or at such places and times as may be directed or approved by the Council.

5. The Commission shall adopt its rules of procedure, subject to the approval of the Council.

Article VI

1. The Commission shall evaluate technical developments relating to the manufacture, marking and detection of explosives.

2. The Commission, through the Council, shall report its findings to the States Parties and international organizations concerned.

3. Whenever necessary, the Commission shall make recommendations to the Council for amendments to the Technical Annex to this Convention. The Commission shall endeavour to take its decisions on such recommendations by consensus. In the absence of consensus the Commission shall take such decision by a two-thirds majority vote of its members.

4. The Council may, on the recommendation of the Commission, propose to States Parties amendments to the Technical Annex to this Convention.

Article VII

1. Any State Party may, within ninety days from the date of notification of a proposed amendment to the Technical Annex to this Convention, transmit to the Council its comments. The Council shall communicate these comments to the Commission as soon as possible for its consideration. The Council shall invite any State Party which comments on or objects to the proposed amendment to consult the Commission.

2. The Commission shall consider the views of States Parties made pursuant to the preceding paragraph and report to the Council. The Council, after consideration of the Commission's report, and taking into account the nature of the amendment and the comments of States Parties, including producer States, may propose the amendment to all States Parties for adoption.

TEL-OREN v. LIBYAN ARAB REPUBLIC
UNITED STATES COURT OF APPEALS,
DISTRICT OF COLUMBIA CIRCUIT.
DECIDED FEB. 3, 1984.

[726 F.2d 774 (1984)]

Concurring opinions filed by Circuit Judge HARRY T. EDWARDS, Circuit Judge [ROBERT H.] BORK, and Senior Circuit Judge ROBB.
PER CURIAM:
Plaintiffs in this action, mostly Israeli citizens, are survivors and representatives of persons murdered in an armed attack on a civilian bus in Israel in March 1978.

. . .

In their complaint, plaintiffs alleged that defendants were responsible for multiple tortious acts in violation of the law of nations, . . .
We affirm the dismissal of this action.

. . .

[HARRY T.] EDWARDS, Circuit Judge, concurring:

. . .

VII. TERRORISM AS A LAW OF NATIONS VIOLATION

I turn next to consider whether terrorism is itself a law of nations violation. [footnote omitted] While this nation unequivocally condemns all terrorist attacks, that sentiment is not universal. Indeed, the nations of the world are so divisively split on legitimacy of such aggression as to make it impossible to pinpoint an area of harmony or consensus. Unlike the issue of individual responsibility, which much of the world has never even reached, terrorism has evoked strident reactions and sparked strong alliances among numerous states. Given this division, I do not believe that under current law terrorist attacks amount to law of nations violations.

To witness the split one need only look at documents of the United Nations. They demonstrate that to some states acts of terrorism, in particular those with political motives, are legitimate acts of aggression and therefore immune from condemnation. For example, a resolution entitled "Basic principles of the legal status of the combatants struggling against colonial and alien domination and racist regimes," G.A.Res. 3103, 28 U.N. GAOR at 512, U.N.Doc. A/9102 (1973), declared:

> The struggle of peoples under colonial and alien dom-
> ination and racist regimes for the implementation of
> their right to self-determination and independence is
> legitimate and in full accordance with the principles of
> international law.

It continued that armed conflicts involving such struggles have the full legal status of international armed conflicts, and that violation of that status "entails full responsibility in accordance with norms of international law." *Id.* at 513. *See also* Definition of Aggression, G.A.Res. 3314, 29 GAOR Supp. (No. 31) at 142 44, U.N.Doc. A/9631 (1974) (nothing in definition of term "aggression" should prejudice right of self-determination or struggle, particularly of peoples under "colonial and racist regimes or other forms of alien domination"). In contrast, there is of course authority in various documents and international conventions for the view that terrorism is an international crime. Many Western nations condemn terrorist acts, either generally, as in the Convention to Prevent and Punish the Acts of Terrorism Taking the Forms of Crime Against Persons and Related Extortion That Are of International Significance, [footnote omitted] or with reference to particular terrorist acts, as in the International Convention Against the Taking of Hostages, [footnote omitted] or the Hague Convention on the Suppression of Unlawful Seizure of Aircraft. [footnote omitted] *See also* R. FRIEDLANDER, TERROR-VIOLENCE: ASPECTS OF SOCIAL CONTROL 38 (1983) (describing the international division on the legitimacy of terrorist acts); *see generally* R. LILLICH, TRANSNATIONAL TERRORISM: CONVENTIONS AND COMMENTARY (1982).

The divergence as to basic norms of course reflects a basic disagreement as to legitimate political goals and the proper method of attainment. Given such disharmony, I cannot conclude that the law of nations—which, we must recall, is defined as the principles and rules that states feel themselves bound to observe, and do commonly observe [footnote omitted]—outlaws politically motivated terrorism, no matter how repugnant it might be to our own legal system.

. . .

[ROBERT H.] BORK, Circuit Judge, concurring:

. . .

In addition, appellants' principal claim, that appellees violated customary principles of international law against terrorism, concerns an area of international law in which there is little or no consensus and in which the disagreements concern politically sensitive issues that are especially prominent in the foreign relations problems of the Middle East. Some aspects of terrorism have been the subject of several international conventions, such as those concerning hijacking, e.g., Convention for the Suppression of Unlawful Acts Against the Safety of Civil Aviation (Montreal Convention), Sept. 23, 1971, 24 U.S.T. 564, T.I.A.S. No. 7570; Convention on the Suppression of Unlawful Seizure of Aircraft (Hague Convention), Dec. 16, 1970, 22 U.S.T. 1641, T.I.A.S. No. 7192, 860 U.N.T.S. 105; Convention on Offenses and Certain Other Acts Committed on Board Aircraft (Tokyo Convention), Sept. 14, 1963, 20 U.S.T. 2941, T.I.A.S. No. 6768, 704 U.N.T.S. 219, and attacks on internationally protected persons such as diplomats, e.g., Convention on the Prevention and Punishment of Crimes Against Internationally Protected Persons, Including Diplomatic Agents (New York Convention), Dec. 14, 1973, 28 U.S.T. 1975, T.I.A.S. No. 8532. But no consensus has developed on how properly to define "terrorism" generally. G. von Glahn, *Law Among Nations* 303 (4th ed. 1981). As a consequence, " '[i]nternational law and the rules of warfare as they now exist are inadequate to cope with this new mode of conflict.' " *Transnational Terrorism: Conventions and Commentary* xv (R. Lillich ed. 1982) (quoting Jenkins, International Terrorism: A New Mode of Conflict 16 (California Seminar on Arms Control and Foreign Policy, Research Paper No. 48, 1975)). "The dismal truth is that the international community has dealt with terrorism ambivalently and ineffectually." Shestack, *Of Private and State Terror—Some Preliminary Observations*, 13 Rutgers L.J. 453, 463 (1982).

Customary international law may well forbid states from aiding terrorist attacks on neighboring states. *See* Lillich & Paxman, *State Responsibility for Injuries to Aliens Occasioned by Terrorist Activities*, 26 Am.U.L.Rev. 217, 251–76 (1977). Although that principle might apply in a case like this to a state such as Libya (which is not a proper party here, *see supra* note 13), it does not, at least on its face, apply to a nonstate like the PLO. More important, there is less than universal consensus about whether PLO-sponsored attacks on Israel are unlawful. One important sign of the lack of consensus about terrorism generally, and about PLO activities in particular, is that accusations of terrorism are often met not by denial of the fact of responsibility but by a justification for the challenged actions. *See* Blum & Steinhardt, *supra* note 10, 22 Harv.Int'l L.J. at 92. Indeed, one of the key documents relied on as evidence of an international law proscription on terrorism, the Declaration on Principles of International Law Concerning Friendly Relations and Co-operation Among States in Accordance with the Charter of the United Nations, G.A.Res. 2625, 25 U.N.GAOR Supp. (No. 28) at 121, U.N.Doc. A/8028 (1970), was said by at least one state at the time of its promulgation not to be applicable to Palestinian terrorist raids into Israel supported by Arab states. 24 U.N.GAOR 297, U.N.Doc. A/C.6/SR 1160 (1969) (remarks of Mr. El Attrash of Syria), discussed in Lillich & Paxman, *supra* 26 Am.U.L.Rev. at 272 (qualification is significant). Attempts to secure greater consensus on terrorism have foundered on just such issues as the lawfulness of violent action by groups like the PLO fighting what some states view as "wars of national liberation." [footnote omitted] *See* Franck & Lockwood, *Preliminary Thoughts Towards and International Convention on Terrorism*, 68 Am.J.Int'l L. 69 (1974); Paust, *"Nonprotected" Persons or Things, in Legal Aspects of International Terrorism* 341, 355–56 (A. Evans & J. Murphy eds. 1978); *cf.* Verwey, *The International Hostages Convention and National Liberation Movements*, 75 Am.J.Int'l L. 69 (1981) (obligations of national liberation movements were major problem in drafting and promulgating International Convention against the Taking of Hostages).

There is, of course, no occasion here to state what international law should be. Nor is there a need to consider whether an extended and discriminating analysis might plausibly maintain that customary international law prohibits the actions alleged in the complaint. It is enough to observe that there is sufficient controversy of a politically sensitive nature about the content of any relevant international legal principles . . .

NOTE: In contrast to the judicial uncertainty about the role of United States courts in the suppression of terrorism, the congressional view has been more decisive. In response to a series of overseas terrorist and unconventional warfare attacks against, among others, American civilians and soldiers during the early to mid-1980s (this included the October 1983 suicide truck bombing in Beirut that left more than two hundred marines dead; the shootings from 1983 to 1985 in front of a café in San Salvador that killed several soldiers; and the December 1985 shootings at the Rome and Vienna airports that left many civilians dead), Congress extended United States criminal jurisdiction over such events even though they took place abroad.

Congressional efforts to legislate against terrorism did not end with the 1986 Act that appears below. Amid widespread revulsion over the P.L.O.'s 1987 hijacking of the Italian cruise ship *Achille Lauro* and the murder of an elderly American confined to a wheelchair who had been a passenger, Congress passed the Antiterrorism Act of 1987. It prohibited establishing or maintaining an office at the behest of, direction of, or with the financial assets of the Palestine Liberation Organization (P.L.O.). The 1987 Act was passed despite resistance from the executive branch, which feared that the Act violated the U.N. Headquarters Agreement. In fact, the Act was not implemented. The Federal District Court in New York ruled that since Congress had not expressly indicated that it wished to violate the Headquarters Agreement, the court would assume that it did not intend any such violation.

Diplomatic Security and Antiterrorism Act of 1986

[Pub.L. No. 99-399, § 1202(a), 100 Stat. 853, 896, codified at 18 U.S.C. § 2331 (1989 & Supp. 1992)]

Chapter 113A—Extraterritorial Jurisdiction Over Terrorist Acts Abroad Against United States Nationals

§ 2331. Terrorist acts abroad against United States nationals

(a) Homicide.—Whoever kills a national of the United States, while such national is outside the United States, shall—

(1) if the killing is a murder as defined in section 1111(a) of this title, be fined under this title or imprisoned for any term of years or for life, or both so fined and so imprisoned;

(2) if the killing is a voluntary manslaughter as defined in section 1112(a) of this title, be fined under this title or imprisoned not more than ten years, or both; and

(3) if the killing is an involuntary manslaughter as defined in section 1112(a) of this title, be fined under this title or imprisoned not more than three years, or both.

(b) Attempt or Conspiracy With Respect to Homicide.—Whoever outside the United States attempts to kill, or engaged in a conspiracy to kill, a national of the United States shall—

(1) in the case of an attempt to commit a killing that is a murder as defined in this chapter, be fined under this title or imprisoned not more than 20 years, or both; and

(2) in the case of a conspiracy by two or more persons to commit a killing that is a murder as defined in section 1111(a) of this title, if one or more of such persons do any overt act to effect the object of the conspiracy, be fined under this title or imprisoned for any term of years or for life, or both so fined and so imprisoned.

(c) Other Conduct.—Whoever outside the United States engages in physical violence—

(1) with intent to cause serious bodily injury to a national of the United States; or

(2) with the result that serious bodily injury is caused to a national of the United States;

shall be fined under this title or imprisoned not more than five years, or both.

(d) Definition.—As used in this section the term "national of the United States" has the meaning given such term in section 101(a)(22) of the Immigration and Nationality Act (8 U.S.C. 1101(a)(22)).

(e) Limitation on Prosecution.—No prosecution for any offense described in this section shall be undertaken by the United States except on written certification of the Attorney General or the highest ranking subordinate of the Attorney General with responsibility for criminal prosecutions that, in the judgment of the certifying official, such offense was intended to coerce, intimidate, or retaliate against a government or a civilian population.

. . . .

NOTE: The U.S. executive branch also has taken forceful measures to combat terrorism. In April 1985, President Reagan ordered a bombing mission of several sites within the Libyan cities of Benghazi and Tripoli. The attack took place ten days after a discotheque frequented by U.S. service members in Berlin was bombed and two American soldiers were killed and scores of others wounded. Technical evidence indicated that Libya directed the attack and also was responsible for numerous other terrorist attacks. The attack was presented by the U.S. government as a lawful measure of self-defense, as was President Clinton's destruction of intelligence facilities in Baghdad in 1993 in response to an alleged Iraqi conspiracy to assassinate former President Bush.

WAR CRIMES

International law generally has attributed responsibility for actions by state representatives to the state as a whole. One significant exception is violations of the laws of war. They are characterized as war crimes, for which the individual who is alleged to have perpetrated them may be held personally responsible—even if he claims to have followed superior orders. Not all of the procedures and safeguards deemed central to criminal law in advanced legal systems have been applied to the prosecution of war crimes. But this has not made it easier to apprehend and convict war criminals. In the case of the former Yugoslavia, the United Nations Commission of Experts to Investigate Allegations of War Crimes, which was established by a United Nations resolution in 1992, has encountered particular difficulties in gathering information and making it available for further legal action. We will consider the most recent developments in this regard at the end of this chapter.

Historically, war crimes have been tried by national courts or military commissions. After World War I, the victors tried to establish a formal international war crimes tribunal. It was largely unsuccessful. At the Paris Peace Conference of February 6, 1920, the Allies demanded that Germany extradite over a thousand suspected war criminals. Germany refused the demand for a host of reasons, the most important of which was probably that the fledgling German government was concerned that complying with the demand might have led to its overthrow. The Allies did not press the issue, but compromised and tried only a handful of suspected war criminals. Twelve were tried, of whom six were found guilty. None received a sentence of more than four years imprisonment.

The major Allied powers of World War II agreed that key Nazi leaders should be tried for their war crimes by an International Military Tribunal. Extracts of the Agreement and the London Charter establishing and governing the Tribunal are set out below; these documents were the legal basis for conduct of the war crimes trials at Nuremberg in 1945 and 1946. Additionally, they served as a framework for the Charter of the International Military Tribunal for the Far East, which was established to try major Japanese war criminals. Although each of these series of trials was attended by some controversy, they appear to have established an important precedent in the law of war.

AGREEMENT BY THE GOVERNMENT OF THE UNITED KINGDOM OF GREAT BRITAIN AND NORTHERN IRELAND, THE GOVERNMENT OF THE UNITED STATES OF AMERICA, THE PROVISIONAL GOVERNMENT OF THE FRENCH REPUBLIC AND THE GOVERNMENT OF THE UNION OF SOVIET SOCIALIST REPUBLICS FOR THE PROSECUTION AND PUNISHMENT OF THE MAJOR WAR CRIMINALS OF THE EUROPEAN AXIS

[82 U.N.T.S. 280, signed on August 8, 1945, at London]

. . . .

CHARTER OF THE INTERNATIONAL MILITARY TRIBUNAL

I. — CONSTITUTION OF THE INTERNATIONAL MILITARY TRIBUNAL

Article 1

In pursuance of the Agreement signed on the 8th August, 1945, by the Government of the United Kingdom of Great Britain and Northern Ireland, the Government of the United States of America, the Provisional

Government of the French Republic and the Government of the Union [of] Soviet Socialist Republics, there shall be established an International Military Tribunal (hereinafter called "the Tribunal") for the just and prompt trial and punishment of the major war criminals of the European Axis.

. . .

II. — JURISDICTION AND GENERAL PRINCIPLES

Article 6

The Tribunal established by the Agreement referred to in Article 1 hereof for the trial and punishment of the major war criminals of the European Axis countries shall have the power to try and punish persons who, acting in the interests of the European Axis countries, whether as individuals or as members of organisations, committed any of the following crimes.

The following acts, or any of them, are crimes coming within the jurisdiction of the Tribunal for which there shall be individual responsibility:—

(a) *Crimes against peace:* namely, planning, preparation, initiation or waging of a war of aggression, or a war in violation of international treaties, agreements or assurances, or participation in a common plan or conspiracy for the accomplishment of any of the foregoing:

(b) *War crimes:* namely, violations of the laws or customs of war. Such violations shall include, but not be limited to, murder, ill-treatment or deportation to slave labour or for any other purpose of civilian population of or in occupied territory, murder or ill-treatment of prisoners of war or persons on the seas, killing of hostages, plunder of public or private property, wanton destruction of cities, towns or villages, or devastation not justified by military necessity;

(c) *Crimes against humanity:* namely, murder, extermination, enslavement, deportation, and other inhumane acts committed against any civilian population, before or during the war, or persecutions on political, racial or religious grounds in execution of or in connection with any crime within the jurisdiction of the Tribunal, whether or not in violation of the domestic law of the country where perpetrated.

Leaders, organisers, instigators and accomplices participating in the formulation or execution of a common plan or conspiracy to commit any of the foregoing crimes are responsible for all acts performed by any persons in execution of such plans.

Article 7
The official position of defendants, whether as Heads of State or responsible officials in Government Departments, shall not be considered as freeing them from responsibility or mitigating punishment.

Article 8
The fact that the Defendant acted pursuant to order of his Government or of a superior shall not free him from responsibility, but may be considered in mitigation of punishment if the Tribunal determines that justice so requires.

Article 9
At the trial of any individual member of any group or organisation the Tribunal may declare (in connection with any act of which the individual may be convicted) that the group or organisation of which the individual was a member was a criminal organisation.

After receipt of the Indictment the Tribunal shall give such notice as it thinks fit that the prosecution intends to ask the Tribunal to make such declaration and any member of the organisation will be entitled to apply to the Tribunal for leave to be heard by the Tribunal upon the question of the criminal character of the organisation. The Tribunal shall have power to allow or reject the application. If the application is allowed, the Tribunal may direct in what manner the applicants shall be represented and heard.

Article 10
In cases where a group or organisation is declared criminal by the Tribunal, the competent national authority of any Signatory shall have the right to bring individuals to trial for membership therein before national, military or occupation courts. In any such case the criminal nature of the group or organisation is considered proved and shall not be questioned.

Article 11
Any person convicted by the Tribunal may be charged before a national, military or occupation court, referred to in Article 10 of this

Charter, with a crime other than of membership in a criminal group or organisation and such court may, after convicting him, impose upon him punishment independent of and additional to the punishment imposed by the Tribunal for participation in the criminal activities of such group or organisation.

Article 12

The Tribunal shall have the right to take proceedings against a person charged with crimes set out in Article 6 of this Charter in his absence, if he has not been found or if the Tribunal, for any reason, finds it necessary, in the interests of justice, to conduct the hearing in his absence.

Article 13

The Tribunal shall draw up rules for its procedure. These rules shall not be inconsistent with the provisions of this Charter.

III. — COMMITTEE FOR THE INVESTIGATION AND PROSECUTION OF MAJOR WAR CRIMINALS

Article 14

Each Signatory shall appoint a Chief Prosecutor for the investigation of the charges against and the prosecution of major war criminals.

. . .

IV. — FAIR TRIAL FOR DEFENDANTS

Article 16

In order to ensure fair trial for the Defendants, the following procedure shall be followed:

(a) The Indictment shall include full particulars specifying in detail the charges against the Defendants. A copy of the Indictment and of all the documents lodged with the Indictment, translated into a language which he understands, shall be furnished to the Defendant at a reasonable time before the Trial.

(b) During any preliminary examination or trial of a Defendant he shall have the right to give any explanation relevant to the charges made against him.

(c) A preliminary examination of a Defendant and his Trial shall be conducted in, or translated into, a language which the Defendant understands.

(d) A Defendant shall have the right to conduct his own defence before the Tribunal or to have the assistance of Counsel.

(e) A Defendant shall have the right through himself or through his Counsel to present evidence at the Trial in support of his defence, and to cross-examine any witness called by the Prosecution.

· · · ·

V. — POWERS OF THE TRIBUNAL AND CONDUCT OF THE TRIAL

· · · ·

Article 19

The Tribunal shall not be bound by technical rules of evidence. It shall adopt and apply to the greatest possible extent expeditious and non-technical procedure, and shall admit any evidence which it deems to have probative value.

· · ·

NOTE: Twenty-two major Nazi war criminals were tried by the Tribunal at Nuremberg. Included below are extracts from the judgment: the introduction; pronouncements concerning Göring and Keitel; and the Tribunal's response to the defendants' argument that they should not be tried for violations of laws that were made *after* the events to which they are to be applied, so-called *ex post facto* laws. The Tribunal's dismissal of this argument is controversial. Some military leaders and prominent judges have not found the Tribunal's *ex post facto* argument compelling. The statements by former Chief of Staff of the United States Army, General Matthew B. Ridgway, and former Associate Justice of the United States Supreme Court, William O. Douglas, are representative of a group whose members could hardly be called unpatriotic but who believed that waging aggressive war was not a violation of international law in 1945 and, consequently, should not have served as a basis of convictions at Nuremberg.

JUDICIAL DECISIONS

INTERNATIONAL MILITARY TRIBUNAL (NUREMBERG), JUDGMENT AND SENTENCES OCTOBER 1, 1946

[Trial of the Major War Criminals Before the International
Military Tribunal, Nuremberg, 14 November 1945—1 October 1946,
Volume I, 411]

JUDGMENT

On 8 August 1945, the Government of the United Kingdom of Great Britain and Northern Ireland, the Government of the United States of America, the Provisional Government of the French Republic, and the Government of the Union of Soviet Socialist Republics entered into an Agreement establishing this Tribunal for the Trial of War Criminals whose offenses have no particular geographical location. In accordance with Article 5, the following Governments of the United Nations have expressed their adherence to the Agreement:

Greece, Denmark, Yugoslavia, the Netherlands, Czechoslovakia, Poland, Belgium, Ethiopia, Australia, Honduras, Norway, Panama, Luxembourg, Haiti, New Zealand, India, Venezuela, Uruguay, and Paraguay.

By the Charter annexed to the Agreement, the constitution, jurisdiction, and functions of the Tribunal were defined.

The Tribunal was invested with power to try and punish persons who had committed Crimes against Peace, War Crimes, and Crimes against Humanity as defined in the Charter.

The Charter also provided that at the Trial of any individual member of any group or organization the Tribunal may declare (in connection with any act of which the individual may be convicted) that the group or organization of which the individual was a member was a criminal organization.

In Berlin, on 18 October 1945, in accordance with Article 14 of the Charter, an Indictment was lodged against the defendants named in the caption above, who had been designated by the Committee of the Chief Prosecutors of the signatory Powers as major war criminals.

A copy of the Indictment in the German language was served upon each defendant in custody, at least 30 days before the Trial opened.

This Indictment charges the defendants with Crimes against Peace by the planning, preparation, initiation, and waging of wars of aggression, which were also wars in violation of international treaties, agreements, and assurances; with War Crimes; and with Crimes against Humanity. The defendants are also charged with participating in the formulation or execution of a common plan or conspiracy to commit all these crimes.

.   .   .

In accordance with Articles 16 and 23 of the Charter, Counsel were either chosen by the defendants in custody themselves, or at their request were appointed by the Tribunal. In his absence the Tribunal appointed counsel for the Defendant Bormann, and also assigned Counsel to represent the named groups or organizations.

The Trial, which was conducted in four languages—English, Russian, French, and German—began on 20 November 1945, and pleas of "Not Guilty" were made by all the defendants except Bormann.

The hearing of evidence and the speeches of Counsel concluded on 31 August 1946.

Four hundred and three open sessions of the Tribunal have been held. Thirty-three witnesses gave evidence orally for the Prosecution against the individual defendants and 61 witnesses, in addition to 19 of the defendants, gave evidence for the Defense.

A further 143 witnesses gave evidence for the Defense by means of written answers to interrogatories.

The Tribunal appointed Commissioners to hear evidence relating to the organizations, and 101 witnesses were heard for the Defense before the Commissioners, and 1,809 affidavits from other witnesses were submitted. Six reports were also submitted, summarizing the contents of a great number of further affidavits.

Thirty-eight thousand affidavits, signed by 155,000 people, were submitted on behalf of the Political Leaders, 136,213 on behalf of the SS, 10,000 on behalf of the SA, 7,000 on behalf of the SD, 3,000 on behalf of the General Staff and OKW, and 2,000 on behalf of the Gestapo.

The Tribunal itself heard 22 witnesses for the organizations. The documents tendered in evidence for the Prosecution of the individual defendants and the organizations numbered several thousands. A complete stenographic record of everything said in Court has been made, as well as an electrical recording of all the proceedings.

.   .   .

Much of the evidence presented to the Tribunal on behalf of the Prosecution was documentary evidence, captured by the Allied armies in German army headquarters, Government buildings, and elsewhere. Some of the documents were found in salt mines, buried in the ground, hidden behind false walls and in other places thought to be secure from discovery. The case, therefore, against the defendants rests in a large measure on documents of their own making, the authenticity of which has not been challenged except in one or two cases.

THE CHARTER PROVISIONS

The individual defendants are indicted under Article 6 of the Charter.

GÖRING

Göring is indicted on all four Counts. The evidence shows that after Hitler he was the most prominent man in the Nazi regime. He was Commander-in-Chief of the Luftwaffe, Plenipotentiary for the Four Year Plan, and had tremendous influence with Hitler, at least until 1943, when their relationship deteriorated, ending in his arrest in 1945. He testified that Hitler kept him informed of all important military and political problems.

CRIMES AGAINST PEACE

From the moment he joined the Party in 1922 and took command of the street-fighting organization, the SA, Göring was the adviser, the active agent of Hitler, and one of the prime leaders of the Nazi movement. As Hitler's political deputy he was largely instrumental in bringing the National Socialists to power in 1933, and was charged with consolidating this power and expanding German armed might. He developed the Gestapo, and created the first concentration camps, relinquishing them to Himmler in 1934, conducted the Röhm purge in that year, and engineered the sordid proceedings which resulted in the removal of Von Blomberg and Von Fritsch from the Army. In 1936 he became Plenipotentiary for the Four Year Plan, and in theory and in practice was the economic dictator of the Reich. Shortly after the Pact of Munich, he announced that he would embark on a five-fold expansion of the Luft-waffe, and speed rearmament with emphasis on offensive weapons.

Göring was one of the five important leaders present at the Hossbach Conference of 5 November 1937, and he attended the other important conferences already discussed in this Judgment. In the Austrian Anschluss he was indeed the central figure, the ringleader. He said in Court: "I must take 100 per cent responsibility. . . . [in original] I even overruled objections by the Führer and brought everything to its final develop-ment." In the seizure of the Sudetenland, he played his rôle as Luftwaffe chief by planning an air offensive which proved unnecessary, and his rôle as politician by lulling the Czechs with false promises of friendship. The night before the invasion of Czechoslovakia and the absorption of Bohemia and Moravia, at a conference with Hitler and President Hacha he threatened to bomb Prague if Hacha did not submit. This threat he admitted in his testimony.

Göring attended the Reich Chancellery meeting of 23 May 1939 when Hitler told his military leaders "there is, therefore, no question of sparing Poland," and was present at the Obersalzberg briefing of 22 August 1939. And the evidence shows that he was active in the diplomatic maneuvers which followed. With Hitler's connivance, he used the Swedish busi-nessman, Dahlerus, as a go-between to the British, as described by Dah-lerus to this Tribunal, to try to prevent the British Government from keeping its guarantee to the Poles.

He commanded the Luftwaffe in the attack on Poland and throughout the aggressive wars which followed.

Even if he opposed Hitler's plans against Norway and the Soviet Union, as he alleged, it is clear that he did so only for strategic reasons; once Hitler had decided the issue, he followed him without hesitation. He made it clear in his testimony that these differences were never ideological or legal. He was "in a rage" about the invasion of Norway, but only because he had not received sufficient warning to prepare the Luftwaffe offensive. He admitted he approved of the attack: "My attitude was perfectly positive." He was active in preparing and executing the Yugoslavian and Greek campaigns, and testified that "Plan Marita," the attack on Greece, had been prepared long beforehand. The Soviet Union he regarded as the "most threatening menace to Germany," but said there was no immediate military necessity for the attack. Indeed, his only objec-tion to the war of aggression against the U.S.S.R. was its timing; he wished for strategic reasons to delay until Britain was conquered. He testi-fied: "My point of view was decided by political and military reasons only."

After his own admissions to this Tribunal, from the positions which he held, the conferences he attended, and the public words he uttered, there can remain no doubt that Göring was the moving force for aggressive war, second only to Hitler. He was the planner and prime mover in the military and diplomatic preparation for war which Germany pursued.

WAR CRIMES AND CRIMES AGAINST HUMANITY

The record is filled with Göring's admissions of his complicity in the use of slave labor.

"We did use this labor for security reasons so that they would not be active in their own country and would not work against us. On the other hand, they served to help in the economic war."

And again:

"Workers were forced to come to the Reich. That is something I have not denied."

The man who spoke these words was Plenipotentiary for the Four Year Plan charged with the recruitment and allocation of manpower. As Luftwaffe Commander-in-Chief he demanded from Himmler more slave laborers for his underground aircraft factories: "That I requested inmates of concentration camps for the armament of the Luftwaffe is correct and it is to be taken as a matter of course."

As Plenipotentiary, Göring signed a directive concerning the treatment of Polish workers in Germany and implemented it by regulation of the SD, including "special treatment." He issued directives to use Soviet and French prisoners of war in the armament industry; he spoke of seizing Poles and Dutch and making them prisoners of war if necessary, and using them for work. He agrees Russian prisoners of war were used to man anti-aircraft batteries.

As Plenipotentiary, Göring was the active authority in the spoliation of conquered territory. He made plans for the spoliation of Soviet territory long before the war on the Soviet Union. Two months prior to the invasion of the Soviet Union, Hitler gave Göring the over-all direction for the economic administration in the territory. Göring set up an economic staff for this function. As Reichsmarshal of the Greater German Reich, "the orders of the Reich Marshal cover all economic fields, including nutrition and agriculture." His so-called "Green" folder, printed by the Wehrmacht, set up an "Economic Executive Staff, East." This directive contemplated plundering and abandonment of all industry in the food deficit regions and, from the food surplus regions, a diversion of food to German needs. Göring claims its purposes have been misunderstood but admits "that as a matter of course and a matter of duty we would have used Russia for our purposes," when conquered.

And he participated in the conference of 16 July 1941 when Hitler said the National Socialists had no intention of ever leaving the occupied countries, and that "all necessary measures—shooting, desettling, etc." should be taken.

Göring persecuted the Jews, particularly after the November 1938 riots, and not only in Germany where he raised the billion-mark fine as stated elsewhere, but in the conquered territories as well. His own utterances then and his testimony now shows this interest was primarily economic—how to get their property and how to force them out of the economic life of Europe. As these countries fell before the German Army, he extended the Reich's anti-Jewish laws to them; the *Reichsgesetzblatt* for 1939, 1940, and 1941 contains several anti-Jewish decrees signed by Göring. Although their extermination was in Himmler's hands, Göring was far from disinterested or inactive, despite his protestations in the witness box. By decree of 31 July 1941 he directed Himmler and Heydrich to "bring about a complete solution of the Jewish question in the German sphere of influence in Europe."

There is nothing to be said in mitigation. For Göring was often, indeed almost always, the moving force, second only to his leader. He was the leading war aggressor, both as political and as military leader; he was the director of the slave labor program and the creator of the oppressive program against the Jews and other races, at home and abroad. All of these crimes he has frankly admitted. On some specific cases there may be conflict of testimony but in terms of the broad outline, his own admissions are more than sufficiently wide to be conclusive of his guilt. His guilt is unique in its enormity. The record discloses no excuses for this man.

CONCLUSION

The Tribunal finds the Defendant Göring guilty on all four Counts of the Indictment.

. . .

KEITEL

Keitel is indicted on all four Counts. He was Chief of Staff to the then Minister of War Von Blomberg from 1935 to 4 February 1938; on that day Hitler took command of the Armed Forces, making Keitel Chief of the High Command of the Armed Forces. Keitel did not have command authority over the three Wehrmacht branches which enjoyed direct access to the Supreme Commander. OKW was in effect Hitler's military staff.

CRIMES AGAINST PEACE

Keitel attended the Schuschnigg conference in February 1938 with two other generals. Their presence, he admitted, was a "military demonstration," but since he had been appointed OKW Chief just one week before [,] he had not known why he had been summoned. Hitler and Keitel then continued to put pressure on Austria with false rumors, broadcasts, and troop maneuvers. Keitel made the military and other arrangements, and Jodl's diary noted "the effect is quick and strong." When Schuschnigg called his plebiscite, Keitel that night briefed Hitler and his generals, and Hitler issued "Case Otto" which Keitel initialed.

On 21 April 1938 Hitler and Keitel considered making use of a possible "incident," such as the assassination of the German Minister at Prague, to preface the attack on Czechoslovakia. Keitel signed many directives and memoranda on "Fall Gruen," including the directive of 30 May containing Hitler's statement: "It is my unalterable decision to smash Czechoslovakia by military action in the near future." After Munich, Keitel initialed Hitler's directive for the attack on Czechoslovakia, and issued two supplements. The second supplement said the attack should appear to the outside world as "merely an act of pacification and not a warlike undertaking." The OKW Chief attended Hitler's negotiations with Hacha when the latter surrendered.

Keitel was present on 23 May 1939 when Hitler announced his decision "to attack Poland at the first suitable opportunity." Already he had signed the directive requiring the Wehrmacht to submit its "Fall Weiss" timetable to OKW by 1 May.

The invasion of Norway and Denmark he discussed on 12 December 1939 with Hitler, Jodl, and Raeder. By directive of 27 January 1940 the Norway plans were placed under Keitel's "direct and personal guidance."

Hitler had said on 23 May 1939 he would ignore the neutrality of Belgium and the Netherlands, and Keitel signed orders for these attacks on 15 October, 20 November, and 28 November 1939. Orders postponing this attack 17 times until spring all were signed by Keitel or Jodl.

Formal planning for attacking Greece and Yugoslavia had begun in November 1940. On 18 March 1941 Keitel heard Hitler tell Raeder complete occupation of Greece was a prerequisite to settlement, and also heard Hitler decree on 27 March that the destruction of Yugoslavia should take place with "unmerciful harshness."

Keitel testified that he opposed the invasion of the Soviet Union for military reasons, and also because it would constitute a violation of the Non-aggression Pact. Nevertheless he initialed "Case Barbarossa," signed by Hitler on 18 December 1940, and attended the OKW discussion with Hitler on 3 February 1941. Keitel's supplement of 13 March established the relationship between the military and political officers. He issued his timetable for the invasion on 6 June 1941, and was present at the briefing of 14 June when the generals gave their final reports before attack. He appointed Jodl and Warlimont as OKW representatives to Rosenberg on matters concerning the Eastern Territories. On 16 June he directed all army units to carry out the economic directives issued by Göring in the so-called "Green Folder," for the exploitation of Russian territory, food, and raw materials.

WAR CRIMES AND CRIMES AGAINST HUMANITY

On 4 August 1942 Keitel issued a directive that paratroopers were to be turned over to the SD. On 18 October Hitler issued the Commando Order which was carried out in several instances. After the landing in Normandy, Keitel reaffirmed the order, and later extended it to Allied missions fighting with partisans. He admits he did not believe the order was legal but claims he could not stop Hitler from decreeing it.

When, on 8 September 1941, OKW issued its ruthless regulations for the treatment of Soviet POW'S, Canaris wrote to Keitel that under international law the SD should have nothing to do with this matter. On this memorandum in Keitel's handwriting, dated 23 September and initialed by him, is the statement:

> "The objections arise from the military concept of chivalrous warfare. This is the destruction of an ideology. Therefore I approve and back the measures."

Keitel testified that he really agreed with Canaris and argued with Hitler, but lost. The OKW Chief directed the military authorities to coöperate with the Einsatzstab Rosenberg in looting cultural property in occupied territories.

Lahousen testified that Keitel told him on 12 September 1939, while aboard Hitler's headquarters train, that the Polish intelligentsia, nobility, and Jews were to be liquidated. On 20 October, Hitler told Keitel the intelligentsia would be prevented from forming a ruling class, the standard of living would remain low, and Poland would be used only for labor forces. Keitel does not remember the Lahousen conversation, but admits there was such a policy and that he had protested without effect to Hitler about it.

On 16 September 1941 Keitel ordered that attacks on soldiers in the East should be met by putting to death 50 to 100 Communists for one German soldier, with the comment that human life was less than nothing in the East. On 1 October he ordered military commanders always to have hostages to execute when soldiers were attacked. When Terboven, the Reich Commissioner in Norway, wrote Hitler that Keitel's suggestion that workmen's relatives be held responsible for sabotage, could work only if firing squads were authorized, Keitel wrote on this memorandum: "Yes, that is the best."

On 12 May 1941, five weeks before the invasion of the Soviet Union, OKW urged upon Hitler a directive of OKH that political commissars be liquidated by the Army, Keitel admitted the directive was passed on to field commanders. And on 13 May Keitel signed an order that civilians suspected of offenses against troops should be shot without trial, and that prosecution of German soldiers for offenses against civilians was unnecessary. On 27 July all copies of this directive were ordered destroyed without affecting its validity. Four days previously he had signed another order that legal punishment was inadequate and troops should use terrorism.

On 7 December 1941, as already discussed in this opinion, the so-called "Nacht und Nebel" Decree, over Keitel's signature, provided that in occupied territories civilians who had been accused of crimes of resistance against the army of occupation would be tried only if a death sentence was likely; otherwise they would be handed to the Gestapo for transportation to Germany.

Keitel directed that Russian POW's be used in German war industry. On 8 September 1942 he ordered French, Dutch, and Belgian citizens to work on the construction of the Atlantic Wall. He was present on 4 January 1944 when Hitler directed Sauckel to obtain 4 million new workers from occupied territories.

In the face of these documents Keitel does not deny his connection with these acts. Rather, his defense relies on the fact that he is a soldier, and on the doctrine of "superior orders," prohibited by Article 8 of the Charter as a defense.

There is nothing in mitigation. Superior orders, even to a soldier, cannot be considered in mitigation where crimes as shocking and extensive have been committed consciously, ruthlessly, and without military excuse or justification.

CONCLUSION

The Tribunal finds Keitel guilty on all four Counts.

.   .   .

TABULATION OF SENTENCES
30 September 1946 [footnote omitted]

Defendant	Counts on Which Convicted	Sentence
Hermann Wilhelm Göring	1, 2, 3, 4	Death by hanging
Rudolf Hess	1, 2	Imprisonment for life
Joachim Von Ribbentrop	1, 2, 3, 4	Death by hanging
Wilhelm Keitel	1, 2, 3, 4	Death by hanging
Ernest Kaltenbrunner	3, 4	Death by hanging
Alfred Rosenberg	1, 2, 3, 4	Death by hanging
Hans Frank	3, 4	Death by hanging
Wilhelm Frick	2, 3, 4	Death by hanging
Julius Streicher	4	Death by hanging
Walter Funk	2, 3, 4	Imprisonment for life
Hjalmar Schacht	Not guilty	
Karl Dönitz	2,3	Ten years' imprisonment
Erick Raeder	1, 2, 3	Imprisonment for life
Baldur Von Schirach	4	Twenty years' imprisonment
Fritz Sauckel	3, 4	Death by hanging
Alfred Jodl	1, 2, 3, 4	Death by hanging
Franc Von Papen	Not guilty	
Arthur Seyss-Inquart	2, 3, 4	Death by hanging

Albert Speer	3, 4	Twenty years' imprisonment
Constantin Von Neurath	1, 2, 3, 4	Fifteen years' imprisonment
Hans Fritzsche	Not guilty	
Martin Bormann	3, 4	Death by hanging

INTERNATIONAL MILITARY TRIBUNAL (NUREMBERG), JUDGMENT AND SENTENCES SEPTEMBER 30, 1946

[Trial of the Major War Criminals Before the International Military Tribunal, Nuremberg, 14 November 1945 1 October 1946, Volume I, 461-2]

JUDGMENT

. . .

It was urged on behalf of the defendants that a fundamental principle of all law—international and domestic—is that there can be no punishment of crime without a pre-existing law. *"Nullum crimen sine lege, nulla poena sine lege."* It was submitted that *ex post facto* punishment is abhorrent to the law of all civilized nations, that no sovereign power had made aggressive war a crime at the time the alleged criminal acts were committed, that no statute had defined aggressive war, that no penalty had been fixed for its commission, and no court had been created to try and punish offenders.

In the first place, it is to be observed that the maxim *nullum crimen sine lege* is not a limitation of sovereignty, but is in general a principle of justice. To assert that it is unjust to punish those who in defiance of treaties and assurances have attacked neighboring states without warning is obviously untrue, for in such circumstances the attacker must know that he is doing wrong, and so far from it being unjust to punish him, it would be unjust if his wrong were allowed to go unpunished. Occupying the positions they did in the Government of Germany, the defendants, or at least some of them must have known of the treaties signed by Germany, outlawing recourse to war for the settlement of international disputes; they must have known that they were acting in defiance of all international law when in complete deliberation they carried out their designs of invasion and aggression. On this view of the case alone, it would appear that the maxim has no application to the present facts.

. . .

NOTE: Contrast the following two views, which criticize some aspects of the post–World War II war crimes tribunals.

GENERAL MATTHEW B. RIDGWAY, USA[2]

"To apprehend, arraign and try an individual for the wanton killing— murder, if you please—of prisoners of war, for example, is one thing. To do likewise to individuals who waged war in the uniform of their nation and under the orders or directives of their superiors, is another and quite different thing. I believe the former is fully justified. I believe the latter is unjustified and repugnant to the code of enlightened governments.["]

"Until such distant date, if this ever transpires, as nations can and will agree on a world political organization with judicial tribunals whose jurisdiction is acknowledged and whose judgments are accepted, I think trials in the second category described above, are steps backwards to the distant past when the fate of a defeated people was determined at the whim of the victor.["][3]

WILLIAM O. DOUGLAS[4]

. . ."I thought at the time and still think that the Nuremberg trials were unprincipled. Law was created *ex post facto* to suit the passion and clamor of the time. The concept of *ex post facto* law is not congenial to the Anglo-American viewpoint on law. Before criminal penalties can be imposed there must be fair warning that the conduct which one undertook was criminal.["]

"There has never been a code of International Law governing aggressive wars. So a punishment within the scope of domestic laws would have been impermissible, and I think that a nation must practice abroad what it practices and preaches at home if it is to take its place among the nations of the world and still be true to its own ideals.["]

"Scholars have searched frantically for little pieces of evidence of whether there was ever an International Law and have pieced together fragments that in their minds justify the conclusion that aggressive war is an international crime—but the reasoning in those cases is shaped to the urgent necessity to find an *ex post facto* justification for what was done."[5]

.   .   .

NOTE: The international community, under the auspices of the International Law Commission, used the Nuremberg trials as a springboard to codify principles that define international crimes.

PRINCIPLES OF INTERNATIONAL LAW RECOGNIZED IN THE CHARTER OF THE NUREMBERG TRIBUNAL AND JUDGMENT OF THE TRIBUNAL

[1950 U.N. GAOR, 5th Sess., Supp. No. 12 (A/1316)]

(The ILC Report on these principles and commentaries thereto appears in *Yearbook of the International Law Commission,* 1950, vol. II.)

PRINCIPLE I. Any person who commits an act which constitutes a crime under international law is responsible therefor and liable to punishment.

PRINCIPLE II. The fact that internal law does not impose a penalty for an act which constitutes a crime under international law does not relieve the person who committed the act from responsibility under international law.

PRINCIPLE III. The fact that a person who committed an act which constitutes a crime under international law acted as Head of State or responsible Government official does not relieve him from responsibility under international law.

PRINCIPLE IV. The fact that a person acted pursuant to order of his Government or of a superior does not relieve him from responsibility under international law, provided a moral choice was in fact possible to him.

PRINCIPLE V. Any person charged with a crime under international law has the right to a fair trial on the facts and law.

PRINCIPLE VI. The crimes hereinafter set out are punishable as crimes under international law:

a. Crimes against peace:
   (i) Planning, preparation, initiation or waging of a war of aggression or a war in violation of international treaties, agreements or assurances;
   (ii) Participation in a common plan or conspiracy for the accomplishment of any of the acts mentioned under (i).
b. War crimes:
   Violations of the laws or customs of war which include, but are not limited to, murder, ill-treatment of prisoners of war or of persons on the seas, killing of hostages, plunder of public or private property, wanton destruction of cities, towns, or villages, or devastation not justified by military necessity.
c. Crimes against humanity:
   Murder, extermination, enslavement, deportation and other inhuman acts done against any civilian population, or persecutions on political, racial or religious grounds, when such acts are done or such persecutions are carried on in execution of or in connection with any crime against peace or any war crime.

PRINCIPLE VII. Complicity in the commission of a crime against peace, a war crime, or a crime against humanity as set forth in Principle VI is a crime under international law.

. . .

NOTE: As noted earlier, the Charter of the International Military Tribunal for the Far East was influenced by the London Charter and the Nuremberg Tribunal. But there were several significant differences. While judges from only the four major Allied powers sat on the Nuremberg Tribunal, judges from thirteen nations (the nine nations that signed the Instrument of Surrender of Japan on September 15, 1945, as well as India and the Philippines) sat on the Far East Tribunal. At Nuremberg, each of the Allies had a prosecutor; in the Far East Tribunal, there was one chief prosecutor, who was an American, and ten associate prosecutors.

Extracts from the Far East Tribunal Indictment and Judgment are set out below. Additionally, portions of the case *Yamashita* v. *Styer* are included. In *Yamashita*, the Supreme Court of the United States reviewed the trial of the Japanese wartime leader, General Tomoyuki Yamashita, and, in so doing, enunciated United States law on numerous aspects of conducting war crimes trials.

INTERNATIONAL MILITARY TRIBUNAL FOR THE FAR EAST[6]

．　．　．

INDICTMENT

．　．　．

GROUP ONE: CRIMES AGAINST PEACE

．　．　．

Count 1

All the accused together with other persons, between the 1st January, 1928, and the 2nd September, 1945, participated as leaders, organisers, instigators, or accomplices in the formulation or execution of a common plan or conspiracy, and are responsible for all acts performed by any person in execution of such plan.

The object of such plan or conspiracy was that Japan should secure the military, naval, political and economic domination of East Asia and of the Pacific and Indian Oceans, and of all countries bordering thereon and islands therein, and for that purpose they conspired that Japan should alone or in combination with other countries having similar objects, or who could be induced or coerced to join therein, wage declared or undeclared war or wars of aggression, and war or wars in violation of international law, treaties, agreements and assurances, against any country or countries which might oppose that purpose.

．　．　．

JUDGMENT OF THE INTERNATIONAL MILITARY TRIBUNAL FOR THE FAR EAST: FINDINGS ON COUNTS OF THE INDICTMENT

[The Tokyo War Crimes Trial, vol. 20, Judgment and Annexes 49,762–72, 49,854–58 (R. John Pritchard and Sonia M. Zaide, eds., 1981) (photocopies of the original Tribunal documents)]

In Count I of the Indictment it is charged that all the defendants together with other persons participated in the formulation or execution of a common plan or conspiracy. The object of that common plan is alleged to have been that Japan should secure the military, naval, political and economic domination of East Asia and of the Pacific and Indian Oceans, and of all countries and islands therein or bordering thereon, and for that purpose should, alone or in combination with other countries having similar objects, wage a war or wars of aggression against any country or countries which might oppose that purpose.

There are undoubtedly declarations by some of those who are alleged to have participated in the conspiracy which coincide with the above grandiose statement, but in our opinion it has not been proved that these were ever more than declarations of the aspirations of individuals. Thus, for example, we do not think the conspirators ever seriously resolved to attempt to secure the domination of North and South America. So far as the wishes of the conspirators crystallized into a concrete common plan we are of opinion that the territory they had resolved Japan should dominate was confined to East Asia, the Western and Southwestern Pacific Ocean and the Indian Ocean, and certain of the islands in these oceans. We shall accordingly treat Count I as if the charge had been limited to the above object.

We shall consider in the first place whether a conspiracy with the above object has been proved to have existed.

Already prior to 1928 Okawa, one of the original defendants, who has been discharged from this trial on account of his present mental state, was publicly advocating that Japan should extend her territory on the continent of Asia by the threat or, if necessary, by use of military force. He also advocated that Japan should seek to dominate Eastern Siberia and the South Sea Islands. He predicted that the course he advocated must result in a war between the East and the West, in which Japan would be the champion of the East. He was encouraged and aided in his advocacy of this plan by the Japanese General Staff. The object of this plan as stated was substantially the object of the conspiracy, as we have defined it. In our review of the facts we have noticed many subsequent declarations of the conspirators as to the object of the conspiracy. These do not vary in any material respect from this early declaration by Okawa.

Already when Tanaka was premier, from 1927 to 1929, a party of military men, with Okawa and other civilian supporters, was advocating this policy of Okawa that Japan should expand by the use of force. The conspiracy was now in being. It remained in being until Japan's defeat in 1945. The immediate question when Tanaka was premier was whether

Japan should attempt to expand her influence on the continent—beginning with Manchuria—by peaceful penetration, as Tanaka and the members of his Cabinet wished, or whether that expansion should be accomplished by the use of force if necessary, as the conspirators advocated. It was essential that the conspirators should have the support and control of the nation. This was the beginning of the long struggle between the conspirators, who advocated the attainment of their object by force, and those politicians and latterly those bureaucrats, who advocated Japan's expansion by peaceful measures or at least by a more discreet choice of the occasions on which force should be employed. This struggle culminated in the conspirators obtaining control of the organs of government of Japan and preparing and regimenting the nation's mind and material resources for wars of aggression designed to achieve the object of the conspiracy. In overcoming the opposition the conspirators employed methods which were entirely unconstitutional and at times wholly ruthless. Propaganda and persuasion won many to their side, but military action abroad without Cabinet sanction or in defiance of Cabinet veto, assassination of opposing leaders, plots to overthrow by force of arms Cabinets which refused to cooperate with them, and even a military revolt which seized the capital and attempted to overthrow the government were part of the tactics whereby the conspirators came ultimately to dominate the Japanese polity.

As and when they felt strong enough to overcome opposition at home and latterly when they had finally overcome all such opposition the conspirators carried out in succession the attacks necessary to effect their ultimate object that Japan should dominate the Far East. In 1931 they launched a war of aggression against China and conquered Manchuria and Jehol. By 1934 they had commenced to infiltrate into North China, garrisoning the land and setting up puppet governments designed to serve their purposes. From 1937 onwards they continued their aggressive war against China on a vast scale, overrunning and occupying much of the country, setting up puppet governments on the above model, and exploiting China's economy and natural resources to feed the Japanese military and civilian needs.

In the meantime they had long been planning and preparing a war of aggression which they proposed to launch against the U.S.S.R.. [sic] The intention was to seize that country's eastern territories when a favorable opportunity occurred. They had also long recognized that their exploitation of East Asia and their designs on the islands in the Western and Southwestern Pacific would bring them into conflict with the United

States of America, Britain, France and the Netherlands who would defend their threatened interests and territories. They planned and prepared for war against these countries also.

The conspirators brought about Japan's alliance with Germany and Italy, whose policies were as aggressive as their own, and whose support they desired both in the diplomatic and military fields, for their aggressive actions in China had drawn on Japan the condemnation of the League of Nations and left her friendless in the councils of the world.

Their proposed attack on the U.S.S.R. was postponed from time to time for various reasons, among which were (1) Japan's preoccupation with the war in China, which was absorbing unexpectedly large military resources, and (2) Germany's pact of nonaggression with the U.S.S.R. in 1939, which for the time freed the U.S.S.R. from threat of attack on her western frontier, and might have allowed her to devote the bulk of her strength to the defence of her eastern territories if Japan had attacked her.

Then in the year 1940 came Germany's great military successes on the continent of Europe. For the time being Great Britain, France and the Netherlands were powerless to afford adequate protection to their interests and territories in the Far East. The military preparations of the United States were in the initial stages. It seemed to the conspirators that no such favorable opportunity could readily recur of realizing that part of their objective which sought Japan's domination of Southwest Asia and the islands in the Western and Southwestern Pacific and Indian Oceans. After prolonged negotiations with the United States of America, in which they refused to disgorge any substantial part of the fruits they had seized as the result of their war of aggression against China, on 7 December 1941 the conspirators launched a war of aggression against the United States and the British Commonwealth. They had already issued orders declaring that a state of war existed between Japan and the Netherlands as from 00.00 hours on 7 December 1941. They had previously secured a jumping-off place for their attacks on the Philippines, Malaya and the Netherlands East Indies by forcing their troops into French Indo-China under threat of military action if this facility was refused to them. Recognizing the existence of a state of war and faced by the imminent threat of invasion of her Far Eastern territories, which the conspirators had long planned and were now about to execute, the Netherlands in self-defence declared war on Japan.

These far-reaching plans for waging wars of aggression and the prolonged and intricate preparation for and waging of these wars of aggression were not the work of one man. They were the work of many leaders acting in pursuance of a common plan for the achievement of a common object. That common object, that they should secure Japan's domination by preparing and waging wars of aggression, was a criminal object. Indeed no more grave crimes can be conceived of than a conspiracy to wage a war of aggression or the waging of a war of aggression, for the conspiracy threatens the security of the peoples of the world, and the waging disrupts it. The probable result of such a conspiracy, and the inevitable result of its execution is that death and suffering will be inflicted on countless human beings.

The Tribunal does not find it necessary to consider whether there was a conspiracy to wage wars in violation of the treaties, agreements and assurances specified in the particulars annexed to Count I. The conspiracy to wage wars of aggression was already criminal in the highest degree.

The Tribunal finds that the existence of the criminal conspiracy to wage wars of aggression as alleged in Count I, with the limitation as to object already mentioned, has been proved.

The question whether the defendants or any of them participated in that conspiracy will be considered when we deal with the individual cases.

The conspiracy existed for and its execution occupied a period of many years. Not all of the conspirators were parties to it at the beginning, and some of those who were parties to it had ceased to be active in its execution before the end. All of those who at any time were parties to the criminal conspiracy or who at any time with guilty knowledge played a part in its execution are guilty of the charge contained in Count I.

. . .

Counts 27 to 36 charge the crime of waging wars of aggression and wars in violation of international law, treaties, agreements and assurances against the countries named in those counts.

In the statement of facts just concluded we have found that wars of aggression were waged against all those countries with the exception of the Commonwealth of the Philippines (Count 30) and the Kingdom of Thailand (Count 34). With reference to the Philippines, as we have heretofore stated, that Commonwealth during the period of the war was not a completely sovereign state and so far as international relations were concerned it was a part of the United States of America. We further stated that it is beyond doubt that a war of aggression was waged in the Philippines, but for the sake of technical accuracy we consider the aggressive war in the Philippines as being a part of the war of aggression waged against the United States of America.

Count 28 charges the waging of a war of aggression against the Republic of China over a lesser period of time than that charged in Count 27. Since we hold that the fuller charge contained in Count 27 has been proved we shall make no pronouncement on Count 28.

Wars of aggression having been proved, it is unnecessary to consider whether they were also wars otherwise in violation of international law or in violation of treaties, agreements and assurances. The Tribunal finds therefore that it has been proved that wars of aggression were waged as alleged. . . .

Count 54 charges ordering, authorizing and permitting the commission of Conventional War Crimes. Count 55 charges failure to take adequate steps to secure the observance and prevent breaches of conventions and laws of war in respect of prisoners of war and civilian internees. We find that there have been cases in which crimes under both those Counts have been proved.

. . .

[Sentences]

Defendant	Sentence
Araki	Life Imprisonment
Dohihara	Hanging
Hashimoto	Life Imprisonment
Hata	Life Imprisonment
Hiranuma	Life Imprisonment
Hirota	Hanging
Hoshino	Life Imprisonment
Itagaki	Hanging
Kaya	Life Imprisonment
Kido	Life Imprisonment
Kimura	Hanging
Koiso	Life Imprisonment
Matsui	Hanging
Minami	Life Imprisonment
Muto	Hanging
Oka	Life Imprisonment
Oshima	Life Imprisonment
Sato	Life Imprisonment

Shigemitsu	7 Years Imprisonment
Shimada	Life Imprisonment
Shiratori	Life Imprisonment
Suzuki	Life Imprisonment
Togo	20 Years Imprisonment
Tojo	Hanging
Umezu	Life Imprisonment

. . .

YAMASHITA V. STYER

. . .

DECIDED FEB. 4, 1946

[327 U.S. 1]

Mr. Chief Justice STONE delivered the opinion of the Court.

. . . .

. . . [I]t appears that prior to September 3, 1945, petitioner was the Commanding General of the Fourteenth Army Group of the Imperial Japanese Army in the Philippine Islands. On that date he surrendered to and became a prisoner of war of the United States Army Forces in Baguio, Philippine Islands. On September 25th, by order of respondent, Lieutenant General Wilhelm D. Styer, Commanding General of the United States Army Forces, Western Pacific, which command embraces the Philippine Islands, petitioner was served with a charge prepared by the Judge Advocate General's [sic] Department of the Army, purporting to charge petitioner with a violation of the law of war. On October 8, 1945, petitioner, after pleading not guilty to the charge, was held for trial before a military commission of five Army officers appointed by order of General Styer. The order appointed six Army officers, all lawyers, as defense counsel. . . .

. . . The trial then proceeded until its conclusion on December 7, 1945, the commission hearing two hundred and eighty-six witnesses, who gave over three thousand pages of testimony. On that date petitioner was found guilty of the offense as charged and sentenced to death by hanging.

The petitions for habeas corpus set up that the detention of petitioner for the purpose of the trial was unlawful for reasons which are now urged as showing that the military commission was without lawful authority or jurisdiction to place petitioner on trial . . .

In *Ex parte Quirin*, 317 U.S. 1, 63 S.Ct. 2, 87 L.Ed. 3, we had occasion to consider at length the sources and nature of the authority to create military commissions for the trial of enemy combatants for offenses against the law of war. We there pointed out that Congress, in the exercise of the power conferred upon it by Article I, § 8, Cl. 10 of the Constitution to "define and punish * * * Offenses against the Law of Nations * * * ," [in original] of which the law of war is part, had by the Articles of War (10 U.S.C. §§ 1471–1593, 10 U.S.C.A. §§ 1471–1593) recognized the "military commission" appointed by military command, as it had previously existed in United States Army practice, as an appropriate tribunal for the trial and punishment of offenses against the law of war. Article 15 declares that "the provisions of these articles conferring jurisdiction upon courts-martial shall not be construed as depriving military commissions * * * or other military tribunals of concurrent jurisdiction in respect of offenders or offenses that by statute or by the law of war may be triable by such military commissions * * * or other military tribunals." [in original] . . .

We further pointed out that Congress, by sanctioning trial of enemy combatants for violations of the law of war by military commission, had not attempted to codify the law of war or to mark its precise boundaries. Instead, by Article 15 it had incorporated, by reference, as within the preexisting jurisdiction of military commissions created by appropriate military command, all offenses which are defined as such by the law of war, and which may constitutionally be included within that jurisdiction. It thus adopted the system of military common law applied by military tribunals so far as it should be recognized and deemed applicable by the courts, and as further defined and supplemented by the Hague Convention, to which the United States and the Axis powers were parties.

We also emphasized in *Ex parte Quirin*, as we do here, that on application for habeas corpus, we are not concerned with the guilt or innocence of the petitioners. We consider here only the lawful power of the commission to try the petitioner for the offense charged. In the present cases it must be recognized throughout that the military tribunals which Congress has sanctioned by the Articles of War are not courts whose rulings and judgments are made subject to review by this Court. . . . They are tribunals whose determinations are reviewable by the military authorities either as provided in the military orders constituting such tribunals or as provided by the Articles of War. Congress conferred on the courts no power to review their determinations save only as it has granted judicial power "to grant writs of habeas corpus for the purpose of an inquiry into the cause of the restraint of liberty. . . . The courts may inquire whether the detention complained of is within the authority of those detaining the petitioner. If the military tribunals have lawful authority to hear, decide and condemn, their action is not subject to judicial review merely because they have made a wrong decision on disputed facts. Correction of their errors of decision is not for the courts but for the military authorities which are alone authorized to review their decisions.

Finally, we held in *Ex parte Quirin* . . . as we hold now, that Congress by sanctioning trials of enemy aliens by military commission for offenses against the law of war had recognized the right of the accused to make a defense. . . .

With these governing principles in mind we turn to the consideration of the several contentions urged to establish want of authority in the commission. . . .

The authority to create the Commission. General Styer's order for the appointment of the commission was made by him as Commander of the United States Armed Forces, Western Pacific. His command includes, as part of a vastly greater area, the Philippine Islands, where the alleged offenses were committed, where petitioner surrendered as a prisoner of war, and where, at the time of the order convening the commission, he was detained as a prisoner in custody of the United States army. The Congressional recognition of military commissions and its sanction of their use in trying offenses against the law of war to which we have referred, sanctioned their creation by military command in conformity to long established American precedents. Such a commission may be appointed by any field commander, or by any commander competent to appoint a general court-martial, as was General Styer, who had been vested with that power by order of the President. . . .

Here the commission was not only created by a commander competent to appoint it, but his order conformed to the established policy of the Government and to higher military commands authorizing his action. In a proclamation of July 2, 1942 . . . the President proclaimed that enemy belligerents who, during time of war, enter the United States, or any territory possession thereof, and who violate the law of war, should be subject to the law of war and to the jurisdiction of military tribunals. Paragraph 10 of the Declaration of Potsdam of July 6, 1945, declared that "* * * stern justice shall be meted out to all war criminals including those who have visited cruelties upon prisoners." [in original] . . . This Declaration was accepted by the Japanese government by its note of August 10, 1945. . . .

By direction of the President, the Joint Chiefs of Staff of the American Military Forces, on September 12, 1945, instructed General MacArthur, Commander in Chief, United States Army Forces, Pacific, to proceed with the trial, before appropriate military tribunals, of such Japanese war criminals "as have been or may be apprehended." By order of General MacArthur of September 24, 1945, General Styer was specifically directed to proceed with the trial of petitioner upon the charge here involved. . . .

It thus appears that the order creating the commission for the trial of petitioner was authorized by military command, and was in complete conformity to the Act of Congress sanctioning the creation of such tribunals for the trial of offenses against the law of war committed by enemy combatants. And we turn to the question whether the authority to create the commission and direct the trial by military order continued after the cessation of hostilities.

. . . .

We cannot say that there is no authority to convene a commission after hostilities have ended to try violations of the law of war committed before their cessation, at least until peace has been officially recognized by treaty or proclamation of the political branch of the Government. In fact, in most instances the practical administration of the system of military justice under the law of war would fail if such authority were thought to end with the cessation of hostilities. For only after their cessation could the greater number of offenders and the principal ones be apprehended and subjected to trial.

No writer on international law appears to have regarded the power of military tribunals, otherwise competent to try violations of the law of war, as terminating before the formal state of war has ended . . .

The Charge. Neither Congressional action nor the military orders constituting the commission authorized it to place petitioner on trial unless the charge preferred against him is of a violation of the law of war. The charge, so far as now relevant, is that petitioner, between

October 9, 1944 [,] and September 2, 1945, in the Philippine Islands, "while commander of armed forces of Japan at war with the United States of America and its allies, unlawfully disregarded and failed to discharge his duty as commander to control the operations of the members of his command, permitting them to commit brutal atrocities and other high crimes against people of the United States and of its allies and dependencies, particularly the Philippines; and he * * * thereby violated the laws of war." [in original]

. . . The first item specifies the execution of "a deliberate plan and purpose to massacre and exterminate a large part of the civilian population of Batangas Province, and to devastate and destroy public, private and religious property therein, as a result of which more than 25,000 men, women and children, all unarmed noncombatant civilians, were brutally mistreated and killed. . . . Other acts specify acts of violence, cruelty and homicide inflicted upon the civilian population and prisoners of war, acts of wholesale pillage and the wanton destruction of religious monuments.

It is not denied that such acts directed against the civilian population of an occupied country and against prisoners of war are recognized in international law as violations of the law of war. Articles 4, 28, 46 and 47, Annex to Fourth Hague Convention, 1907. . . . The question then is whether the law of war imposes on an army commander a duty to take such appropriate measures as are within his power to control the troops under his command for the prevention of the specified acts which are violations of the law of war and which are likely to attend the occupation of hostile territory by an uncontrolled soldiery, and whether he may be charged with personal responsibility for his failure to take such measures when violations result. . . .

It is evident that the conduct of military operations by troops whose excesses are unrestrained by the orders or efforts of their commander would almost certainly result in violations which it is the purpose of the law of war to prevent. Its purpose to protect civilian populations and prisoners of war from brutality would largely be defeated if the commander of an invading army could with impunity neglect to take reasonable measures for their protection. Hence the law of war presupposes that its violation is to be avoided through the control of the operations of war by commanders who are to some extent responsible for their subordinates.

This is recognized by the Annex to Fourth Hague Convention of 1907, respecting the laws and customs of war on land. Article I lays down as a condition which an armed force must fulfill in order to be accorded the rights of lawful belligerents, that it must be "commanded by a person responsible for his subordinates." . . .

We do not here appraise the evidence on which petitioner was convicted. We do not consider what measures, if any, petitioner took to prevent the commission, by the troops under his command, of the plain violations of the law of war detailed in the bill of particulars, or whether such measures as he may have taken were appropriate and sufficient to discharge the duty imposed upon him. These are questions within the peculiar competence of the military officers composing the commission and were for it to decide. . . .

. . . But we conclude that the allegations of the charge, tested by any reasonable standard, adequately allege a violation of the law of war and that the commission had authority to try and decide the issue which it raised. . . .

The Proceedings before the Commission. The regulations prescribed by General MacArthur governing the procedure for the trial of petitioner by the commission directed that the commission should admit such evidence "as in its opinion would be of assistance in proving or disproving the charge, or such as in the commission's opinion would have probative value in the mind of a reasonable man," and that in particular it might admit affidavits, depositions or other statements taken by officers detailed for that purpose by military authority. . . . Petitioner argues as ground for the writ of habeas corpus, that Article 25 [footnote omitted] of the Articles of War prohibited the reception in evidence by the commission of depositions on behalf of the prosecution in a capital case, and that Article 38 [footnote omitted] prohibited the reception of hearsay and of opinion evidence.

We think that neither Article 25 nor Article 38 is applicable to the trial of an enemy combatant by a military commission for violations of the law of war. Article 2 of the Articles of war enumerates "the persons * * * subject to these articles," who are denominated, for purposes of the Articles, as "persons subject to military law." [in original] In general, the persons so enumerated are members of our own Army and of the personnel accompanying the Army. Enemy combatants are not included among them. . . .

It thus appears that the order convening the commission was a lawful order, that the commission was lawfully constituted, that petitioner was charged with violation of the law of war, and the commission had authority to proceed with the trial, and in doing so did not violate any military, statutory or constitutional command. . . . We therefore conclude that the detention of petitioner for trial and his detention upon his conviction, subject to the prescribed review by the military authorities were lawful, and that the petition for certiorari, and leave to file in this Court petitions for writs of habeas corpus and prohibition should be, and they are Denied.

. . .

Mr. Justice MURPHY, dissenting [Mr. Justice RUTLEDGE filed a separate dissenting opinion].

. . . The grave issue raised by this case is whether a military commission so established and so authorized may disregard the procedural rights of an accused person as guaranteed by the Constitution, especially by the due process clause of the Fifth Amendment.

The answer is plain. The Fifth Amendment guarantee of due process of law applies to "any person" who is accused of a crime by the Federal Government or any of its agencies. No exception is made as to those who are accused of war crimes or as to those who possess the status of an enemy belligerent. Indeed, such an exception would be contrary to the whole philosophy of human rights which makes the Constitution the great living document that it is. The immutable rights of the individual, including those secured by the due process clause of the Fifth Amendment, belong not alone to the members of those nations that excel on the battlefield or that subscribe to the democratic ideology. They belong to every person in the world, victor or vanquished, whatever may be his race, color or beliefs. They rise above any status of belligerency or outlawry. . . .

The failure of the military commission to obey the dictates of the due process requirements of the Fifth Amendment is apparent in this case. . . .

. . . No military necessity or other emergency demanded the suspension of the safeguards of due process. Yet petitioner was rushed to trial under an improper charge, given insufficient time to prepare an adequate defense, deprived of the benefits of some of the most elementary rules of evidence and summarily sentenced to be hanged. In all this needless and unseemly haste there was no serious attempt to charge or to prove that he committed a recognized violation of the laws of war. He was not charged with personally participating in the acts of atrocity or with ordering or condoning their commission. Not even knowledge of these crimes was attributed to him. . . .

The petitioner was accused of having "unlawfully disregarded and failed to discharge his duty as commander to control the operations of the members of his command, permitting them to commit brutal atrocities and other high crimes." . . .

In other words, read against the background of military events in the Philippines subsequent to October 9, 1944, these charges amount to this: "We, the victorious American forces, have done everything possible to destroy and disorganize your lines of communication, your effective control of your personnel, your ability to wage war. In those respects we have succeeded. We have defeated and crushed your forces. And now we charge and condemn you for having been inefficient in maintaining control of your troops during the period when we were so effectively besieging and eliminating your forces and blocking your ability to maintain effective control. Many terrible atrocities were committed by your disorganized troops. Because these atrocities were so widespread we will not bother to charge or prove that you committed, ordered or condoned any of them. We will assume that they must have resulted from your inefficiency and negligence as a commander. In short, we charge you with the crime of inefficiency in controlling your troops. We will judge the discharge of your duties by the disorganization which we ourselves created in large part. Our standards of judgment are whatever we wish to make them."

Nothing in all history or in international law, at least as far as I am aware, justifies such a charge against a fallen commander of a defeated force. To use the very inefficiency and disorganization created by the victorious forces as the primary basis for condemning officers of the defeated armies bears no resemblance to justice or to military reality.

. . . . .

NOTE: The following case involves the only known instance of a war crimes trial arising in the European Theater during World War II in which the accused was charged with the offense of violating Article 2(2) of the 1929 Geneva Convention relative to the Treatment of Prisoners of War. This Convention requires combatants to protect prisoners of war from insults and public curiosity, a provision now found in Article 13 of the 1949 Geneva Convention relative to the Treatment of Prisoners of War. This violation of the laws of war has been committed frequently since then. At the outset of the Gulf War, Iraq paraded United States POWs in front of television cameras as mentioned in Chapter 4. General condemnation of this conduct seems to have moved Iraq to suspend it promptly, suggesting that public outcry concerning war crimes can effectively moderate behavior under certain circumstances.

TRIAL OF LIEUTENANT GENERAL KURT MAELZER (U.S. MILITARY COMMISSION, FLORENCE, ITALY, 9–14 SEPTEMBER 1946)[7]

1. THE CHARGE

The accused was charged with ". . . exposing prisoners of war . . . in his custody . . . to acts of violence, insults and public curiosity." [in original]

2. THE EVIDENCE

Some time in January, 1944, Field Marshal Kesselring, commander-in-chief of the German forces in Italy, ordered the accused who was commander of Rome garrison to hold a parade of several hundreds of British and American prisoners of war in the streets of the Italian capital. This parade, emulating the tradition of the triumphal marches of ancient Rome, was to be staged to bolster the morale of the Italian population in view of the recent allied landings, not very far from the capital. The accused ordered the parade which took place on 2nd February, 1944. 200 American prisoners of war were marched from the Coliseum, through the main streets of Rome under armed German escort. The streets were lined by forces under the control of the accused. The accused and his staff officers attended the parade. According to the Prosecution witnesses (some of whom were American ex-prisoners of war who had taken part in the march), the population threw stones and sticks at the prisoners, but, according to the defence witnesses, they threw cigarettes and flowers. The prosecution also alleged that when some of the prisoners were giving the "victory sign" with their fingers the accused ordered the guards to fire. This order, however, was not carried out. A film was made of the parade and a great number of photographs taken which appeared in the Italian press under the caption "Anglo-Americans enter Rome after all . . . [in original] flanked by German bayonets." The accused pleaded in the main that the march was planned and ordered by his superiors and that his only function as commander of Rome garrison was to guarantee the safe conduct and security of the prisoners during the march, which he did. He stated that the march was to quell rumours of the German defeat and to quieten the population of Rome, not to scorn or ridicule the prisoners.

3. FINDINGS AND SENTENCE

The accused was found guilty and sentenced to 10 years' imprisonment. The sentence was reduced to three years' imprisonment by higher military authority.

. . .

NOTE: When a war ends in the total surrender of one side, the victor, now in control of the enemy, can conduct war crimes trials as it wishes. But when a war criminal escapes and is in the territory of another state, apprehension of the criminal can be difficult. Adolf Eichmann, a Nazi officer who played a major role in the destruction of European Jewry during World War II, evaded capture after the war and escaped to South America. He was captured by Israeli secret service personnel in Argentina in 1960 and was tried, convicted, and executed in 1962 for war crimes. The abduction prompted diplomatic protests by Argentina, which brought the issue to the Security Council. A major issue in the case was who is entitled to try and punish war criminals.

THE ATTORNEY-GENERAL OF THE GOVERNMENT OF ISRAEL v. EICHMANN
DISTRICT COURT OF JERUSALEM;
JUDGMENT OF DEC. 11, 1961.

[56 A.J.I.L. 805 (1962)]

Adolf Eichmann was abducted from Argentina and brought to trial in Israel under the Nazi Collaborators (Punishment) Law, enacted after Israel became a state and after the events charged against Eichmann during the Nazi era in Germany. Section 1(a) of the law provides:

A person who has committed one of the following offences—

1) did, during the period of the Nazi regime, in a hostile country, an act constituting a crime against the Jewish people;
2) did, during the period of the Nazi regime, in a hostile country, an act constituting a crime against humanity;
3) did, during the period of the Second World War, in a hostile country, an act constituting a war crime;

is liable to the death penalty.

Counsel for Eichmann objected to the jurisdiction of the Court, *inter alia*, on grounds based on international law. [Excerpted opinion follows.] [in original]

. . . . . [in original]

8. Learned Counsel does not ignore the fact that the Israel law applicable to the acts attributed to the accused vests in us the jurisdiction to try this case. His contention against the jurisdiction of the Court is not based on this law, but on international law. He contends—

(a) that the Israel law, by inflicting punishment for acts done outside the boundaries of the State and before its establishment, against persons who were not Israel citizens, and by a person who acted in the course of duty on behalf of a foreign country ("Act of State") conflicts with international law and exceeds the powers of the Israel legislator;

. . .

30. We have discussed at length the international character of the crimes in question because this offers the broadest possible, though not the only, basis for Israel's jurisdiction according to the law of nations. No less important from the point of view of international law is the special connection the State of Israel has with such crimes, seeing that the people of Israel (Am Israel)—the Jewish people (Ha'am Ha'yehudi— to use the term in the Israel legislation)—constituted the target and the victim of most of the crimes in question. The State of Israel's "right to punish" the accused derives, in our view, from two cumulative sources: a universal source (pertaining to the whole of mankind) which vests the right to prosecute and punish crimes of this order in every State within the family of nations; and a specific or national source which gives the victim nation the right to try any who assault their existence.

. . .

32. We have already stated above the view of Grotius on "the right to punish," a view which is also based on a "linking point" between the

criminal and his victim: Grotius holds that the very commission of the crime creates a legal connection between the offender and the victim, and one that vests in the victim the right to punish the offender or demand his punishment. According to natural justice the victim may himself punish the offender, but the organisation of society has delegated that natural right to the sovereign State. One of the main objects of the punishment is—continues the author of "The Law of Peace and War" (Book 2, chapter 20)—to ensure that "the victim shall not in future suffer a similar infliction at the hands of the same person or at the hands of others" . . .

. . .[T]he very term "connection" or "linking point" is useful for the elucidation of the problem before us.

.   .   .

34. The connection between the State of Israel and the Jewish people needs no explanation. The State of Israel was established and recognised as the State of the Jews. The proclamation of Iyar 5, 5705 (14.5.48) (Official Gazette No. 1) opens with the words: "It was in the Land of Israel that the Jewish people was born," dwells on the history of the Jewish people from ancient times until the Second World War, refers to the Resolution of the United Nations Assembly of 29.11.47 which demands the establishment of a Jewish State in Eretz Israel, determines the "natural right of the Jewish people to be, like every other people, self-governing, in its sovereign State." It would appear that there is hardly need for any further proof of the very obvious connection between the Jewish people and the State of Israel: this is the sovereign State of the Jewish people.

Moreover, the proclamation of the establishment of the State of Israel makes mention of the very special tragic link between the Nazi crimes, which form the theme of the law in question, and the establishment of the State:

> "The recent holocaust which consumed millions of
> Jews in Europe, provides fresh and unmistakable proof
> of the necessity of solving the problem of the home-
> lessness and lack of independence of the Jewish people
> by re-establishing the Jewish State which would fling
> open the gates of the fatherland to every Jew and would
> endow the Jewish people with equality of status within
> the family of nations.
>
> "The remnants of the disastrous slaughter of the

Nazis in Europe together with Jews from other lands persisted in making their way to the Land of Israel in defiance of all difficulties, obstacles and dangers. They have not ceased to claim their right to a life of dignity, freedom and honest toil in their ancestral home.["]

"In the Second World War the Jewish people in Palestine made its full contribution to the struggle of the freedom and peace-loving nations against the Nazi forces of evil. Its war effort and the blood of its soldiers entitled it to rank with the peoples that made the covenant of the United Nations."

These words are no mere rhetoric, but historical facts, which international law does not ignore.

In the light of the recognition by the United Nations of the right of the Jewish people to establish their State, and in the light of the recognition of the established Jewish State by the family of nations, the connection between the Jewish people and the State of Israel constitutes an integral part of the law of nations. . . . [in original]

36. Counsel contended that the protective principle cannot apply to this case because that principle is designed to protect only an existing State, its security and its interests, while the State of Israel had not existed at the time of the commission of the crime. . . .

In our view Learned Counsel errs when he examines the protective principle in this retroactive law according to the time of the commission of the crimes, as is the case in an ordinary law. . . .

38. . . . Indeed, this retroactive law is designed to supplement a gap in the laws of Mandatory Palestine, and the interests protected by this law had existed also during the period of the Jewish National Home. The Balfour Declaration and the Palestine Mandate given by the League of Nations to Great Britain constituted an international recognition of the Jewish people, . . . the historical link of the Jewish people with Eretz Israel and their right to re-establish their National Home in that country. . . . The Jewish "Yishuv" in Palestine constituted during that period a "State-on-the-way," as it were, which reached in due time a sovereign status. The want of sovereignty made it impossible for the Jewish "Yishuv" in the country to enact a criminal law against the Nazi crimes at the time of the commission thereof, but these crimes were also directed against that "Yishuv" who constituted an integral part of the Jewish people, and the enactment with retroactive application of the law in

question by the State of Israel filled the needs which had already existed previously.

.   .   .

39. We should add that the well-known judgment of the International Court of Justice at The Hague in the "Lotus Case" has ruled that the principle of territoriality does not limit the power of the State to try crimes and, moreover, any argument against such power must point to a specific rule in international law which negates the power. . . .

NOTE: The United States military, like many other national militaries, prosecutes its own soldiers when it believes that they may have committed war crimes. In the United States, these proceedings are not called war crimes trials but are prosecuted as criminal charges under the United States Uniform Code of Military Justice. The United States Army's policy is enunciated in the following extract from the field manual, *The Law of Land Warfare*:

THE LAW OF LAND WARFARE

[The United States Army, *The Law of Land Warfare* 182 (Field Manual (FM) 27-10 1956)]

507. *Universality of Jurisdiction*

.   .   .

b. Persons Charged with War Crimes. The United States normally punishes war crimes as such only if they are committed by enemy nationals or by persons serving the interests of the enemy State. Violations of the law of war committed by persons subject to the military law of the United States will usually constitute violations of the Uniform Code of Military Justice and, if so, will be prosecuted under that Code. Violations of the law of war committed within the United States by other persons will usually constitute violations of federal or state criminal law and preferably will be prosecuted under such law (see pars. 505 and 506). Commanding officers of United States troops must insure that war crimes committed by members of their forces against enemy personnel are promptly and adequately punished.

NOTE: The United States conducted many trials against its own officers and men during the Vietnam War. The *Griffen* and *Calley* cases provide useful discussions in their judgments of the considerations that military officers bring to bear when they appraise action in terms of the law of war.

UNITED STATES V. STAFF SERGEANT (E-6) WALTER GRIFFEN (U.S. ARMY BOARD OF REVIEW, 2 JULY 1968)

[39 C.M.R. 586 (1968); petition for review denied
18 U.S.C.M.A. 622, 39 C.M.R. 293 (1968)]

. . . .

PORCELLA, Judge Advocate:

In this contested case, the accused was found guilty of acting jointly with others in committing an unpremeditated murder in violation of Article 118 of the Uniform Code of Military Justice. After reducing the period of confinement from ten years, the convening authority approved a sentence of total forfeitures, confinement at hard labor for seven years and reduction to the lowest enlisted grade.

In their assignment of errors, counsel for the appellant contend that the law officer erred prejudicially in failing to instruct the court on the applicable law of the defense of obedience to superior orders. In considering this contention, we will recite those facts which appear pertinent to our disposition of the case.

On 4 April 1967, in Vietnam, a platoon of the 1st Cavalry Division was providing security for an engineer element near Bong Son. About 10 o'clock in the morning, members of the platoon apprehended an indigenous male of military age who, after evacuation and interrogation by a higher echelon, was "confirmed" to be a member of the hostile Viet Cong. Later that day, as the platoon was preparing to cross a large, open rice paddy, a security element on the right flank found an unarmed male native about 40 to 45 years old in a bunker. He was brought to the command post area, and a helicopter was requested for his evacuation. Meanwhile, the accused noticed that activities of his platoon were being observed by a native he suspected might be a member of the Viet Cong.

A patrol was dispatched to apprehend him. However, the search was unsuccessful. While the patrol was reconnoitering by fire and discharging grenades in bunkers, one of its members was injured by a secondary explosion. Using radio communications, overheard by several witnesses, Lieutenant Patrick, the platoon leader, conversed with Captain Ogg, the company commander. He arranged for the air evacuation of the wounded man but was told this prisoner would not be evacuated by helicopter. The precise conversation concerning the disposition of the prisoner is not clear. However, the understanding of Captain Ogg's order appears to have been that the prisoner should be killed. There is evidence that Lieutenant Patrick gave the accused a direct order to the same effect. Specialist Garcia, the medical technician attached to the platoon, removed the prisoner from the command post area and escorted him, his hands tied behind his back, to an embankment, where the accused and Private First Class Woods each fired several shots at him with M-16 rifles. The prisoner expired as a result. His body contained numerous fragments from M-16 bullets.

The accused testified, in part, to the following effect: He overheard Captain Ogg state in his radio transmission that the prisoner should be killed. Then Lieutenant Patrick said: "Sergeant Griffen, take him down the hill and shoot him. Come back and let me know." The accused admitted firing his rifle at the prisoner and thereafter reporting back to Lieutenant Patrick. He committed the act because he had been ordered to do so and for the safety of his men. He believed the order to be legal because his platoon leader, a lieutenant, had once been relieved when a prisoner who had been securely tied escaped during the night. Also, he felt that the security of the platoon would have been violated if the prisoner were kept, since their operations had already been observed by another suspect. In addition, several months earlier, all the members of his platoon had either been killed or wounded in that same general area after their positions had been observed.

Prior to argument, the defense submitted a proposed instruction on obedience of orders as a defense to the offense charged. The law officer did not give the requested instruction. Rather, he instructed the court as follows on this subject:

> "Now, the general rule is that the acts of a subordinate, done in good faith in compliance with his supposed duty or orders, are justifiable. This justification does not exist, however, when those acts are manifestly

beyond the scope of his authority, or the order is such that a man of ordinary sense and understanding would know it to be illegal.

"I tell you as a matter of law that if instructions or orders were received over that radio or were given to the accused in this case to kill the prisoner suspect who was helpless there before them, such an order would have been manifestly an illegal order. You are advised as a matter of law, any such command, if in fact there was such a command, was an illegal order. "A soldier or airman is not an automaton but a reasoning agent who is under a duty to exercise judgment in obeying the orders of a superior officer to the extent, that where such orders are manifestly beyond the scope of the issuing officer's authority and are so palpably illegal on their face that a man of ordinary sense and understanding would know them to be illegal, then the fact of obedience to the order of a superior officer will not protect a soldier for acts committed pursuant to such illegal orders. This is the law in regard to superior orders."

In deciding the issues in this case, we will assume that a superior officer ordered the accused to kill the native male then in the platoon's custody.

The intentional killing of another person without premeditation, provocation, justification, or excuse and not while in the perpetration of a felony is unpremeditated murder. (UCMJ, Art 188, 10 USC § 918). However, a homicide committed in the proper performance of a legal duty is justifiable and not a crime. Thus, killing to prevent the escape of a prisoner if no other reasonably apparent means are adequate or killing an enemy in battle are cases of justifiable homicide. (MCM, US, 1951, ¶ 197b). Conversely, the killing of a docile prisoner taken during military operations is not justifiable homicide. . . . In his authoritative work, Winthrop stated:

> "That the act charged as an offense was done in obedience to the order—verbal or written—of a military superior, is, in general, a good defense at military law.
>
>   * * * * * * * [in original]

". . . Where the order is apparently regular and lawful on its face, he is not to go behind it to satisfy himself that his superior has proceeded with authority, but is to obey it according to its terms, the only exceptions recognized to the rule of obedience being cases of orders so manifestly beyond the legal power of discretion of the commander as to admit of no rational doubt of their unlawfulness." (Winthrop, Military Law and Precedents, 2d Ed. (1920 reprint) 296–297.)

The Manual for Courts-Martial, U.S. Army, 1921 (¶ 4156, page 355) stated:

"To justify from a military point of view a military inferior in disobeying the order of a superior, the order must be one requiring something to be done which is palpably a breach of law and a crime or an injury to a third person, or is of a serious character (not involving unimportant consequences only) and if done would not be susceptible of being righted. An order requiring the performance of a military duty or act can not be disobeyed with impunity unless it has one of these characteristics."

The Manual for Courts-Martial, United States, 1951 (¶ 197b, p. 351, contains the following discussion relating to the defense of duty or orders as justification for a homicide:

". . . the acts of a subordinate, done in good faith in compliance with his supposed duties or orders are justifiable. *This justification does not exist, however, when* those acts are manifestly beyond the scope of his authority, or *the order is such that a man of ordinary sense and understanding would know it to be illegal. . .*" (Emphasis supplied.) [in original]

.   .   .

Having considered the foregoing authorities, we accept the following principle for application in this case (¶ 197b, MCM, US, 1951, quoted supra): The act of a subordinate, done in good faith in compliance with the supposed order of a superior, is not justifiable when the order is such that a man of ordinary sense and understanding would know it to be illegal. (See ACM 7321, Kinder, 14 CMR 742, 773 (1954)).

We now turn to the question: Did the law officer err in failing to give an appropriate instruction on justification as a defense to a homicide committed in good faith compliance with the order of a superior? As previously noted, the defense counsel made a request for such an instruction, but the law officer instructed contradictorily. He informed the court to the effect that if an order to kill the prisoner had been given, it would have been manifestly illegal.

A law officer is required to give an appropriate instruction when there is some evidence that will allow a reasonable inference that a defense is in issue (United States v. Black, 12 USCMA 571, 31 CMR 157 (1961)). Evaluating the record, we find the evidence clear and convincing that an unarmed, unresisting prisoner whose hands were bound behind his back was killed at close range by rifle fire discharged by the accused and another soldier. We note no evidence which could provide an inference suggestive of self-defense, or that the killing was to prevent the escape of the prisoner, or for that matter, any other justification or excuse for the killing. Also, there are strong moral, religious, and legal prohibitions in our society against killing others which should arouse the strongest scruples against killings of this kind. In fact, it is difficult to conceive of a military situation in which the order of a superior would be more patently wrong. Accordingly, we view the order as commanding an act so obviously beyond the scope of authority of the superior officer and so palpably illegal on its face as to admit of no doubt of its unlawfulness to a man of ordinary sense and understanding. As there was no evidence which would have allowed a reasonable inference that the accused justifiably killed the prisoner pursuant to the order of a superior officer, it follows, as a matter of law, that this defense was not in issue, the law officer did not err by refusing to give an instruction on it, and that the law officer properly instructed the court that such an order would have been manifestly illegal.

· · ·

United States v. William L. Calley, Jr.
(U.S. Court of Military Appeals,
21 December 1973)

[22 U.S.C.M.A. 534 (1973), 48 C.M.R. 19 (1973),
habeas corpus granted sub nom. Calley v. *Calloway,*
382 F.Supp. 650 (M.D. Ga. 1974), *rev'd* 519 F.2d. 184
(5th Cir. 1975), *cert. denied sub nom. Calley* v. *Hoffman,*
425 U.S. 911 (1976)]

.   .   .

QUINN, Judge:
First Lieutenant Calley stands convicted of the premeditated murder
of 22 infants, children, women, and old men, and of assault with intent
to murder a child of about 2 years of age. All the killings and the assault
took place on March 16, 1968 [,] in the area of the village of My Lai
in the Republic of South Vietnam. The Army Court of Military Review
affirmed the findings of guilty and the sentence, which, as reduced by
the convening authority, includes dismissal and confinement at hard labor
for 20 years. The accused petitioned this Court for further review, alleging
30 assignments of error. We granted three of these assignments.

.   .   .

Lieutenant Calley was a platoon leader in C Company, a unit that
was part of an organization known as Task Force Barker, whose mission
was to subdue and drive out the enemy in an area in the Republic of
Vietnam known popularly as Pinkville. Before March 16, 1968, this
area, which included the village of My Lai 4, was a Viet Cong stronghold.
C Company had operated in the area several times. Each time the unit
had entered the area it suffered casualties by sniper fire, machine gun
fire, mines, and other forms of attack. Lieutenant Calley had accompanied his platoon on some of the incursions.

On March 15, 1968, a memorial service for members of the company
killed in the area during the preceding weeks was held. After the service
Captain Ernest L. Medina, the commanding officer of C Company,
briefed the company on a mission in the Pinkville area set for the next
day. C Company was to serve as the main attack formation for Task Force
Barker. In that role it would assault and neutralize My Lai 4, 5, and 6
and then mass for an assault on My Lai 1. Intelligence reports indicated

that the unit would be opposed by a veteran enemy battalion, and that all civilians would be absent from the area. The objective was to destroy the enemy. Disagreement exists as to the instructions on the specifics of destruction.

Captain Medina testified that he instructed his troops that they were to destroy My Lai 4 by "burning the hootches, to kill the livestock, to close the wells and to destroy the food crops." Asked if women and children were to be killed, Medina said he replied in the negative, adding that, "You must use common sense. If they have a weapon and are trying to engage you, then you can shoot back, but you must use common sense." However, Lieutenant Calley testified that Captain Medina informed the troops they were to kill every living thing—men, women, children, and animals—and under no circumstances were they to leave any Vietnamese behind them as they passed through the villages enroute to their final objective. Other witnesses gave more or less support to both versions of the briefing.

On March 16, 1968, the operation began with interdicting fire. C Company was then brought to the area by helicopters. Lieutenant Calley's platoon was on the first lift. This platoon formed a defense perimeter until the remainder of the force was landed. The unit received no hostile fire from the village.

Calley's platoon passed the approaches to the village with his men firing heavily. Entering the village, the platoon encountered only unarmed, unresisting men, women, and children. The villagers, including infants held in their mothers' arms, were assembled and moved in separate groups to collection points. Calley testified that during this time he was radioed twice by Captain Medina, who demanded to know what was delaying the platoon. On being told that a large number of villagers had been detained, Calley said Medina ordered him to "waste them." Calley further testified that he obeyed the orders because he had been taught the doctrine of obedience throughout his military career. Medina denied that he gave any such order.

One of the collection points for the villagers was in the southern part of the village. There, Private First Class Paul D. Meadlo guarded a group of between 30 to 40 old men, women, and children. Lieutenant Calley approached Meadlo and told him, " 'You know what to do,' " and left. He returned shortly and asked Meadlo why the people were not yet dead. Meadlo replied he did not know that Calley had meant that they should be killed. Calley declared that he wanted them dead. He and Meadlo then opened fire on the group, until all but a few children fell. Calley then personally shot these children. He expended 4 or 5 magazines from his M-16 rifle in the incident.

Lieutenant Calley and Meadlo moved from this point to an irrigation ditch on the east side of My Lai 4. There, they encountered another group of civilians being held by several soldiers. Meadlo estimated that this group contained from 75 to 100 persons. Calley stated, " 'We got another job to do, Meadlo,' " and he ordered the group into the ditch. When all were in the ditch, Calley and Meadlo opened fire on them. Although ordered by Calley to shoot, Private First Class James J. Dursi refused to join in the killings, and Specialist Four Robert E. Maples refused to give his machine gun to Calley for use in the killings. Lieutenant Calley admitted that he fired into the ditch, with the muzzle of his weapon within 5 feet of people in it. He expended between 10 to 15 magazines of ammunition on this occasion.

With his radio operator, Private Charles Sledge, Calley moved to the north end of the ditch. There, he found an elderly Vietnamese monk, whom he interrogated. Calley struck the man with his rifle butt and then shot him in the head. Other testimony indicates that immediately afterwards a young child was observed running toward the village. Calley seized him by the arm, threw him into the ditch, and fired at him. Calley admitted interrogating and striking the monk, but denied shooting him. He also denied the incident involving the child.

Appellate defense counsel contend that the evidence is insufficient to establish the accused's guilt. They do not dispute Calley's participation in the homicides, but they argue that he did not act with the malice or *mens rea* essential to a conviction of murder; that the orders he received to kill everyone in the village were not palpably illegal; that he was acting in ignorance of the laws of war; that since he was told that only "the enemy" would be in the village, his honest belief that there were no innocent civilians in the village exonerates him of criminal responsibility for their deaths; and, finally, that his actions were in the heat of passion caused by reasonable provocation.

.   .   .

The testimony of Meadlo and others provided the court members with ample evidence from which to find that Lieutenant Calley directed and personally participated in the intentional killing of men, women, and children, who were unarmed and in the custody of armed soldiers of C Company. If the prosecution's witnesses are believed, there is also ample evidence to support a finding that the accused deliberately shot the Vietnamese monk whom he interrogated, and that he seized, threw into a ditch, and fired on a child with the intent to kill.

. . .

Enemy prisoners are not subject to summary execution by their captors. Military law has long held that the killing of an unresisting prisoner is murder. Winthrop's Military Law and Precedents, 2d ed., 1920 Reprint, at 788–91.

> While it is lawful to kill an enemy "in the heat and exercise of war," yet "to kill such an enemy after he has laid down his arms . . . is murder." Digest of Opinions of the Judge Advocates General of the Army, 1912, at 1074–75 n.3.

Conceding for the purposes of this assignment of error that Calley believed the villagers were part of "the enemy," the uncontradicted evidence is that they were under the control of armed soldiers and were offering no resistance. In his testimony, Calley admitted he was aware of the requirement that prisoners be treated with respect. He also admitted he knew that the normal practice was to interrogate villagers, release those who could satisfactorily account for themselves, and evacuate the suspect among them for further examination. Instead of proceeding in the usual way, Calley executed all, without regard to age, condition, or possibility of suspicion. On the evidence, the court-martial could reasonably find Calley guilty of the offenses before us.

. . .

At trial, Calley's principal defense was that he acted in execution of Captain Medina's order to kill everyone in My Lai 4. Appellate defense counsel urge this defense as the most important factor in assessment of the legal sufficiency of the evidence. The argument, however, is inapplicable to whether the evidence is *legally* sufficient. Captain Medina denied that he issued any such order, either during the previous day's briefing or on the date the killings were carried out. Resolution of the conflict between his testimony and that of the accused was for the triers of the facts. United States v. Guerra, 13 USCMA 463, 32 CMR 403 (1963). The general findings of guilty, with exceptions as to the number of persons killed, does not indicate whether the court members found that Captain Medina did not issue the alleged order to kill, or whether, if he did, the court members believed that the accused knew the order was illegal. For the purpose of the legal sufficiency of the evidence, the record supports the findings of guilty.

In the third assignment of error, appellate defense counsel assert gross deficiencies in the military judge's instructions to the court members. Only two assertions merit discussion. . . . [T]he second allegation is that the defense of compliance with superior orders was not properly submitted to the court members.

. . .

We turn to the contention that the judge erred in his submission of the defense of superior orders to the court. After fairly summarizing the evidence, the judge gave the following instructions pertinent to the issue:

> The killing of resisting or fleeing enemy forces is generally recognized as a justifiable act of war, and you may consider any such killings justifiable in this case. The law attempts to protect those persons not actually engaged in warfare, however; and limits the circumstances under which their lives may be taken.
>
> Both combatants captured by and noncombatants detained by the opposing force, regardless of their loyalties, political views, or prior acts, have the right to be treated as prisoners until released, confined, or executed, in accordance with law and established procedures, by competent authority sitting in judgment of such detained or captured individuals. Summary execution of detainees or prisoners is forbidden by law. Further, it's clear under the evidence presented in this case, that hostile acts or support of the enemy North Vietnamese or Viet Cong forces by inhabitants of My Lai (4) at some time prior to 16 March 1968, would not justify the summary execution of all or a part of the occupants of My Lai (4) on 16 March, nor would hostile acts committed that day, if, following the hostility, the belligerents surrendered or were captured by our forces. I therefore instruct you, as a matter of law, that if unresisting human beings were killed at My Lai (4) while within the effective custody and control of our military forces, their deaths cannot be considered

justified, and any order to kill such people would be, as a matter of law, an illegal order. Thus, if you find that Lieutenant Calley received an order directing him to kill unresisting Vietnamese within his control or within the control of his troops, *that order would be an illegal order*.

A determination that an order is illegal does not, of itself, assign criminal responsibility to the person following the order for acts done in compliance with it. Soldiers are taught to follow orders, and special attention is given to obedience of orders on the battlefield. Military effectiveness depends upon obedience to orders. On the other hand, the obedience of a soldier is not the obedience of an automaton. A soldier is a reasoning agent, obliged to respond, not as a machine, but as a person. The law takes these factors into account in assessing criminal responsibility for acts done in compliance with illegal orders.

The acts of a subordinate done in compliance with an unlawful order given him by his superior are excused and impose no criminal liability upon him unless the superior's order is one which a man of *ordinary sense and understanding* would, under the circumstances, know to be unlawful, or if the order in question is actually known to the accused to be unlawful.

. . . . . [in original]

. . . [in original] In determining what orders, if any, Lieutenant Calley acted under, if you find him to have acted, you should consider all of the matters which he has testified reached him and which you can infer from other evidence that he saw and heard. Then, unless you find beyond a reasonable doubt that he was not acting under orders directing him in substance and effect to kill unresisting occupants of My Lai (4), you must determine whether Lieutenant Calley actually knew those orders to be unlawful.

. . . In determining whether or not Lieutenant Calley had knowledge of the unlawfulness of any order found by you to have been given, you may consider all relevant facts and circumstances, including Lieutenant

Calley's rank; educational background; OCS schooling; other training while in the Army, including basic training, and his training in Hawaii and Vietnam; his experience on prior operations involving contact with hostile and friendly Vietnamese; his age; and any other evidence tending to prove or disprove that on 16 March 1968, Lieutenant Calley knew the order was unlawful. If you find beyond a reasonable doubt, on the basis of all the evidence, that *Lieutenant Calley actually knew* the order under which he asserts he operated was unlawful, the fact that the order was given operates as no defense.

Unless you find beyond reasonable doubt that the accused acted with actual knowledge that the order was unlawful, you must proceed to determine whether, under the circumstances, *a man of ordinary sense and understanding would have known the order was unlawful. Your deliberations on this question do not focus on Lieutenant Calley and the manner in which he perceived the legality of the order found to have been given him. The standard is that of a man of ordinary sense and understanding under the circumstances.*

Think back to the events of 15 and 16 March 1968 . . . [in original] Then determine, in light of all the surrounding circumstances, whether the order, which to reach this point you will have found him to be operating in accordance with, is one which a man of ordinary sense and understanding would know to be unlawful. Apply this to each charged act which you have found Lieutenant Calley to have committed. Unless you are satisfied from the evidence, beyond a reasonable doubt, that a man of ordinary sense and understanding would have known the order to be unlawful, you must acquit Lieutenant Calley for committing acts done in accordance with the order. (Emphasis added.) [in original]

Appellate defense counsel contend that these instructions are prejudicially erroneous in that they require the court members to determine that Lieutenant Calley knew that an order to kill human beings in the circumstances under which he killed was illegal by the standard of whether "a man of ordinary sense and understanding" would know the order was illegal. They urge us to adopt as the governing test whether the order is so palpably or manifestly illegal that a person of "the commonest understanding" would be aware of its illegality. They maintain the standard stated by the judge is too strict and unjust: that it confronts members of the armed forces who are not persons of ordinary sense and understanding with the dilemma of choosing between the penalty of death for disobedience of an order in time of war on the one hand and the equally serious punishment for obedience on the other. Some thoughtful commentators on military law have presented much the same argument. [footnote omitted]

The "ordinary sense and understanding" standard is set forth in the present Manual for Courts-Martial, United States, 1969 (Rev) and was the standard accepted by this Court in United States v. Schultz, 18 USCMA 133, 39 CMR 133 (1969) and United States v. Keenan, 18 USCMA 108, 39 CMR 108 (1969). It appeared as early as 1917. Manual for Courts-Martial, U.S. Army 1917, paragraph 442. Apparently, it originated in a quotation from F. Wharton, Homicide § 485 (3d ed. 1907). Wharton's authority is Riggs v. State, 3 Coldwell 85, 91 American Decisions 272, 273 (Tenn 1866), in which the court approved a charge to the jury as follows:

> "[I]n its substance being clearly illegal, so that a man of ordinary sense and understanding would know as soon as he heard the order read or given that such order was illegal, would afford a private no protection for a crime committed under such order."

. . .

In the stress of combat, a member of the armed forces cannot reasonably be expected to make a refined legal judgment and be held criminally responsible if he guesses wrong on a question as to which there may be considerable disagreement. But there is no disagreement as to the illegality of the order to kill in this case. For 100 years, it has been a settled rule of American law that even in war the summary killing of an enemy, who has submitted to, and is under, effective physical control, is murder. Appellate defense counsel acknowledge that rule of law and its continued viability, but they say that Lieutenant Calley should not be held accountable for the men, women and children he killed because the court-martial could have found that he was a person of "commonest understanding" and such a person might not know what our law provides; that his captain had ordered him to kill these unarmed and submissive people and he only carried out that order as a good disciplined soldier should.

.   .   .

Whether Lieutenant Calley was the most ignorant person in the United States Army in Vietnam, or the most intelligent, he must be presumed to know that he could not kill the people involved here. The United States Supreme Court has pointed out that "[t]he rule that 'ignorance of the law will not excuse' [a positive act that constitutes a crime] [in original] . . . is deep in our law." Lambert v. California, 355 US 225, 228 (1957). An order to kill infants and unarmed civilians who were so demonstrably incapable of resistance to the armed might of a military force as were those killed by Lieutenant Calley is, in my opinion, so palpably illegal that whatever conceptional difference there may be between a person of "commonest understanding" and a person of "common understanding," that difference could not have had any "impact on a court of lay members receiving the respective wordings in instructions," as appellate defense counsel contend. In my judgment, there is no possibility of prejudice to Lieutenant Calley in the trial judge's reliance upon the established standard of excuse of criminal conduct, rather than the standard of "commonest understanding" presented by the defense, or by the new variable test postulated in the dissent, which, with the inclusion of such factors for consideration as grade and experience, would appear to exact a higher standard of understanding from Lieutenant Calley than that of the person of ordinary understanding.

In summary, as reflected in the record, the judge was capable and fair, and dedicated to assuring the accused a trial on the merits as provided by law; his instructions on all issues were comprehensive and correct. Lieutenant Calley was given every consideration to which he was entitled, and perhaps more. We are impressed with the absence of bias or prejudice on the part of the court members. They were instructed to determine the *truth* [in original] according to the law and this they did with due deliberation and full consideration of the evidence. Their findings of guilty represent the truth of the facts as they determined them to be and there is substantial evidence to support those findings. No mistakes of procedure cast doubt upon them.

Consequently, the decision of the Court of Military Review is affirmed.

. . .

NOTE: As the international community becomes more integrated, there appears to be a growing tendency to characterize certain types of socially destructive behavior as criminal. The International Law Commission's elaboration of a Convention on State Responsibility assumed that some actions by states could be so harmful that compensation alone would be insufficient. Hence their characterization as an international crime. Article 19 of the Draft, adopted in 1976, has major implications for the law of war.

◆

DRAFT ARTICLES ON STATE RESPONSIBILITY

ARTICLE 19

[Report of the International Law Commission to the General Assembly on the work of its thirty-second session, (1980) 2 Y.B. Int'l L. Comm'n 26, 32]

INTERNATIONAL CRIMES AND INTERNATIONAL DELICTS

1. An act of a State which constitutes a breach of an international obligation is an internationally wrongful act, regardless of the subject-matter of the obligation breached.

2. An internationally wrongful act which results from the breach by a State of an international obligation so essential for the protection of fundamental interests of the international community that its breach is recognized as a crime by that community as a whole constitutes an international crime.

3. Subject to paragraph 2, and on the basis of the rules of international law in force, an international crime may result, *inter alia*, from:

(a) a serious breach of an international obligation of essential importance for the maintenance of international peace and security, such as that prohibiting aggression;

(b) a serious breach of an international obligation of essential importance for safeguarding the right of self-determination of peoples, such as that prohibiting the establishment or maintenance by force of colonial domination;

(c) a serious breach on a widespread scale of an international obligation of essential importance for safeguarding the human being, such as those prohibiting slavery, genocide and *apartheid*;

(d) a serious breach of an international obligation of essential importance for the safeguarding and preservation of the human environment, such as those prohibiting massive pollution of the atmosphere or of the seas.

4. Any internationally wrongful act which is not an international crime in accordance with paragraph 2 constitutes an international delict.

. . .

NOTE: In September 1982, after Israeli forces had advanced through Lebanon to the capital, Beirut, the Phalange, one of the armies of Lebanon that was collaborating with Israel, entered two Palestinian refugee camps in a sector controlled by the Israeli Defense Forces and massacred a large number of civilians. In the face of international condemnation, the Israeli government appointed a commission of inquiry that considered the events in terms of the law of war.

The Commission of Inquiry into the Events at the Refugee Camps in Beirut[8]
1983
Final Report
(Authorized Translation)
Yitzhak Kahan,
President of the Supreme Court, Commission Chairman
Aharon Barak, Justice of the Supreme Court
Yona Efrat, Major General (Res.), Israel Defense Forces

[22 I.L.M. 473 (1983)]

. . . .

. . . The expression "Lebanese Forces" refers to an armed force known by the name "Phalangists" or "Keta'ib" (henceforth, Phalangists). . . .

The Direct Responsibility

. . .[A]ll the evidence indicates that the massacre was perpetrated by the Phalangists between the time they entered the camps on Thursday, 16.9.82, at 18.00 hours, and their departure from the camps on Saturday, 18.9.82, at approximately 8:00 A.M. The victims were found in those areas where the Phalangists were in military control during the afore-mentioned time period. No other military force aside from the Phalangists was seen by any one of the witnesses in the area of the camps where the massacre was carried out, or at the time of the entrance into or exit from this area. . . .

Our conclusion is therefore that the direct responsibility for the per-petration of the acts of slaughter rests on the Phalangist forces. No evi-dence was brought before us that Phalangist personnel received explicit orders from their command to perpetrate acts of slaughter, but it is evident that the forces who entered the area were steeped in hatred for the Palestinians, in the wake of the atrocities and severe injuries done to the Christians during the civil war in Lebanon by the Palestinians and those who fought alongside them; and these feelings of hatred were com-pounded by a longing for revenge in the wake of the assassination of the

Phalangists' admired leader Bashir and the killing of several dozen Phalangists two days before their entry into the camps. The execution of acts of slaughter was approved for the Phalangists on the site by the remarks of the two commanders to whom questions were addressed over the radios, as was related above.

THE INDIRECT RESPONSIBILITY

. . . If it indeed becomes clear that those who decided on the entry of the Phalangists into the camps should have foreseen—from the information at their disposal and from things which were common knowledge—that there was danger of a massacre, and no steps were taken which might have prevented this danger or at least greatly reduced the possibility that deeds of this type might be done, then those who made the decisions and those who implemented them are indirectly responsible for what ultimately occurred, even if they did not intend this to happen and merely disregarded the anticipated danger. A similar indirect responsibility also falls on those who knew of the decision; it was their duty, by virtue of their position and their office, to warn of the danger, and they did not fulfill this duty. It is also not possible to absolve of such indirect responsibility those persons who, when they received the first reports of what was happening in the camps, did not rush to prevent the continuation of the Phalangists' actions and did not do everything within their power to stop them. . . . If the territory of West Beirut may be viewed at the time of the events as occupied territory—and we do not determine that such indeed is the case from a legal perspective—then it is the duty of the occupier, according to the rules of usual and customary international law, to do all it can to ensure the public's well-being and security. Even if these legal norms are invalid regarding the situation in which the Israeli government and the forces operating at its instructions found themselves at the time of the events, still, as far as the obligations applying to every civilized nation and the ethical rules accepted by civilized peoples go, the problem of indirect responsibility cannot be disregarded. . . .

As has already been said above, the decision to enter West Beirut was adopted in conversations held between the Prime Minister and the Defense Minister on the night between 14–15 September 1982. . . . There is great sense in the supposition that had I.D.F. [Israel Defense Forces] troops not entered West Beirut, a situation of total chaos and battles between various combat forces would have developed, and the number of victims among the civilian population would have been far greater than it ultimately was. The Israeli military force was the only real force nearby which could take control over West Beirut so as to maintain the peace and prevent a resumption of hostile actions between various militias and communities. . . .

The demand made in Israel to have the Phalangists take part in the fighting was a general and understandable one; and political, and to some extent military, reasons existed for such participation. The general question of relations with the Phalangists and cooperation with them is a saliently political one. . . .

It is a different question whether the decision to have the Phalangists enter the camps was justified in the circumstances that were created. From the description of events cited above and from the testimony before us, it is clear that this decision was taken by the Minister of Defense with the concurrence of the Chief of Staff and that the Prime Minister did not know of it until the Cabinet session in the evening hours of 16.9.82. . . .

The heads of Government in Israel and the heads of the I.D.F. who testified before us were for the most part firm in their view that what happened in the camps was an unexpected occurrence, in the nature of a disaster which no one had imagined and which could not have been— or, at all events, need not have been—foreseen. . . .

In our view, everyone who had anything to do with events in Lebanon should have felt apprehension about a massacre in the camps, if armed Phalangist forces were to be moved into them without the I.D.F. exercising concrete and effective supervision and scrutiny of them. All those concerned were well aware that combat morality among the various combatant groups in Lebanon differs from the norm in the I.D.F., that the combatants in Lebanon belittle the value of human life far beyond what is necessary and accepted in wars between civilized peoples, and that various atrocities against the non-combatant population had been widespread in Lebanon since 1975. It was well known that the Phalangists harbor deep enmity for the Palestinians, viewing them as the source of all the troubles that afflicted Lebanon during the years of the civil war. The fact that in certain operations carried out under close I.D.F. supervision the Phalangists did not deviate from disciplined behavior could not serve as an indication that their attitude toward the Palestinian population had changed, or that changes had been effected in their plans— which they made no effort to hide—for the Palestinians. To this backdrop of the Phalangists' attitude toward the Palestinians were added the profound shock in the wake of Bashir's death along with a group of Phalangists in the explosion at Ashrafiya, and the feeling of revenge that event must arouse, even without the identity of the assailant being known.

The written and oral summations presented to us stressed that most of the experts whose remarks were brought before the commission—both Military Intelligence personnel and Mossad personnel—had expressed the view that given the state of affairs existing when the decision was taken to have the Phalangists enter the camps, it could not be foreseen that the Phalangists would perpetrate a massacre, or at all events the probability of that occurring was low; . . . In contrast to the approach of these experts, there were cases in which other personnel, both from Military Intelligence, from other I.D.F. branches, and from outside the governmental framework, warned—as soon as they learned of the Phalangists' entry into the camps, and on earlier occasion when the Phalangists' role in the war was discussed—that the danger of a massacre was great and that the Phalangists would take advantage of every opportunity offered them to wreak vengeance on the Palestinians. Thus, for example, Intelligence Officer G. (whose name appears in Section 1 of Appendix B), a branch head in Military Intelligence/Research, stated that the subject of possible injury by the Phalangists to the Palestinian population had come up many times in internal discussions (statement No. 176). Similarly, when Intelligence Officer A. learned on Thursday, in a briefing of Intelligence officers, that the Phalangists had entered the camps, he said, even before the report arrived about the 300 killed, that he was convinced that the entry would lead to a massacre of the refugee camps' population. . . . Captain Nahum Menahem relates that in a meeting he had with the Defense Minister on 12.9.82, he informed the Defense Minister of his opinion, which was based on considerable experience and on a study he had made of the tensions between the communities in Lebanon, that a "terrible" slaughter could ensue if Israel failed to assuage the inter-communal tensions in Lebanon. . . .

To sum up this chapter, we assert that the atrocities in the refugee camps were perpetrated by members of the Phalangists, and that absolutely no direct responsibility devolves upon Israel or upon those who acted in its behalf. At the same time, it is clear from what we have said above that the decision on the entry of the Phalangists into the refugee camps was taken without consideration of the danger—which the makers and executors of the decision were obligated to foresee as probable—that the Phalangists would commit massacres and pogroms against the inhabitants of the camps, and without an examination of the means for preventing this danger. Similarly, it is clear from the course of events that when the reports began to arrive about the actions of the Phalangists in the camps, no proper heed was taken of these reports, the correct conclusions were not drawn from them, and no energetic and immediate actions were taken to restrain the Phalangists and put a stop to their actions. . . .

PERSONAL RESPONSIBILITY

. . .

THE PRIME MINISTER, MR. MENACHEM BEGIN

. . .

The Prime Minister testified that only in the Cabinet session of 16.9.82 did he hear about the agreement with the Phalangists that they would operate in the camps, and that until then, in all the conversations he had held with the Defense Minister and with the Chief of Staff, nothing had been said about the role of the Phalangists or their partic pation in the operations in West Beirut. He added that since this matter had not come up in the reports he received from the Defense Minister and the Chief of Staff, he had raised no questions about it. . . .

We have cited above passages from remarks made at the Cabinet session of 16.9.82, during which the Prime Minister learned that the Phalangists had that evening begun to operate in the camps. Neither in that meeting nor afterward did the Prime Minister raise any opposition or objection to the entry of the Phalangists into the camps. Nor did he react to the remarks of Deputy Prime Minister Levy which contained a warning of the danger to be expected from the Phalangists' entry into the camps. . . .

. . .[B]ecause of things that were well known to all, it should have been foreseen that the danger of a massacre existed if the Phalangists were to enter the camps without measures being taken to prevent them from committing acts such as these. We are unable to accept the Prime Minister's remarks that he was absolutely unaware of such a danger. According to what he himself said, he told the Chief of Staff on the night between 14 and 15 September 1982, in explaining the decision to have the I.D.F. occupy positions in West Beirut, that this was being done "in order to protect the Moslems from the vengeance of the Phalangists," and he could well suppose that after the assassination of Bashir, the

Phalangists' beloved leader, they would take revenge on the terrorists. The Prime Minister was aware of the mutual massacres committed in Lebanon during the civil war, and of the Phalangists' feelings of hate for the Palestinians, whom the Phalangists held responsible for all the calamities that befell their land. The purpose of the I.D.F.'s entry into West Beirut—in order to prevent bloodshed—was also stressed by the Prime Minister in his meeting with Ambassador Draper on 15.9.82. . . . [W]e are unable to accept the position of the Prime Minister that no one imagined that what happened was liable to happen, or what follows from his remarks: that this possibility did not have to be foreseen when the decision was taken to have the Phalangists move into the camps.

As noted, the Prime Minister first heard about the Phalangists' entry into the camps about 36 hours after the decision to that effect was taken, and did not learn of the decision until the Cabinet session. When he heard about the Phalangists' entry into the camps, it had already taken place. According to the "rosy" reports the Prime Minister received from the Defense Minister and the Chief of Staff, the Prime Minister was entitled to assume at that time that all the operations in West Beirut had been performed in the best possible manner and had nearly been concluded. We believe that in these circumstances it was not incumbent upon the Prime Minister to object to the Phalangists' entry into the camps or to order their removal. On the other hand, we find no reason to exempt the Prime Minister from responsibility for not having evinced, during or after the Cabinet session, any interest in the Phalangists' actions in the camps. It has already been noted above that no report about the Phalangists' operations reached the Prime Minister, except perhaps for the complaint regarding the Gaza Hospital, until he heard the BBC broadcast towards evening on Saturday. For two days after the Prime Minister heard about the Phalangists' entry, he showed absolutely no interest in their actions in the camps. This indifference would have been justifiable if we were to accept the Prime Minister's position that it was impossible and unnecessary to foresee the possibility that the Phalangists would commit acts of revenge; but we have already explained above that according to what the Prime Minister knew, according to what he heard in the Thursday Cabinet session, and according to what he said about the purpose of the move into Beirut, such a possibility was not unknown to him. It may be assumed that a manifestation of interest by him in this matter, after he had learned of the Phalangists' entry, would have increased the alertness of the Defense Minister and the Chief of Staff to the need to take appropriate measures to meet the expected danger. The Prime Minister's lack of involvement in the entire matter casts on him a certain degree of responsibility.

THE MINISTER OF DEFENSE, MR. ARIEL SHARON

. . .[T]he Minister of Defense also adopted the position that no one had imagined the Phalangists would carry out a massacre in the camps and that it was a tragedy that could not be foreseen. . . .

. . .[I]t is impossible to justify the Minister of Defense's disregard of the danger of a massacre. We will not repeat here what we have already said above about the widespread knowledge regarding the Phalangists' combat ethics, their feelings of hatred toward the Palestinians, and their leaders' plans for the future of the Palestinians when said leaders would assume power. Besides this general knowledge, the Defense Minister also had special reports from his not inconsiderable [number of] [in original] meetings with the Phalangist heads before Bashir's assassination.

. . . The sense of such a danger should have been in the consciousness of every knowledgeable person who was close to this subject, and certainly in the consciousness of the Defense Minister, who took an active part in everything relating to the war. His involvement in the war was deep, and the connection with the Phalangists was under his constant care. If in fact the Defense Minister, when he decided that the Phalangists would enter the camps without the I.D.F. taking part in the operation, did not think that decision could bring about the very disaster that in fact occurred, the only possible explanation for this is that he disregarded any apprehensions about what was to be expected because the advantages—which we have already noted—to be gained from the Phalangists' entry into the camps distracted him from the proper consideration in this instance.

As a politician responsible for Israel's security affairs, and as a Minister who took an active part in directing the political and military moves in the war in Lebanon, it was the duty of the Defense Minister to take into account all the reasonable considerations for and against having the Phalangists enter the camps, and not to disregard entirely the serious consideration mitigating against such an action, namely that the Phalangists were liable to commit atrocities and that it was necessary to forestall this possibility as a humanitarian obligation and also to prevent the political damage it would entail. From the Defense Minister himself we know that this consideration did not concern him in the least, and that this matter, with all its ramifications, was neither discussed nor examined in the meetings and discussions held by the Defense Minister. In our view, the Minister of Defense made a grave mistake when he ignored the danger of acts of revenge and bloodshed by the Phalangists against the population in the refugee camps.

. . .

We do not believe that responsibility is to be imputed to the Defense Minister for not ordering the removal of the Phalangists from the camps when the first reports reached him about the acts of killing being committed there. As was detailed above, such reports initially reached the Defense Minister on Friday evening; but at the same time, he had heard from the Chief of Staff that the Phalangists' operation had been halted, that they had been ordered to leave the camps, and that their departure would be effected by 5:00 A.M. Saturday. These preventive steps might well have seemed sufficient to the Defense Minister at that time, and it was not his duty to order additional steps to be taken, or to have the departure time moved up, a step which was of doubtful feasibility.

. . .

THE CHIEF OF STAFF, LIEUTENANT GENERAL RAFAEL EITAN

. . .

. . .[T]he Chief of Staff took a position similar to that of the Minister of Defense which was discussed above and which we have rejected. The Chief of Staff stated in his testimony before us that it had never occurred to him that the Phalangists would perpetrate acts of revenge and bloodshed in the camps. He justified this lack of foresight by citing the experience of the past, whereby massacres were perpetrated by the Christians only before the "Peace for Galilee" War and only in response to the perpetration of a massacre by the Muslims against the Christian population, and by citing the disciplined conduct of the Phalangists while carrying out certain operations after the I.D.F.'s entry into Lebanon.

. . .

Past experience in no way justified the conclusion that the entry of the Phalangists into the camps posed no danger. The Chief of Staff was well aware that the Phalangists were full of feelings of hatred towards the Palestinians and that their feelings had not changed since the "Peace for Galilee" War. The isolated actions in which the Phalangists had participated during the war took place under conditions that were completely different from those which arose after the murder of Bashir Jemayel; and as one could see from the nature of [those] [in original] operations, in the past there had been no case in which an area populated by Palestinian refugees had been turned over to the exclusive control of the Phalangists. . . .

The decision to send the Phalangists into the camps was taken by the Minister of Defense and the Chief of Staff, and the Chief of Staff must be viewed as a partner to this decision and as bearing responsibility both for its adoption and for its implementation. . . .

If the Chief of Staff did not imagine at all that the entry of the Phalangists into the camps posed a danger to the civilian population, his thinking on this matter constitutes a disregard of important considerations that he should have taken into account. Moreover, considering the Chief of Staff's own statements quoted above, it is difficult to avoid the conclusion that the Chief of Staff ignored this danger out of an awareness that there were great advantages to sending the Phalangists into the camps, and perhaps also out of a hope that in the final analysis, the Phalangist excesses would not be on a large scale. This conclusion is likewise prompted by the Chief of Staff's behavior during later stages, once reports began to come in about the Phalangists' excesses in the camps.

It has been argued by the Chief of Staff, and in his behalf, that appropriate steps were taken to avoid the danger. A similar claim has been made by Major General Drori and Brigadier General Yaron. In our opinion, this claim is unfounded.

As stated, one of the precautions was a lookout posted on the roof of the forward command post and on another roof nearby. It may be that this lookout was of value in obtaining certain military information on combat operations, but it was worthless in terms of obtaining information on the Phalangists' operations within the camps. Another step was taken to obtain information on exchanges over the communications sets between the Phalangist forces in the field and their commanders. It is difficult to regard this step as an efficient way to discover what was going on in the camps, . . .

The claim that every possible step was taken to obtain detailed information on the excesses of the Phalangists—in the event that such excesses would take place—is not congruent with the claim that such excesses were not foreseen at all. But we do not wish to go into this logical contradiction, as in any case it is clear that the steps which were adopted fell far short of satisfying the need to know what was going on in the camps; and in fact, the truth about what was happening there only came out after the Phalangists left the camps.

We find that the Chief of Staff did not consider the danger of acts of vengeance and bloodshed being perpetrated against the population of the refugee camps in Beirut; he did not order the adoption of the appropriate steps to avoid this danger; and his failure to do so is tantamount to a breach of duty that was incumbent upon the Chief of Staff.

The other matter for which a notice was sent to the Chief of Staff under Section 15(A) was that when reports reached him about acts of killing or actions that deviated from usual combat operations, he did not check the veracity of these reports and the scope of these actions and did not order the cessation of the operations, the removal of the Phalangists from the camps as quickly as possible, and the adoption of steps to protect the population of the camps. In a meeting with the Phalangist commanders on the morning of 17.9.82, he approved the continuation of their operations until the morning of 18.9.82 and ordered that they be provided with assistance for that purpose.

．　　．　　．

The outstanding impression that emerges from the Chief of Staff's testimony is that his refraining from raising the issue of the Phalangists' excesses against the population in the camps stemmed from a fear of offending their honor; but this fear was out of place and should not have been a cause for the lack of any clarification of what had happened, when the Chief of Staff had gotten reports that should have served as a warning about the grave harm caused to the population in the camps and when, as a result of these reports, Major General Drori had issued an order to halt the advance of the Phalangists. Not only did the Chief of Staff not raise the subject of the Phalangists' behavior in the camps at the meeting which was called to clarify what was happening in the camps, but he expressed his satisfaction with the Phalangist operation and agreed to their request to provide them with tractors so they could complete their operations by Saturday morning. It is difficult to avoid the conclusion that this conduct on the Chief of Staff's part during the meeting at the Phalangists' headquarters stemmed from his disregard of the suspicions that the Phalangists were perpetrating acts of slaughter, and this disregard went so deep that even the information that had arrived in the meanwhile and reached the Chief of Staff did not shake it.

.   .   .

In our opinion, after the Chief of Staff received the information from Major General Drori in a telephone conversation that the Phalangists had "overdone it" and Major General Drori had halted their operation, this information should have alerted him to the danger that acts of slaughter were being perpetrated in the camps and made him aware of his obligation to take appropriate steps to clarify the matter and prevent the continuation of such actions if the information proved to be of substance. Toward that end, the Chief of Staff should have held a detailed clarification [session] [in original] with Major General Drori, Brigadier General Yaron, and other officers of the division, as well as with the Phalangist commanders, immediately upon his arrival in Beirut. . . .

We determine that the Chief of Staff's inaction, described above, and his order to provide the Phalangist forces with tractors, or a tractor, constitute a breach of duty and dereliction of the duty incumbent upon the Chief of Staff.

.   .   .

DIVISION COMMANDER BRIGADIER GENERAL AMOS YARON

.   .   .

We determined in the specification of the facts that Brigadier General Yaron received reports of acts of killing in the evening and night hours of 16.9.82. He received the first report from Lieutenant Elul, and from it should have been clear to him that the Phalangists were killing women and children in the camps. Brigadier General Yaron heard an additional report that same evening from the division intelligence officer concerning the fate of the group of 45 people who were in the Phalangists' hands. A third report was delivered by the Phalangists' liaison officer, G., about 300 killed, a number which was later reduced to 120. Even if we suppose that the first and second report were considered by Brigadier General Yaron to be about the same event, nevertheless, from all the reports, it became known to Brigadier General Yaron that the Phalangists were perpetrating acts of killing which went beyond combat operations, and were killing women and children as well. That evening he was satisfied with reiterating the warnings to the Phalangists' liaison officer and to Elie Hobeika not to kill women and children; but beyond that he did nothing to stop the killing. He did not pass on the information that he had received to Major General Drori that evening nor on the following day in the morning call, nor when they met before noon. When Brigadier General Yaron heard from the division intelligence officer, in the briefing on 16.9.82, about the report indicating the danger that women and children were being killed, he interrupted him—and it appears from the transcript of the conversation that took place then that Brigadier General Yaron wished to play down the importance of the matter and to cut off the clarification of the issue at that briefing. Brigadier General Yaron testified that he was, indeed, aware that the Phalangists' norms of behavior during wartime are different from those of the I.D.F. and that there is no sense in arguing with them to change their combat ethics; but since in previous Phalangist operations conducted jointly with the I.D.F. they had not behaved aberrantly, he trusted that his reiterated warnings not to kill women and children would suffice, the Phalangist commanders' promises would be kept, and the steps that he had taken in order to obtain information on the Phalangists' operations would enable him to follow their actions. We are not prepared to accept this explanation. We have already determined that the means of supervision over what the Phalangists were doing in the camps could not ensure the flow of real and immediate information on their actions. It is difficult to understand how Brigadier General Yaron relied on these warnings and assurances, when he knew about the Phalangists' combat ethics. He also did not take into account the influence of the assassination of Bashir on the fanning of the Phalangists' feelings of revenge. Already shortly after the Phalangists' entrance into the camps, he started receiving reports which should have clarified to him the gravity of the danger of a massacre being perpetrated in the camps and which should have spurred him to take immediate steps, whether on his own cognizance or by authorization from the G.O.C. or the Chief of Staff, to prevent the continuation of operations of these kinds. No action was taken by Brigadier General Yaron, and neither did he see to conveying the information in his possession to his superiors.

.   .   .

We have already cited Brigadier General Yaron's statement at the Senior Command Meeting in which he admitted with laudable candor that this was an instance of "insensitivity" on his part and on the part of others concerned. As we have already stated above, Brigadier General Yaron's desire was to save I.D.F. soldiers from having to carry out the operation in the camps, and this appears to be the main reason for his insensitivity to the dangers of the massacre in the camps. This concern of a commander for the welfare of his men would be praiseworthy in other circumstances; but considering the state of affairs in this particular instance, it was a thoroughly mistaken judgment on the part of Brigadier General Yaron, and a grave error was committed by a high-ranking officer of an I.D.F. force in this sector.

We determine that by virtue of his failings and his actions, detailed above, Brigadier General Yaron committed a breach of the duties incumbent upon him by virtue of his position.

◆

PROSECUTION AND PUNISHMENT

PROTOCOL ADDITIONAL TO THE GENEVA CONVENTIONS OF 12 AUGUST 1949, AND RELATING TO THE PROTECTION OF VICTIMS OF NON-INTERNATIONAL ARMED CONFLICTS (PROTOCOL II)

[1125 U.N.T.S. 609, adopted on June 8, 1977, at Geneva]

. . .

PART II
HUMANE TREATMENT

. . .

Article 6
Penal Prosecutions

1. This Article applies to the prosecution and punishment of criminal offences related to the armed conflict.

2. No sentence shall be passed and no penalty shall be executed on a person found guilty of an offence except pursuant to a conviction pronounced by a court offering the essential guarantees of independence and impartiality. In particular:

(a) the procedure shall provide for an accused to be informed without delay of the particulars of the offence alleged against him and shall afford the accused before and during his trial all necessary rights and means of defence;

(b) no one shall be convicted of an offence except on the basis of individual penal responsibility;

(c) no one shall be held guilty of any criminal offence on account of any act or omission which did not constitute a criminal offence, under the law, at the time when it was committed; nor shall a heavier penalty be imposed than that which was applicable at the time when the criminal offence was [committed] [in original; footnote omitted] if, after the commission of the offence, provision is made by law for the imposition of a lighter penalty, the offender shall benefit thereby;

(d) anyone charged with an offence is presumed innocent until proved guilty according to law;

(e) anyone charged with an offence shall have the right to be tried in his presence;

(f) no one shall be compelled to testify against himself or to confess guilt.

3. A convicted person shall be advised on conviction of his judicial and other remedies and of the time-limits within which they may be exercised.

4. The death penalty shall not be pronounced on persons who were under the age of eighteen years at the time of the offence and shall not be carried out on pregnant women or mothers of young children.

5. At the end of hostilities, the authorities in power shall endeavour to grant the broadest possible amnesty to persons who have participated in the armed conflict, or those deprived of their liberty for reasons related to the armed conflict, whether they are interned or detained.

◆ ◆ ◆

◆

INVESTIGATION OF ALLEGED WAR CRIMES IN THE FORMER YUGOSLAVIA

In 1992 journalistic accounts of concentration camps, mass executions and mass rapes, expulsions of civilian population, and the intentional targeting of civilians in the conflict in the former Yugoslavia poured in. In response, the Security Council, by Resolution 780 (1992), established a Commission of Experts to examine and analyze information that was submitted and to try to gather further information on its own with regard to grave breaches of the Geneva Conventions and other violations of international humanitarian law committed in the territory of the former Yugoslavia. The five-member commission issued an interim report to the secretary-general on February 10, 1993.[9] The commission defined its mandate as gathering of evidence "not merely to establish the existence of certain patterns of criminality but also to obtain specific evidence such as an investigative body would need for prosecution purposes."[10] Despite the fact that some of the conflicts were "internal," the commission decided to apply the law applicable in international armed conflicts to the entirety of the armed conflicts in the territory of the former Yugoslavia.[11]

.　　.　　.

INTERIM REPORT OF THE COMMISSION OF EXPERTS UNITED NATIONS DOCUMENT S/25274, JANUARY 2, 1993

3.　GRAVE BREACHES, WAR CRIMES, CRIMES AGAINST HUMANITY

47. The Geneva Conventions and Additional Protocol I contain rules on the treatment of grave breaches. While "grave breaches" are carefully defined in each of these instruments, they fall under the general heading of war crimes. The Commission understands the general notion of war crimes as comprising any violation of the law of international armed conflicts, sufficiently serious and committed with the requisite intent to be regarded as a crime.

48. A war crime is usually a crime committed by a person demonstrably linked to one side of an armed conflict against persons or property on the other side. The perpetrator may be a member of the armed forces

(as defined in article 43 of Protocol I) or a civilian. The issue of a demonstrable link is of particular relevance where victims and offenders are of the same nationality or from countries which are on the same side of a conflict. The Commission intends to address this issue in due course.

49. The notion of crimes against humanity as defined in conventional international law and as applied in customary international law is considered by the Commission to be applicable to these conflicts. The Commission regards as crimes against humanity gross violations of fundamental rules of humanitarian and human rights law committed by persons demonstrably linked to a party to the conflict, as part of an official policy based on discrimination against an identifiable group of persons, irrespective of war and the nationality of the victim.

50. The Commission notes that fundamental rules of human rights law often are materially identical to rules of the law of armed conflict. It is therefore possible for the same act to be a war crime and a crime against humanity.

4. COMMAND RESPONSIBILITY

51. A person who gives the order to commit a war crime or crime against humanity is equally guilty of the offence with the person actually committing it. This principle, expressed already in the Geneva Conventions of 1949, applies both to military superiors, whether of regular or irregular armed forces, and to civilian authorities.

52. Superiors are moreover individually responsible for a war crime or crime against humanity committed by a subordinate if they knew, or had information which should have enabled them to conclude, in the circumstances at the time, that the subordinate was committing or was going to commit such an act and they did not take all feasible measures within their power to prevent or repress the act.

53. Military commanders are under a special obligation, with respect to members of the armed forces under their command or other persons under their control, to prevent and, where necessary, to suppress such acts and to report them to competent authorities.

5. Superior Orders

54. A subordinate who has carried out an order of a superior or acted under government instructions and thereby has committed a war crime or a crime against humanity, may raise the so-called defence of superior orders, claiming that he cannot be held criminally liable for an act he was ordered to commit. The Commission notes that the applicable treaties unfortunately are silent on the matter. The Commission's interpretation of the customary international law, particularly as stated in the Nuremberg principles, is that the fact that a person acted pursuant to an order of his Government or of a superior does not relieve him from responsibility under international law, provided a moral choice was in fact available to him.

6. "Ethnic Cleansing"

55. The expression "ethnic cleansing" is relatively new. Considered in the context of the conflicts in the former Yugoslavia, "ethnic cleansing" means rendering an area ethnically homogeneous by using force or intimidation to remove persons of given groups from the area. "Ethnic cleansing" is contrary to international law.

56. Based on the many reports describing the policy and practices conducted in the former Yugoslavia, "ethnic cleansing" has been carried out by means of murder, torture, arbitrary arrest and detention, extrajudicial executions, rape and sexual assault, confinement of civilian population in ghetto areas, forcible removal, displacement and deportation of civilian population, deliberate military attacks or threats of attacks on civilians and civilian areas, and wanton destruction of property. Those practices constitute crimes against humanity and can be assimilated to specific war crimes. Furthermore, such acts could also fall within the meaning of the Genocide Convention.

57. The Commission is mindful of these considerations in the examination of reported allegations.

7. Rape and Other Forms of Sexual Assault

58. Throughout the various phases of the armed conflicts in the former Yugoslavia, reports have referred to allegations of widespread and

systematic rape and other forms of sexual assault. Such reports have become more frequent, raising urgent concerns, and have led to several specific investigations into these allegations.

59. Acts such as rape, enforced prostitution or any form of sexual assault against women are explicitly prohibited in the relevant treaties in force. Superiors who authorize or tolerate the commission of such acts or who fail to take all practicable measures to prevent or suppress them are also culpable.

60. The Commission will examine the question whether the systematic commission of such acts, or the development and encouragement of a policy encouraging such acts, should be regarded as crimes in themselves and, if so, as war crimes or crimes against humanity.[12]

[The Commission concluded its Interim Report by addressing the question of jurisdiction for war crimes and the establishment of an international tribunal.]

.   .   .

72. Jurisdiction for war crimes is governed by the universality principle and, hence, is vested in all States, whether parties to the conflict or not. Although the Genocide Convention emphasizes territorial jurisdiction, it also establishes the jurisdictional basis for an international tribunal. It is well recognized that the principle of universality can also apply to genocide as well as to other crimes against humanity.

73. States may choose to combine their jurisdictions under the universality principle and vest this combined jurisdiction in an international tribunal. The Nuremberg International Military Tribunal may be said to have derived its jurisdiction from such a combination of national jurisdictions of the States parties to the London Agreement setting up that Tribunal.

74. The Commission was led to discuss the idea of the establishment of an ad hoc international tribunal. In its opinion, it would be for the Security Council or another competent organ of the United Nations to establish such a tribunal in relation to events in the territory of the former Yugoslavia. The Commission observes that such a decision would be consistent with the direction of its work.[13]

NOTE: In the nature of international politics, wars may be decisively won, but political conclusions are often indecisive. This has had a direct effect on the application of the law of war to war crimes. Where neither side in a war wins decisively or where a winner decides that the loser must remain politically and militarily viable in order to maintain a regional balance of power, there may be a reluctance to press war crimes prosecutions after hostilities have ceased. A number of coalition political leaders spoke of conducting international war crimes trials after the war with Iraq; Security Council resolutions confirmed this consensus. And the United States in its Department of Defense report on the Gulf War concluded:

> Iraqi war crimes were widespread and premeditated. They included the taking of hostages, forcible deportation, torture and murder of civilians, in violation of the CC [Fourth Geneva Convention]; looting of civilian property in violation of Hague IV, looting of cultural property, in violation of the 1954 Hague Cultural Property Convention; indiscriminate attacks in the launching of Scud missiles against cities rather than specified military objectives, in violation of customary international law; violation of Hague VIII in the method of using sea mines; and unnecessary destruction in violation of Article 23(g) of the Annex to Hague IV, as evidenced by the unlawful and wanton release of oil into the Persian Gulf and the unlawful and wanton sabotage of hundreds of Kuwaiti oil wells.[14]

Nonetheless, any programs for such trials appear to have been shelved. The international law of war, it seems, cannot be severed from international politics. This uneasy union obviously limits the full normative force of the codified law of war. Still, as long as combatants share some common goals and values, if nothing other than to limit the pain and suffering inflicted upon one's own troops, the law of war, in broadest form, can obtain benefits.

Then Secretary of State Lawrence S. Eagleburger stated to the delegates at a conference on the fighting in the Balkans on December 16, 1992:

> We know that crimes against humanity have occurred, and we know when and where they occurred. . . . We know, moreover, which forces committed those crimes, and under whose command they operated. And we know, finally, who the political leaders are and to whom

those military commanders were—and still are—responsible. . . . In waiting for the people of Serbia, if not their leaders, to come to their senses . . . we must make them understand that their country will remain alone, friendless and condemned to economic ruin and exclusion from the family of civilized nations for as long as they pursue the suicidal dream of a Greater Serbia. They need, especially, to understand that a second Nuremberg awaits the practitioners of ethnic cleansing, and that the judgment and opprobrium of history awaits the people in whose name their crimes were committed. . . . I want to make it clear that, in naming names, I am presenting the views of my Government alone. . . . The information I have cited has been provided to the U.N. War Crimes Commission, whose decision it will be to prosecute or not. . . . There is another category of fact which is beyond dispute . . . namely the fact of political and command responsibility for the crimes against humanity which I have described. Leaders such as Slobodan Milosevic, the President of Serbia, Radovan Karadzic, the president of the self-declared Serbian Bosnian republic, and Gen. Ratko Mladic, commander of Bosnian Serb military forces, must eventually explain whether and how they sought to insure, as they must under international law, that their forces complied with international law.[15]

On February 22, 1993, the Security Council decided "that an international tribunal shall be established for the prosecution of persons responsible for serious violations of international humanitarian law committed in the territory of the former Yugoslavia since 1991."[16]

At the instruction of the Council, the Secretary-General prepared a Statute.

STATUTE OF THE INTERNATIONAL TRIBUNAL

[Security Council Resolution 827 (1993), May 25, 1993]

Having been established by the Security Council acting under Chapter VII of the Charter of the United Nations, the International Tribunal for the Prosecution of Persons Responsible for Serious Violations of International Humanitarian Law Committed in the Territory of the Former Yugoslavia since 1991 (hereinafter referred to as "the International Tribunal") shall function in accordance with the provisions of the present Statute.

Article 1
Competence of the International Tribunal

The International Tribunal shall have the power to prosecute persons responsible for serious violations of international humanitarian law committed in the territory of the former Yugoslavia since 1991 in accordance with provisions of the present Statute.

Article 2
Grave breaches of the Geneva Conventions of 1949

The International Tribunal shall have the power to prosecute persons committing or ordering to be committed grave breaches of the Geneva Conventions of 12 August 1949, namely the following acts against persons or property protected under the provisions of the relevant Geneva Convention:

(a) wilful killing;

(b) torture or inhuman treatment, including biological experiments;

(c) wilfully causing great suffering or serious injury to body or health;

(d) extensive destruction and appropriation of property, not justified by military necessity and carried out unlawfully and wantonly;

(e) compelling a prisoner of war or a civilian to serve in the forces of a hostile power;

(f) wilfully depriving a prisoner of war or a civilian of the rights of fair and regular trial;

(g) unlawful deportation or transfer or unlawful confinement of a civilian;

(h) taking civilians as hostages.

Article 3
Violations of the Laws or Customs of War

The International Tribunal shall have the power to prosecute persons violating the laws or customs of war. Such violations shall include, but not be limited to:

(a) employment of poisonous weapons or other weapons calculated to cause unnecessary suffering;
(b) wanton destruction of cities, towns or villages, or devastation not justified by military necessity;
(c) attack, or bombardment, by whatever means, of undefended towns, villages, dwellings, or buildings;
(d) seizure of, destruction or wilful damage done to institutions dedicated to religion, charity and education, the arts and sciences, historic monuments and works of art and science;
(e) plunder of public or private property.

Article 4
Genocide

1. The International Tribunal shall have the power to prosecute persons committing genocide as defined in paragrah 2 of this article or of committing any of the other acts enumerated in paragraph 3 of this article.

2. Genocide means any of the following acts committed with intent to destroy, in whole or in part, a national, ethnical, racial or religious group, as such:

(a) killing members of the group;
(b) causing serious bodily or mental harm to members of the group;
(c) deliberately inflicting on the group conditions of life calculated to bring about its physical destruction in whole or in part;
(d) imposing measures intended to prevent births within the group;
(e) forcibly transferring children of the group to another group.

3. The following acts shall be punishable:

(a) genocide;
(b) conspiracy to commit genocide;
(c) direct and public incitement to commit genocide;
(d) attempt to commit genocide;
(e) complicity in genocide.

Article 5
Crimes against humanity

The International Tribunal shall have the power to prosecute persons responsible for the following crimes when committed in armed conflict, whether international or internal in character, and directed against any civilian population:

(a) murder;
(b) extermination;
(c) enslavement;
(d) deportation;
(e) imprisonment;
(f) torture;
(g) rape;
(h) persecutions on political, racial and religious grounds;
(i) other inhumane acts.

Article 6
Personal jurisdiction

The International Tribunal shall have jurisdiction over natural persons pursuant to the provisions of the present Statute.

Article 7
Individual criminal responsibility

1. A person who planned, instigated, ordered, committed or otherwise aided and abetted in the planning, preparation or execution of a crime referred to in articles 2 to 5 of the present Statute, shall be individually responsible for the crime.

2. The official position of any accused person, whether as Head of State or Government or as a responsible Government official, shall not relieve such person of criminal responsibility nor mitigate punishment.

3. The fact that any of the acts referred to in articles 2 to 5 of the present Statute was committed by a subordinate does not relieve his superior of criminal responsibility if he knew or had reason to know that the subordinate was about to commit such acts or had done so and the superior failed to take the necessary and reasonable measures to prevent such acts or to punish the perpetrators thereof.

4. The fact that an accused person acted pursuant to an order of a Government or of a superior shall not relieve him of criminal responsibility, but may be considered in mitigation of punishment if the International Tribunal determines that justice so requires.

Article 8
Territorial and temporal jurisdiction

The territorial jurisdiction of the International Tribunal shall extend to the territory of the former Socialist Federal Republic of Yugoslavia, including its land surface, airspace and territorial waters. The temporal jurisdiction of the International Tribunal shall extend to a period beginning on 1 January 1991.

Article 9
Concurrent jurisdiction

1. The International Tribunal and national courts shall have concurrent jurisdiction to prosecute persons for serious violations of international humanitarian law committed in the territory of the former Yugoslavia since 1 January 1991.

2. The International Tribunal shall have primacy over national courts. At any stage of the procedure, the International Tribunal may formally request national courts to defer to the competence of the International Tribunal in accordance with the present Statute and the Rules of Procedure and Evidence of the International Tribunal.

Article 10
Non-bis-in-idem

1. No person shall be tried before a national court for acts constituting serious violations of international humitarian law under the present Statute, for which he or she has already been tried by the International Tribunal.

2. A person who has been tried by a national court for acts constituting serious violations of international humanitarian law may be subsequently tried by the International Tribunal only if:

(a) the act for which he or she was tried was characterized as an ordinary crime; or

(b) the national court proceedings were not impartial or independent, were designed to shield the accused from international criminal responsibility, or the case was not diligently prosecuted.

3. In considering the penalty to be imposed on a person convicted of a crime under the present Statute, the International Tribunal shall take into account the extent to which any penalty imposed by a national court on the same person for the same act has already been served.

Article 11
Organization of the International Tribunal
The International Tribunal shall consist of the following organs:
(a) The Chambers, comprising two Trial Chambers and an Appeals Chamber;
(b) The Prosecutor; and
(c) A Registry, servicing both the Chambers and the Prosecutor.

Article 12
Composition of the Chambers
The Chambers shall be composed of eleven independent judges, no two of whom may be nationals of the same State, who shall serve as follows:
(a) Three judges shall serve in each of the Trial Chambers;
(b) Five judges shall serve in the Appeals Chamber.

Article 13
Qualifications and election of judges
1. The judges shall be persons of high moral character, impartiality and integrity who possess the qualifications required in their respective countries for appointment to the highest judicial offices. In the overall composition of the Chambers due account shall be taken of the experience of the judges in criminal law, international law, including international humanitarian law and human rights law.

2. The judges of the International Tribunal shall be elected by the General Assembly from a list submitted by the Security Council, in the following manner:
(a) The Secretary-General shall invite nominations for judges of the International Tribunal from States Members of the United Nations and non-Member States maintaining permanent observer missions at United Nations Headquarters;
(b) Within sixty days of the date of the invitation of the Secretary-General, each State may nominate up to two candidates meeting the qualifications set out in paragraph 1 above, no two of whom shall be the same nationality;
(c) The Secretary-General shall forward the nominations received to the Security Council. From the nominations received the Security Council shall establish a list of not less than twenty-two and not more than thirty-three candidates, taking due account of the adequate representation of the principal legal systems of the world;

(d) The President of the Security Council shall transmit the list of candidates to the President of the General Assembly. From that list the General Assembly shall elect the eleven judges of the International Tribunal. The candidates who receive an absolute majority of the votes of the States Members of the United Nations and of the non-Member States maintaining permanent observer missions at United Nations Headquarters, shall be declared elected. Should two candidates of the same nationality obtain the required majority vote, the one who received the higher number of votes shall be considered elected.

3. In the event of a vacancy in the Chambers, after consultation with the Presidents of the Security Council and of the General Assembly, the Secretary-General shall appoint a person meeting the qualifications of paragraph 1 above, for the remainder of the term of office concerned.

4. The judges shall be elected for a term of four years. The terms and conditions of service shall be those of the judges of the International Court of Justice. They shall be eligible for re-election.

Article 14
Officers and members of the Chambers

1. The judges of the International Tribunal shall elect a President.

2. The President of the International Tribunal shall be a member of the Appeals Chamber and shall preside over its proceedings.

3. After consultation with the judges of the International Tribunal, the President shall assign the judges to the Appeals Chamber and to the Trial Chambers. A judge shall serve only in the Chamber to which he or she was assigned.

4. The judges of each Trial Chamber shall elect a Presiding Judge, who shall conduct all of the proceedings of the Trial Chamber as a whole.

Article 15
Rules of procedure and evidence

The judges of the International Tribunal shall adopt rules of procedure and evidence for the conduct of the pre-trial phase of the proceedings, trials and appeals, the admission of evidence, the protection of victims and witnesses and other appropriate matters.

Article 16
The Prosecutor

1. The Prosecutor shall be responsible for the investigation and prosecution of persons responsible for serious violations of international humanitarian law committed in the territory of the former Yugoslavia since 1 January 1991.

2. The Prosecutor shall act independently as a separate organ of the International Tribunal. He or she shall not seek or receive instructions from any Government or from any other source.

3. The Office of the Prosecutor shall be composed of a Prosecutor and such other qualified staff as may be required.

4. The Prosecutor shall be appointed by the Security Council on nomination by the Secretary-General. He or she shall be of high moral character and possess the highest level of competence and experience in the conduct of investigations and prosecutions of criminal cases. The Prosecutor shall serve for a four-year term and be eligible for reappointment. The terms and conditions of service of the Prosecutor shall be those of an Under-Secretary-General of the United Nations.

5. The staff of the Office of the Prosecutor shall be appointed by the Secretary-General on the recommendation of the Prosecutor.

Article 17
The Registry

1. The Registry shall be responsible for the administration and servicing of the International Tribunal.

2. The Registry shall consist of a Registrar and such other staff as may be required.

3. The Registrar shall be appointed by the Secretary-General after consultation with the President of the International Tribunal. He or she shall serve for a four-year term and be eligible for reappointment. The terms and conditions of service of the Registrar shall be those of an Assistant Secretary-General of the United Nations.

4. The staff of the Registry shall be appointed by the Secretary-General on the recommendation of the Registrar.

Article 18
Investigation and preparation of the indictment

1. The Prosecutor shall initiate investigations *ex-officio* or on the basis of information obtained from any source, particularly from Governments, United Nations organs, intergovernmental and non-governmental or-

ganizations. The Prosecutor shall assess the information received or obtained and decide whether there is sufficient basis to proceed.

2. The Prosecutor shall have the power to question suspects, victims and witnesses, to collect evidence and to conduct on-site investigations. In carrying out these tasks, the Prosecutor may, as appropriate, seek the assistance of the State authorities concerned.

3. If questioned, the suspect shall be entitled to be assisted by counsel of his own choice, including the right to have legal assistance assigned to him without payment by him in any such case if he does not have sufficient means to pay for it, as well as to necessary translation into and from a language he speaks and understands.

4. Upon a determination that a prima facie case exists, the Prosecutor shall prepare an indictment containing a concise statement of the facts and the crime or crimes with which the accused is charged under the Statute. The indictment shall be transmitted to a judge of the Trial Chamber.

Article 19
Review of the indictment

1. The judge of the Trial Chamber to whom the indictment has been transmitted shall review it. If satisfied that a prima facie case has been established by the Prosecutor, he shall confirm the indictment. If not so satisfied, the indictment shall be dismissed.

2. Upon confirmation of an indictment, the judge may, at the request of the Prosecutor, issue such orders and warrants for the arrest, detention, surrender or transfer of persons, and any other orders as may be required for the conduct of the trial.

Article 20
Commencement and conduct of trial proceedings

1. The Trial Chambers shall ensure that a trial is fair and expeditious and that proceedings are conducted in accordance with the rules of procedure and evidence, with full respect for the rights of the accused and due regard for the protection of victims and witnesses.

2. A person against whom an indictment has been confirmed shall, pursuant to an order or an arrest warrant of the International Tribunal, be taken into custody, immediately informed of the charges against him and transferred to the International Tribunal.

3. The Trial Chamber shall read the indictment, satisfy itself that the rights of the accused are respected, confirm that the accused under-

stands the indictment, and instruct the accused to enter a plea. The Trial Chamber shall then set the date for trial.

4. The hearings shall be public unless the Trial Chamber decides to close the proceedings in accordance with its rules of procedure and evidence.

Article 21
Rights of the accused

1. All persons shall be equal before the International Tribunal.

2. In the determination of charges against him, the accused shall be entitled to a fair and public hearing, subject to article 22 of the Statute.

3. The accused shall be presumed innocent until proved guilty according to the provisions of the present Statute.

4. In the determination of any charge against the accused pursuant to the present Statute, the accused shall be entitled to the following minimum guarantees, in full equality:

   (a) to be informed promptly and in detail in a language which he understands of the nature and cause of the charge against him;
   (b) to have adequate time and facilities for the preparation of his defence and to communicate with counsel of his own choosing;
   (c) to be tried without undue delay;
   (d) to be tried in his presence, and to defend himself in person or through legal assistance of his own choosing; to be informed, if he does not have legal assistance, of this right; and to have legal assistance assigned to him, in any case where the interests of justice so require, and without payment by him in any such case if he does not have sufficient means to pay for it;
   (e) to examine, or have examined, the witnesses against him and to obtain the attendance and examination of witnesses on his behalf under the same conditions as witnesses against him;
   (f) to have the free assistance of an interpreter if he cannot understand or speak the language used in the International Tribunal;
   (g) not to be compelled to testify against himself or to confess guilt.

Article 22
Protection of victims and witnesses

The International Tribunal shall provide in its rules of procedure and evidence for the protection of victims and witnesses. Such protection measures shall include, but shall not be limited to, the conduct of *in camera* proceedings and the protection of the victim's identity.

Article 23
Judgment

1. The Trial Chambers shall pronounce judgments and impose sentences and penalties on persons convicted of serious violations of international humanitarian law.

2. The judgment shall be rendered by a majority of the judges of the Trial Chamber, and shall be delivered by the Trial Chamber in public. It shall be accompanied by a reasoned opinion in writing, to which separate or dissenting opinions may be appended.

Article 24
Penalties

1. The penalty imposed by the Trial Chamber shall be limited to imprisonment. In determining the terms of imprisonment, the Trial Chambers shall have recourse to the general practice regarding prison sentences in the courts of the former Yugoslavia.

2. In imposing the sentences, the Trial Chambers should take into account such factors as the gravity of the offence and the individual circumstances of the convicted person.

3. In addition to imprisonment, the Trial Chambers may order the return of any property and proceeds acquired by criminal conduct, including by means of duress, to their rightful owners.

Article 25
Appellate proceedings

1. The Appeals Chamber shall hear appeals from persons convicted by the Trial Chambers or from the Prosecutor on the following grounds:
   (a) an error on a question of law invalidating the decision; or
   (b) an error of fact which has occasioned a miscarriage of justice.

2. The Appeals Chamber may affirm, reverse or revise the decisions taken by the Trial Chambers.

Article 26
Review proceedings

Where a new fact has been discovered which was not known at the time of the proceedings before the Trial Chambers or the Appeals Chamber and which could have been a decisive factor in reaching the decision, the convicted person or the Prosecutor may submit to the International Tribunal an application for review of the judgment.

Article 27
Enforcement of sentences

Imprisonment shall be served in a State designated by the International Tribunal from a list of States which have indicated to the Security Council their willingness to accept convicted persons. Such imprisonment shall be in accordance with the applicable law of the State concerned, subject to the supervision of the International Tribunal.

Article 28
Pardon or commutation of sentences

If, pursuant to the applicable law of the State in which the convicted person is imprisoned, he or she is eligible for pardon or commutation of sentence, the State concerned shall notify the International Tribunal accordingly. The President of the International Tribunal, in consultation with the judges, shall decide the matter on the basis of the interests of justice and the general principles of law.

Article 29
Cooperation and judicial assistance

1. States shall cooperate with the International Tribunal in the investigation and prosecution of persons accused of committing serious violations of international humanitarian law.

2. States shall comply without undue delay with any request for assistance or an order issued by a Trial Chamber, including, but not limited to:

   (a) the identification and location of persons;
   (b) the taking of testimony and the production of evidence;
   (c) the service of documents;
   (d) the arrest or detention of persons;
   (e) the surrender or the transfer of the accused to the International Tribunal.

Article 30
The status, privileges and immunities of the International Tribunal

1. The Convention on the Privileges and Immunities of the United Nations of 13 February 1946 shall apply to the International Tribunal, the judges, the Prosecutor and his staff, and the Registrar and his staff.

2. The judges, the Prosecutor and the Registrar shall enjoy the privileges and immunities, exemptions and facilities accorded to diplomatic envoys, in accordance with international law.

3. The staff of the Prosecutor and of the Registrar shall enjoy the privileges and immunities accorded to officials of the United Nations under articles V and VII of the Convention referred to in paragraph 1 of this article.

4. Other persons, including the accused, required at the seat of the International Tribunal shall be accorded such treatment as is necessary for the proper functioning of the International Tribunal.

Article 31
Seat of the International Tribunal

The International Tribunal shall have its seat at The Hague.

Article 32
Expenses of the International Tribunal

The expenses of the International Tribunal shall be borne by the regular budget of the United Nations in accordance with Article 17 of the Charter of the United Nations.

Article 33
Working languages

The working languages of the International Tribunal shall be English and French.

Article 34
Annual report

The President of the International Tribunal shall submit an annual report of the International Tribunal to the Security Council and to the General Assembly.

.   .   .

NOTE: The judges have been elected, the Prosecutor has been selected, and the new court has begun its work on what is widely hoped will be an important advance in the implementation of the international law of armed conflict.

1. Commander, 8th Army in Korea, 1950–51; Supreme Allied Commander in Europe, 1952–53; and Chief of Staff, United States Army, 1953–55.
2. *Doenitz at Nuremberg: A Reappraisal; War Crimes and the Military Professional* (H. K. Thompson, Jr., and Henry Strutz, eds., 1976), p. 181.
3. Associate Justice, Supreme Court of the United States, 1939–75.
4. *Doenitz at Nuremberg*, p. 194.
5. United States Department of State, *Trial of Japanese War Criminals, Documents*, Publication 2613 45-62 (1946).
6. Howard S. Levie, *International Law Studies*, vol. 60, *Documents on Prisoners of War* (1979), p. 355.
7. Reproduced from the text provided to *International Legal Materials* by the Embassy of Israel, Washington, D.C. The text is the authorized English translation.
8. Interim Report of the Commission of Experts established pursuant to Security Council Resolution 780 (1992), S/25274, January 26, 1993, distributed with a letter from the secretary-general to the president of the Security Council on February 10, 1993 in Doc. S/25274.
9. *Ibid.*, p. 11, para. 31.
10. *Ibid.*, p. 14, para. 45.
11. *Ibid.*, pp. 15–17.
12. *Ibid.*, p. 20.
13. United States: Department of Defense Report to Congress on the Conduct of the Persian Gulf War— Appendix O on the Role of the Law of War (April 10, 1992), reprinted in 31 I.L.M. 612, 632–33 (1992).
14. Elaine Sciolino, "U.S. Names Figures it Wants Charged with War Crimes," *The New York Times*, Dec. 17, 1992, p. A1.
15. Security Council Resolution 808 (1993), February 22, 1993.

CHART OF MULTILATERAL TREATIES

The following chart notes which states have become party to seventeen of the multilateral treaties reproduced in this book. For brevity's sake, the names of treaties indexed in the chart have been shortened. Where diplomatic representatives of a state merely have signed a treaty text, thereby attesting to the authenticity of the text, no entry has been made in the chart. However, where diplomatic representatives have made known a state's intention, pursuant to the procedures prescribed by a particular treaty (i.e., via deposit of instruments of ratification), to be bound by such treaty, the year that such treaty went into effect for that state is noted. The year that each treaty was signed, not the year that each treaty came into force, is listed.

When a state formally undertakes to be bound by a treaty, it may attach one or more reservations (r), declarations (d), understandings (u), and statements (s) (for our purposes, collectively, "conditions") to becoming party to the treaty. In addition, a state already bound by a treaty may file an objection (o) where, for example, such state wishes to voice its opposition to another state becoming party to a treaty.

Consider several of the more common conditions to treaty ratification. A state may announce that its adherence to a treaty in no way constitutes recognition of another state that already is party to the treaty. A state may contract out of a particular portion of a treaty, such as a clause that mandates a particular manner of settling disputes. A very common condition attached to being bound by a treaty is that a state shall consider itself bound only vis-à-vis other contracting states and, even as to them, only to the extent that these other states continue to observe the treaty. This chart does not catalogue the multitude of conditions that accompany most treaties. However, their existence is noted in the chart utilizing the abbreviations above.

The Treaty Section of the Office of Legal Affairs at the United Nations was most helpful in compiling the chart. Data for each convention is current to early 1994. We have made several assumptions. First, we assume that, notwithstanding changes in sovereignty in the former U.S.S.R., the new states of Belarus, Russia, and Ukraine remain bound by the treaties to which the Byelorussian S.S.R., the U.S.S.R., and the Ukrainian S.S.R., respectively, were bound. Second, we assume that Serbia remains bound by treaties to which the former Yugoslavia was bound, due to statements its government has made and the conclusions of the Badinter Commission. While every effort was made to ensure the accuracy of the chart, we apologize should there be any omissions or errors therein.

	Poisonous Gases (1925)	Biological & Toxin Weapons (1972)	Injurious Weapons (1980)	Genocide (1948)
Afghanistan	1986	1975		1956
Albania				1955
Algeria				1963
Andorra				
Angola	1990r			
Antigua & Barbuda	1989			1988
Argentina	1969	1979		1956rdo
Armenia				1993
Australia	1930o	1977	1983	1949o
Austria	1928r	1975r	1983	1958
Bahamas		1986		1975
Bahrain	1988rs	1988s		1990
Bangladesh	1989	1985		
Barbados	1966	1975		1980
Belarus		1975	1983	1954

	Poisonous Gases (1925)	Biological & Toxin Weapons (1972)	Injurious Weapons (1980)	Genocide (1948)
Belgium	1928r	1979		1951o
Belize		1981		
Benin	1986	1975	1980(I&III)	
Bhutan	1979			
Bolivia	1985	1975		
Bosnia-Herzegovina				1992
Botswana		1992		
Brazil	1970	1975		1952o
Brunei		1991		
Bulgaria	1934ro	1975	1983	1950d
Burkina Faso	1971	1991		1965
Burundi				
Cameroon	1989			
Canada	1930r	1975		1952
Cape Verde	1991			
C. African Republic	1970			
Chad				
Chile	1935r	1980		1953
China	1929rd	1984	1983s	1983dro
Colombia				1959
Comoros				
Congo				
Costa Rica		1975		1950
Côte d'Ivoire	1970			
Croatia		1993		1992
Cuba	1966o	1976	1987	1953
Cyprus	1966	1975	1989d	1982o
Czech Republic				1993
Democratic Kampuchea	1983r			1950o
Dem. Yemen	1986			1987d
Denmark	1930	1975	1983	1951o

	Geneva IV (Civilians) (1949)	Protocol I (1977)	Protocol II (1977)	Environmental Modification (1976)
Afghanistan	1957			
Albania	1957r			
Algeria		1989d	1989	1991
Andorra				
Angola	1985r	1985		
Antigua & Barbuda	1981	1987	1987	1988
Argentina	1957	1987d	1987d	1987d
Armenia				
Australia	1959r	1991d	1991	1984
Austria	1954	1983r	1983r	1990r
Bahamas	1973	1980	1980	
Bahrain	1972	1987	1987	
Bangladesh	1972	1981	1981	1979
Barbados	1966d	1990	1990	
Belarus	1955r	1989d	1989	1988
Belgium	1953	1986d	1986	1982
Belize	1984	1984	1984	
Benin		1986	1986	1986
Bhutan	1991			
Bolivia	1977	1984	1984	
Bosnia-Herzegovina				
Botswana	1968	1979	1979	
Brazil	1957o	1992	1992	1984
Brunei	1991	1991	1991	
Bulgaria	1955r	1989	1989	
Burkina Faso	1960d	1988	1988	1978
Burundi				
Cameroon	1963d	1984	1984	
Canada	1965	1991	1991rd	1981
Cape Verde	1984			1979
C. African Republic	1960	1985	1985	
Chad	1971			
Chile	1951	1991d		

	Geneva IV (Civilians) (1949)	Protocol I (1977)	Protocol II (1977)	Environmental Modification (1976)
China	1957r	1984r	1984	
Colombia	1962			
Comoros	1986	1986	1986	
Congo	1960	1984	1984	
Costa Rica	1970	1984	1984	
Côte d'Ivoire	1960	1989	1989	
Croatia	1992	1992	1992	
Cuba	1954	1983		1978
Cyprus	1962	1979		1978
Czech Republic				1993
Democratic Kampuchea	1959			
Dem. Yemen	1977d			
Denmark	1951	1982rd	1982	1978

	Cultural Property (1954)	Geneva I Land (1949)	Geneva II (Sea) (1949)	Geneva III (POWs) (1949)
Afghanistan		1957	1957	1957
Albania	1961	1957r	1957r	1957r
Algeria				
Andorra				
Angola		1985r	1985r	1985r
Antigua & Barbuda		1981	1981	1981
Argentina	1989	1957	1957	1957
Armenia				
Australia		1959s	1959s	1959s
Austria	1962	1954	1954	1954
Bahamas		1973	1973	1973
Bahrain		1972	1972	1972
Bangladesh		1971	1971	1971
Barbados		1966	1966	1966
Belarus	1957o	1955r	1955r	1955r
Belgium	1960	1953	1953	1953
Belize		1984	1984	1984
Benin				
Bhutan				
Bolivia		1977	1977	1977
Bosnia-Herzegovina				
Botswana		1968	1968	1968
Brazil	1958	1957o	1957o	1957o
Brunei		1991	1991	1991
Bulgaria	1959o	1955r	1955r	1955r
Burkina Faso	1970	1960	1960	1960
Burundi		1962	1962	1962
Cameroon	1962	1960d	1960d	1960d
Canada		1965	1965	1965
Cape Verde		1984	1984	1984
C. African Republic		1960	1960	1960
Chad		1971	1971	1971

	Cultural Property (1954)	Geneva I Land (1949)	Geneva II (Sea) (1949)	Geneva III (POWs) (1949)
Chile		1951	1951	1951
China		1957r	1957r	1957r
Colombia		1962	1962	1962
Comoros		1986	1986	1986
Congo		1960	1960	1960
Costa Rica		1970	1970	1970
Côte d'Ivoire	1980	1960	1960	1960
Croatia		1992	1992	1992
Cuba	1958	1954	1954	1954
Cyprus	1964	1962	1962	1962
Czech Republic				
Democratic Kampuchea	1962	1959	1959	1959
Dem. Yemen		1977d	1977d	1977d
Denmark		1951	1951	1951

	Diplomatic Agents (1973)	Hostages (1979)	Offenses/ Aircraft (1963)	Seizure/ Aircraft (1970)	Safety of Civil Aviation (1971)
Afghanistan			1977		
Albania					
Algeria					
Andorra					
Angola					
Antigua & Barbuda		1986	1985		1985
Argentina	1982do		1971	1972d	1973
Armenia					
Australia	1977	1990	1970	1972	1973
Austria	1977	1986	1974	1974	1974
Bahamas	1986	1983	1973	1976	
Bahrain			1984rd	1983	1983
Bangladesh			1978		

	Diplomatic Agents (1973)	Hostages (1979)	Offenses/ Aircraft (1963)	Seizure/ Aircraft (1970)	Safety of Civil Aviation (1971)
Barbados	1979	1983	1972	1973	1976
Belarus	1977rd	1987d	1988dr	1972r	1973r
Belgium			1970	1973	1976
Belize	1979				
Benin					
Bhutan	1989	1983	1989	1989	1989
Bolivia			1979		
Bosnia-Herzegovina					
Botswana			1979		
Brazil			1970	1972r	1973r
Brunei		1988	1986	1986	1986
Bulgaria	1974d	1988rd	1989	1971r	1973r
Burkina Faso			1969		
Burundi	1980r		1971		
Cameroon	1992	1988	1988		1971
Canada	1977	1985	1976	1972	1973
Cape Verde			1989		
C. African Republic					
Chad			1970	1972	1973
Chile	1977	1983s	1971	1972	1974
China	1987d	1993	1979r		
Colombia			1973		
Comoros					
Congo			1979		1987
Costa Rica	1977		1973	1971	1973
Côte d'Ivoire		1989	1970		1973
Croatia	1992				
Cuba					
Cyprus	1977		1972	1972	1973
Czech Republic	1993	1993			
Democratic Kampuchea					
Dem. Yemen	1977r				
Denmark	1977	1987	1969	1972r	1973r

	Poisonous Gases (1925)	Biological & Toxin Weapons (1972)	Injurious Weapons (1980)	Genocide (1948)
Djibouti				
Dominica		1975		1970
Dom. Republic	1970	1975		
Ecuador	1970	1975	1983	1949o
Egypt	1928			1952
El Salvador				1950
Eq. Guinea	1989	1992		
Estonia		1993		1991
Ethiopia	1935o	1975		1949
Fiji	1979r	1975		1973
Finland	1929	1975	1983	1959d
France	1926o	1984	1988(I&II)dsr	1950
Gabon				1983
Gambia	1966			1978
Georgia				
Germany	1929	1983		1954
Ghana	1967	1975		1958
Greece	1931	1975	1992	1954o
Grenada	1989	1986		1970
Guatemala	1983	1975	1983	1950
Guinea				
Guinea-Bissau	1989			
Guyana				
Haiti				1950
Honduras				1952
Hungary	1952o	1975	1983	1952
Iceland	1967	1975		1949
India	1930r	1975d	1984	1959
Indonesia	1971			1959
Iran	1929	1975		1956
Iraq	1931r			1959
Ireland	1930	1975d		1976o
Israel	1969ro			1950
Italy	1928	1975		1952o
Jamaica	1970	1975		1968

	Poisonous Gases (1925)	Biological & Toxin Weapons (1972)	Injurious Weapons (1980)	Genocide (1948)
Japan	1970	1982	1983	
Jordan	1977r	1975		1950
Kazakhstan				
Kenya	1970	1976		
Kiribati				
Korea, North	1989s			1989
Korea, South	1989s	1987d		1950
Kuwait	1971r	1975us		
Kyrgizstan				
Lao People's Dem. Rep.	1989	1975	1983	1950
Latvia				1992
Lebanon	1969	1975		1953
Lesotho	1972	1977		1974
Liberia	1927			1950
Libya	1971r			1989

	Geneva IV (Civilians) (1949)	Protocol I (1977)	Protocol II (1977)	Environmental Modification (1976)
Djibouti	1977	1991		
Dominica	1981			1992
Dom. Republic	1958			
Ecuador	1955	1979	1979	
Egypt	1953			1982
El Salvador	1953	1979	1979	
Eq. Guinea	1987	1987	1987	
Estonia				
Ethiopia	1970			
Fiji	1970			
Finland	1955	1981rd	1981	1978
France	1951		1984d	
Gabon	1960	1980	1980	
Gambia	1965d	1989	1989	

	Geneva IV (Civilians) (1949)	Protocol I (1977)	Protocol II (1977)	Environmental Modification (1976)
Georgia				
Germany	1955d	1991	1991	1983
Ghana	1959	1978	1978	
Greece	1956	1989		1983
Grenada	1974			
Guatemala	1952	1988	1988	1988r
Guinea	1984	1985	1985	
Guinea-Bissau	1974r	1987	1987	
Guyana	1966	1988	1988	
Haiti	1957			
Honduras	1966			
Hungary	1955dr	1989	1989	
Iceland	1966	1987rd	1987	
India	1951			1978
Indonesia	1959			
Iran	1957			
Iraq	1956			
Ireland	1963			1982
Israel	1952dr			
Italy	1952	1986d	1986d	1981
Jamaica	1962	1987d	1987	
Japan	1953			1982
Jordan	1951	1979	1979	
Kazakhstan	1991	1991	1991	
Kenya	1967			
Kiribati	1979			
Korea, North	1958r	1988		1984
Korea, South	1966rd	1982d	1982	1986u
Kuwait	1968d	1985	1985	1986ru
Kyrgyzstan	1991	1991	1991	
Lao People's Dem. Rep.	1957	1981	1981	1978
Latvia				
Lebanon	1951			
Lesotho	1966			
Liberia	1954	1988	1988	
Libya	1956	1978	1978	

THE LAWS OF WAR

	Cultural Property (1954)	Geneva I Land (1949)	Geneva II (Sea) (1949)	Geneva III (POWs) (1949)
Djibouti		1977	1977	1977
Dominica		1978	1978	1978
Dom. Republic	1960	1958	1958	1958
Ecuador	1957	1955	1955	1955
Egypt	1956o	1953	1953	1953
El Salvador		1953	1953	1953
Eq. Guinea		1987	1987	1987
Estonia				
Ethiopia		1970	1970	1970
Fiji		1970	1970	1970
Finland		1955	1955	1955
France	1957	1951	1951	1951
Gabon	1962	1960	1960	1960
Gambia		1965	1965	1965
Georgia				
Germany	1967d	1955o	1955o	1955o
Ghana	1960	1959	1959	1959
Greece	1981	1956	1956	1956
Grenada		1974	1974	1974
Guatemala	1986	1952	1952	1952
Guinea	1960	1985	1985	1985
Guinea-Bissau		1974r	1974r	1974r
Guyana		1966	1966	1966
Haiti		1957	1957	1957
Honduras		1966	1966	1966
Hungary	1956	1955r	1955r	1955r
Iceland		1956	1956	1956
India	1958o	1951	1951	1951
Indonesia	1967	1959	1959	1959
Iran	1959	1957	1957	1957
Iraq	1968	1956	1956	1956
Ireland		1963	1963	1963
Israel	1958	1952rd	1952r	1952d
Italy	1958o	1952	1952	1952
Jamaica		1962	1962	1962
Japan		1953	1953	1953

	Cultural Property (1954)	Geneva I Land (1949)	Geneva II (Sea) (1949)	Geneva III (POWs) (1949)
Jordan	1958	1951	1951	1951
Kazakhstan		1991	1991	1991
Kenya		1967	1967	1967
Kiribati		1979	1979	1979
Korea, North		1958r	1958r	1958r
Korea, South		1966d	1966d	1966rd
Kuwait	1969	1968d	1968d	1968d
Kyrgyzstan		1991	1991	1991
Lao People's Dem. Rep.		1957	1957	1957
Latvia				
Lebanon	1960	1951	1951	1951
Lesotho		1966	1966	1966
Liberia		1954	1954	1954
Libya	1958	1956	1956	1956

	Diplomatic Agents (1973)	Hostages (1979)	Offenses/ Aircraft (1963)	Seizure/ Aircraft (1970)	Safety of Civil Aviation (1971)
Djibouti					
Dominica		1986u			
Dom. Republic	1977		1971		1973
Ecuador	1977d	1988	1970	1971	
Egypt	1986	1983	1975r		
El Salvador	1980d	1983r	1980		
Eq. Guinea			1991	1991	
Estonia					
Ethiopia			1979r	1979r	1979r
Fiji			1970	1972	1973
Finland	1978r	1983	1971	1972	1973
France			1970	1972	1976r
Gabon	1981		1970	1971	
Gambia			1979		
Georgia					

	Diplomatic Agents (1973)	Hostages (1979)	Offenses/ Aircraft (1963)	Seizure/ Aircraft (1970)	Safety of Civil Aviation (1971)
Germany	1977o	1983	1970	1974	1978
Ghana	1977r	1987	1974		1974
Greece	1984	1987	1971	1973	1974
Grenada		1990	1978		
Guatemala	1983s	1983	1971r		1973
Guinea					
Guinea-Bissau					
Guyana			1973		
Haiti	1980	1989	1984		
Honduras		1983	1987r		
Hungary	1977	1987	1971r	1971r	1973r
Iceland	1977	1983	1970	1973	1973
India	1978d		1975r	1982	1982
Indonesia			1976r		
Iran	1978	1976	1976	1972	1973
Iraq	1978d		1974d	1972d	1974
Ireland			1976	1975	1976
Israel	1980dros		1969	1971	1973
Italy	1985o	1986	1969	1974	1974
Jamaica	1978d		1983		
Japan	1987	1987	1970	1971	1974
Jordan	1984	1986d	1973	1971	1973
Kazakhstan					
Kenya		1983d	1970		
Kiribati					
Korea, North	1982d		1983r		
Korea, South	1983		1971		1973d
Kuwait	1989r	1989d	1980d	1979	1979s
Kyrgizstan					
Lao People's Dem. Rep.			1973	1989	1989
Latvia					
Lebanon			1974		
Lesotho		1980	1972		
Liberia	1977				
Libya			1972		1974

	Poisonous Gases (1925)	Biological & Toxin Weapons (1972)	Injurious Weapons (1980)	Genocide (1948)
Liechtenstein	1991	1991	1989	
Lithuania				
Luxembourg	1936	1976		1981
Macedonia				
Madagascar	1967			
Malawi	1970			
Malaysia	1970	1991r		
Maldives	1967d			1984
Mali				1974
Malta	1964	1975		
Mauritania				
Mauritius	1968o	1975		
Mexico	1932	1975d	1983	1952
Moldova				1993
Monaco		1967		1950
Mongolia	1968ro	1975	1983	1967d
Morocco	1970			1958d
Mozambique				1983
Myanmar				1956r
Namibia				
Nauru				
Nepal	1969			1969
Netherlands	1930ro	1981	1987u	1966o
New Zealand	1930r	1975		1978
Nicaragua	1990	1975		1952
Niger	1967	1975	1992	
Nigeria	1968r	1975		
Norway	1932	1975	1983	1949o
Oman		1992		
Pakistan	1960	1975	1985	1957
Panama	1970	1975		1950
Papua New Guinea	1975r	1980		1982
Paraguay	1933	1976		
Peru	1985	1985		1960

	Poisonous Gases (1925)	Biological & Toxin Weapons (1972)	Injurious Weapons (1980)	Genocide (1948)
Philippines	1973	1975		1950d
Poland	1929o	1975	1983	1950d
Portugal	1930r	1975		
Qatar	1976	1975		
Romania	1929r	1979		1950d
Russia	1928ro	1975ds	1983	1954
Rwanda	1964	1975		1975d
St. Kitts			1992	
St. Lucia	1988	1979		1970
St. Vincent				1981
San Marino		1975		
São Tome & Principe				
Saudi Arabia	1971	1975		1950
Senegal	1977	1975		1983

	Geneva IV (Civilians) (1949)	Protocol I (1977)	Protocol II (1977)	Environmental Modification (1976)
Liechtenstein	1951	1989dr	1989r	
Lithuania				
Luxembourg	1954	1989	1989	
Macedonia				
Madagascar	1960	1992	1992	
Malawi	1968	1991	1991	1978
Malaysia	1963			
Maldives	1991	1991	1991	
Mali	1965	1989	1989	
Malta	1964	1989dr	1989r	
Mauritania	1960	1980	1980	
Mauritius	1968	1982	1982	1992
Mexico	1953	1983		

	Geneva IV (Civilians) (1949)	Protocol I (1977)	Protocol II (1977)	Environmental Modification (1976)
Moldova				
Monaco	1951			
Mongolia	1959d			1978
Morocco	1957			
Mozambique	1983	1983		
Myanmar	1992			
Namibia	1984	1984	1984	
Nauru				
Nepal	1964			
Netherlands	1955r	1987d	1987	1983d
New Zealand	1959r	1988d	1988d	1984d
Nicaragua	1954			
Niger	1960	1979	1979	1993
Nigeria	1961	1988	1988	
Norway	1952	1982d	1982	1979
Oman	1974	1984d	1984d	1986
Pakistan	1951r			1986
Panama	1956			
Papua New Guinea	1975			1980
Paraguay	1962	1991	1991	
Peru	1956	1989	1989	
Philippines	1953		1987	
Poland	1955dr			1978
Portugal	1961od	1992	1992	
Qatar	1976	1988d		
Romania	1954dor	1990	1990	1983
Russia	1954dr	1989d	1989d	1978
Rwanda	1962	1985	1985	
St. Kitts	1983	1986	1986	
St. Lucia	1981	1983	1983	1993
St. Vincent	1981	1983	1983	
San Marino	1954			
São Tome & Principe	1976			1979
Saudi Arabia	1963	1988r		
Senegal	1960d	1985	1985	

	Cultural Property (1954)	Geneva I Land (1949)	Geneva II (Sea) (1949)	Geneva III (POWs) (1949)
Liechtenstein	1960	1951	1951	1951
Lithuania				
Luxembourg	1961	1954	1954	1954s
Macedonia				
Madagascar	1962o	1960	1960	1960
Malawi		1968	1968	1968
Malaysia	1961	1963	1963	1963
Maldives		1991	1991	1991
Mali	1961	1965	1965	1965
Malta		1964	1964	1964
Mauritania		1960	1960	1960
Mauritius		1968	1968	1968
Mexico	1956o	1953	1953	1953
Moldova				
Monaco	1958	1951	1951	1951
Mongolia	1965	1959d	1959d	1959d
Morocco	1968	1957	1957	1957
Mozambique		1983	1983	1983
Myanmar		1992	1992	1992
Namibia		1984	1984	1984
Nauru				
Nepal		1964	1964	1964
Netherlands	1959o	1955d	1955d	1955d
New Zealand		1959d	1959d	1959d
Nicaragua	1960	1954	1954	1954
Niger	1977	1960	1960	1960
Nigeria	1961	1960	1960	1960
Norway	1961r	1952	1952	1952
Oman	1978	1974	1974	1974
Pakistan	1959	1951	1951	1951
Panama	1962	1956	1956	1956
Papua New Guinea		1975	1975	1975
Paraguay		1962	1962	1962
Peru	1989	1956	1956	1956
Philippines		1953	1953	1953

	Cultural Property (1954)	Geneva I Land (1949)	Geneva II (Sea) (1949)	Geneva III (POWs) (1949)
Poland	1956o	1955rd	1955rd	1955rd
Portugal		1961do	1961do	1961do
Qatar	1973	1976	1976	1976
Romania	1958o	1954ro	1954ro	1954ro
Russia	1957o	1954r	1954r	1954r
Rwanda		1962	1962	1962
St. Kitts		1983	1983	1983
St. Lucia		1979	1979	1979
St. Vincent		1981	1981	1981
San Marino	1956	1954	1954	1954
São Tome & Principe		1976	1976	1976
Saudi Arabia	1971	1963	1963	1963
Senegal	1987	1960d	1960d	1960

	Diplomatic Agents (1973)	Hostages (1979)	Offenses/ Aircraft (1963)	Seizure/ Aircraft (1970)	Safety of Civil Aviation (1971)
Liechtenstein					
Lithuania					
Luxembourg		1991	1972	1978	1982
Macedonia					
Madagascar			1970		
Malawi	1977d	1986d	1973r		1973r
Malaysia			1985	1985	1985
Maldives	1990	1990	1987	1987	1987
Mali		1990	1971	1971	1973
Malta					
Mauritania			1977		
Mauritius		1983	1983		1989
Mexico	1980	1987d	1969	1972	1974
Moldova					

	Diplomatic Agents (1973)	Hostages (1979)	Offenses/ Aircraft (1963)	Seizure/ Aircraft (1970)	Safety of Civil Aviation (1971)
Monaco			1983	1983	1983
Mongolia	1977d	1992		1971r	1973r
Morocco			1976d		
Mozambique					
Myanmar					
Namibia					
Nauru			1984		
Nepal	1990	1990	1979	1979	1979
Netherlands	1988dr	1988rd	1970d	1973d	1973d
New Zealand	1985r	1985	1974	1974	1974
Nicaragua	1977		1973		1973
Niger	1985		1969	1971	1973
Nigeria			1970	1973	1973
Norway	1980	1983	1969	1971	1973
Oman	1988	1988	1977rd	1977dr	1977dr
Pakistan	1977d		1973	1973	1974
Panama	1980	1983	1971	1972	1973
Papua New Guinea			1975r	1975r	1975r
Paraguay	1977		1971	1972	1974
Peru	1978r		1978r	1978	1978
Philippines	1977	1983	1969		1973
Poland	1982r		1971r	1972r	1975r
Portugal			1969	1972	1973
Qatar			1981		
Romania	1978r	1990	1974r	1972r	1975r
Russia	1977r	1987rd	1988dr	1972r	1973r
Rwanda	1977		1971		
St. Kitts		1991			
St. Lucia			1984		
St. Vincent					
San Marino		1991			
São Tome & Principe					
Saudi Arabia		1991d	1970		1974r
Senegal		1987	1972	1978	1978

	Poisonous Gases (1925)	Biological & Toxin Weapons (1972)	Injurious Weapons (1980)	Genocide (1948)
Serbia	1929r	1975	1983	1950
Seychelles		1979		1992
Sierra Leone	1967	1976		
Singapore		1975		1981
Slovak Republic		1993		
Slovenia		1991	1992	1992
Solomon Is.	1978	1978		
Somalia				
South Africa		1975		
Spain	1929r	1979		1968ro
Sri Lanka	1954	1986		1950o
Sudan	1980			
Suriname		1993		
Swaziland		1992		
Sweden	1930	1976	1983	1952o
Switzerland	1932	1976d	1983	
Syria	1968r			1955
Taiwan		1975d		
Thailand	1931	1975		
Togo	1971			1984
Tonga	1970	1976		1972
Trinidad & Tobago	1962			
Tunisia	1967	1975	1987	1956
Turkey	1929	1975		1950
Turkmenistan				
Tuvalu				
Uganda	1965	1992		
Ukraine		1975	1983	1954
United Arab Emirates				
United Kingdom	1930r	1975d		1970o
United Rep. of Tanzania	1963			1984

	Poisonous Gases (1925)	Biological & Toxin Weapons (1972)	Injurious Weapons (1980)	Genocide (1948)
USA	1975r	1975		1988ru
Uruguay	1977			1967
Uzbekistan				
Vanuatu				
Vatican City	1966			
Venezuela	1928	1978		1960d
Vietnam	1980o			1981d
Western Sahara				
Western Samoa				
Yemen	1971			1989
Zaire		1975		1962
Zambia				
Zimbabwe		1990		1991

	Geneva IV (Civilians) (1949)	Protocol I (1977)	Protocol II (1977)	Environmental Modification (1976)
Serbia	1950	1979d	1979	
Seychelles	1985	1985d	1985d	
Sierra Leone	1961	1987	1987	
Singapore	1973			
Slovak Republic				
Slovenia	1992	1992	1992	
Solomon Is.	1978	1988	1988	1981
Somalia	1963			
South Africa	1952			
Spain	1953	1989d	1989d	1978
Sri Lanka	1959			1978
Sudan	1958			
Suriname	1975r	1986	1986	
Swaziland	1973			

	Geneva IV (Civilians) (1949)	Protocol I (1977)	Protocol II (1977)	Environmental Modification (1976)
Sweden	1954	1980rd	1980	1984
Switzerland	1950	1982r	1982	1988r
Syria	1954	1984r		
Taiwan				
Thailand	1955			
Togo	1960	1984	1984	
Tonga	1970			
Trinidad & Tobago	1964			
Tunisia	1957	1980	1980	1978
Turkey	1954			
Turkmenistan	1991	1992	1992	
Tuvalu	1978			
Uganda	1964	1991		
Ukraine	1955dr	1990d	1990	1978
United Arab Emirates	1972	1983d	1983d	
United Kingdom	1958od			1978
United Rep. of Tanzania	1961d	1983	1983	
USA	1956dr			1980
Uruguay	1969r	1986	1986	
Uzbekistan				1993
Vanuatu	1982	1985	1985	
Vatican City	1951	1986d	1986d	
Venezuela	1956			
Vietnam	1957rd	1982		1980
Western Sahara				
Western Samoa		1985	1985	
Yemen	1971	1990	1990d	1977
Zaire	1966	1982		
Zambia	1967			
Zimbabwe	1983			

	Cultural Property (1954)	Geneva I Land (1949)	Geneva II (Sea) (1949)	Geneva III (POWs) (1949)
Serbia	1956	1950r	1950r	1950r
Seychelles		1985	1985	1985
Sierra Leone		1961	1961	1961
Singapore		1973	1973	1973
Slovak Republic				
Slovenia		1992	1992	1992
Solomon Is.		1978	1978	1978
Somalia		1963	1963	1963
South Africa		1952d	1952d	1952d
Spain	1960	1953	1953	1953
Sri Lanka		1959	1959	1959
Sudan	1970	1958	1958	1958
Suriname		1975	1975	1975
Swaziland		1973	1973	1973
Sweden	1985	1954	1954	1954
Switzerland	1962	1950	1950	1950
Syria	1958	1954	1954	1954
Taiwan				
Thailand	1958	1955	1955	1955
Togo		1960	1960	1960
Tonga		1970	1970	1970
Trinidad & Tobago		1964	1964	1964
Tunisia	1981	1957	1957	1957
Turkey	1966	1954	1954	1954
Turkmenistan		1991	1991	1991
Tuvalu		1978	1978	1978
Uganda		1964	1964	1964
Ukraine	1957	1955r	1955r	1955r
United Arab Emirates		1972	1972	1972
United Kingdom		1958do	1958do	1958do
United Rep. of Tanzania	1971	1961d	1961d	1961
USA		1956ro	1956ro	1956ro
Uruguay		1969	1969	1969r
Uzbekistan				

	Cultural Property (1954)	Geneva I Land (1949)	Geneva II (Sea) (1949)	Geneva III (POWs) (1949)
Vanuatu		1983	1983	1983
Vatican City	1958	1951	1951	1951
Venezuela		1956	1956	1956
Vietnam		1954r	1954r	1954ro
Western Sahara				
Western Samoa		1962	1962	1962
Yemen	1970	1971	1971	1971
Zaire	1961	1960	1960	1960
Zambia		1967	1967	1967
Zimbabwe		1983	1983	1983

	Diplomatic Agents (1973)	Hostages (1979)	Offenses/ Aircraft (1963)	Seizure/ Aircraft (1970)	Safety of Civil Aviation (1971)
Serbia	1977	1985d	1971	1972	1973
Seychelles	1980		1979	1979	1979
Sierra Leone			1971	1974	
Singapore			1971	1978	1978
Slovak Republic					
Slovenia	1992	1992			
Solomon Is.			1978	1971	1978
Somalia					
South Africa			1972r	1972r	1973r
Spain	1985	1984	1969	1972	1973
Sri Lanka	1991		1978	1978	1978
Sudan		1990			
Suriname		1983	1975		
Swaziland					
Sweden	1977	1983	1969	1971	1973
Switzerland	1985d	1985d	1971	1971	1978
Syria	1988d		1980r		
Taiwan			1969	1972	1973
Thailand			1972	1978	1978

	Diplomatic Agents (1973)	Hostages (1979)	Offenses/ Aircraft (1963)	Seizure/ Aircraft (1970)	Safety of Civil Aviation (1971)
Togo	1979	1986	1971		
Tonga				1977	1977
Trinidad & Tobago	1979d	1983	1972	1972	1973
Tunisia	1977d		1975r	1981r	1981r
Turkey	1981	1989r	1976	1973	
Turkmenistan					
Tuvalu					
Uganda			1982	1972	
Ukraine	1977r	1987rd	1988dr	1972r	1973r
United Arab Emirates			1981r	1981r	1981r
United Kingdom	1979os	1983	1969d	1971	1973d
United Rep. of Tanzania			1983		
USA	1977	1985	1989	1971	1973
Uruguay	1978		1977		
Uzbekistan					
Vanuatu			1989	1989	1989
Vatican City					
Venezuela		1988d	1983r		
Vietnam			1980		
Western Sahara					
Western Samoa					
Yemen	1987		1986	1987	1987
Zaire	1977d		1977		
Zambia			1971		
Zimbabwe			1989	1989	1989

INDEX

Page numbers in **boldface** refer to excerpts from official documents.

Attorney-General of the Government of
Israel v. Eichmann (1961), **352–56**
Austria, 329

Badinter Commission, 407
Balkans, see Yugoslavia
Barak, Aharon, 373
Barbados, 44
Begin, Menachem, 377–79
Beirut:
  Palestinian refugees massacred in,
    372–85
  suicide truck bombing in, 314
Belarus, 407
Belgium, 133, 331
biological weapons, 57–59, 407–8,
    414–15, 420–21, 426–27
blockades, 76
Blomberg, Werner Von, 325, 329
Bokassa, Emperor of Central Africa, 33
bombardments, 47, 80–84, 89
  cultural property and, 94
  by naval forces, 81–82, 94
bombardments, aerial, 83–84, 95–
    97, 394
  in Vietnam War, 106–15, 119–24
booby-traps, 50–54
  in Grenada invasion, 129
  recording of location of, 53–54
Bork, Robert H., 310, 312
Bormann, Martin, 324, 333
Bosnia-Hercegovina, see Yugoslavia,
    former
Bothe, Michael, 37
Brezhnev Doctrine, 30
Bryan, Roberto, xxvii–xxviii
bullets, expanding, 49
Bureau of Prisons, U.S. (BOP), 220,
    223, 224, 228, 230n
Burundi, 86
Bush, George, 30–31, 316

Calley, William L., Jr., trial of, 362–
    71

Cambodia:
  Khmer Rouge in, 86
  Vietnamese invasion of, 33
  in Vietnam War, 111, 112, 123, 127
Canada, Persian Gulf War and, 71
Canaris, Wilhelm Franz, 330–31
capitulations, 130
Central African Republic, 33
Central Information Agency, 265,
    266, 268, 273, 275–77
Central Prisoners of War Information
    Agency, 195, 215–16, 229n
cessation of hostilities, 130–31
  repatriation of prisoners of war
    after, 211–13
chemical weapons, 57–58, 60–65,
    407–8, 414–15, 420–21, 426–27
  in Iran-Iraq War, xix–xx
children, 235, 239, 242, 246, 258,
    260, 274
China:
  Kellogg-Briand Pact and, 4
  U.N. Security Council and, 8
  World War II and, 339, 340, 342
civilian objects, military objectives
    vs., 26, 72, 87, 89–93, 247
  in former Yugoslavia, 394
  in Grenada invasion, 129
  see also cultural property
civilian populations, 72, 84–93
  bombardment of, 80–84, 89, 109,
    111–12, 114, 120–21, 124,
    125–26
  definition of, 88
  in Grenada invasion, 128, 129
  incendiary weapons and, 55
  mines and, 51, 52
  in Vietnam War, 109, 110, 111–
    12, 114, 115, 117–18, 120–21,
    124, 125–26, 362–71
  see also Geneva Conventions
    (1949), (IV) Relative to the
    Protection of Civilian Persons
    in Time of War; genocide;

Hoshino, Naoki, 342
hospitals, 94, 129, 236–37, 248
   emblems of, 95, 237, 280
hospital ships, 95, 158, 160–63,
   165–66, 170
hospital trains and convoys, 237–38
hospital zones, 171, 177–79, 235,
   279–81
hostage-taking, 154, 241, 293, 304,
   331, 391, 393
   U.N. convention on, 29–30, 300–
   302, 311, 412–13, 418–19,
   424–25, 430–31
humanitarian law, xxi–xxii
human rights, xxi, 32
human rights law, xxi–xxii
Hussein, Saddam, 219

Identify Friend or Foe (IFF) system, 45
identity discs, 159, 165, 169
identity documents, 183, 184, 195,
   237, 262
incendiary weapons, 54–55
   in Vietnam War, 115
India, 336
   decolonization of, 33
indiscriminate attacks, 88–89, 391
indiscriminate use of mines, 51
Indonesia, 33
Information Bureaux, 212, 214–19,
   266, 275–77
Institute of International Law, 150
Inter-American Treaty of Reciprocal
   Assistance, 15
International Civil Aviation Organization, 298, 305, 306, 309–10
International Committee of the Red
   Cross (ICRC), 219, 222
   founding of, xxi
   Geneva conferences sponsored by,
   xxix, 151–52
   Geneva Conventions commentary
   of, 221, 223, 226, 227, 228
   hospital zones and, 171, 235–36

occupation and internment and,
   240, 249, 261, 264, 266, 267,
   276, 277, 278, 283
   and prisoners of war, 181, 196,
   198, 199, 216, 217
   and sick and wounded, 154, 155
International Convention against the
   Recruitment, Use, Financing
   and Training of Mercenaries
   (U.N.; 1989), 44
International Convention Against the
   Taking of Hostages (U.N.;
   1979), 29–30, 300–302, 311
   adherents to, 412–13, 418–19,
   424–25, 430–31
International Court of Justice (ICJ),
   xix, 67, 356
   see also Nicaragua v. United States
International Explosives Technical
   Commission, 309–10
International Law Commission,
   U.N., 26–27, 371
international legal system:
   case law in, xxvi
   sanction and, xxii–xxiii
   "soft law" in, xxii–xxiii
   terrorism and, 310–13
   war crimes and, 353–56, 389
internationally protected persons,
   299–300, 312
International Maritime Organization,
   305
International Military Commission,
   48
International Military Tribunal at
   Nuremberg, xix, xxvi, 318–33,
   390
   charter of, 318–22, 335–36
   judgments in, 323–34
   principles of international law in
   charter of, 335–36
   sentences of, 332–33
International Military Tribunal for
   the Far East, xxvi, 318, 337–43

Kuwait:
  Iran-Iraq War and, 148
  see also Persian Gulf War

Laos, in Vietnam War, 123, 124, 127
Latvia, 33
Lauterpacht, Sir Hersch, 26
Law of Land Warfare, The (U.S.
    Army), **36–37, 356–57**
laws of war:
  implementation of, xxvii
  origin of, xviii
  as unorganized legal system, xvii–
    xviii
League of Nations, 32, 340, 355
  Versailles Covenant of, **3–4**
Lebanon, 231, 293
  Palestinian refugee camp massacres
    in, 372–85
Levy, David, 377
Libya, 310–13
  U.S. attack on (1985), 316
Lieber, Francis, 131*n*, 150
Lieber Instructions, 131*n*
Lincoln, Abraham, 131*n*
Lithuania, 33
London Charter of the International
    Military Tribunal (1945), **318–
    22**, 336, 390
London Naval Treaty (1930), 77–78

MacArthur, Douglas, 346
Maelzer, Kurt, trial of (1946), 351–
    52
mail, *see* postal correspondence
Malaya, 340
Maldives, 44
Manual for Courts-Martial (U.S.
    Army), **360**, 369
maritime activity:
  commercial, 56, 73–77, 143
  neutrality and, 138–39, 143–48
  scientific, religious, or philan-
    thropic, 76, 144

submarine, 77–78, 144
  see also naval warfare; watercraft
Maritime Neutrality (Inter-American)
    (Havana; 1928), **143–48**
Matsui, Iwane, 342
Mauritius, 59
media, role of, in war, xxiv, 219
medical aircraft, 163, 164, 238
medical personnel, 163, 169, 171–
    75, 181, 237
  internees and, 258–59
  and prisoners of war, 189–90
  see also wounded and sick
medical transports, 163–64, 237–38
  emblem for, 164
mercenaries:
  Geneva Protocol I on, **44–45**, 152
  qualifications of, 44–45
merchant ships, 56, 73–77, 143
military force:
  and cessation of hostilities, 130–
    31, 211–13
  laws on resorting to, 3–34
  use of, 35–132
Milosevic, Slobodan, 392
Minami, Jiro, 342
mines, 50–54
  in Grenada invasion, 129
  recording of location of, 53–54
  remotely delivered, 50, 52
  submarine contact, 56, 82, 141, 391
Mixed Medical Commissions, 199, 210
Mladic, Ratko, 392
Monroe Doctrine, 30
Montreal Convention for the
    Suppression of Unlawful Acts
    Against the Safety of Civil Avia-
    tion (1971), 288, **296–98**, 312
  adherents to, 412–13, 418–19,
    424–25, 430–31
Montreal Convention on the Mark-
    ing of Plastic Explosives for the
    Purpose of Detection (1991),
    306–10

torture and inhuman treatment, 153,
    157, 176, 182, 183, 201, 202,
    218, 241, 269, 279, 391, 393
  see also war crimes
treaties, xix, xx
  charts of adherents to, 406–31
  conditions to, 406–7
  self-executing, 225–26
Treaty for the Renunciation of War as
    an Instrument of National Policy
    (Paris; 1928), 4–5
Treaty of Amity and Commerce
    (1785), 150

Uganda, 33
Ukraine, 44, 407
Umezu, Yoshijiro, 343
United Nations, 54, 305, 311
  New York Charter of, 5–9, 21, 22,
    27, 29, 30, 66, 225, 302, 393
  Persian Gulf War and, xxv, 71
  War Crimes Tribunal proposed by,
    xxvi
  see also General Assembly, U.N.;
    Security Council, U.N.
United Nations Commission of Ex-
    perts to Investigate Allegations of
    War Crimes, 317, 387, 392
  Interim Report of, 387–90
United Nations Headquarters Agree-
    ment, 314
United Nations Military Staff Com-
    mittee, 7
United Nations Treaty Section of the
    Office of Legal Affairs, 407
United States, 30
  on biological and chemical
    weapons, 58
  Civil War in, 131n, 150
  on combatant vs. noncombatant
    aircraft, 45–46
  "environmental" warfare letter of,
    71–73
  Geneva Conventions and, 152

Geneva Protocols and, xxix, 69
Iran-Iraq War and, 148
and League of Nations, 3–4
neutrality in, 133
Nicaragua's suit against, xxx, 12–23
nuclear weapons and, 67
Nuremberg trials and, 318, 323
Peace Movement in, xviii
Prussia's treaty with, 150
Somalia intervention of, 33–34
U.N. Security Council and, 8, 9
on use of force, 30–32
war crimes in forces of, 356–71
and war crime trials against Japa-
    nese, 336, 343–50
in World War II, 339–40, 351
see also Grenada, U.S. invasion of;
    Panama, U.S. invasion of; Per-
    sian Gulf War; Vietnam War
United States Uniform Code of Mili-
    tary Justice, 356
United States v. Manuel Antonio
    Noriega (1992), 220–30
United States v. Staff Sergeant (E-6)
    Walter Griffen (1968), 357–61
United States v. William L. Calley,
    Jr. (1973), 362–71
Universal Postal Convention (1947),
    266

Versailles Covenant of the League of
    Nations (1919), 3–4
Vienna airport shooting (1985), 314
Vienna Convention, 289
Vietnam, Cambodia invaded by, 33
Vietnam War:
  Bertrand Russell and, xxvi
  "environmental" warfare in, xxix,
    69
  U.S. rules of engagement in, 106–
    28
  war crimes in, 357–71
Vincennes, Iranian Airbus downed
    by, 45

war crimes, 317–405
  in former Yugoslavia, 386–404
  Germany and, 317–33, 351–56
  Japan and, 337–50
  in U.S. forces, 356–71
  in Vietnam War, 357–71
  in World War I, 317–18
  in World War II, 318–56
War Crimes Tribunal, xxvi
wars of annihilation, wars of control
    vs., xviii
"wars of expulsion," xxxin
Washington Pact for the Protection of
    Artistic and Scientific Institu-
    tions and of Historic Monu-
    ments (1935), 104
watercraft:
  in Vietnam War, 118–19, 121–22,
    126–27
  see also maritime activity
water supplies:
  documents on, 90, 93
  in Grenada invasion, 129
  internment and, 258, 272
  in Persian Gulf War, xxviii
Weinberger, Caspar, 108
West Bank (Judea and Samaria), 231,
    232, 284, 291
Wheeler, Earle, 106
women:
  alien, 242
  interned, 258, 261, 262, 271
  mothers with infants and young
    children, 235, 242, 274
  in occupied territories, 235, 240,
    254
  pregnant and nursing, 235, 242,
    258, 262, 274
  prisoners of war, 182, 187, 188,
    201, 204, 208
  wounded and sick, 157
World Health Organization, 67

World War I, 3
  prisoners of war in, 151
  war crimes in, 317–18
World War II, xxix, 78, 233, 285,
    287, 288, 289, 291
  genocide in, 84, 85, 328, 331,
    352–56
  prisoners of war in, 330, 331, 347,
    351–52
  slave labor in, 327
  war crimes in, 318–56
wounded and sick:
  abuses and infractions against,
    167–68, 176–77
  alien, 242
  civilian, 235, 236–38
  emblems and, 164–66, 175, 178
  in field, 168–79
  information on, 159
  interned, 255, 258–59, 260, 265,
    271, 274
  medical transports for, 163–64,
    175
  medical units for, 170–71, 174
  in naval forces, 153–67
  neutrality and, 137
  occupation and, 247, 248, 254
  as prisoners of war, 153–67, 168–
    79, 184–85, 188–89, 192, 209–
    10
  and religious and medical person-
    nel, 163, 169, 171–75, 181, 237
  see also hospitals

Yamashita, Tomoyuki, 336, 343–50
Yamashita v. Styer (1946), 336, 343–
    50
Yaron, Amos, 381, 383–85
Yugoslavia, in World War II, 326, 330
Yugoslavia, former, 407
  war crimes in, 86, 386–404
  wars in, 219, 317